DREAMS
AND
SHADOWS

DREAMS

AND

SHADOWS

The Future of the Middle East

ROBIN WRIGHT

THE PENGUIN PRESS

New York

2008

THE PENGUIN PRESS
Published by the Penguin Group
Penguin Group (USA) Inc., 375 Hudson Street, New York, New York 10014, USA
• Penguin Group (Canada), 90 Eglinton Avenue East, Suite 700, Toronto, Ontario,
Canada M4P 2Y3 (a division of Pearson Penguin Canada Inc.) • Penguin Books
Ltd, 80 Strand, London WC2R 0RL, England • Penguin Ireland,
25 St. Stephen's Green, Dublin 2, Ireland (a division of Penguin Books Ltd) • Penguin
Books Australia Ltd, 250 Camberwell Road, Camberwell, Victoria 3124, Australia
(a division of Pearson Australia Group Pty Ltd) • Penguin Books India Pvt Ltd,
11 Community Centre, Panchsheel Park, New Delhi–110 017, India • Penguin
Group (NZ), 67 Apollo Drive, Rosedale, North Shore 0632, New Zealand
(a division of Pearson New Zealand Ltd) • Penguin Books (South Africa)
(Pty) Ltd, 24 Sturdee Avenue, Rosebank, Johannesburg 2196, South Africa

Penguin Books Ltd, Registered Offices:
80 Strand, London WC2R 0RL, England

First published in 2008 by The Penguin Press,
a member of Penguin Group (USA) Inc.

Library of Congress Cataloging-in-Publication Data

Wright, Robin B., 1948–
Dreams and shadows : the future of the Middle East / Robin Wright.
p.   cm.
Includes bibliographical references and index.
ISBN: 978-1-59420-111-0
1. Middle East—Politics and government—21st century.   I. Title.
DS44.W87 2008
956.05'4—dc22
2007046267

Printed in the United States of America
1 3 5 7 9 10 8 6 4 2

Map by Jeffrey L. Ward

For my wondrous Nani

All men dream: but not equally. Those who dream
by night in the dusty recesses of their minds wake
in the day to find that it was vanity. But the dreamers
of the day are dangerous men, for they may act their
dream with open eyes, to make it possible.

—T. E. LAWRENCE, *SEVEN PILLARS OF WISDOM*

I am certain that this night of darkness will not last.
The moon of freedom will emerge from behind
the clouds of religious tyranny.

—IRANIAN DISSIDENT AKBAR GANJI, IN A LETTER FROM PRISON
ON THE FORTY-THIRD DAY OF A HUNGER STRIKE, JULY 23, 2005

CONTENTS

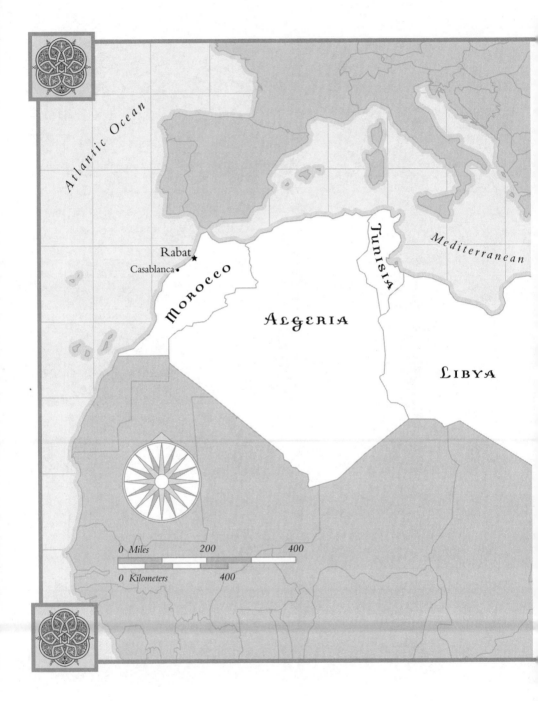

Atlantic Ocean

Mediterranean

Rabat ★
Casablanca •

MOROCCO

TUNISIA

ALGERIA

LIBYA

0 Miles   200   400

0 Kilometers   400

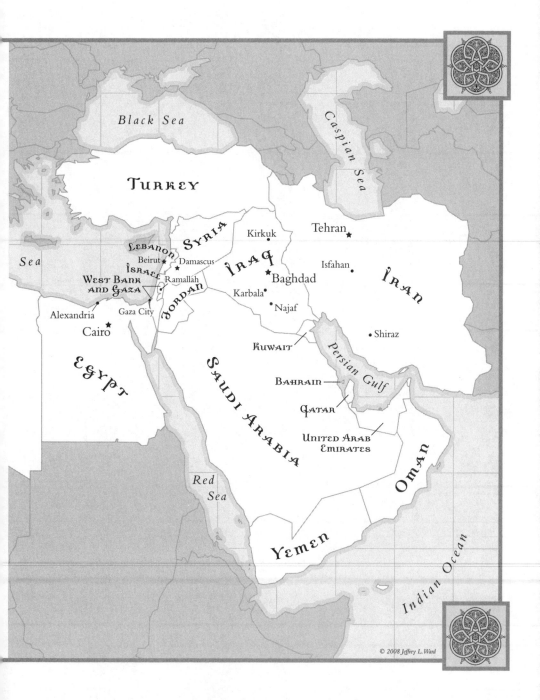

THE

MIDDLE EAST

The Prospects

We're coming out of a bad millennium in the Arab world.

—PALESTINIAN POLITICAL ANALYST RAMI KHOURI

We have learned that we have to gain our freedom

ourselves, and that only we can nourish that freedom and

create a political system that can sustain it. Ours is a

difficult struggle; it could even be a long one.

—IRANIAN DISSIDENT AKBAR GANJI[1]

On a warm spring day in April 1983, I stood across from what had been the United States Embassy in Beirut and watched as rescuers picked through tons of mangled steel and concrete littered with glass shards. Tenderly, emergency crews put salvaged bits of bodies in small blue plastic bags. Forensic experts later matched up the pieces so they could be buried together. More than sixty Americans were killed in that lunchtime bombing.

Some of the dead had been my friends.

The attack was the first by a Muslim suicide bomber against an American target—anywhere in the world. Over the next eighteen months, Islamic extremists blew up a second American embassy and the U.S. Marine peacekeeping compound in Lebanon. The Marine bombing is still the largest loss of American military life in a single incident since World War II, larger than any attack in Vietnam or Iraq. I heard those bombs thunder through Beirut too and again watched weeks of rescue efforts. The three terrorism spectaculars marked a turning point for the Middle East.

Since then, Islamic extremism has progressively grown into the most energetic force in the Middle East—and the gravest threat to Western interests. Out of my own sense of anguish, I tracked the trend as it unfolded in country after country and wrote one of the first books, in 1985, about this new form of sacred rage that has since redefined the world's political divide. Fear of its explosive potential will define American foreign policy for years, potentially decades, to come. Al Qaeda and a growing array of offshoots continue to push their tentacles deeper throughout the region—and beyond.

Yet a generation later, Islamic extremism is no longer the most important, interesting, or dynamic force in the Middle East. The hard-core terrorists in al Qaeda or Islamic Jihad have repeatedly proven that they can destroy. But they have yet to provide tangible solutions or viable new models for problems plaguing the region.

In the early twenty-first century, a budding culture of change is instead imaginatively challenging the status quo—and even the extremists. New public voices, daring publications, and increasingly noisy protests across two dozen countries are giving shape to a vigorous, if disjointed, trend. It includes defiant judges in Cairo, rebel clerics in Tehran, satellite television station owners in Dubai, imaginative feminists in Rabat and the first female candidates in Kuwait, young techies in Jeddah, daring journalists in Beirut and Casablanca, and brave writers and businessmen in Damascus.

For all, peaceful empowerment has become the preferred means of making political decisions and producing change.

The tiny minority willing to go out and kill has had such impact in part because there have been so few other political ideas and activists in the region offering alternatives. Now, increasingly, there are. A trend struggling for decades to take root has finally begun—and, I stress, *only* begun—to have impact.

Impatience and frustration fueled by education, technology and the miracles of instant media, demographics, globalization, and change elsewhere in the world have altered the equation.

The mujahedeen, or holy warriors, have long dominated the headlines. Today, however, the so-called pyjamahedeen, or pajama warriors, are increasingly capturing the public imagination too. They campaign for change not with bombs on battlefields, but from laptops at home.[2] Web sites and blogs have become the twenty-first-century chroniclers of police crackdowns, human-rights abuses, and election irregularities. In countries where I once sought out clandestine cells, I now also look for computer nerds. So, tellingly, are government security forces. Some of the pyjamahedeen have already gone to prison.

"Governments have a new kind of opponent," said Egyptian blogger Wael Abbas. His blog has posted cell-phone videos of police brutality, including one of a detainee writhing in pain as he was sodomized by police with a broomstick. Started in 2004, Abbas' blog was getting up to 30,000 hits a day—and up to 45,000 during a crisis—by 2007.

"We are not bound by government rules, like the political parties. We can use the language of freedom," he told me. "We offer an alternative voice, especially for the young."

The issue in the Middle East is no longer whether to engage in political transformation. The issue today is how to get there.

"In the Arab world, the status quo is not sustainable," reflected Marwan Muasher, a former Jordanian foreign minister who became a World Bank vice president. "What worked forty years ago—when the state could decide things and expect people to follow—does not work now. Unless the state is responsive and aware, it is in for major trouble."

Pressure is now mounting on virtually every Middle East regime.

Even the conservative Gulf sheikhdoms have had to respond, albeit in the smallest feasible steps. Saudi Arabia held its first (male only) elections for local councils in 2005, while Kuwait's parliament ended a long boycott and finally granted women the rights to vote and run for office in 2006.

"Regimes are increasingly unable to deliver what they promised or protect their people, and they certainly provide no direction for the future," explained Nader Said, a Palestinian pollster and political sociologist. "Mix that with a constituency that is more demanding, and more aware, and more in search of rights.

"Most in the Arab world now think they deserve better."

Regimes have been forced to adopt the language of democracy, whatever their real intentions or conniving to prevent it. The definition publicly embraced in the Middle East is the same as it is everywhere else, reflected in the Alexandria Statement produced at a meeting of 165 civil society leaders and government officials from eighteen Muslim countries at Egypt's rebuilt Alexandria Library in 2004.

> *When we talk of democratic systems, we mean, without ambiguity, genuine democracy. This may differ in form and shape from one country to another due to cultural or historical variations; but the essence of democracy remains the same. Democracy refers to a system where freedom is the paramount value that ensures actual sovereignty of the people, and government by the people through political pluralism, leading to transfer of power. Democracy is based in respect of . . . freedom of thought and expression and the right to organize under the umbrella of effective political institutions, with an elected legislature, an independent judiciary, a government that is subject to both constitutional and public accountability, and political parties of different intellectual and ideological orientations.*[3]

Few governments have begun yet to honor those words. What makes this era different are the activists now trying to hold them to account. They are no longer limited to the intellectual elite. And the numbers engaged—especially compared to the small cells of suicide bombers—are striking. Roughly one quarter of Lebanon's entire population took to the streets, peacefully, in 2005 to demand the government's resignation and an end to Syria's twenty-nine-year military occupation. Despite dangers from an escalating insurgency, Iraqis poured out in three elections that made the purple ink-stained finger famous. Participation increased with each vote.

More than 100,000 people turned out in the Jordanian capital to protest after suicide bombers simultaneously struck three Amman hotels in 2005. "Burn in hell," they shouted, in rhythmic unison, after the al Qaeda leader in Iraq claimed credit.

And none of these were rent-a-crowds, the usual means of producing mass turnouts in the region.

"These initial signs were intoxicating. They produced wonderment," mused Ghassan Salameh, Lebanon's former minister of culture. "A region long dead politically suddenly had a pulse."

Violence is increasingly unacceptable to the majority, according to public opinion polls and petitions. In 2004, more than 2,000 Muslim intellectuals signed a petition calling on the United Nations to sponsor a new international treaty that would outlaw the use of religion to incite violence. It proposed that the Security Council create a new international tribunal to try "the theologians of terror" and the "sheikhs of death" who provide religious cover for terrorism. The petition also urged members of the world body to prevent broadcasts of "the mad musings of the theologians of terror."[4]

Even as people turn to political Islam, they are turning against Islamic extremism. Clerics and theologians have begun to challenge bin Laden and al Qaeda with their own *fatwas* in what has been dubbed the "counter-jihad."[5] Even in Iraq, some Sunni tribal leaders turned on al Qaeda cells after they went too far in kidnapping and killing the local populations.

Militant movements are under pressure too. A few of the groups that began as secretive cells have also begun to emerge from the underground to run for office. Motives are often suspect, but it is also striking that they are appealing to voters on platforms that deal with everyday issues such as better garbage collection, improved health care, and less corruption.

The new momentum has spurred talk of a *nahda,* Arabic for "awakening" or "renaissance."[6]

"Is it something real? Is this finally an Arab spring?" asked my old friend Saad Eddin Ibrahim, the leading human rights activist in Cairo, who was jailed three times and left crippled by prison abuse. "Our desert region is famous for its mirages. But these are real visions of change.

"The despots in the Arab world are on their last gasp," he reflected. "Just like any last-ditch battles, they will do a lot of stupid things and leave a lot of destruction. But these will be the last battles. People have already broken the fear barrier. They are as ready for change and democracy as Eastern Europe was in the 1980s and as Latin America was in the 1970s. History is moving. The moment is ours."

That's the good news.

The so-called "Arab spring" of 2005, which offered greater promise than at any time since most countries gained independence, did not endure. It did not set off the toppling dominoes of regional change, as the fall of the Berlin Wall did in Eastern Europe. For much of the Middle East, the challenge of change is today tougher than anywhere else in the world.

The Middle East, concluded a United Nations survey in 2005, faces an "acute deficit of freedom and good governance." Most Arabs live in a "black hole...in which nothing moves and from which nothing escapes."[7] The region has the largest proportion of ruling monarchies (eight) and family political dynasties (four) in the world.*

The dangers of change are also already visible.

Democracy is about differences—and they are bound to flourish once disparate sides of society are really free for the first time to speak and make their own specific demands. Unity in opposition to tyranny almost never translates into unity once in power. In a region rife with vulnerable minorities and shifting demographics, opening up politics endangers deepening the problems it is meant to solve.

---

*The monarchies include Saudi Arabia, Kuwait, the United Arab Emirates, Qatar, Bahrain, and Oman in the Persian Gulf, plus Jordan and Morocco. The budding family dynasties include countries where sons have taken over or are being groomed to assume power: Syria, Egypt, Libya, and Yemen.

As Iraq has illustrated too vividly, democracy unleashes existential dilemmas.

Opening new space also does not guarantee what or who will fill it. Because the political debate in the Middle East is grounded in its own experience, the face of change will be too. More often than not, Islam will be the dominant idiom of opposition and change. Indeed, the region may not be transformed without tapping into its religious traditions—because of their appeal and legitimacy, but also by default.

Shortly before he was killed in 2005 by a bomb placed underneath his car in Beirut, Lebanese historian Samir Kassir opined in a little book entitled *Being Arab,*

> *Not only can the current regimes not give, or restore, to their states the ability to take the initiative in international affairs, they also forbid their citizens any license—if not to change these regimes, then at least to breathe new life into them through popular participation. . . . The crisis of faith in the political process then runs its course, until there is nothing left but religion to channel people's frustrations and express their demands for change.*
>
> *Although today militant Islam appears primarily to target the West, it was initially a product of the impasse in Arab states. . . . The rise of political Islam took the form of a re-Islamization of society in response to what were considered to be inefficient, iniquitous or impious governments, rather than a reaction to the culture of modernism.[8]*

The period of change will often witness an uneven contest pitting inexperienced democratic activists with limited resources against both well-heeled autocrats who have no intention of ceding control and Islamists who believe they have a mission from God and a flock of the faithful to tap into. It will be an unfair battle from the start.

Nothing will happen quickly, either. Even regimes that acknowledge the need to open up politically talk about gradual steps, in phases, over years or decades or generations.

"Change is a future notion," reflected Marwan Muasher, the former Jordanian foreign minister. "The trick is putting it in the present."

In 1995, Sheikh Hamad bin Khalifa al Thani of Qatar—the little emirate jutting off Saudi Arabia into the Persian Gulf—became the first of a younger generation of Gulf princes to assume power. He did it by overthrowing his father, the region's most autocratic leader in what was then the Middle East's most closed society. To the consternation of neighboring sheikhdoms, Sheikh Hamad then invited Israel to open a commercial office in Doha, the United States to headquarter Central Command in Qatar, and American and European universities, including Cornell and Georgetown, to open up Qatari branches. He also launched al Jazeera, the first all-news Arab satellite channel. All were bold, controversial moves. Yet Qatar's emir is still pacing the spread of political participation.

"We have no intention of waving some magic wand and changing our entire culture and society overnight," Sheikh Hamad told me.

"To hurry change would only invite the social instability we seek to avoid, so we have chosen a middle course for change. Compared to radical changes in other nations since the end of the Cold War, our changes might appear small, but they are well-planned. We must be careful to change at a pace that meets the needs and desires of our people, as well as our traditional culture steeped in thousands of years of Arab and Islamic history."

Qatar has held three municipal elections since 1999, conducted a referendum for the first constitution in 2003, and scheduled the first elections for a new national legislature in 2007. Women are able to vote and run for office.

Yet Qatar's new legislature will have thirty elected seats with fifteen more appointed by the emir—still giving the palace effective veto power. The emir's rule is still absolute.

"The Arab world is developing. Nothing can stop what is happening. But for now, the trend is toward participatory despotism," said Harvard-educated Paul Salem, head of the Beirut branch of the Carnegie Endowment for International Peace and son of a former Lebanese foreign minister.

"Most of the Arab states are making that shift, and it's important. That's how it started in the West: The king allowed a parliament and eventually parliament got stronger. After that, the dynamic will be slow liberalization within authoritarian systems that accept and integrate, to varying degrees, the principle of participation in parliament, in local government, in open discussion of the budget, and with emerging press freedoms, nongovernment organizations, more political parties, and more human rights groups.

"It will happen," Salem said, "but with much grinding of the wheels and sluggishness and tension."

And tokenism. Elections engineered to produce token participation are preempting real democracy in several states.

In 2006, the seven sheikhdoms in the United Arab Emirates—the most opulent and liberal society on the Arabian Peninsula, complete with bikini beaches and restaurants serving alcohol and pork—held their first election. More than 400 candidates ran, including sixty-five women. The process, however, was a political charade. Only 6,595 people, all handpicked by the government out of 300,000 citizens over the age of eighteen, were allowed to vote. The stakes—twenty seats on a new Federal National Council—were also a token. Another twenty seats were appointed by the ruling tribal royal families. And the new council had no powers. It was only an advisory body that could be ignored.[9] The first elected body was not a credible political entity in the twenty-first century, even as a transition device.

Several Middle East regimes, particularly the eight oil-rich members of OPEC, can literally afford tokenism. The wealth of so-called "rentier" states—which survive off the "rent" of foreign payments from petroleum products—can limit both public leverage and foreign pressure.

Petroleum and democracy do not mix well. "Tyranny has a full tank," said Marina Ottaway of the Carnegie Endowment for International Peace.[10] And the push for change began just as oil prices soared to unprecedented highs.

Petrodollar wealth can also breed political apathy in traditional societies.

In little Qatar, which has the world's second-largest gas reserves, the emir worried that people with one of the world's highest per capita incomes would not be interested in politics. Qatar's stock market is instead the national obsession.

"To get people to accept a constitution or the idea of voting took us time. Some people didn't see it as important," Sheikh Hamad told me in Doha, the construction-crazed capital, in 2006. "Our society is tribal. It means that tribes select their eldest as their leader, and they just listen to his order and his wisdom. People are still comfortable with that system. They don't see any reason to work in politics."

The election turnout for the 2003 municipal election was 32 percent. In 2007, it was 51 percent. Only a minority of citizens, however, was registered to vote for either election.

As change does play out, the emerging governments will also be weaker and far from full democracies for a long, long time to come. New leaders will remain vulnerable.

"America is different from everywhere else. It was full-born in a constitution. The rest of the world had to work toward a constitution," Paul Salem said. "Remember that when you make calculations about the Middle East."

The disastrous miscalculations in Iraq will further slow and complicate the process. The American intervention was, in the end, often counterproductive to the cause of democracy in the region. It disillusioned many about both the costs and benefits.

All the factors contributing to change will also make the region susceptible to greater turmoil and divisions during the transitions. The stimulants pose hazards.

Among them, a major engine of change is youth. The Middle East—including North Africa, the Levant, and the Persian Gulf—has witnessed a sevenfold explosion in population over only three generations, from 60 million in the 1930s to 415 million by 2006.[11] The majority today are young. In some countries, up to seventy percent are under age thirty. They are hungry for change. As they come of working age, economists contend that they offer the potential for the kind of economic growth witnessed with the Asian Tigers. Many of the young are willing to act politically, too. And numbers are on their side.

Yet as governments are increasingly unable to provide education, employment, and housing, today's frustrated youth are also looking for fast answers. Regionwide, roughly one in three young people is unemployed.[12] The highest youth unemployment rate in the world also provides an exploitable flashpoint to build sympathy or support for extremist movements.

"Tens of millions of educated but underemployed, unemployed, restive and frustrated young men and women have given unnatural birth to thousands of active terrorists and anarchists, targeting our own and foreign lands," wrote my colleague and friend Rami Khouri, a columnist for Lebanon's *Daily Star* and head of the American University of Beirut's think tank.[13]

The many arms of information technology and the media have also had a huge impact, again to good and bad effect. The Internet, even with government censorship or restrictions, provides access to the outside world as never before. In some countries, up to seventy percent of the young were using the Internet on a weekly basis in 2006, surveys show.[14] The cell phone text message has become the medium to organize antigovernment rallies. And satellite television has revolutionized a region where all media were state-controlled not so long ago.

After decades with only one or two heavily censored television channels, the first Arab satellite news station debuted in 1996, providing access for the first time to news not controlled by local governments in a language most in the region could understand. By 2007, dozens of unregulated satellite stations beamed in via rooftop satellite dishes began making people far more aware—of what is really happening in their own countries, of change happening in other parts of the world, and of international standards for political life.

"Arab media is in the midst of a highly dynamic transition, fuelled by the emergence of low-cost and accessible satellite broadcast technology," a report by the United States Institute of Peace concluded in 2005.

> *It is the satellite channels that show the greatest potential for ushering in political change in the region.... No matter how hard they try, regimes can no longer control the information environment.... The fact that Arab governments call in to television [talk] programs to defend their human rights record indicates some advancement.*[15]

But technology's wizardry also allows Osama bin Laden and his affiliates to distribute worldwide their diatribes, threats, and beheadings on satellite television, while terrorist groups tap into the resources and riches of the Internet. Propaganda has a new tool with unprecedented reach.

For now, Middle East societies are caught in an awkward stage in transition. In 2003, the Lebanese Broadcasting Corporation launched *Star Academy,* a mixture of *American Idol* and *Big Brother* that brings together Arab youth from all over the region to compete for a singing contract. An affiliate station tracks the competitors all day, every day, as they sing, dance, play, interact, cook, and sleep. Conservative clerics quickly condemned the show. Saudi Arabia's Grand Mufti Abdul Aziz al Sheikh, the kingdom's highest religious authority, issued an edict calling the show an open invitation to sin. He warned Muslims to avoid it. Nevertheless, it became wildly popular.

Finally, greater exposure to ideas in the outside world has helped inform and change public attitudes in the Middle East. Some of the most popular books in the region are written by or about Western politicians, philosophers, and political analysts. The osmosis of globalization has spurred a rich new discourse on democracy and how to adapt it to their own cultures.

Yet exposure has also alienated those fearing foreign encroachment—again. Many of the most ardent Iranian revolutionaries were educated in the United States; one group was often referred to as the "Berkeley mafia" because they all attended the University of California. In the very worst case, Mohammed Atta, who masterminded the terrorist spectaculars against the World Trade Center and the Pentagon on September 11, 2001, spent almost a decade in Europe.

Change and its agents will produce some troubling consequences. Many in the region will question whether the short-term dangers are worth the eventual benefits—and the price paid along the way.

The Middle East is not really one place, so change will have many faces.

The region today is arguably more stereotyped than any other part of the world. But the peoples, histories, religions, political systems, and economies actually differ widely among countries, even within them. It is the world's only bloc spread across two continents.

"Democracy," said Paul Salem, "will be a country-by-country phenomenon."

The Middle East includes the tribal societies of the Arabian Peninsula, from where Islam and the Arabs originated. It includes the cosmopolitan cities of new Beirut and old Damascus. It includes Palestinians who have lived more than a half century in squalid refugee camps as well as Gulf princes who own multiple palaces because of oil found under the desert sands. It includes the desert-dwelling Berbers and Bedouin nomads who roam with their camel-hair tents across the Sahara, the Sinai, and the vast expanses of Arabia. And it includes Kurds, who are the world's largest minority without a state. Although they are not Arabs, they have significant numbers in Iraq, Iran, Syria, and Turkey.

Political starting points vary just as deeply. Saudi Arabia has strict Sunni religious rule, while Iran is a Shiite-dominated Islamic republic with a constitution that draws on European law. Syria and Libya are secular states based on socialist ideologies. Kuwait, Jordan, and Morocco are still ruled by traditional monarchies.

The range of freedoms is reflected in the region's fashions: In Arabia, the national dress for men is the traditional loose-fitting white *thobe,* which looks like a shirt that extends to the ankles; for women in public, it is a shapeless black cloak with four layers of black veils. In contrast, Lebanese men can wear tight Speedo briefs on mixed-gender beaches, while many women favor whatever fashion is the sassiest, flashiest, or skimpiest.

Economically, the peoples of the Middle East also have vastly different resources as tools for a transition. The region includes the earth's richest nations, like glitzy Qatar, the tiny thumb off Saudi Arabia's eastern coast that sits atop the world's largest field of natural gas and has a per-capita income of $38,000. On the other extreme is exotic but densely populated Yemen on Saudi Arabia's southern border, where the per capita income is a mere $500.

The broader Middle East is not even a single geographic unit. The two dozen nations spread from northern Africa to western Asia. They stretch from Morocco on the Atlantic Ocean to Lebanon and Syria on the Mediterranean, from Egypt and Yemen on opposite sides of the Red

Sea, to Iraq and Iran at the top of the Persian Gulf and Oman at its mouth. The region spans four time zones and 4,000 miles from east to west.

Languages differ too. Using French and English, I once translated between Moroccans and Saudis who could not understand each other's Arabic. Most Iranians speak Farsi and haughtily note their Indo-European rather than Arab roots. Kurds have their own language too.

Although the region is associated with Islam, it is rich with religious minorities. One out of every ten Egyptians is a Coptic Christian. About fifteen percent of the Palestinians belong to disparate Christian faiths. The region is also home to Alawites, Armenian Orthodox and Catholics, Baha'i, Chaldeans, Druze, Greek Orthodox, Maronites, and many others.

I once visited a fire temple of the Zoroastrians, who worship light as the symbol of a good and omnipotent God. Iran is the world center for the faith founded six centuries before Christianity. As the symbol of light, fires at the altars of their temples have burned continuously for centuries. Zoroastrian ideas about the devil, hell, a future savior, the struggle between good and evil ending with a day of judgment, the resurrection of the dead, and an afterlife had great impact on all monotheistic faiths, and even Buddhism.

The largest Jewish population in the Middle East outside of Israel is also in Iran, which still has kosher butchers, Jewish schools, synagogues, and a first-rate hospital favored by many of the ayatollahs. In Tehran, I have attended a Hebrew class for children as well as a Catholic service at which wine was served—with government permission, in a country that otherwise outlaws alcohol—as part of communion. Iran's parliament has five especially reserved (and proportionate) seats for Jews, Christians, and Zoroastrians.

Because of the region's diversity, rivalries and backstabbing can become bitter and intense. Middle East nations can also be miserly with each other.

On a 1981 trip to Libya, I covered Yasser Arafat's quest for financial aid. In a bizarre scene, Libyan leader Moammar Qaddafi escorted a fatigues-clad Arafat through the opening of a new People's Store in Tripoli, showing off French fashions, German toys, Italian appliances, and Japanese electronics. At a rooftop ceremony afterward, the two men prayed, shared dates and goat's milk, then exchanged gifts. Arafat gave Qaddafi an exquisite antique camel saddle. Qaddafi presented the Palestinian leader, who was still in exile, with a set of Samsonite luggage.

"That's all he's likely to get from Qaddafi," complained one of Arafat's aides as we watched from the sidelines. "Qaddafi has promised us millions but never delivered a single cent."

More than two decades later, several Arab governments that had pledged billions to help rebuild Iraq had failed to pay up several years after making their commitments—even though Iraq's instability was affecting them all.

Opening up political systems may spark further friction, at least in the short term, as the balance of power shifts both within countries and between them. People long excluded will now want their say too. Indeed, whatever the rhetoric, the greatest tension in the region may not be between Arabs and Israelis. Sunnis, who long monopolized power, are particularly apprehensive about the growing leverage of Shiites, Islam's so-called second sect. In an interview in 2004, Jordan's King Abdullah warned me about the danger of an emerging "Shiite arc," or crescent, stretching from Iran through Iraq into Syria and Lebanon—the kind of domino theory that once scared the West about communism.[16] The phrase set off a firestorm; it is still used to describe the region's growing sectarian split.

The Middle East has already gone through enormous change.

In the twentieth century, three pivotal events redefined the region. The collapse of the Ottoman Empire, which dominated the Middle East for five centuries, redrew the map and gave birth to modern states after World War I. The creation of Israel in 1948 changed the region's political dynamics and spawned the world's longest conflict. And the 1979 Iranian revolution introduced Islam as an alternative political idiom. All three had spillover worldwide.

By coincidence, I first landed in the Middle East on October 6, 1973, arriving in Beirut during the chaotic outbreak of the fourth modern Middle East war. The Arabs had just launched a surprise attack on Israel. "Egyptian troops have crossed the Suez Canal," an American tourist leaned over and whispered to me.

Oil was then only $3.12 per barrel—yes, barrel, not gallon—and the sheikhdoms of the Arabian Peninsula were considered poor developing countries. In Saudi Arabia, schools for girls had only been around for nine years and a single-channel television service for seven; both had been introduced over serious objections by conservative clergy. The strict Saudi version of Islam did not tolerate the human image in art or literature, much less on the small screen.

Iran was then one of two pillars of United States policy in the region. Some 40,000 Americans—military trainers and government advisers, businessmen, Peace Corps volunteers and tourists—passed through each year. It was spy heaven for the Central Intelligence Agency, which trained and worked closely with its Iranian counterpart. In Tehran in 1973, I stayed at the high-rise Hilton, which had just hosted a pageant of exotic and scantily clad beauties competing for the Miss Iran title.

Lebanon was the region's playground, a cosmopolitan tourist haven of Mediterranean beaches and scenic ski slopes with decadent night-time pleasures, casinos, and nightclubs. And Washington still had dip-lomatic relations with Baghdad, which was ruled by the Baath Party of an up-and-coming politician named Saddam Hussein.

During more than thirty years of living in and traveling to the region, I've witnessed extraordinary transformations of all kinds. I've covered Middle East wars as well as the first phase of peace between Egypt and Israel. In the 1970s, I covered the Shah of Iran as well as the revolution that ousted him. I covered Yasser Arafat as the world's most notorious terrorist in the 1980s, as a signatory to a Palestinian-Israeli peace accord on the White House south lawn in the 1990s, and as the obstacle to a final peace in the 2000s. I covered Saddam Hussein's war with Iran in the 1980s, and with Kuwait in the 1990s, and then flew into Baghdad weeks after he was ousted in 2003. Along the way, I've talked to thousands of people—on the streets and in palaces, in the bunkers of war zones and the tranquility of religious sites, on university campuses as well as in banks, shops, and factories, in newspaper offices and Internet cafes, in shantytown slums and luxurious villas, in the corridors of power and the back-alley hideouts of extremist cells.

For this book, I wandered across the region again to write about the crises of change that have begun to redefine the Middle East in the twenty-first century. There are many fine books about the Arab-Israeli conflict, Islamic extremism, the Iraq war, and Iran's turmoil. I deliberately set out to look through a different prism. This is a book about disparate experiments with empowerment in the world's most troubled region. My goal was to probe deep inside societies of the Middle East for the emerging ideas and players that are changing the political environment in ways that will unfold for decades to come.

The trauma of the 9/11 attacks and the Iraq war—and other turmoil that almost certainly lies ahead—makes understanding the Middle East even more important. The central flaw behind the American intervention in Iraq was ignorance of the country and its people. Policy was ill informed. The U.S. decision to go to war was often based on wishful thinking and armchair projections at great distance.

"The United States didn't have relations with Iraq for well over a decade, so there were very few U.S. officials who had any direct experience of the country," reflected Charles Duelfer, who served for seven years as a UN weapons inspector in Iraq and returned after the war for the United States to write the final report on Saddam's weapons of mass destruction.

"The analysts who were making judgments, making assessments, didn't have a tactile feel for Iraq," he said. "Many of them had never even met a real Iraqi. Their reality came from a computer screen. Some policy makers made decisions not knowing—or caring—how catastrophically ignorant they were about Iraq. They had no concept of the ground truth of Iraqi politics and society. They had only a cartoonist's understanding of Saddam. They did not know what made Iraq Iraq."

The United States and its allies cannot afford to make that kind of mistake again. The Iraq war has carried costs—in lives, resources, and both human and political relationships—that are still incalculable.

This book reflects the voices in the region, not the pundits from afar. It covers the full spectrum of politics, not just the new democrats or heroes of change. I tracked down the heads of militant Palestinian and Lebanese movements as well as the inspiring activists of Egypt and Morocco and the reformers risking their lives in Syria and Iran. Some countries, like Saudi Arabia, I left out because the system has prevailed and the voices of change are not yet noisy enough. I also did not include Israel because it teems with political diversity and open debate. I deliberately selected a variety of countries experiencing the dynamic tension of change and used each to reflect a different slice of it.

Not all of the new actors will succeed. Some may only nudge the door ajar for those who follow. And others will be totally unacceptable to the West, creating tensions and diversions for both sides along the path of change.

I have seen up close how volatile the period ahead will be. When I started out on this latest journey, the region was full of dreams. As I finished it, serious shadows loomed in many places. I chose the title of this book from a lament by Mustafa Kemal Ataturk, the Islamic world's great twentieth-century modernizer, who molded today's Turkey from the ruins of the old Ottoman Empire. "Neither sentiment nor illusion must influence our policy. Away with dreams and shadows!" he said. "They have cost us dear in the past."[17]

The Middle East will, unquestionably, continue to spur anxiety, threaten security, and drain resources. Yet even as the war in Iraq steadily escalated and the United States was increasingly discredited on democracy promotion, the majority of the people in the Middle East still wanted the kind of political change that has swept the rest of the world over the past quarter century.

What is most inspiring is not the dreams the outside world has for the people of the Middle East. It is instead the aspirations and goals they have genuinely set for themselves.

one

THE PALESTINIANS

The Conundrum

We are not to expect to be transported from despotism to liberty in a featherbed.

—THOMAS JEFFERSON

The rise of political Islam is not a statement about its strength or ideology as much as it is about the failure of elites that are corrupt and dictatorial.

—IRAQ'S DEPUTY PRIME MINISTER BARHAM SALIH

On January 25, 2006, the Palestinians became the first Arabs to peacefully and democratically reject the status quo. They took their uprising to the ballot box. It started out as quite a party.

I woke up on Election Day to horn-tooting and deafening loud-speakers. Caravans of battered cars, pickup trucks and taxis were driving through the rocky hills of the West Bank, blaring party slogans, get-out-to-vote appeals, and even hip-hop campaign ditties for their candidates. Big party flags billowed from car rooftops, little banners on suction cups flapped from the back. One procession would fade into the distance, and another would soon roar noisily down the street.

Eleven parties were running. It was a raucous morning.

"I truly believe things will never be the same again," Nader Said, a political sociologist and pollster at Birzeit University, told me almost giddily as he organized staff to run exit polls at voting sites. "These elections are a real threshold for the Palestinians. Even those who were hesitant or who refused to participate before are being brought into the game."

The pollsters, however, seriously underestimated the scope of change in store—and the direction.

The Palestinian election was a dicey experiment for the Middle East. Over the previous century, big political change had more often been determined by bloody purges, coups d'état, revolutions or civil wars. Autocratic monarchies and one-party rule have long been the norm; real opposition is not tolerated. While most countries did conduct elections, most were a sham. Opening them up—fairly—to all who wanted to run was a rarity. The few earlier attempts had been manipulated, sabotaged, or aborted.

When fifty-four parties competed in Algeria to replace one-party rule in 1992, the military launched a coup on the eve of the final vote because it feared the projected winners. The election was abandoned. After a serious opposition party emerged in Jordan in 1989 and won a large chunk of parliamentary seats, the government redistricted to disperse its constituency for the next election. After Egypt's president faced real opposition in a popular vote for the first time in 2005, his leading opponent was arrested.

The Palestinians also reflected the central conundrum of change in the Middle East—that perilous condition when both the status quo and the available alternatives are problematic, but delaying change could make the situation even worse. For just that reason, most key players— among Palestinians, Israel, the international community, and especially the United States—decided that long-delayed democratic elections should go forward. It was, however, the most thoroughly monitored election ever held in the Middle East.

The Palestinians are among the smaller Arab communities, but they are the savviest politically. They have the highest education rates in the Arab world. They have long interacted with worldly ideas and experienced diversity in the hub of the three great monotheistic religions. And in an ironic twist they have been exposed to Israel's democracy.

About 2.4 million Palestinians live in the fertile West Bank, an area the size of Delaware positioned between Israel and Jordan. Another 1.4 million reside in the tiny but teeming Gaza Strip, which is less than 140 square miles, or twice the size of Washington, D.C., and is squished between Israel's southern border and giant Egypt. More than half of the Palestinians, somewhere between four to six million, are scattered among twenty-two Arab nations and the six inhabited continents. Without a state for almost six decades, the Palestinian political experience has been unique among the Arabs.

Yet the Palestinians have defined the Arab agenda since 1948. And on election eve, politicians throughout the Middle East knew that the outcome would have disproportionate impact regionwide.

"We are the wound in the Arab world," added Said, the pollster, as he toyed with the yellow and light green magic markers on his desk. "And everyone watches what happens to us."

The pattern of change globally—communism's demise in Eastern Europe, the end of Latin America's military dictatorships, and apartheid's collapse in Africa—has a common denominator: Change begins with breaking the monopoly of an autocratic leader, party, government, or ideology. It can take decades. Once accomplished, it is still only the starting point.

In the Middle East, the Palestinians were the first to reach that stage—on their own steam.

I watched the election for a new government in Ramallah, the embryonic Palestinian capital and a bustling city of some 60,000 in the West Bank, or biblical Judea. It is the first city across the border from Israel, about ten miles slightly north of Jerusalem, in the middle niche of the peanut-shaped West Bank. Palestinians often say that the road to peace is not through Damascus or Baghdad but through Ramallah.

Ramallah is the most liberal and cosmopolitan Palestinian city. It launched its own international film festival in 2004. You can browse downtown at the Miami Beach Arcade, shop at Cowboy 2000 Jeans, and get coiffed at Just 4 U Hair, Face and Nails. Among the dining options are Mickey Mouse Subs, Angelo's Pizzeria, the Titanic Coffee Shop, the Pollo-Loco Mexican restaurant, and a Chinese take-out. Its basketball teams—both men and women—have competed regionally; the poster shop downtown features a blowup of American basketball star Allen Iverson in the window. Ramallah is known for its poets and writers, artists and musicians. It is also home to the leading Palestinian university, Birzeit.

In Arabic, the city's name—*ram allah*—means "God's hill." Allah is the Arabic word for God—not an Islamic God, but the same monotheistic God worshiped by Muslims, Christians, and Jews. In Ramallah's case, the reference was originally Christian. The city was founded by tribes of Christian Arabs in the sixteenth century. To this day, about fifteen percent of all Palestinians worldwide are Christian.

Many families in Ramallah can trace their ancestors to the eight original Christian clans.[1] The mayor's job in Ramallah is still reserved for a Christian.

"It's not *exactly* a law. It's a custom," explained Janet Michael, Ramallah's first female mayor and a Greek Orthodox who descends from a founding clan, when I dropped by her office in City Hall. Michael, a graying former school headmistress, had been selected by the city council two weeks earlier. She had even won the votes of the three city council members from an Islamist party, she told me, pointedly.

Ramallah was redefined after the birth of Israel in 1948, when refugees flooded into what was then Jordan and transformed the city's quaint pastoral life. Its numbers more than doubled, even as many Christians fled to the United States and Europe. Squalid refugee camps grew up on its outskirts. Ramallah was quickly converted from a prosperous Christian town of some 6,000 into a burgeoning community of Muslims who had abandoned or lost almost everything.

The city was transformed again a generation later after Israel captured the West Bank from Jordan in the 1967 war. Jewish settlements grew up quickly near Ramallah, sometimes built on confiscated Palestinian land with Palestinian labor. The city became economically dependent on Israel and paid Israeli taxes.

Yet Ramallah's early identity has not disappeared. Many Christian customs have endured despite big demographic shifts. The Quaker Friends School, opened in 1869, is still the choice of elites, both Muslim and Christian; many prominent politicians and intellectuals are among its alums. The Sabbath is still observed on Sunday, not Friday, the Muslim Sabbath; church bells from several denominations echo through Ramallah's hills. And on Election Day, exactly one month after Christmas, an artificial Christmas tree decorated with miniature gift boxes, gold bulbs, and a star of Bethlehem—named for a city that is less than fifteen miles down the road, as the crow flies—was still up in the lobby of the Best Eastern Hotel.

"We won't take it down until the end of January. That's the tradition," the reception clerk told me.

Ramallah, originally an agricultural center, is still surrounded by gently tiered hills of olive groves, citrus orchards, and vineyards. "God's hill" refers more to the area's fertility and scenic beauty than its history.

For there is certainly nothing more sacred in Ramallah than politics.

The Palestinian campaign was quite intense, right down to a competitive new election chic. Parties distributed thousands of baseball caps, in party colors, inscribed with party slogans. Packs of campaign workers handing out party literature on downtown streets looked like rival teams who had showed up to play ball. Others produced pageant-like sashes and headbands with campaign logos. An Islamic party organized children wearing green sashes—printed with the Muslim creed, "There is no deity but God and Mohammed is his messenger"—and accompanied by drummers to parade through West Bank towns. Ramallah, a city of creamy stone buildings and dirty streets, was plastered with candidates' faces on utility poles, shops, fences, billboards, traffic intersections, even monuments. The Third Way, a group of independents trying to carve out a new middle ground, rolled huge ads down the sides of buildings, top floor to bottom, and made downtown Manara Square look like a modest version of Times Square. And the array of posters, placards, and banners was constantly changing. Overnight, one long row of a candidate's picture would be covered by another contestant's face until, in the brief three-week campaign, posters were layers thick. It was as if political parties calculated that each poster might produce another vote, so whoever put up the most would triumph.

Or perhaps the Palestinians were making up for lost time.

Ramallah is also home to the Muqata, which means "something separated." It is an imposing compound of white stone buildings that has the commanding presence of a fortress. Britain built the Muqata in 1920, during its mandate of Palestine, as a prison. After the British left in 1948, Jordan turned the Muqata into a military base. When Israel captured the West Bank in the 1967 war, it was converted back again into a prison and a center for occupation troops.

In 1994, the Muqata became the West Bank headquarters for the first Palestinian government. It was Yasser Arafat's domain.

For almost a half century, Palestinian politics was dominated by one man—and one party. In the mid-1950s, as a young engineer working in Kuwait, Arafat gave up a lucrative job and his beloved two-tone pink Thunderbird convertible to establish a new Palestinian political movement. Arafat's creation was Fatah. It translates from Arabic as "victory" or "conquest," but it is also the backward acronym for Harakat al-Tahrir al-Falistiniya, or the Palestine Liberation Movement.[2] In a macabre twist, the acronym spelled forward is *hataf,* or "death."

The first conflict among Fatah's founding members—mostly engineers and teachers trained in Egypt, when Arafat was president of the Union of Palestine Students at Cairo University—was over leadership. They decided against a single leader, opting for collective power. A fifteen-member central committee was the ultimate authority and was supposed to vote on all major decisions.*

But Arafat—a surprisingly short man with a potbelly, a perpetual three-day stubble, bulbous lips, and a cunning charisma—quickly developed a chokehold over Fatah. It became his personal political tool.

Over the next five decades, Arafat did pretty much what he pleased— and, shrewdly, used the others as his advisers, emissaries, shields, and decoys for the party's darker activities. Among them was cofounder Abu

---

*Fatah's Palestine Liberation Movement should not to be confused with the Palestine Liberation Organization, the larger umbrella group for many factions.

Iyad, the nom de guerre of the portly intelligence chief with bushy black eyebrows who created Black September, the notorious network that carried out the 1972 Munich Olympics massacre of eleven Israeli athletes and other dirty deeds. Arafat usually wanted to be one step removed from the airplane hijackings, bombings, and assassinations that killed hundreds of Israelis—and far more Palestinians in Israeli counterstrikes. He preferred to put himself above it all as the father of the Palestinian people, not the executioner of its youth or the master terrorist.

I encountered Arafat many times during the years I lived in Lebanon. I got an anecdotal glimpse of his hold over Fatah's leadership during an anniversary rally on New Year's Eve 1981. Fatah had no fireworks, but it had plenty of weapons. Arafat's fighters fired round after noisy round of flares, tracers, automatic rifles, and even antiaircraft guns into Beirut's night sky to celebrate. Most of Fatah's central committee, including Abu Iyad, had gathered in an underground bunker behind the dais; it was one of many in a subterranean network under Beirut built by the PLO to hide its fighters and arsenal. I tagged along with one of Arafat's advisers to get inside. The bunker was almost bourgeois—paneled walls, modern chrome furniture, shag carpeting. The thick stink of many cigarettes permeated the poorly ventilated room.

The centerpiece of the evening was Arafat's long speech exhorting Palestinian fighters on to victory against Israel and promising refugees that they would soon go home. Alternately waving his fist and a rifle in the air, Arafat appealed,

> *Let all rifles gather. Let all wills unite. And let all our people in the good Holy Land come together, because victory is near. . . . This is the year of the victorious march in the direction of Palestine. . . . We have a rendezvous with our steadfast kinfolk. Our flag which will fly over the minarets, churches, plains, hills, and mountains of liberated Jerusalem. We can already smell the scent of the land.*

As Arafat spoke, not one member of the central committee bothered to leave the bunker for the outdoor rally just a few steps away. They all stayed behind, smoking and talking among themselves.

The evening, like Palestinian politics, was a one-man show.

Over the years, in frustration and anger, rivals occasionally split off to form their own factions. Most of them were leftist. Fatah, ironically, had little ideology; it basically had a leader and a mission—to eliminate the state of Israel and expel all Jews who arrived after 1917. Arafat acquired weapons from the Soviet Union, China, and the eastern bloc, but the PLO was quite capitalist. It invested in Wall Street, through intermediaries, and ran a string of businesses, farms, and factories that produced furniture, clothing, toys, and kitchenware. Its conglomerate was often referred to as PLO, Inc.[3] For all his claims of leading a simple life, Arafat wore a Rolex watch. His uniforms were custom-made Italian khakis. And his late-in-life wife and daughter led a luxurious life in Paris.

Arafat usually coerced or cajoled most of his rivals back together under the broader umbrella of the Palestine Liberation Organization. And he often took the toughest decisions to his inner circle as well as the Palestinian National Council, a parliament in exile. But it was usually to provide him cover to do what he wanted. Wily Arafat almost always prevailed.

Little changed after he returned from exile in 1994. From the Muqata, Arafat ran the new Palestinian Authority for the next decade as autocratically as he had the Palestine Liberation Organization. He also ensured that Fatah dominated all branches of government, the best private sector jobs, monopolies on lucrative imports, and the top security positions. Patronage was the lever of power. Laws passed by an elected legislature, including some impressive judicial and executive-branch reforms, sat on his desk ignored and unsigned for years.[4] Critics were often picked up and released at his whim rather than the dictates of a court.

In 2004, a public opinion poll found that eighty-seven percent of Palestinians surveyed believed that Arafat's government was corrupt and that its leaders were opportunists who became rich off their powers. Ninety-two percent wanted sweeping political reform of the Palestinian government.[5]

"Arafat became the curse of the Palestinian people. He was like a pharaoh," Palestinian journalist Sufian Taha told me. "He had the blood of many Palestinians on his hands during the years he was in Jordan and Beirut. We also suffered when he came back.

"Arafat wanted people to be corrupt, because that was the way he could control them," Taha said. "He could look them in the eye and know he could tell them what to do, because he knew what they were doing. He was like Don Corleone."

Disdain was widespread. Reflected Said, the pollster, "For Fatah, power was like having an open credit card, and it was all free. They had a 'shop 'til you drop' attitude."

In 2006, the Palestinian attorney general revealed that 700 million dollars in state funds had been squandered or stolen over the previous few years. Some of the money lost in fifty separate cases had been transferred to personal accounts locally and abroad. Twenty-five people had been arrested, but ten had fled overseas. The fraud included construction of fictitious factories and land deals that existed only on paper. The Palestinian Authority had received five billion dollars in foreign aid over the previous five years, but was still on the verge of bankruptcy.[6]

"I thought Arafat and his people would be accountable once they were face-to-face with the people, in a way they hadn't been when in exile. But I was mistaken," said Samir Abdullah, director of the Palestine Economic Policy Research Institute, when we met at the Ramallah Coffee Shop, the hub of political gossip. Abdullah had been a delegate to peace negotiations in the 1990s and was an early deputy minister of economy. But he quit in disgust, he told me.

"Arafat was like any dictator who relied on the few around him. He wouldn't listen. He never changed," Abdullah said.

When he died in late 2004, Arafat was buried at the Muqata, in a space cleared in the parking lot next to his old headquarters. The grave was lined with soil imported from Jerusalem's Dome of the Rock, the resplendent tiled shrine erected in the seventh century to mark the spot where Muslims believe the prophet Mohammed began his night journey into the heavens, mounted on a winged steed and in the company of the archangel Gabriel, to receive the word of God. I visited the grave site four months after Arafat's death. I was among the press traveling to the Muqata with Secretary of State Condoleezza Rice for talks with Arafat's successor, President Mahmoud Abbas. Rice's motorcade deliberately whizzed past Arafat's grave. I ambled back to take a look. Arafat's familiar black-and-white checkered kaffiyeh headdress was at the top of the grave. Self-conscious about his bald pate, Arafat had always covered it; he refused to be seen in public or to allow pictures without his headdress or military cap.

On a drizzling February day, the grave site seemed a forlorn place. It was inside a simple glass enclosure; plans were in the works to build a larger shrine and mosque around the grave. Three of the men who had protected Arafat in life stood at attention guarding his tomb. But there were no visitors. Arafat had quickly passed into history.

Arafat's death was one in a convergence of catalysts that has begun to spur change in the Middle East. It symbolized the gradual—and ongoing—passage of the old guard of leaders who emerged between the 1960s and the 1980s and then hung on to power for decades. That early generation of leaders may have started out with popular ideology or nationalist zeal, but they all ended up corrupt, ineffective, or autocratic—and often all three. Each miscalculated the costs to their societies of monopolizing power. They became the obstacles to progress.

Each also insured that the pace of change in the Middle East would be slower and its course more complex than anywhere elsewhere in the world.

After decades of autocratic rule, the search for alternatives can divide societies. Change unleashes not only new democrats. Transitions can produce the unexpected and even the extreme, and the process is complicated by conflict.

During the final week of the campaign, I called on Khalil Shikaki, who heads the Palestine Center for Policy and Survey Research. Born in 1953, Shikaki is a sturdily built man who dresses impeccably, usually in dark suits, fashionably classic ties, and wing-tip shoes. He wears large aviator glasses and has a neatly trimmed mustache and beard. His center, which is on the third floor of a small office building in Ramallah, was bustling with young researchers at computers, preparing for the election.

The vote, Shikaki told me, was the most important turning point since the Palestinian Authority was founded twelve years earlier.

"Politics here was dominated for so long by Arafat and Fatah. Palestinians for the first time have a lot of options," he explained, in his husky American-accented voice, as we chatted in a sunlit office. "So this election will go a long way in defining our future."

Shikaki has spent his professional life chronicling the evolution of Palestinian politics in international foreign-affairs journals and at prominent American and European think tanks. But his own family reflected the evolving diversity too. The son of refugees, Shikaki came from a family that had farmed citrus, apricots, cucumbers, and wheat for generations in the village of Zarnouga, near Rehovot, in what is now central Israel. His parents fled in 1948. He was one of eight children brought up in a refugee camp in the Gaza Strip. Education was often the only way out of rampant poverty among refugees; both he and his older brother Fathi won scholarships outside Gaza.

The Shikaki brothers, close in age and appearance, then chose opposite paths.

Khalil Shikaki earned a doctorate in political science at Columbia University in New York. He returned in 1986 to teach at a West Bank university. He later founded the first fully independent political research center in the Arab world. He became an outspoken advocate of democracy for the Palestinians and of peace with Israel, frequently speaking to Jewish groups and working with Israeli colleagues.

His older brother Fathi Shikaki took a medical degree at Egypt's Zagazig University, a campus with a restive Islamist movement. He returned to the Gaza Strip in 1981 to practice medicine. He soon cofounded Islamic Jihad, the Palestinians' most militant movement, and became its first leader. The goal of secret underground cells under his command was to eliminate the "Zionist entity" and reestablish old Palestine in a state based on Islamic law.

Khalil Shikaki refuses to talk about his older brother, a relationship that has complicated his own life and sparked controversy despite their estrangement.[7] He responded only generically to my question about the political range—and contradictions—within a single family.

"Education was important in giving Palestinians the ability to express their own opinions," he told me. "It's not an issue now for family members to have quite different views and tactics. You'll find it in dozens of cases, even in this election."

The evolution of new leadership usually unfolds in uneven stages. For the Palestinians, it has been a particularly circuitous path because of the Arab-Israeli conflict. The goals and tactics of Palestinian politics have evolved through four stages since the so-called *Nakba,* the "disaster" or "cataclysm," of 1948.

The early leaders who rejected a United Nations proposal to partition Palestine into separate Arab and Jewish states were the traditional powers, including feudal landowners, clan patriarchs, and community figures like the Grand Mufti of Jerusalem. The exodus in 1948 of some 700,000 Palestinians—more than half of the population, according to United Nations and British figures—left the Palestinians largely rudderless and in disarray. For a generation, the Palestinian issue was managed by other Arabs. Egypt created the original Palestine Liberation Organization, which was only years later wrested away by Arafat's Fatah to become the umbrella for many Palestinian factions.

The first power shift began in the mid-1960s, as traditional leaders lost ground to a modern and secular nationalist movement no longer based on class and clan. It took two forms. Exiles in the Diaspora were the most visible. Over the next two decades, the eight factions in the Palestine Liberation Organization mobilized fighters from refugee camps in Egypt, Jordan, Syria, and Lebanon to wage war on Israel.

A second leadership also quietly emerged inside the territories after Israel occupied the West Bank and Gaza in 1967. It was tentative and fragmented. Its focus was local affairs. It deferred to the PLO to pressure Israel. But to fend for themselves, the internal Palestinians developed a vibrant array of institutions more diverse, independent, and active than in any other part of the Arab world.

"In order to work together against Israel, Palestinians had to overlook major differences among themselves," Shikaki explained. "That created a de facto pluralism. It opened the door for a new civil society that emerged in context of the occupation—and having to respect each other's role in fighting it."

Among those who witnessed the shift between 1967 and the mid-1980s was Ghassan Khattib, a tall man with a neat black mustache and a modest deference. He was eleven when Israel captured the West Bank and Gaza Strip. I also visited him during the final campaign week.

"We had a different experience from other Arab countries. The occupation didn't allow the emergence of an elite powerful enough to dominate the community or prevent elections among us or suppress whole strata of society, as happened elsewhere," Khattib told me. "But because we didn't have our own government, we built grassroots nongovernment organizations—charitable societies, trade unions, a women's movement, youth and sports groups, professional organizations, a lawyers' bar, a medical association.

"Almost all of them were structured on a democratic basis, with leadership that was elected, most of them annually," he said. "The student-union elections at universities were very prominent. People all over the country would stay up all night to see the results of the student elections."

I had occasionally covered those elections, which generated great interest in Israel and the wider Middle East too. They first revealed the takeover of Palestinian politics inside the territories by the nationalists. The student council votes then became the strongest indicator of political trends and effectively the only form of public-opinion polling.

Khattib was one of the early student leaders. He was elected to the Birzeit University council five times.

"So we've been living in a society with the beginnings of democratic ambitions for quite some time," he told me, then added pointedly, "and this did not come from the PLO in Beirut."

Khattib later held three cabinet posts in the Palestinian government. He was minister of planning, a pivotal post in a nascent state, when we spoke.

The second big power shift followed Israel's 1982 lightning invasion of Lebanon. Israel routed the Palestinians in one week, then besieged west Beirut for three months, until Arafat was forced to pull out of Lebanon altogether. Only six months after his New Year's Eve vow that 1982 would mark "the year of the victorious march" to Jerusalem, Arafat was instead dispatched even further away. I watched him sail off from Beirut's port to distant Tunis in North Africa—not even on the same continent. Palestinian fighters were dispersed as far away as Yemen and Algeria.

It was the biggest defeat for the Palestinians since 1948. Almost three decades after Fatah's creation and almost two decades after the PLO was founded, the exiled Palestinian leadership had achieved virtually nothing.

Hundreds of miles from the action, the defeated PLO soon lost its leverage—with Israel, the international community and, most of all, its own people.

"The defeat of the PLO created a vacuum," Shikaki told me. "Leaders in the territories were quick to take charge, and from 1982 until 1988, the inside leadership became stronger than the leadership outside."

In 1987, angry young Palestinians in the West Bank and Gaza for the first time took action against Israel into their own hands with a grassroots revolt. Tensions with Israel had been compounded by growing unemployment, soaring poverty, and high birth rates in small spaces. The situation was combustible. It took only the spark of a traffic accident in which an Israeli military truck crashed into a van, killing four Palestinians from a Gaza refugee camp, to set it off.[8] Rioting erupted and quickly spread across Gaza and into the West Bank. Young Palestinians initially confronted Israeli troops with rocks, but later with Molotov cocktails and barricades of burning tires.

The uprising—popularly called the intifada, literally the "shaking off"—marked the rise of the Palestinian internal leadership. It altered the political dynamics too.

"The intifada," Shikaki explained, "produced two phenomena. It introduced political Islam as a mobilizing force. It also produced a new young guard of nationalists who posed a challenge to the dominance of the PLO's old guard in exile."

The PLO in Tunis tried to claim credit for the intifada and manipulate its activities from afar. But the heart of the uprising was really run by local leaders. In the West Bank, Ramallah was the center for the intifada's Unified Command, a new umbrella for young leftist, nationalist, and religious activists who banded together. Every week, its leadership passed out bulletins on Ramallah's streets with schedules of protests or strikes. The intifada raged on year after year in sporadic angry bursts.

Overtaken and increasingly irrelevant, Arafat was forced to cede to the internal leaders—and, more importantly, their quite different agenda.

The PLO Covenant formulated in 1968 had pledged "armed struggle" until all of old Palestine was "liberated." Articles Twenty and Twenty-one in the covenant ruled out Jewish rights to a country.

Jewish claims of historical or religious ties with Palestine are incompatible with the facts of history and the true conception of what constitutes state-hood. Judaism, being a religion, is not an independent nationality. Nor do Jews constitute a single nation with an identity of its own; they are citizens of the states to which they belong.

The Arab Palestinian people, expressing themselves by the armed Palestinian revolution, reject all solutions which are substitutes for the total liberation of Palestine and reject all proposals aiming at the liquidation of the Palestinian problem.

But the Palestinians inside the territories had moved in a different direction. Thousands worked in Israel. Many spoke Hebrew. And significant numbers appeared willing, albeit begrudgingly, to accept Israel's right to exist and a two-state solution in which Israel and a Palestinian state would coexist.

"The occupation was by Israel, a democratic country, not a dictatorship. Palestinians worked in Israel, watched Israeli television, read Israeli newspapers, and what they saw was that Israel had the kind of democracy that they wanted," Shikaki explained to me.

"This was very different from the PLO elite, who lived in countries that were dictatorships—Syria, Iraq, Tunisia, Algeria, Libya, Yemen, or Syrian-controlled Lebanon—that weren't tolerant. These were societies with guns that were used to enforce views.

"The outside leadership was made up of refugees whose solution was the return of all of Israel. The leadership inside had only one goal: to create a Palestinian state," Shikaki said. "Every time the inside leadership gained prominence, the PLO had to moderate its positions."

In 1988, to avoid becoming irrelevant as the intifada raged on, Arafat was forced to take the two steps he had long avoided—renouncing terrorism and recognizing Israel's right to exist. He had little choice. It was the only way to get back in the game. His concessions opened the way for the PLO to become a player in diplomatic efforts. In exchange, Arafat won diplomatic recognition of the PLO by the United States, the primary broker of peace.

The uprising did not wind down completely until peace talks began in Madrid in 1991 and led, on a circuitous and initially secret route, to talks in Oslo and the first phase of a peace agreement. The formal pact was signed in 1993 by Arafat and Israeli Prime Minister Yitzhak Rabin on the south lawn of the White House. The Oslo Accords established the Palestinian Authority, a tiny new pre-state, with powers limited to policing and municipal services in parts of the West Bank and Gaza Strip.

The Shikaki brothers were among the new internal leaders.

Khalil Shikaki was part of back-channel contacts between Palestinians and Israelis in London in 1992. It was a parallel process to the secret negotiations in Oslo that produced the peace accords. He also conducted the first public-opinion poll to test whether Palestinians would embrace peace after more than four decades of war. The process took nine months. The idea of getting Palestinians to say what they really thought—which had never been done before, and was complicated by the Israeli occupation—proved far harder than anticipated.

"During the initial tests, four out of ten homes refused to talk to us. We had to take dozens of tests just to find out what was preventing people from allowing us into their homes," Shikaki said. With little basic data to work from, field teams had to draw their own maps of some areas and figure out from scratch the local demographics to ensure a representative sampling. They eventually got rejections down to two percent.

"On the day that the Oslo agreement was signed on the White House lawn, we released our first survey. We asked whether people supported or opposed the plan," he recalled.

"Two thirds supported it," he said, cracking a small smile. Shikaki usually speaks with a professor's serious precision. "It was very exciting."

Over the same period, however, his older brother was committed to undermining peace. Often described as a charismatic man, Fathi Shikaki was twice jailed by the Israelis, for a year in 1983 and for three years beginning in 1986. In 1988, he was deported to Lebanon. By 1992, he was headquartered in Syria, and Iran had become Islamic Jihad's main source of funds, arms, and training.

"We reject a negotiation process, because it legitimizes the occupation of our land and neglects the Palestinians who are without a country or identity," Fathi Shikaki told an interviewer in 1992, the same year his brother was negotiating with Israelis. "I do not know how the Palestinian is described as a terrorist when he screams from his pain and suffering and is defending his land against Jewish Russian soldiers, who never—neither he nor his forefathers—set foot in any inch of Palestine."[9]

Islam, he added, "is the ideology that must be adhered to in achieving liberation and independence as well as development and progress. This is what the PLO lacked from the very beginning."

After the 1993 Oslo Accords were signed, the older Shikaki helped launch the National Alliance, a coalition of ten hard-line Palestinian groups that rejected the peace plan. It, too, was headquartered in Syria.

On October 26, 1995, Shikaki was in Malta, reportedly in transit between Libya and Syria. All Islamic Jihad activities are clandestine. All its members operate in covert cells. Shikaki's movements were all secret. According to accounts from the time, Shikaki walked out of his hotel and was approached by two men on a motorcycle. One pulled out a gun with a silencer and shot Shikaki five times. The Maltese government described the assassination as a professional hit. The motorcycle was later found abandoned. It had false license plates. The gunmen were never identified or caught.

The assassination was widely attributed to, but never acknowledged by, Israeli intelligence. Fathi Shikaki's funeral in Damascus was reportedly attended by some 40,000 people.

The third shift in power followed the breakdown of peace efforts in 2000.

The 1993 Oslo Accords called for a final peace agreement within five years. Its Declaration of Principles tackled the thorny issues of statehood and borders, Jerusalem, refugees, and Jewish settlements. But the Oslo goal proved elusive. And a last-ditch effort by the United States to negotiate in 2000 broke down when Arafat balked at terms offered by Israeli Prime Minister Ehud Barak.

With the death of the Oslo process, tensions again reached breaking point. Another intifada erupted within weeks.[10]

The second uprising was far more sophisticated, down to the onions and perfume handed out by teenage girls as antidotes to Israeli tear gas. It was also deadlier.[11] Rock-throwing escalated into low-intensity warfare after two Israeli soldiers were captured and taken to Ramallah's police station. A mob stormed the facility, beat the two Israelis to death, then mutilated their bodies. Israeli helicopter gunships retaliated by demolishing the police station. It was the first Israeli air strike on the Palestinian territories in thirty-three years, since the 1967 war.

The second intifada featured the bloodiest cycle of violence ever between Israelis and Palestinians. Suicide bombings soared against Israeli civilian targets, including hotels, discos, a bustling café, a pizzeria, a pub, a shopping mall, and several bus stations.[12] Israel struck back hard against both Palestinian street fighters and government sites. In 2002, Israeli troops reoccupied big chunks of the Palestinian territories and began construction of a controversial wall to cordon off the West Bank. Arafat came under siege in the Muqata.

The Palestinian Authority, unable to deliver either stability or basic governance, started to disintegrate. Its legislature had to meet by video-conference because Gazan lawmakers were unable to travel to headquarters in Ramallah. The United States orchestrated a new "road map" for peace, which stalled when Arafat did not end the violence against Israel. Temporary cease-fires were organized but frequently violated. Much of daily life came to a standstill. Unemployment, lawlessness, and despair became rampant.

Fatah also increasingly fragmented. Arafat, ailing and stubborn, refused to leave the Muqata for fear he would not be allowed back. Bitter and sometimes bloody power struggles erupted within Fatah. Its young guard—which included both moderates and militants, both rising politicians and armed thugs—increasingly went out on their own. Younger Fatah politicians like Marwan Barghouti, almost by default, took the political initiative away from Arafat and his cronies. And young thugs in the security forces effectively became militias that initiated their own attacks against Israel and ruled the Palestinian streets by intimidation, racketeering, and gangsterism.

As order broke down, Hamas increasingly filled the political space. During this third shift in power, the Islamic party moved from the margins to the mainstream.

Hamas differed significantly from Islamic Jihad, the first militant movement. Islamic Jihad had remained tiny, totally underground, engaged only in violence, with leaders either forced into exile or eliminated in Israel's "targeted assassinations." Hamas was not clandestine. It was also dual-purpose. Created in 1987 during the first intifada, its well-armed al Qassam Brigade became notorious for some of the most brazen suicide and rocket attacks against Israel.[13] But Hamas also used the 1990s to establish a huge network of social services, schools, clinics, welfare organizations, and women's groups—a parallel civil society. Up to ninety percent of its resources and staff were devoted to public-service enterprises.[14] When the Palestinian Authority failed to deliver, Hamas institutions increasingly did.

"Hamas emerged as a credible political and security alternative to Fatah and a challenge to its long-standing dominance," Shikaki explained.

"The shift did not mean a greater religiosity in society. Hamas responded to the perception of a heightened threat more than anyone else. Palestinians were subject to collective punishment, so there was a great deal of public anger. Suicide attacks became very popular. The Palestinian public wanted it in the same way Ariel Sharon's brutality against the Palestinians was popular among Israelis."

Support for Hamas more than doubled between the outbreak of the intifada in 2000 and 2004, Shikaki's surveys found. Support for Fatah had meanwhile tumbled, with Arafat's personal standing cut in half, from a high of sixty-five percent support in 1996, when he won the presidency in the first Palestinian election, to thirty-five percent in 2004.[15]

And then Arafat suddenly died, opening the way for long-deferred elections—and even more dramatic change.

Voters, when offered real choices for the first time, often go to the polls to get revenge for the past. Early victors are not always long-term winners. They are simply the ones not rejected.

The day before the election, I drove to Hebron. Twenty miles south of Jerusalem, it is now the West Bank's largest city. While Ramallah is the most liberal town, dusty Hebron is the most conservative. It is rich with religious history, centered around the Tomb of the Patriarchs, where Abraham is buried, along with Sarah, Isaac and Rebecca, Jacob and Leah, the patriarchs and matriarchs of Judaism. The tomb is a venerated place for Jewish pilgrimages; 500 Jewish settlers reestablished a presence in Hebron, under the protection of 2,000 Israeli troops, to be near it. But Muslims also revere Abraham. Religious tradition holds that he fathered the Arabs through his son Ismail and the Israelites through his son Isaac. He is mentioned more than two dozen times in the Koran. In Arabic, Hebron is called al-Khalil, short for *Ibrahim al-Khalil al-Rahman,* or "City of Abraham, the Friend of God." Muslims also pray at the tomb.

Some of the most dramatic violence in the Palestinian-Israeli conflict has happened at the tomb. In 1980, Palestinians murdered six Jewish yeshiva students and wounded twenty others as they returned from prayers at the Tomb of the Patriarchs. In 1994, American-born Israeli physician Baruch Goldstein opened fire on Muslim worshippers at the tomb, killing twenty-nine and wounding 125.

I went to Hebron, however, because of a different rivalry. One of the world's oldest cities had the most interesting contest in the Palestinian election: A top Fatah official who had once been considered an heir apparent to Arafat was running against a popular Muslim preacher with Hamas.

They, too, happened to be brothers.

The Rajoub boys, Jibril and Nayef, came from a family of thirteen children. Both born in the 1950s, they grew up in Dura, on Hebron's outskirts. In 2006, they symbolized Palestinian politics fifteen months after Arafat's death. Although eleven parties were competing, the election for the 132-seat parliament and a new government had boiled down to a contest between two: Fatah and Hamas.

The Rajoubs represented the conundrum of choices.

Jibril Rajoub—Jibril is Arabic for Gabriel—is the older brother and a Palestinian legend. He is a bear of a man, now balding and paunchy, with a tough-guy swagger. His career has been checkered. In 1969, at age sixteen, he was caught throwing grenades at Israeli troops in the West Bank. He was imprisoned for seventeen years, until 1985. After the first intifada erupted, he was deported. He went to Tunisia and joined the Fatah inner circle around Arafat.

After the Oslo Accords, Rajoub returned with Arafat and was put in charge of West Bank security, a pseudo-defense minister's job for a nonstate. The job included liaising with Israel—ironically, using the Hebrew he had picked up in an Israeli prison to deal with his former jailers—and the United States. A bit of a braggart, Rajoub made no secret of ties to the Central Intelligence Agency. During a 2001 trip to Washington, he boasted that the CIA always provided him with an armor-plated limousine during his visits.[16] An autobiographical collection of his interviews includes a picture with former CIA Director George Tenet, with whom he worked closely during Tenet's brief mission in Middle East diplomacy.

By Palestinian standards, the older Rajoub was a tough pragmatist willing to do Arafat's dirty work. He reined in militants of Hamas and Islamic Jihad to stop attacks against Israelis during peace efforts. He also quashed dissent against Arafat. His Preventive Security Force made calls or visits to media outlets, nongovernmental organizations, and academics that became too critical of Arafat's autocratic rule. More feared than popular, Rajoub was sometimes referred to as the king of the West Bank.

On Israel, however, Rajoub straddled the line. After the second uprising erupted in 2000, he supported the intifada against Israeli troops in the occupied territories, but he opposed attacks inside Israel.

"Suicide bombs and violence will not serve the Palestinian cause," Rajoub told Voice of Palestine Radio after two Palestinians were killed while preparing a bomb near the site of the Maccabiah Games, Israel's Olympics-like athletic competition, in 2001.

"Resistance against the occupation is one thing, and using perni-
cious means to kill people, just because they are people, is something
else," he added. "These should stop because it is not in our interests, it
does not serve us."[17]

On Islamic militancy, he took a tough line. He publicly blasted
Islamic schools for teaching "dangerous things" about the faith. "No
one," he said in 2001, "has a right to dictate their crazy vision to our
children."[18]

In the 2006 election, Rajoub's base of support was hard-core Fatah
loyalists and the bloated Palestinian security services. The West Bank
force had 5,000 personnel, but Palestinians told me that almost 60,000
were on the payroll—one of the ways Fatah maintained support.
Rajoub's well-financed campaign was partially footed, according to
West Bank scuttlebutt, by ill-gotten profits off the Palestinian Authority's import monopolies. His entourage tooled around in armored vans
and European luxury cars. He used the conference center of Hebron's
best hotel to meet local leaders. A large staff of handlers arranged rallies, answered calls, and distributed glossy brochures. He even had a
campaign song, with a refrain, "Jibril Rajoub is the lion of the south;
he *is* the strong man."

Rajoub ran on Fatah's Future List. The split within Fatah had deepened in the run-up to the election. The young guard, who came from
inside the territories, felt it should assume more power after Arafat's
death. When the old guard balked, the younger generation threatened
to break away and run on its own. In a last-minute compromise, they
agreed to field candidates from both factions, sometimes in the same
districts. Each district had multiple seats; Hebron was the largest district, with nine seats up for grabs. Conceivably, candidates from both
factions could win. It proved a fateful decision.

Fatah's young guard was led by Marwan Barghouti, the most popular Fatah politician. Barghouti came from Ramallah. He had been
student-body president at Birzeit University and later a leader in the
first intifada. Israel deported him to Jordan in 1987; he was allowed to
return after the Oslo Accords. In the 1996 election, he won a seat in the
Palestinian legislature. Barghouti advocated peace with Israel, but after
the Oslo process died and the second intifada erupted, he was again a

major figure as a leader of the new Tanzim militia that emerged within Fatah.

Israel arrested Barghouti after it reoccupied the West Bank in 2002. He was charged with the murder of four Israelis and a Greek monk carried out by the Tanzim. It was largely guilt by leadership. He was sentenced to five life sentences. Nevertheless, in 2006 he was running, from prison, for reelection to the Palestinian legislature. As part of the compromise between the old and young guards, he headed Fatah's list. He became Fatah's election poster boy. Ramallah and other West Bank cities were festooned with billboards and placards of Barghouti in brown prison garb, smiling and waving his shackled hands above his head, as if in victory.

Fatah did not have much to offer besides Barghouti's popular appeal. The whole campaign played out over the party's failures.

During the final campaign week, the eleven parties held a debate at Ramallah's Cultural Palace. Candidates from each party sat at a desk on stage for two hours of intense questioning by four independent moderators. Each answer was limited to two minutes. Throughout the evening, I kept thinking back to Arafat rambling on interminably and making impossible promises, his inner circle unwilling to rein him in, at Fatah's 1981 anniversary event. In 2006, eleven parties had to present detailed political platforms in a program televised throughout the Arab world. Each party outlined an agenda centered on ending corruption, investigating government abuses, limiting leaders' special powers, and strengthening an independent judiciary—all reforms playing off Arafat's failures.

Rajoub also had little to run on, except his past power. He was often on the defensive and quite elusive to journalists. I set up several appointments to see him. But his assistant, a harried young woman named Rima, called back frequently to change the day or time—until it was finally election eve. When I got to Hebron, she told me that Jibril had had to leave town on short notice and would be unavailable. He may have gotten tired of talking about the competition. On the few occasions when the press did corner him, the subject inevitably turned to Hamas.

"We have nothing to learn from Hamas," Rajoub told *The New*

York Times. "Hamas believes armed struggle is the only way to confront Israel. I hope they will adopt a pragmatic, realistic platform. But they should learn from us. We have led the revolution. We have led the Palestinian people for forty-one years."[19]

Rajoub, like most of the political analysts and pollsters, thought he was a shoo-in. The only question was which brother would come in first.

It was much easier to see Sheikh Nayef, as his younger brother is known in deference to his role as a mosque preacher in the Dura suburb of Hebron. Every time I called a telephone number I had been given, he answered. He was always amenable to shifting the time to accommodate the needs of his brother and rival. He invited me to meet him at his home.

Sheikh Nayef is a towering man with a full beard accented by gray wisps under the lip. He has strikingly large hands and long eyelashes. He was born five years after his older brother and has a fraternal twin named Yasser. We sat on worn velvet couches in a receiving room in front of the house. The sheikh was dressed informally in a V-neck sweater and a tan jacket with a zipper. He was as low-key as his brother was intense.

Sheikh Nayef was running on Hamas's Change and Reform ticket. It was a low-budget campaign. He had to borrow his twin brother's dented, secondhand car to drive around Hebron.

"Jibril is part of the Palestinian Authority, so he has tremendous assets available to him," the sheikh told me, as the youngest of his eight children waddled into the room and over to her father. The two-year-old was wearing a green Hamas baseball cap and green Hamas sash over a pink sweater. "Our campaign is so modest that I had to borrow one thousand dollars to register as a candidate. I have yet to pay it off." To supplement his income, the neighborhood sheikh was also a beekeeper. He was well known around Hebron for his honey.

Hamas underplayed its assets, however, and its strategy. Before the election, the party signed an election code of conduct not to exploit places of worship to win votes. But the younger Rajoub had an edge simply by preaching at the mosque every Friday. His campaign was also staffed by the faithful, including several women in conservative Muslim dress. And Hamas's technologically hip campaign did not shy away from invoking higher powers.

"Vote for the green crescent of Hamas. Forward this message and you will be blessed by God," was one of several text messages sent to cell phones throughout the territories, including my rental.

Like his brother, Sheikh Nayef had a checkered past. He had been arrested four times by Israel—and once by his brother.

Educated in Jordan, he joined Hamas when it emerged in 1987 out of the first intifada. Detained four times by Israel, he and his twin had been part of a mass expulsion in 1992 after the deaths of six Israeli soldiers, including one who was kidnapped and later found bound and stabbed. More than 400 Islamists, mainly from Hamas, were rounded up, blindfolded and handcuffed, and driven to the Lebanese border. When Lebanon refused to allow them to cross, the deportees ended up living in tents for a year in a no-man's land between the two countries. Jibril Rajoub had visited his younger brothers; Sheikh Nayef had a picture in his receiving room of the three of them standing along the border. The deportees were eventually allowed to return as a by-product of the Oslo Accords. Seven of the nine Hamas candidates in Hebron had been among those deportees.

The sheikh and his twin were arrested by their big brother during Arafat's 1996 crackdown on Hamas.

"It was nothing personal," the sheikh said, smiling. Neither was held very long.

Ironically, Hamas and Fatah have the same roots. Both emerged from the Muslim Brotherhood founded in Egypt. Arafat had been a member of the Brotherhood as a student in Cairo in the 1950s. Hamas had been created by the crippled but charismatic Muslim preacher Sheikh Ahmed Yassin, who headed the Palestinian branch of the Brotherhood in Gaza.

Hamas is an acronym for *Harakat al-Muqawama al-Islamiyya,* or the Islamic Resistance Movement. Arab organizations often look for double entendre in their titles. Hamas means "zeal."

The Hamas charter lauds the PLO, since it "contains the father and the brother, the next of kin and the friend" who share a common enemy and a common fate. But it scolds the PLO for its secular platform. "Whoever takes his religion lightly," the charter declares, "is a loser." The Koran is the movement's constitution. Its goal is to see "the banner of Allah over every inch of Palestine."

The Hamas charter is venomous about Israel, which it charges is trying to consume territory from the Nile to the Euphrates. It echoes the Palestine Liberation Organization's original covenant in its pledge to obliterate the Jewish state.

> *The Islamic Resistance Movement believes that the land of Palestine is an Islamic endowment consecrated for future Muslim generations until Judgment Day. . . . It, or any part of it, should not be given up. . . . There is no solution for the Palestinian question except through Jihad. Initiatives and so-called peaceful solutions and international conferences are in contradiction to the principles of the Islamic Resistance Movement. . . . These conferences are only ways of setting infidels in the land of Muslims as arbiters. When did the infidels do justice to the believers? . . . All [are] a waste of time and vain endeavors.*

Since it rejected the peace process, Hamas boycotted the Palestinian Authority that the Oslo Accords had produced. The movement did not run in either the 1996 election or the 2005 presidential election to replace Arafat. Participating in national politics would have compromised its mission and goals. Arafat had never been keen to include Hamas anyway. His strategy was a mix of squeezing, confronting, and clamping down on potential rivals, especially the Islamists.

But the post-Arafat era changed the dynamics—and the strategy of both Fatah and Hamas.

After he was elected to replace Arafat, President Mahmoud Abbas opted to try to integrate Hamas into the political process.[20] He had few choices. The white-haired Fatah cofounder, who had just turned seventy, did not have the political leverage to contain Hamas, even though Israel had eliminated its founder, Sheikh Yassin, his successor, the chief bomb-maker, and other top leaders in a string of "targeted assassinations." Hamas simply had too much local legitimacy. Its autonomous armed wing was too much of a threat both to Israel and the Palestinian Authority. And its institutions were on the verge of creating a parallel state.

Abbas could no longer establish order in the territories or negotiate with Israel without an arrangement with Hamas.

The turning point was local elections. Hamas, a grassroots movement, had long pressed for a vote in towns and cities; local councils had nothing to do with the Oslo Accords. Arafat had stalled, even after he agreed to hold them, aware that Hamas might gain further legitimacy.

After Arafat's death, Abbas reversed course in an attempt to co-opt Hamas.

Five months after Arafat's death and two months after Abbas took office, Egypt negotiated an agreement between the new Palestinian leadership and thirteen political groups. The Cairo Declaration in March 2005 called for all sides to honor a *tahdiya,* or period of calm, and to hold local and legislative elections without delay.[21]

In staggered votes over the next nine months, Hamas surprised even Hamas. By the final vote in December 2005, the Islamist party had won full or partial control of councils in most major towns, including historically Christian Bethlehem and other former Fatah strongholds. The one exception was Ramallah. In contrast, Fatah proved strong mainly in the politically marginal rural areas.[22]

A month later, Hamas was running for the first time in national elections.

In both votes, Hamas ran on a twenty-point platform of everyday issues—more health care, better education, improved infrastructure— though not piety. Like many of the Middle East's rising Islamist movements, Hamas was moving deliberately, but practically.

"We need to change many things, but step by step," Sheikh Nayef told me.

"We have two big priorities," he explained. "The first is corruption. Betraying the people's trust is one of the main reasons for people's disenchantment with Fatah and why they are turning to Hamas.

"The second is dealing with the chaos and lawlessness in the territories," he continued, in Arabic, relying on a reporter from aljazeera .net who said he had studied at the University of Oklahoma and Southern Illinois University. "Those responsible for this insecurity are the Palestinian security agencies. We have to reconstruct them. They are entirely bloated and yet they have utterly failed to end the chaos. Over half of the 58,000 on the payroll draw a salary but never leave their homes. It is nepotism and graft and cronyism."

I pointed out that his brother had controlled the West Bank security force.

"I am aware," he said, with a bemused grin.

To a lot of ears, the security-force issue was doublespeak for peace with Israel. Whoever controlled Palestinian security determined whether the Palestinian forces were used for peace or to pressure Israel.

On election eve, the big debate among both Palestinians and Israelis was over whether a democratically elected Hamas would moderate its position—specifically by implicitly honoring the principles and agreements made by the PLO even if it did not formally sign on. In other words, would Hamas be willing to repeat what Fatah did in 1988 in formally renouncing terrorism and accepting Israel's right to exist? Hamas had launched its first suicide bomb in 1993. Since the second intifada began in 2000, the militant movement was linked to more than 400 terrorist attacks—including over fifty suicide bombs—in which hundreds of Israelis had died and more than 2,000 had been injured.[23]

Some Hamas leaders hinted at the possibility of an indefinite *hudna,* or ceasefire, if Israel returned all territory occupied in the 1967 war. But none of them suggested that Hamas would accept a permanent peace.

I asked the sheikh—who had been released just four months earlier after eight months in Israeli detention—how far apart he was from his older brother on peace with Israel. "We agree when diagnosing political problems, but we differ on how to treat them," he replied, as his fingers flicked through a large set of worry beads. "Jibril's approach is based on negotiating with Israel. The Islamic movement's experience in negotiating has been dismal and disastrous. The Palestinian Authority was eventually reduced to a vanquished supplicant begging Israel for everything. This giant fiasco will not be repeated by us."

I noted that he had not totally rejected negotiations with Israel. For decades, Arafat had deftly skirted the same issue. Time and again, he came close in deliberately suggestive but ambiguous language, only to back off again when asked to clarify. Only when Arafat began to lose his political grip did he formally cave.

"What you said is true," Sheikh Nayef replied. "If negotiations have the potential to serve the interests of the Palestinian people or improve the lot of average Palestinians, yes, there is room for that. But it should not be conducted under conditions reflecting Israeli insolence and arrogance of power and blackmail and so on."

"Look," he said, "I am a moderate. There is a Koranic verse that says 'Allah has made you a moderate nation, so that you may be witness upon mankind and so that the prophet will be a witness unto you.' And I believe this."

I asked the sheikh if he would allow his own eight children to become suicide bombers. Hebron had gained fame as the hometown of several suicide bombers. Eight members of a local soccer team, including a coach, had all become suicide bombers.

"You have a totally gruesome picture of us that is inaccurate," he replied, his fingers flicking faster through the worry beads. "Martyrdom operations are not a fixed feature of the Islamic movement. They are not a pillar of our policy. They should be viewed instead as a reaction to Israeli oppression. We earnestly appeal to the Israelis to refrain from murdering Palestinian civilians so that we can put an end to martyrdom operations once and for all. We can not get rid of the effect unless we get rid of the cause."

I repeated my question about his children.

"Yes, I would allow them to carry out martyrdom operations, but I would much rather focus on ruling out the causes of what has made this inevitable," he said. "Martyrdom operations are the result of Jewish Nazism. The Israelis have presented us with two choices—either we die submissively like meek sheep or we die in suicide bombings in the streets of Tel Aviv or Netanya."

For the first time, the sheikh's voice rose. "We might forgive the Israelis for murdering our innocent civilians," he said, "but we will never forgive them for forcing us to kill their civilians."

Before I left, I pressed Sheikh Nayef for his election predictions. All public-opinion polls indicated Fatah was in the lead, but Hamas was pulling closer—anywhere from two to ten percentage points behind Fatah. The day before, both parties had held large rallies in Hebron. Some 4,000 had turned out for Jibril Rajoub and Fatah, but 35,000 had turned out for Sheikh Nayef and the Hamas candidates.

I asked how the sheikh thought his own siblings were likely to vote.

He chuckled. "I honestly don't know," he told me. "Some will probably vote for Jibril, and some will probably vote for me."

Even during their campaigns against each other, the two men had kept in touch.

"We see each other every two or three days, and we talk by telephone every day. We're very close," the sheikh said. "There's an Arab proverb—'A difference in opinion does not corrupt friendly relations.'

"This political diversity is a sign of the sophistication and maturity that members of one family can espouse different ideologies and political views," he continued. "Our parents' home was the epitome of Palestinian political plurality. We're proud of it.

"But," he added, "I think both of us will win."

On election night, the results were announced at Ramallah's Cultural Palace. They trickled in district by district amid great anticipation since, for the first time in an Arab election, no one knew the outcome in advance.

In the end, Hamas swept liberal Ramallah, except for the one seat reserved for a Christian. The Islamic party won all the seats in Jerusalem, except for two reserved for Christians. It took all but one seat allocated to Nablus. Even in historically Christian Bethlehem, Hamas won all but the two seats reserved for Christians.

The outcome stunned Palestinians—including the Rajoub brothers—as well as the outside world. Mused Secretary of State Condoleezza Rice, "Certainly I've asked why nobody saw it coming, and I hope that we will take a hard look, because it does say something about perhaps not having had a good enough pulse on the Palestinian population."[24]

In Hebron, Sheikh Nayef received more votes than any candidate in the entire West Bank. His older brother Jibril did not even make a decent showing. He lost. Hamas won all nine seats in Hebron.

Defying every exit poll, Hamas won an outright majority. It did not mop up, however. It won fifty-six percent of the seats in the legislature—and the right to form a government—but only forty-four percent of the vote. Fatah's fatal mistake was running too many candidates, dividing its own vote. Pollsters later said Fatah could have won—with the same vote—by fielding fewer candidates.

Nevertheless, Palestinian voters had sent a decisive message. "This was the only way to stop Fatah," said Samir Abdullah, director of the Palestine Economic Policy Research Institute, a delegate to peace negotiations in the 1990s, and an early deputy minister of economy. "Fatah leaders showed no willingness to change."

Added Nader Said, "If it had rained, Fatah would have lost out even more. You have to be motivated to vote."

After a half century of dominating Palestinian politics, Fatah's monopoly had ended. It was the first time an Arab electorate ousted autocratic leadership in free and fair elections—a message that resonated throughout the region.

Jibril Rajoub, jobless, decided to go back to school.

Sheikh Nayef became minister of religious affairs in the new government.

The coming conundrum in the Middle East is that free and fair elections may not initially produce a respectable democracy. After decades of autocratic rule, the political spectrum has become so skewed that the choices, and winners, may not all be peace-loving or tolerant moderates. The transition to stable democracy worldwide—in Russia, South Africa, and Venezuela, to name but a few still struggling in disparate ways—is a rocky process that requires time. But in the Middle East, transitions may be the messiest.

The Palestinians were the test case.

After winning several city-council elections in 2005, Hamas politicians sent mixed signals about their intentions. They often streamlined budgets, eliminated waste, and went after pervasive corruption. They also allied with Christian politicians in Ramallah and Bethlehem and did not try to change the tradition of councils appointing Christian mayors ruling over Muslim majorities. And they did not propose adopting Islamic law—yet.

"The implementation of Sharia is not a priority at this juncture,"

Sheikh Nayef Rajoub told al Jazeera. "This doesn't mean, however, that we will not seek to amend some of the existing laws to make them more even-handed."[25]

But the atmospherics clearly changed. Islam may not have become the law, but its rules were increasingly becoming the practice. In the West Bank town of Qalqilya, the city council cancelled a popular music festival because the music was too Westernized. The local sheikh said the festival violated Sharia. "There are times when the municipality acts as a brake on the Palestinian Authority decisions that are against Islam," the mayor explained.[26] In Gaza, a clampdown by Islamist vigilantes targeted shops selling liquor and pharmacies carrying birth-control pills. Traditionally more religious than the West Bank, more men in Gaza also grew beards, and more women wore head scarves, some even donning face veils, a practice virtually unknown a generation earlier.

So Hamas's decision to run for national office in 2006 deepened the debate about whether Islamists would honor democratic principles once elected. Views differed sharply.

"I have not seen any group as willing to be co-opted and integrated into a system that is not of their own making," reflected Nader Said, the U.S.-educated pollster in Ramallah. "The Palestinian Authority is still the umbrella of power, the Americans are still the interlocutors, and Israel is still the neighbor. So whatever they say, Hamas has to give up a great deal to participate.

"Things will never be the same for Hamas. And they have willingly accepted this change. Hamas decided that participation is part of the Muslim Brotherhood tradition. And this is the best time to integrate and compromise. They are not god-given angels anymore. They are running to fix things, not just to serve God. Their rhetoric has changed 180 degrees."

The region's rulers firmly believed otherwise. They have long argued that their control is the main safeguard against an Islamist political wave and potential theocratic rule.

"We should follow a style of reform that will not undermine stability and encourage the forces of radicalism and fundamentalism to direct the course of reform toward their objectives," opined Egypt's President

Hosni Mubarak. "What would happen if extremists won a majority in Arab parliaments?"[27]

After the election, I went to see the Hamas leadership outside the Palestinian territories—the men who had not participated in the historic vote—to get a sense of their vision of the future. The Palestinians faced two immediate challenges: First, developing their nascent democracy amid one of the fiercest political rivalries in the Arab world. And second, achieving statehood after many false starts. The way ahead was not clear because Hamas, like the Palestine Liberation Organization during its years in exile, has both inside and outside branches. Unlike the PLO, Hamas has a binding ideology. Yet views still differ within the movement.

My ultimate goal was to see Khaled Mashaal, the leader of Hamas. Getting access to him in Syria was hard enough. But security around Mashaal had also been tightened after an Israeli assassination attempt in 1997, which followed a series of suicide bombs in Israel. Benjamin Netanyahu, the Israeli prime minister at the time, called Mashaal the "preeminent figure responsible for the murder of innocent Israeli civilians." Israel came close to getting its revenge when two Israeli agents disguised as Canadian tourists tracked down Mashaal in Jordan and injected poison into his ear. The operatives were captured, and an enraged King Hussein demanded the antidote from Israel to save Mashaal's life. As part of the deal, Jordan freed the two Israelis in a prisoner exchange that included Israel's release of Sheikh Ahmed Yassin, the founding father of Hamas who had been imprisoned for eight years. Jordan later expelled Mashaal. He ended up in Syria.

Seven years later, Mashaal became head of Hamas by a process, literally, of elimination. In 2004, Israeli helicopter gunships swooped down over Gaza and fired a missile as Sheikh Yassin, who was partially paralyzed in a childhood sports accident, was being wheeled out of morning prayer services. Yassin, his bodyguards, and nine bystanders were killed. Abdel Aziz Rantisi, a cofounder of Hamas, succeeded Yassin. Less than a month later, an Israeli helicopter fired a missile at a car carrying Rantisi, his bodyguards, and his son. It was incinerated. Mashaal then assumed leadership of Hamas.

To get to Mashaal, I went first to Beirut in search of Osama Hamdan, whom I had met in the mid-1990s when he headed the Hamas office in Tehran. As a primary supplier of aid and arms to Hamas, Tehran was an important posting. Nevertheless, Hamdan once grumbled about how hard he had to lobby the Iranian government. "It's not as easy a job as you might think," he once told me. As a Sunni Arab, he also felt somewhat out of place among the Shiite Persians. He spoke Arabic and English, but he needed an interpreter to speak to the Iranians.

From Tehran, Hamdan moved to head the Beirut office in 1998. He also became a member of the Hamas politburo. In 2003, he was one of six senior Hamas leaders named by President Bush as a "specially designated global terrorist," which automatically froze personal assets in the United States and prohibited business transactions with Americans. I found his office in Beirut's poor southern suburbs, which is also the stronghold of Hezbollah, another Iranian ally.

Born in 1965, Hamdan still had youthful eyes, even as he had grown from the leanness of youth in 1994 to the heft of middle age in 2006. His brown beard and hair had not changed; they were both cropped short and neat.

We had a long conversation about the election and the future. I asked him if Hamas might modify its position on Israel, perhaps under an arrangement where President Abbas continued peace efforts as leader of the Palestine Liberation Organization. The PLO was the signatory to earlier agreements committing the Palestinians to peace in exchange for their own state. The compromise widely proffered after the election envisioned Hamas running day-to-day government, while Abbas brokered a solution for a Palestinian state coexisting with Israel.

"No," Hamdan replied, shaking his head with certainty.

"The Jews have the right to return to the places they came from, or they can live in the region as citizens, with their rights as Jews and as humans—but not in a state on our occupied land. Why did the French resist the German occupation during World War II? Why didn't the Afghans let the Russians occupy their country? The Israelis know they are occupying our homeland.

"So they will have their choice: They can accept that they are Jewish Palestinians, or they can go back to their homelands. It's their choice. No one will be forced to take one decision or the other."

Hamdan's answer was like going back thirty years in time, to the aggressive rhetoric from the days Yasser Arafat waged his campaign against Israel from the same southern suburbs of Beirut. Ironically, Hamdan invoked Arafat as justification for his view.

"In 1988, Arafat believed that recognizing Israel would win back part of our rights—and that he could get a Palestinian state with the 1967 borders. We met him several times after 1988, and he really believed that," Hamdan said. "But what happened? The Oslo agreement in 1993 called for a Palestinian state by 1998. It didn't happen. Since then, big chunks of West Bank lands have been taken by the Israelis. And the numbers of settlers tripled.

"It was all a grave mistake," he said, shaking his head. "No one will think to do that again."

On every issue, Hamdan represented the toughest positions within Hamas. His ideal state was a caliphate, ruled by a caliph, God's representative on earth, which would incorporate several Muslim countries as well as modern Israel. I asked him if he really thought a caliphate was viable in the twenty-first century.

"It's the right of people to dream that this may happen one day," he replied. "If someone had talked in the fifteenth century about France existing without a kingdom, no one would have believed it. If I had said eighty years ago that there will be a European Union, no one would have believed it. If someone had talked about unifying Germany twenty years ago, no one would believe it. But they all happened.

"Understand, I'm not talking about going back to living in old times. It doesn't mean riding camels or living in tents. It's only the principles we want to revive."

He was also dismissive of the American commitment to democracy for the Palestinians, even as he claimed Hamas was willing to talk to Washington's envoys.

"The United States is like the prince in search of Cinderella," he told me. "The Americans have the shoe, and they want to find the kind of people who fit the shoe. If the people who are elected don't fit into the American shoe, then the Americans will reject them for democracy."

Before leaving, I asked Hamdan if he would give me a contact to see Mashaal in Syria. Hamdan knew I disagreed with him, quite profoundly. I once told him that my father had been an officer in the U.S. Third Army unit that seized Ohrdruf, the first Nazi camp to be liberated by American troops. Ohrdruf was part of the Buchenwald network of camps. I had grown up on my father's stories about what the Nazis had done to Europe's Jews. Hamdan always argued with me that the Palestinians should not have to pay the price for Germany's atrocities. Neither of us ever got anywhere with the other on the subject of the Holocaust. Nevertheless, Hamdan pulled out his cell phone and called Damascus.

A week later, I was in a large room filled with green overstuffed chairs at Hamas headquarters in Syria. On one wall was a large poster of Sheikh Yassin surrounded with smaller pictures of fourteen other Hamas officials who had died in Israeli "targeted assassinations." A television tuned to al Jazeera was in one corner; a large model of Jerusalem's Dome of the Rock was in another.

Khalid Mashaal is a beefy man with silvering hair and penetrating dark eyes; his short beard is still black except for two silver streaks under the two sides of his mouth. He was wearing a light blue shirt, open-necked, and a navy suit. He greeted me when he strode into the room, but before we began talking he paused to intone, "In the name of God the compassionate and merciful."

Born in 1956 outside Ramallah, Mashaal had a reputation as a brainy kid from a conservative religious family. The family fled when Israel occupied the West Bank in 1967. The bitterness lingers.

"I'm from Ramallah," he said when I told him that I been at the Palestinian election. "I can't go there. But you, an American, just came from there."

Mashaal had spent half his life, almost a quarter century, in Kuwait. At Kuwait University, he studied physics and founded an Islamic student movement called the List of the Islamic Right to counter Arafat's Fatah. In the late 1980s, he was one of the original members of Hamas. He led the branch in Kuwait. Mashaal taught school until the 1990 Iraqi invasion of Kuwait, after which he fled again, this time to Jordan. In 1996, he became political director of Hamas.

Mashaal, a serious man not prone to smiling, was almost gleeful about the election results. "I was confident of winning, but not by this much," he told me. "Our people in the West Bank and Gaza said a week before the election that they thought we would do well. But it was much more than I expected."

What Hamas had not counted on was forming a government alone. The widespread assumption among many Palestinians, whatever the election outcome, was that Fatah and Hamas would end up in a coalition government. After Hamas's decisive win, however, Fatah opted to become the formal opposition. The result was a political mishmash: Fatah still controlled the presidency, while Hamas won the right to pick the prime minister, form a cabinet, and run the day-to-day government.

The rivalry between the two parties only deepened. Both sides violated the spirit of democracy.

Fatah refused to heed the message of its electoral defeat. In a preemptive move during the old legislature's final session, Fatah transferred many of the prime minister's powers to the president's office—effectively from Hamas to Fatah. Fatah ministers also filled vacancies and promoted followers in the civil service so it would be top-heavy with Fatah loyalists. President Abbas assumed control of lucrative border crossings from the interior ministry, and transferred authority over the Palestinian Broadcasting Corporation and the Palestinian News Agency from the information ministry to the president's office.[28] He also failed to clean up rampant corruption. After promising to rebuild the party from the ground up, Abbas instead allowed the old-boys' network to largely remain in place. Adding to the political tensions, Fatah's militias roamed the streets as if they still owned them.

At a rally in Damascus shortly before my visit, Mashaal condemned Fatah as "traitorous" for "robbing us of our powers as well as our people's rights."

Hamas, in turn, used the network of mosques to lambaste Fatah. The Islamic party, which already had the largest Palestinian militia, the al Qassam Brigade, mobilized a new government security force loyal only to its officials. It used tunnels, some almost 100 feet deep, dug by profiteering Gaza clans under the eight-mile border with Egypt, to bring in arms.[29] It also refused to recognize Israel, renounce violence, and accept either past peace deals or future negotiations—even though every public-opinion poll before and after the election showed the majority of Palestinians favored peace with Israel and a two-state solution.

Mashaal tried to straddle the divergent views within Hamas about how to achieve a Palestinian state. In an op-ed piece in Britain's *Guardian* newspaper a week after the vote, Mashaal invoked the old rhetoric opposing a Jewish state while at the same time proposing a long-term truce with Israel.

> *Our message to the Israelis is this: we do not fight you because you belong to a certain faith or culture. Jews have lived in the Muslim world for 13 centuries in peace and harmony; they are in our religion "the people of the book" who have a covenant from God and His Messenger Muhammad (peace be upon him) to be respected and protected. Our conflict with you is not religious but political. We have no problem with Jews who have not attacked us—our problem is with those who came to our land, imposed themselves on us by force, destroyed our society and banished our people.*
>
> *We shall never recognize the right of any power to rob us of our land and deny us our national rights. We shall never recognize the legitimacy of a Zionist state created on our soil in order to atone for somebody else's sins or solve somebody else's problem. But if you are willing to accept the principle of a long-term truce, we are prepared to negotiate the terms. Hamas is extending a hand of peace to those who are truly interested in a peace based on justice.[30]*

I asked Mashaal what "peace based on justice" really meant: Was Hamas willing to explore an arrangement that would effectively allow a permanent peace, or was it just positioning itself until demographics, regional support, and the military balance were more in its favor to claim all of old Palestine?

"Wars and struggles have favored Israel. These are historical facts," he replied. "The issue is complicated, so that's why we in Hamas have announced that we're ready to establish a Palestinian country on the borders of 1967, with the right of Palestinian refugees to come back to the cities they came from, then there can be an agreement for a truce. After that, the coming generations will decide the future."

His terms—the 1967 border and return of Palestinian refugees—were unacceptable to Israel. And, like Arafat at his slipperiest, Mashaal dodged the question—for ninety minutes—of recognizing the Jewish state.

"Israel does not recognize my rights. Who needs to be recognized—me the victim, or the killer and occupier?" he said.

Hamas's immediate crisis, however, was governing the little Palestinian Authority. Unwilling to deal with a violent extremist movement, the outside world suspended foreign aid needed to develop the nascent state, from building schools and paving roads to fostering civil society. Israel also withheld some fifty-five million dollars a month in Palestinian tax revenues that it collected—and that paid one-half of the Palestinian government's payroll, from teachers and police to medical staff and utility workers. Mashaal had been scrambling to raise tens of millions of dollars from a limited number of Muslim countries willing to help pay the Palestinian government's bills.

As revenues and aid dried up, Fatah loyalists agitated unpaid government workers to organize sit-ins and protests, deepening tensions. Within months, Fatah politicians urged Abbas to call early elections, ostensibly to end the political deadlock but also because they were unwilling to wait until 2010 to have a shot at ruling again.

"All these measures are to make the Hamas government fail," Mashaal told me.

The Palestinian Authority suffered from a political vacuum and rumbling disorder. The most vocal supporters of Hamas were other extremists. The day before I saw Mashaal, al Jazeera had aired a new audiotape from Osama bin Laden. The al Qaeda chief raged at the West for cutting off aid to the Palestinians after Hamas's victory.

"The European and American rejection of the current Palestinian government is a Zionist-Crusader war against Muslims," bin Laden said.

To the outside world, al Qaeda and Hamas fell into the same camp of militant groups built around a zealous religious ideology that justified suicide bombers and called for societies built strictly around Islamic law. With the rise of political Islam, cells of al Qaeda affiliates or wannabes had also emerged in Gaza. The Swords of Islamic Righteousness was one of the shadowy new renegade groups that attacked music

stores, recreational clubs, Internet cafés, and cultural centers. "Get back
to Allah and away from all those dirty, corruption things, because you
will never withstand the fire of hell and the torture at the end of your
life," the Swords warned after an Internet café attack.[31] The new cells
were widely linked to the mysterious deaths of three prostitutes.

Hamas and al Qaeda, however, were often also at odds. After the
Hamas election, Ayman al Zawahiri, the second-in-command, issued
a statement from hiding that scolded Hamas and appealed to the Palestinian movement not to work with the "secularist traitors" of Fatah.

> How come they did not demand an Islamic constitution for Palestine
> before entering any elections? Are they not an Islamic movement? ...
> Accepting the legitimacy of Mahmoud Abbas ... is an abyss that will
> ultimately lead to eliminating the jihad and recognizing Israel.[32]

Mashaal struggled to distance himself from al Qaeda. "Hamas has
very different policies," he told me. "Bin Laden thinks it's wrong to
participate in elections, while we participate. We also limit our struggle
against the Israeli occupation to Palestine. We don't take our attacks
outside Israel. The world must make a clear distinction between us and
al Qaeda."

Before leaving, I asked Mashaal to look at the Middle East a decade
down the road.

"There will be a general escalation in the region, because of the
Israeli occupation, the war in Iraq, and the expected American war in
Iran over its nuclear program," he offered. "So the region in the com-
ing years will have no real stability.

"But despite the difficulties in the coming years," he said, "the Palestinians will get their own state."

Over the next year, however, Palestinian politics instead drifted
deeper into a dysfunctional political deadlock. Talks between Hamas
and Fatah repeatedly collapsed; rival security forces and militias increasingly attacked each other. Deaths from factional violence mounted.

Tensions with Israel also escalated. On June 25, 2006, Hamas gunmen and militants from two other groups sneaked through a tunnel

under Gaza and attacked an Israeli army post. Two Israelis were killed, three were injured. The gunmen seized nineteen-year-old Corp. Gilad Shalit, then fled back to Gaza. They then demanded freedom for 1,500 Palestinian prisoners in exchange for the lone Israeli soldier.

Israel blamed Mashaal personally for the kidnapping. It also pledged not to succumb to extortion. Three days later, Israeli troops launched Operation Summer Rains, invading Gaza and launching raids across the West Bank to arrest Hamas members of parliament—thirty-eight in all, including the speaker of parliament and several cabinet ministers. Among them was Sheikh Nayef Rajoub.

The Israeli offensive did not end until a cease-fire was declared in November. Little was gained by either side during the five-month confrontation. Shalit was still a hostage; Rajoub and the Hamas politicians were still in an Israeli prison.

Amid military hostilities with Israel and Palestinian political tensions, life in the territories deteriorated rapidly. A year after the election, roughly two thirds of the Palestinians lived below the poverty line—or on less than three dollars a day.[33] A public-opinion survey found that three out of four Palestinians were disappointed with their government and the direction of their society. More than one half of the Palestinians polled blamed both Fatah and Hamas for failing to form a viable unity government—and for their economic plight.

In February 2007, Saudi Arabia intervened to end the year-long deadlock. Assembling leaders of the rival factions in Mecca, King Abdullah brokered a deal for a unity government and a cease-fire. Hamas retained the prime minister's job, while a Fatah official became his deputy. Cabinet posts were divvied up: Hamas got nine ministries, Fatah six, left-wing parties four, and independents five. Abbas accepted the Mecca Accord for Fatah, Mashaal for Hamas.

Al Qaeda again railed at its fellow Islamists in Hamas. "The Hamas leadership has finally joined the surrender train of [former Egyptian President Anwar] Sadat for humiliation and capitulation....Hamas went to a picnic with the U.S. Satan and his Saudi agent," Zawahiri said in another statement from hiding.[34]

The uneasy calm didn't last long, however. The fierce rivalry among militias soon flared anew. Tensions began to tear the two territories apart—from each other.

Although they are only thirty miles apart, the West Bank and Gaza had always been distinct places since they became the refuge for almost 500,000 fleeing Palestinians after Israel's creation in 1948. The two territories were ruled by different countries: The West Bank was annexed by Jordan. Gaza was administered by Egypt.

Under Jordanian rule, the West Bank—a mix of cosmopolitan cities and rustic agricultural areas with both Christians and Muslims—evolved into a society where religion was largely in the private domain. The West Bank was the center of Palestinian intellectual life. West Bank Palestinians often went to university in Lebanon, Syria, or Jordan. The middle class filled the ranks of Fatah and a slew of leftist factions under the Palestine Liberation Organization umbrella.

Under Egyptian rule, the Palestinians in the narrow Gaza Strip—which had one teeming city, three towns, and eight densely congested refugee camps—were initially influenced by Arab nationalism. But the poor in refugee camps had few cultural outlets beyond the mosque. The young who gravitated to universities in Egypt, including the leaders of Hamas, often came under the spell of the Muslim Brotherhood. Islamic charities often provided badly needed services, from dental care to food banks and summer camps.

Israel's conquest of large chunks of Egypt, Jordan, and Syria in the 1967 war brought the two territories together. Even under common occupation, however, the West Bank and Gaza continued on their own ways culturally and economically. They had distinct education systems, legal systems, and local leadership in nongovernment groups.

The territories finally came under common Arab rule in the new Palestinian Authority after the 1993 Oslo Accords. Israel agreed to treat the two areas as a single unit and guarantee safe passage between them. A winding road—for Palestinian use only—connected the West Bank and Gaza for the first time. The tenuous link lasted for seven years, until Israel imposed travel bans after the second intifada began in 2000.

Yet after almost fifteen years together, the two territories still had disparate profiles: The West Bank was occupied by Israeli troops but it was economically viable. It had more resources; its economy was diverse. Less than six percent of its population lived in refugee camps. In contrast, Gaza was free of Israeli troops, which had been withdrawn in 2005, but was economically strapped. One third of Gazans were stuck in overcrowded refugee camps of cinder-block homes and rutted allies. With few resources, at least one half of Gaza's labor force was out of work by 2007. Roughly eight out of ten Gazans relied on some form of United Nations food aid.

The new rupture began on June 9, 2007. Tensions building over the eighteen months since the election literally exploded. Weeks of escalating attacks between rival forces loyal to Fatah and Hamas turned into open street battles in Gaza. The narrow strip echoed with the staccato of gunfire, as smoke rose into the air from rocket and mortar attacks on government buildings. Bands of masked fighters roamed Gaza City, waged gun battles in the streets, and executed captives on the spot. Both Hamas and Fatah reportedly hurled opponents from high-rise buildings, with gunmen hunting down wounded rivals in hospital wards to finish them off.[35] Hamas executed a Fatah commander and paraded his body through a refugee camp. Another Fatah official escaped by tying Hamas hostages to the front and roof of his pickup truck.

The Gaza showdown quickly began to look like civil war. "I think we are in Iraq, not Gaza," a father of six told Reuters.[36] "Snipers on rooftops killing people. Bodies mutilated and dumped in the streets in very humiliating ways. What else does civil war mean but this?"

The security forces loyal to President Abbas had far greater numbers but no strategy. Hamas forces had more arms and greater discipline. Hamas systematically seized Fatah's outlying positions, then closed in on the four security headquarters in Gaza City. Hamas claimed its goal was only to end the factional fighting and restore order by bringing all armed factions under control of the unity government.

"What happened in Gaza was a necessary step. The people were suffering from chaos, and the lack of security drove the crisis toward explosion, so this treatment was needed," Mashaal told a press conference in Damascus. But the timing may also have been linked to an American plan to train, arm, and upgrade Abbas's personal Presidential Guards with over forty million dollars in aid. It was a little-disguised effort to give Abbas more muscle, which Hamas leaders suspected was designed to oust them from power. Their offensive was in part a pre-emptive strike.

It was also an opportunity for revenge. During the decade of Arafat's rule, Fatah officials had often been ruthless with Hamas. Leaders and fighters had been jailed. Some were tortured; many had their beards, a sign of piety, forcibly shaved to humiliate them. As Hamas got its turn, Muslim clerics issued fatwas over the Hamas television and radio stations calling the battle "a war between Islam and the non-believers."[37]

In a last-ditch effort to end the fighting, hundreds of men, women, and children marched down a main Gaza City street waving the Palestinian flag. One banner warned: "History will judge you. The street will not forgive you."[38] Fatah gunmen used the crowd as a shield to open fire at Hamas fighters. Hamas gunmen fired back. Two of the demonstrators were killed.

The finale to eighteen months of confrontation proved to be a rout, however. It was over in five days. Hamas won easily. Fatah's fighters went to ground or simply fled, by land or sea, to Egypt. More than 140 Palestinians died in the process; three dozen were civilians, including women and children.

After it was over, Hamas fighters commandeered seafront villas owned by Fatah politicos, security officers, and moneymen. They ransacked the home of the Fatah security chief, ripping off crystal chandeliers, silk carpets, even a bathtub, the clay roof tiles, and the palm trees in a courtyard. Looters expressed astonishment at the opulence.[39] At Gaza's presidential compound, masked Hamas gunmen celebrated by pillaging the president's Gaza office, with skirmishes breaking out among militants over who got the last television.[40] The murals of both Arafat and Abbas were riddled with bullet holes. Outside, two bright green Hamas flags flew on the front gate.

Hamas declared June 14 the day of Gaza's "second liberation." The first had been from Israel in 2005, the second in 2007 from "the collaborators."

From the West Bank, Abbas responded by declaring a state of emergency, dismantling the three-month-old unity government, and appointing a new prime minister. Fatah gunmen also asserted their authority in the West Bank. They showed up at government offices and ordered elected Hamas mayors and city-council members to go home—and not return. They also attacked and set fire to Islamic schools and charities. Local imams also disappeared.[41]

The nascent Palestinian state had fractured into two pieces—with dueling governments. Fatah leaders ruled the West Bank. Hamas consolidated its control of Gaza.

In eighteen months, the two largest Palestinian parties had destroyed the euphoria of the Arabs' most democratic election ever, anywhere.

"I do believe it is the end of Palestinian democracy," Ayman Shaheen, a political scientist at Gaza's al Azar University, told an American journalist.[42]

The Palestinian saga was far from over. The Palestinians' sense of national identity is arguably stronger than any other Arab community outside of Egypt. Fatah and Hamas continued to share many goals, including the end of Israeli occupation, creation of a Palestinian state, and release of thousands of political prisoners. Even as the two halves split, the focus in the territories and the region was on how to get them back together. On their first day apart, the West Bank cleric at Ramallah's main mosque called for reconciliation, while Hamas offered an amnesty to Fatah fighters in Gaza. In Damascus, Mashaal told a press conference that there would be "no two governments and no division of the homeland." He also acknowledged Abbas's leadership. "Abbas has legitimacy, there's no one who would question or doubt that he is an elected president, and we will cooperate with him for the sake of national interest."[43]

All was not forgiven by either side, for sure. But both felt a sense of loss.

In the end, Hamas understood that it had only achieved a military victory over Fatah. Neither party had achieved a political monopoly in either territory. Indeed, since the 2006 election, Fatah had gained politically in Gaza as life deteriorated under Hamas rule, while Hamas had made gains in the West Bank because Fatah still refused to clean up its act.[44]

The Palestinians have always been a harbinger of political trends in the Middle East. They showed that the Arabs did have a thirst for open political societies. And they proved that the Arabs were capable of holding robust and free multiparty elections.

But the first eighteen months of the Palestinian experiment with democracy also reflected the volatility of change and, after decades without freedom, the passions that can be unleashed in a free vote.

TWO

EGYPT

The Turning Points

We are usually convinced more easily by reasons we have

found ourselves than by those which have occurred to others.

—French philosopher Blaise Pascal

Never doubt that a small group of thoughtful

committed citizens can change the world. Indeed,

it is the only thing that ever has.

—American anthropologist Margaret Mead

However powerful the forces of history, the precise catalysts of change are often unpredictable. So, too, are its
agents.

To understand how change is picking up momentum in the Middle
East, I went to see Ghada Shahbender in Cairo. At age forty-two,
Shahbender was a middle-aged soccer mom with four teenagers.
She had never voted, never joined a party, never even signed up for
one of Egypt's little pink voting cards. She was, in that way, typically
Egyptian. By law, everyone over the age of eighteen is required to

vote. But, for decades, more than seventy percent of Egyptians did not bother to cast a ballot for anything.

"I didn't believe in Egypt's elections or referendums—or the whole political process," Shahbender explained the first time we met in a middle-class neighborhood of Cairo in early 2006. "It was all fake."

Yet, virtually overnight, Shahbender had become one of the new faces of change in Egypt, the most important country in the Arab world.

Egypt's extraordinary history, its regional might, and its sheer bulk—one out of every four Arabs today is an Egyptian—make it the leading trendsetter among the twenty-two Arab countries. It is the heart and intellectual center of the Arab world, reflected in one of my favorite sayings about the region: "Books are written in Egypt, printed in Lebanon, and read in Iraq."

Egypt has the clout to bestow legitimacy on any idea—and to change the direction of the region. In shaping the Middle East over the past century, Egypt rallied other Arabs to make war on Israel, but could then defy Arab sentiment to make peace with its Jewish neighbor. In shaping politics inside Arab countries for the next century, what happens among Egyptians will again have the greatest influence in defining the path and pace of change.

I called on Shahbender at an unmarked ground-floor apartment that had been converted into a makeshift office and equipped—down to the glasses—by donations from friends. She is a slim woman with an easy demeanor. Her tawny brown hair has the casually smart cut of privilege, and she was wearing a thin beige turtleneck to ward off the winter chill. We sat around an old table in the dining nook of the apartment that served as a conference area. Cradling one of the donated glasses, which was filled with a milky coffee, Shahbender told me her story as if she did not quite believe what was happening to her life.

"I graduated from university, got married, had my first child, then twins, then a fourth child, all in six years," she explained. "I was convinced that the best thing I could do was to give these kids a good education, support my husband in his career, work hard at whatever job—I worked different jobs due to the kids—and I'd be fulfilling my parental, civic, social, and national duties."

The turning point for her was May 25, 2005, a day that symbolized Egypt at a crossroads. Under pressure both at home and from abroad, Egypt began to dabble in the subject of political change in 2005. To start off a big election year, President Hosni Mubarak offered to let Egyptians vote on who would elect their leader—a rubber-stamp parliament, as it had been done for a half century, or the people. If the referendum passed in May, Egyptians would go to the polls in September to choose for the first time among multiple presidential candidates, and then return to the polls to elect a new parliament, in three stages based on geographic location, in November and December.

The referendum was supposed to signal Mubarak's willingness to open up politically after twenty-four years of unchallenged rule. But the offer was not all it seemed: To nominate a presidential candidate, a party would have to already hold five percent of the seats in both houses of the People's Assembly and to have been legal—or licensed by Mubarak's government—for at least five years. Independent candidates would need endorsements from at least 230 elected officials. And specific quotas of support would be required from the national legislature as well as local city councils.

Most parties, including the largest opposition movement, could not meet those conditions.

So the fledgling new Egyptian dissident movement Kefaya, which means "Enough," organized a demonstration to coincide with the May 25 referendum. Its protest in downtown Cairo was to demand more meaningful democratic reforms.

Shahbender was not interested in either the election or the protest. "I thought, 'Really, what difference would either of these events make?'" she told me, with a shrug. "What difference could I make?" So on referendum day, she instead went to hand in her final term paper.

With her marriage failing, Shahbender had gone back to school to qualify to teach English as a foreign language. She was submitting the paper when her cell phone rang.

"It was a friend, a journalist, and she was so upset I could barely understand her," Shahbender recalled. "She was at the Kefaya rally, and there was a lot of noise."

The protest, her friend reported, had disintegrated into a melee.

A large group of thugs had descended on the crowd, as police stood watching, and begun to beat protesters.

In Egypt, "thugs" is the widely accepted euphemism for the well-muscled young men, usually dressed in dark but informal clothing, who turn up conveniently at protests or polling stations to contain the opposition, always without leaving visible government connections. I saw them show up twice in one week at two small rallies where protesters were already grossly outnumbered by police. Some of them had short but thick truncheons in their hands. Without saying a word, the police stepped aside to let the thugs into the cordon and then watched, either ordered or mesmerized into inaction, as the thugs raised their arms and began beating people.

But the attack on May 25 was different. The thugs had gone after only the women, Shahbender's friend told her. Females old and young had been groped, beaten, mauled, and then had their clothes ripped off. Her friend, a journalist who was covering the event, was also manhandled and hurt. Police failed to intervene even after women were dragged down the street partially unclothed.

Shahbender could only listen. "I wasn't sure what to tell her. I had to go to a farewell lunch for the wife of the Libyan envoy to the Arab League. Many Egyptian women, educated women, working women, and ambassadors' wives were sitting around discussing the referendum on the presidency, and they were making jokes about it.

"Then I thought of my friend at the demonstration," Shahbender recalled, "and I left the lunch and walked through the park. It's one of the most Egyptian parts of Cairo. You look out and see the Citadel and the City of the Dead."

The medieval Citadel was built by Saladin, a hero for many Arabs even though he was actually a Kurd, not an Arab, born in what is today Iraq. Saladin ruled and revitalized Egypt and then forced European Crusaders to retreat from Jerusalem in the twelfth century, ending almost ninety years of Christian control of the Holy Land. For the next eight centuries, the massive walled fortress he built in Cairo continued to be the center of Egypt's government; it remains the capital's most prominent landmark today. In the twenty-first century, Egyptians and other Arabs also still talk about how much they need another Saladin to lead the Arab world.

The nearby City of the Dead is a cemetery, or rather several of them that have grown together to form a virtual suburb of graves and dusty mausoleum chambers. Because of Cairo's chronic housing shortage, the City of the Dead has also become home to more than one million of the living, mainly the destitute and people who have created jobs as grave-tenders.

Together, the two landmarks represent Egypt's former greatness and its chronic current woes.

"I was standing there, looking around, and I kept thinking: What is happening to Egypt? And why did they go after the women?" Shahbender recalled, shaking her head.

"I went home, turned on the television, and was immediately hit with the images from the demonstration. I saw one of the women dragged down the street and clothes pulled off her and onlookers doing nothing. I saw police open barricades to allow the thugs to go in," she said, pausing in the narrative.

"Of course, it was on al Jazeera and CNN and Fox, not Egyptian television. There are so many satellite stations—thank God for the open skies. I kept switching around and seeing the same thing," she added, pulling her hand through shoulder-length hair.

"My children were there. I turned on the Internet to see if we could get updates, and that's when I was slapped in the face because of my children's reaction. My daughter said, 'Why do you get so upset? We can't do anything about it. People are harassed every day.' And my son Abdelazziz said, 'Why were the women there anyway?'"

"I was very upset, really, and I told them, 'This is a violation of our norms, values, and beliefs—and it's on television. The entire world is watching it. It's unacceptable. Would you accept this being done to your sister or being in her place? We sat there arguing forever," Shahbender continued.

"And then I found myself saying, 'Well, I *can* do something about it,'" she recalled, shrugging as if she were still not sure where the thought had come from.

The next day, the government announced that the referendum passed with over eighty percent approval—of those who had turned out to vote. It claimed that just over one half of registered Egyptian voters participated, although every Egyptian voter, nonvoter, election analyst, and foreign diplomat I talked to dismissed the official numbers and said the turnout, again, was a distinct minority. There were no independent monitors.

The referendum was supposed to mark a turning point that gave Egyptians more of a stake in politics by directly electing their president. But throughout Cairo—a city where satellite dishes crowd rooftops, bringing al Jazeera and other foreign news programs even into the City of the Dead—the public buzz was instead about the attack on Egypt's women. The abuse had crossed a threshold.

In the end, the vote set in motion a chain of events that certainly politicized Egyptians, but not in the way Mubarak's government intended.

Among the movements born out of the May 25 confrontation were The Street Is Ours movement and the Egyptian Mothers' Association. The new groups called for a day of public mourning on June 1, one week after the referendum. Urging women to mass at the site of the original demonstration, the mothers dubbed their event Black Wednesday and called on everyone in Egypt to wear black to mark it. They also demanded the resignation of Egypt's powerful interior minister, the top official in charge of both elections and internal security. Their statement was unusually blunt.

> *On the first of June, all of Egypt will be dressed in black, for the sake of our daughters who were assaulted and had their clothes torn in the street because they dared to say 'Enough' instead of remaining silent. We will go out this time . . . to tell the interior minister whose role it was to protect us: the game is over.*
>
> *. . . We emphasize that we . . . do not belong to any political force, legal or otherwise. But when the Egyptian woman pays the price of her political participation with the sanctity of her body and her honor, then every Egyptian mother and all of Egypt will go out in clothes of mourning to tell the Interior Minister: We want your resignation today, now.*

We will see you all on Wednesday, the first of June, a normal day, in our black clothes, calmly, and in bitter silence, for the sake of a free future.

The day after the referendum, Shahbender also contacted friends to figure out what they could do too. They initially thought small, very small.

"All we wanted was a government apology for the brutality," she told me. Piggybacking on the other movements, they set about making thousands of little white lapel ribbons to symbolize their demand.

"We said, 'Wear your ribbons on Black Wednesday but also when you go to work or go shopping or take your kids to the zoo—whatever you're doing and even if you're not going to the demonstration," Shahbender explained.

Shahbender smiled as she recalled the images. "On Black Wednesday, I put on my black dress and my white ribbon. I'd never been to a demonstration. It was a huge learning experience for me. I had to go through lines of security officers to join it," she said. "I didn't know how it was going to turn out—whether I'd get beaten up or whether it'd be quiet."

"When I got in, an elderly woman turned to me and said she thought I was new and did I have 100 [Egyptian] pounds," she recalled.

" 'Why 100 pounds?' I asked her."

"She told me: 'That's what you need for bail,'" Shahbender recalled.

"At times it was very scary, and at other moments it was exhilarating—just for the fact that 500 people bothered to show up. By our standards, that's big."

Emergency law, a sporadic feature of Egyptian life since 1967, has been in force continuously since the 1981 assassination of President Anwar Sadat. It is Egypt's equivalent of martial law, and it requires any group of more than five people to get a government permit if they want to hold a meeting. The government sometimes looks the other way when events are aimed at regional crises—expressions of support for the Palestinians or against the invasion of Iraq. But any group of more than five who meets to discuss Egyptian politics faces arrest. For decades, emergency law has smothered political life in Egypt more than any other instrument of repression.

Although it was illegal, Black Wednesday went off without incident. But the next day, reality hit. "People who had supported us called and said, 'So you haven't gotten an apology. What are you going to do next?' It was like they expected something from us," Shahbender added, pushing her glasses up onto her head.

"Over the previous week I had met people I would never know if this hadn't happened—women in the mothers' association, journalists who were harassed, people in the Kefaya movement and the Muslim Brotherhood, and human-rights activists. I started talking with them about why people don't participate in public life, about the culture of fear, and about how we could break through with Big Brother watching us."

Somewhat ironically, no people in the Arab world have a greater sense of national identity or pride than Egyptians. Most Arab countries were created or had their borders defined by European powers in the twentieth century. Egypt dates back more than 5,000 years, however, to around 3100 B.C., when two disparate cultures that grew up along the world's longest river—the fertile northern delta that pours into the Mediterranean and the southern desert-fringed Nile Valley—were united into one of the world's earliest civilizations.

Yet ever since Egypt became a republic in 1952, the majority of its people have been largely passive about politics. Creating a citizenry willing to claim ownership of local politics is one of the greatest challenges facing Egypt—and the region.

"I thought it was very important to start by letting the government know, for a change, that we're watching them and everything they're doing," Shahbender recalled. "And, after all the brainstorming and concepts and theories we considered, we decided it boiled down to something that simple: 'We're watching you.' And that's what we became."

Two months after the Referendum Day demonstration, on August 4, 2005, Shahbender and her friends formally launched a new movement called We're Watching You to monitor Egypt's government. The phrase in Arabic is *Shayfeencom*. In a play on the language, they dubbed their new website—to publicize government misdeeds and provide Egyptians a mechanism to file complaints—www.shayfeen.com.

"We put the government on notice that we are going to identify wrongs and then pressure them to set it right," she said. "Monitoring is our tool, and reporting our findings on a Web site and through the media is our weapon."

After starting small, the new group ambitiously decided to make the presidential election—then only one month away—its first project. Mubarak was seeking his fifth consecutive six-year term, against nine other candidates, and there was a critical vacuum: International monitors were not allowed at the election, so there would be no recognized nongovernment arbiter of whether the poll was free and fair.

Shahbender admitted that the group had virtually no idea what to do, especially with thousands of polling stations involved. It had no legal status, no government license, no resources, no database, no office, and no official role in the polling. We're Watching You had no choice but to rely on voters to report what happened.

"We came up with violation checklists, which we put on the Web and sent to the 500 people who joined us in the first month," Shahbender said. "Our only instructions were that we needed people to report by Internet or by phone if they saw anything. We bought two mobile numbers. We set up an operations room in an advertising agency that was willing to host us for the day."

She shook her head, smiling. "Frankly, when we first announced our group, we got more attention than we deserved—from the media, the public, and State Security. And the day before the election, we were all asking: 'Are we really going to get reports? Will people phone us? Will there be any movement, or will we just sit there all day? Will we be able to pull it off? We had no idea if we amounted to anything or not."

But on Election Day, September 7, 2005, the telephones began ringing early and did not stop all day; the group's Internet site was also inundated. By midnight, Shayfeencom had received reports of more than 1,000 alleged violations.

"We had an extraordinary wealth of information—and so much participation that we didn't know what to do with all of it," Shahbender recalled. "It was unbelievable, really." As information poured in, task forces scrambled to figure out how to collate complaints—by voting district, violation, or according to the group's own checklist. Maybe they should make charts, a volunteer wondered.

One of the earliest issues was the ink. To prevent multiple balloting, voters were required to dip their finger in a dark ink that takes several days to wear off. "Around 10:30 in the morning we got a report that there was no ink at one station, and at another station the ink came off if you rubbed it with nail polish remover or chlorine," Shahbender told me.

"When we started announcing complaints, Egyptian television called and said we were spreading rumors. Then an Interior Ministry official called to complain, so I sent him a list of places where the ink was coming off and the one place where there was no ink at all."

Shahbender laughed as she told me the government official called her back later to say he had been personally assured that ink was now at the polling station.

"We knew we were having an impact. But we were also terrified after Egyptian television said we were spreading rumors—you can go to prison for that in this country." The allegation was not merely a comment; Egyptian television is state-owned and tightly state-controlled.

Reports of violations came from an array of sources. A university professor in Alexandria phoned on the hour, every hour, each time from a different polling station, to report what was happening. A young man from Port Said reported serious violations carried out by members of parliament from the ruling National Democratic Party. "That was the violation that concerned us the most," Shahbender said.

Lawmakers—who faced their own elections within weeks—were offering money or meals, voters reported. Party representatives sat inside some polling rooms filling in ballot papers or demanding to see who voters selected, Egyptians complained to Shayfeencom.[1]

In Port Said, the young volunteer reported, local workers in government-owned factories had been rounded up and transported in buses to polling stations. The volunteer recorded all the bus numbers. He also talked with workers who said they had been promised a bonus after the vote—based on the percentage that went for Mubarak. Others told him local legislators helped arrange for distribution of workers' pink voting cards.

"He called us all the time," Shahbender recalled. "He was using a mobile phone with prepaid cards. It was a huge expense for him, but he wanted to do it. And he was quite brave."

Other reports cited threats to café owners: Their government licenses could be in jeopardy if they didn't support Mubarak's reelection effort. Egypt is a café society; Egyptians use the cozy, often overcrowded neighborhood hangouts to debate, court, smoke hubble-bubble pipes, watch videos, and drink round after round of coffee or tea.

"There is an omnipotent power structure in Egypt that does not allow for diversity," Shahbender reflected. "If local councils and parliament and the national government are all one and the same, there is no way out. It affects every aspect of life. And the system is quite resistant to change.

"But," she added, "There are also quite a few who are beginning to act. This young man spends a whole day and a lot of money because he won't stand for it any more."

The day after the vote, We're Watching You released its findings—and blasted the government. "Such habits were customary during the old parliament elections; repeating them in this historical election is not only illegal, but led some of the voters to doubt if their vote will ever make a difference," Shayfeencom charged.[2]

The group was besieged for comment by the local, regional, and international media. Egypt's State Security, Shahbender noted, wanted a copy of its report too.

Besides the array of problems at polling stations, the group uncovered a discrepancy between the new law, passed in the referendum, and the instructions from the Interior Ministry to the judiciary that officially supervised the polling.

"When we uncovered it, we at first thought we were wrong. All we did was put the law next to the instructions—and there were important differences that could have been an opening for fraud," Shahbender said.

The law said the counting and announcement of results would happen in each constituency. But the government's instructions to Egypt's judges said votes would be tallied in each district—then given to the government to total up and announce forty-eight hours later.

"The law meant that anyone with a calculator could keep track and say Mubarak got this many and other candidates got that many," Shahbender explained. "But the instructions given to the judges would allow a gap of forty-eight hours where there would be no transparency. We made an issue of that."

To no one's surprise, Mubarak won with eighty-eight percent of the vote—from those who turned out. The second highest candidate, Ayman Nour of the new Tomorrow Party, scored just over seven percent.

No other candidate really had much of a chance. Mubarak carried the weight of the state, the influence of the state-controlled media, and the resources of a party whose membership dominated the private sector. The most popular opposition movement, the Muslim Brotherhood, was outlawed. And the official campaign was less than three weeks long—in a country with almost thirty percent illiteracy.[3]

Egypt's political history in the lifetime of most voters has also hardly been conducive to democracy. Egypt became a republic after the 1952 revolution, when the Free Officers' Movement ousted flamboyant King Farouq. Farouq was nicknamed "the thief of Cairo" because of his lavish palaces, hundreds of cars, playboy lifestyle, and spending sprees abroad at a time of chronic poverty among his people. Lore has it that the king had a penchant for pickpocketing and pilfering, even during state visits; his purloined treasures allegedly included a pocket watch belonging to Winston Churchill and a ceremonial sword owned by the Shah of Iran.

Over the next half century, Egypt's new republic had only four presidents—Mohammed Naguib, Gamal Abdel Nasser, Anwar Sadat and Hosni Mubarak. All four came to power as military men. The first was forced to step down, and the next two died in office. Mubarak was a little-known and politically untested Air Force commander when he inherited power in 1981, after Sadat was gunned down by Islamic extremists as he reviewed a military parade. By the 2005 election, however, Mubarak had served almost as long as all his predecessors combined. Most Egyptians had known little else politically.

Mubarak's reelection was, as a result, a virtual given. Yet We're Watching You was still pleased with its inaugural venture into democracy. It empowered ordinary Egyptians. It held the government to account. And its impact reached beyond Egypt's borders, inspiring the birth of similar groups in Jordan and Lebanon.

In the United States' annual human rights report for 2005, the State Department cited widespread violations in Egypt's presidential election—voters lists with the names of people long dead, termination of voter registration eight months before the election, and ruling-party control over polling stations.[4] Part of the report was based on the data collected and made public by Shayfeencom's volunteers.[5] Shahbender "typifies a new generation of activists," wrote *Democracy Digest,* a publication of the Transatlantic Democracy Network.[6]

Buoyed by the initial reaction, We're Watching You scrambled to get ready for the parliamentary election just two months later. This time, some 7,000 candidates were running in 222 constituencies. The election would play out in three phases around the country from early November to early December. This time, Shayfeencom mobilized task forces to inspect polling sites. It organized training on how to monitor elections. And it found a cameraman.

"We have something called *negarrasoh* in Egypt," Shahbender explained. "It means 'ring bells,' like about someone's shame. During the Fatimid period, if someone did something wrong, he'd be put backwards on a donkey and walked through town. A man next to him would ring bells and say, 'This man stole two chickens. He is a thief'— or whatever he did wrong. Shame is very effective in Egypt," she said. "We have a long tradition of *negarrasoh.* This is the weapon we were trying to use."

By the legislative elections, We're Watching You also had a critical new asset—name recognition.

"In many places, people were waiting for our task forces. 'Oh, you Shayfeecom people are here at last,' they'd say," Shahbender recalled.

Throughout the four weeks of elections, calls poured in from people who were not volunteers but had violations to report—some to telephone numbers that had not been released. "I had no idea how people got my private cell phone," Shahbender said.

Egypt's legislative elections differed significantly from the presidential poll in one pivotal respect: The Muslim Brotherhood was allowed to run, sort of. The party—like all religious parties—was formally outlawed from engaging in politics. But the government sporadically allowed its candidates to run as independents. Several Egyptian analysts told me that the government's decision to let the Brotherhood participate had dual benefits. It would counter criticism that Egypt was not opening up enough, while also scaring the West into backing a slower pace of change, out of fear that the Brotherhood would be the alternative.

But in 2005, the government miscalculated the Brotherhood's support. In the first round alone, the Islamic party won thirty-five seats, already doubling the total it had held in the previous parliament. Abruptly, the next two stages of the election turned nasty. In key districts, voters for ruling-party candidates were brought in to vote early, then police closed down polling stations or harassed voters to discourage voting.[7]

"From phase one to phase three, there was a buildup of violence and vote-rigging," Shahbender told me. "We decided that we didn't want only to monitor the vote. We wanted to prevent wrongdoing from happening. So when polling stations were closed up, we put up a fight for voters to be able to get in. And in some places we succeeded."

On the final day of voting, Shahbender was in the village of Kafr Mit Bashar. The district was important because one of the candidates was the brother of Mubarak's chief of staff. The polling was actually a rerun because of irregularities in the first balloting. A Western diplomat who monitored the local vote later told me that the ruling party had used the first vote to figure out where the opposition votes were—and then blocked them during the rerun.[8]

Shahbender arrived to find the polling station, at a local school, barricaded by police. "Villagers had put a ladder around the school and started jumping over and into the polling station. The police then moved the ladder," Shahbender recalled. "We stood there and tried to negotiate with the head of the riot police. We said, 'Look, let them in ten by ten, women first.' We tried to ask nicely. We asked, 'Why are they keeping them out? Where did the orders come from?'"

"It was a routine for them," Shahbender added. "The same thing had happened in other villages in earlier rounds of voting."

Then the shooting began.

"There were about 200 voters, men and women—their children were playing in the dust behind them—waiting to get into the polling station. They were confronted by rows of riot police. Our volunteers were on the front line between riot police and voters," she said, mapping it out with her fingers on the table.

"The police started beating us with batons. They fired rubber bullets and then live ammunition," she said, pausing to add, "I now know the difference between the sound of rubber bullets and live ammunition."

"Then they fired nine canisters of tear gas—for a crowd of 200 peasants who were not in any way armed. And then it was chaos. Children were running around calling for their mothers or fathers. One child had suffered a broken arm from a baton—you could see it—and he was crying.

"We hid behind our car, but we were suffocating from the tear gas. The villagers were shouting at the police, 'Where are the Israeli forces that you are fighting?' I told one of the kids to get onions. A journalist had told me that onions help with tear gas. Villagers were soon coming out of the field with onions.

"Our cameraman is a giant, but he was scared," Shahbender continued. "We were all keeping an eye on the cameraman. He was our proof of what happened. In fact, I didn't fully comprehend what happened until I saw it later on film.

"Afterwards, I understood that this was not about elections or change. It was about resistance to change, and I began to really understand what a big job we have ahead of us."

At each stage of the voting, We're Watching You issued public reports. By the third round, the group charged that the electoral process had lost credibility.[9] After eleven Egyptians died in clashes at polling stations, it also charged that Mubarak's government was responsible for the most violent election in Egyptian history.

"Security services perpetrated a great deal of unwarranted violence against voters, the media and civil society activists and prevented them from entering polling stations, taking pictures, and even prevented judicial officials from carrying out their jobs and monitoring the elections," the Shayfeencom report concluded.[10]

We're Watching You was quoted throughout the Middle East, by the international press, and by human-rights groups around the world. Only four months had passed since the launching of Shayfeencom, less than seven months since Black Wednesday.

After the election, the group began to diversify its focus. When I stopped in to see Shahbender, We're Watching You had just begun to track avian flu. Rooftop poultry breeders are a Cairo fixture, and the disease had just hit Egypt. In a panic, breeders were dumping their dead chickens into the Nile, which is the main source of drinking water for millions of Egyptians.

Shayfeencom had received information about more than 100 patients hospitalized with suspicious symptoms. It was organizing doctors to quietly probe the cases, because government officials were saying little publicly. Five people were soon confirmed with avian flu, and two immediately died.

Before leaving, I asked Shahbender if she was going to get her pink voting card when registration opened up again. "Yes," she laughed. "Of course."

I also asked if she was worried about becoming a target of the Egyptian government, particularly its massive State Security intelligence service.

She pulled slowly on a cigarette. Shahbender said she had quit smoking several years earlier, but took it up again after Black Wednesday.

"Yes, I have to be realistic," she said. "Besides, they make a point of letting us know that their ears are listening."

The State Security intelligence headquarters is on Lazoghly Square, not too far from Shayfeencom's office. A heavily guarded building set behind a black marble arch, it is the most feared address in Cairo. Amnesty International and other human-rights groups cite it as a place where detainees are regularly interrogated and tortured.[11] As shorthand, Egyptians often refer to State Security simply as Lazoghly.

When we met, Shahbender's divorce had been finalized a month earlier. At the same time, she had acquired a little black Pekingese puppy. She named it Lazoghly.

"Now I walk around home or the office," Shahbender chuckled, "and I say, 'Here, Lazoghly. Here, Lazoghly. Where are you, Lazoghly?'"

The agents of change in the Middle East are not always outsiders or newcomers. A new generation of whistle-blowers is emerging from within.

Noha al Zeiny has been on the Egyptian government payroll since she graduated from Cairo University Law School in 1976. She immediately joined the Ministry of Justice and rose through the ranks until she became a top official in the chief prosecutor's office. In 2005, she was sufficiently senior—and trusted—that the government dispatched her to supervise a key constituency in Egypt's parliamentary elections.

That's when Zeiny dared to speak out.

It was not an easy decision, she told me, when I caught up with her at Cairo's military hospital, where she and her sister were tending to their critically ill mother.

Like a growing number of Egyptian women, Zeiny wears *hejab,* or modest Islamic clothing. When we met, her black hair was covered by a dark piece of cloth that tightly encircled her face and was pinned together right under her chin. Her wholesomely round face bore no makeup, and she was dressed in a comfortably loose navy blue sweat suit. The effect was a stark contrast to the stylish Shahbender, who is distinctly secular in appearance and outlook.

Sitting on a hospital-room chair as her sister spoon-fed supper to their mother, Zeiny spoke in the deliberate, sequential language of a lawyer building a case. She speaks basic English but was more comfortable using technical terms through an interpreter. At the end of each translation, she would nod her head in approval and then continue.

The turning point for Zeiny was November 12, 2005. "I was sent to Damanhur to help supervise the election," she began. Judges supervise elections, but there were not enough judges for all the polling stations, so the government had also dispatched senior staff from the Ministry of Justice.

Damanhur is a microcosm of testy Egyptian politics. The city of more than 200,000 people is about two thirds of the way from Cairo to the historic Mediterranean port of Alexandria. Damanhur survives off the fertile cotton, date, and potato fields on the Nile Delta, but it is not a backwater. Ahmed Zewail, who won the Nobel Prize for chemistry in 1999, was born in Damanhur.

Zeiny was supposed to show up the morning of the election, but she decided to arrive the night before. "It was midnight," she recounted, "and from the minute I got there, I heard people shouting, 'Heshmat, Heshmat, We are with you.' It went on all night. One group would chant for awhile, and then another group would pick up and continue.

"For me, this was a strange experience," she explained. "I'd never seen or heard anything like it."

Gamal Heshmat was the incumbent—kind of. The Damanhur election in 2005 was really about how much democracy—and Islam—Egyptian politics would tolerate. Heshmat was a key to the answer.

The son of a Ministry of Education official, Heshmat had joined the Muslim Brotherhood when he was in medical school. "It was the idea of purity, the idea of religion for the sake of religion, of serving the people without payback," he told *The Los Angeles Times*.[12]

Heshmat went on to become a family doctor and university professor. But in 2000, he decided to put his political beliefs into practice and run for parliament. He won.

The Muslim Brotherhood was outlawed in 1954, but since 1984 its members have run as barely disguised "independents" or in alliance with—effectively under the protective cover of—secular parties. It is part of a political game Mubarak played with the movement; the government does not want to legalize any religious party, but it also has to deal with the reality of the Brotherhood's popularity. Heshmat was one of seventeen Brotherhood "independents" elected in 2000.[13]

The clean-shaven doctor, whose balding pate still has a lonely tuft of hair in the front, quickly gained attention as an upstart legislator. He made daring allegations about government corruption. He assembled a report on torture by State Security, notably at Lazoghly Square.[14] He also campaigned against controversial literature, charging that three popular novels had implicitly pornographic passages and a fourth was blasphemous.[15]

The fourth book was *Banquet for Seaweed*, a book first published in 1983 and cleared for reprinting by Egypt's Ministry of Culture almost a generation later. In it, two Iraqi intellectuals escape Saddam Hussein's regime and end up blaming oppression in the Arab world on dictators and conservatives. But one passage describes God as a failed artist. That was enough to spark protests in Cairo and Heshmat's demand for its banishment. The government withdrew approval of the book.

The flap over the book won public attention because it suddenly pitted moral values against freedom of expression—and spurred a heated debate about political correctness in Egypt. Islamists were outraged. Intellectuals counterprotested. Columnists filled newspapers with criticism. Officials resigned from the Ministry of Culture.[16]

And Heshmat was soon stripped of his seat in parliament. It happened circuitously. In late 2002, two years after his election, the People's Assembly rammed through approval—in twenty-four hours—of a government report citing irregularities in Damanhur's 2000 election and calling for a new vote. Heshmat was forced to run again—with four days' notice of the new poll.[17] This time, he lost. The State Department's annual Human Rights Report noted "heavy-handed police interference on polling day" in favor of Heshmat's opponent.[18]

A few months later, Heshmat was jailed. Members of Egypt's parliament have immunity from prosecution. Once he lost his seat, however, he was vulnerable. Heshmat was arrested for membership in an illegal organization—the Muslim Brotherhood. He was held for four months, although never officially charged or tried.

After his release, Heshmat decided to run for parliament again in 2005. That's where Zeiny came in.

"I was asked to supervise one of the polling stations in a primary school on November 12," Zeiny told me. The vote actually went smoothly. Her station stayed open late because, as often happens in the Middle East, many voters showed up at the end of the day.

"This is important," Zeiny stressed, "because that means I was also one of the last stations to close." Afterward, she accompanied the ballot boxes under heavy security to a large tent set up in a military-school compound where votes from each Damanhur polling place were individually counted.

"We were sitting around counting, and we could all hear each other," Zeiny recalled. "Representatives of the candidates attended the process, which was the first time this happened and was one of the most positive things about the election."

Heshmat's chief opponent was Mustafa Fiqi, who had served as chairman of parliament's Foreign Relations Committee as well as Egypt's ambassador to Austria and the International Atomic Energy Agency.

But Fiqi had never run for office. Egypt's legislature, which has 454 seats, includes ten members appointed by the president. They often go to Egypt's minority Coptic Christians and women—and Mubarak allies in the National Democratic Party. Fiqi had always been one of the ten. Born in a village near Damanhur, Fiqi had moved to Cairo as a student and never returned.[19] He went back in 2005, only to run against a popular local doctor.

"It was quite clear by the end of a long night," Zeiny recalled, "that Heshmat had won an overwhelming majority. All of the polling stations were announcing 'Heshmat.' 'Heshmat.' 'Heshmat.'" She calculated that Heshmat had about 25,000 votes to about 7,000 for Fiqi. Fiqi's representatives were visibly disappointed.

It was almost dawn when Zeiny finished; most of her counterparts were long gone. She lingered to hear the final result, but as the process was wrapping up, she was asked to leave. She thought the request strange, since she was one of the supervising authorities. But the results were so obvious that she returned to her hotel.

The next morning, the government announced that Fiqi had won. Zeiny was stunned. She immediately contacted other officials who had supervised the poll to discuss what happened.

At this point she paused in her story. "There is some information that I can't tell you," she said. "I was told in confidence by other officials, and I can't repeat it unless I am called to testify. All I can tell you is that two high-ranking officials confessed to me that in cases like this documents are changed. But I don't know how it's done."

Zeiny agonized about what to do. When she got back to Cairo, she decided to pull together all the threads of what she had witnessed in a document.

"I hesitated, and I was feeling very anxious," she recalled. "I had colleagues calling me and saying, 'Let it go.'"

Zeiny stayed up all night working on language, but she was still not sure what to do when she finished the draft. Then she picked up her morning newspapers. Every day, Zeiny told me, she gets three newspapers delivered to her door. Two are government-owned, *Al-Ahram* and *Al-Akhbar.* The third is the new independent *Al-Masri al-Youm,* or *The Egyptian Today,* which then had only been publishing for seventeen months.

"By complete chance, the new paper was on top of the pile, and there was a picture of Mustafa Fiqi on the front declaring that there was no fraud," Zeiny recalled, laughing.

Fiqi had made a big deal during his campaign about not seeking preferential treatment because of his government connections. "I've announced from the beginning that I'll quit if there's any rigging," he had said at his last campaign rally, the night Zeiny arrived in Damanhur. "I believe in my freedom and the freedom of others."[20] He said the same thing after the election.

"When I saw this statement, all hesitation ended," Zeiny said. "That's when I decided to call the new paper and give it my testimony." It proved to be a fateful liaison.

The day after I talked to Zeiny I called on Hisham Kassem, publisher of *The Egyptian Today.* He also happens to be the president of the Egyptian Organization of Human Rights, and he had run as an independent in the 2000 parliamentary elections but lost. Kassem is a tall man with silver-flecked black hair and a well-groomed mustache that fits the contours of his mouth right up to the ends of his upper lip. He chain smokes Kents, sometimes double-puffing.

The Egyptian Today was the country's first independent daily in Arabic. Others had tried as weeklies or in English, including Kassem's own *Cairo Times,* but eventually closed. *The Egyptian Today* opened in June 2004 with a run of only 500 papers. Early issues, Kassem told me, "were a disaster. The first six months were hell."

But the paper soon settled into a groove of bold, hard-hitting, but fact-based stories and wryly sharp editorial cartoons, both mainly about regime shortfalls. Its first rule was that pictures of Egypt's leadership would not be a fixture on the front page.

"Other papers put Mubarak on the front page at least 320 days a year, and the only reason they don't do it 365 days is because they can't say the only thing he did that day was go to the toilet," Kassem said.

Starting a quality paper in a country with long-standing press restrictions was "like flying a 747 jetliner," Kassem lamented, moving his hands slowly like the lumbering aircraft. "It's so big you have to move gradually. It's not like a Cessna that can dart in and out of the skies." He focused particularly on recruiting young reporters who had not been jaded by work in the government-controlled media.

Kassem vividly remembered the morning that his editor walked in with Zeiny's four-page testimony in his hand.

"He was very excited, and he said, 'This document is from a judge who says the election was rigged.' I closed the door because this was a very serious charge. It was the biggest story we'd ever had," Kassem said. "Then I called our lawyer. He said we needed to get her signature on the document, or she could always deny it the next day—and then the paper would be closed down. We'd only been publishing a short time.

"So the editor and I went to her together. The paper was already late, and I had to call every two or three minutes to keep it open. We'd have to remake the front page," Kassem continued. "When Zeiny said she would sign it, we decided to go with it. That's when I turned off my cell phone and stopped taking calls on the office phone from anyone, even the paper's shareholders."

Zeiny's testimonial, which ran in full, began starkly. "I was there. I was part of the whole thing." She continued:

> This is a testament for truth's sake. If I did not record it, I would be accountable before God on the Day of Judgment. By what I write here, I do not intend to support or defame any party. It is merely a question of telling the truth, to which I have devoted my life, and to honor the justice that I have vowed to uphold.

Point by point, Zeiny outlined suspicious activity during the vote count. The presence of a State Security official at the table where the final vote was tallied "was in itself a dangerous indication to me," she wrote. She questioned the inappropriate involvement of a government lawyer as "well beyond my comprehension that a state lawyer and defender became part of an authority to adjudicate and supervise the competition between two people, one of whom represents the government."

When the vote count was coming to a close, she wrote, she heard officials "intensively" using their mobile phones to relay the results; she heard the word "sweeping" in several conversations to describe Heshmat's victory. She also heard one colleague comment, "Fiqi's defeat will turn the world upside down."

Because she is an observant Muslim, Zeiny added a personal note in her testimonial.

"To spare any political shows, I would like to say that I disagree with the Muslim Brotherhood organization with regards to many of their orientations and views." Before the election, she added, she had hoped Heshmat would not run again, "after all the troubles he went through in the last session of parliament.

"However," she continued, "as he had already presented himself for elections, we should respect his supporters' will and, above all, carry out the responsibility delegated to us as neutral supervisors."

During our conversation at the hospital, Zeiny had also volunteered her deep disagreement with the Brotherhood. She had never joined any political movement, she said. Candidly, she added, she had never even voted.

At the end of her testimony in *The Egyptian Today,* Zeiny appealed to other official witnesses to join her in revealing the truth. "One of the judges told me that he could not sleep after he saw what had happened," she wrote.

Zeiny's testimony was published three days after the Damanhur election. *The Egyptian Today* publisher told me that he was so nervous about attempts to block its publication that he did not turn on his cell phone again until nine that morning. The first call, he said, was from his mother. She reported that the paper was not available anywhere on newsstands.

Kassem panicked. He immediately called the paper's distribution manager and asked him to contact vendors. It would not be the first time publications had been "removed," as he put it, by government agents or allies.

"By one P.M., we finally found out what had happened," Kassem told me. "No one had touched it. The paper had just sold out—very, very early.

"Then people started calling and asking us to run the story again the next day. And that's what we did—for the next four days. Vendors were reporting that customers were reserving copies overnight and paying for them in advance. Some people wanted several copies!" Kassem said.

"In January, our circulation was only 3,000. It was increasing steadily about 500 copies a month, but after we ran this story, it jumped to 30,000. Now it's around 40,000," he added. "Today, we're the fourth largest newspaper in the country."

I asked Kassem if he was concerned about repercussions. Three of his reporters had recently been charged with libel for an article about alleged corruption by Egypt's Minister of Housing.

"We get new cases against us regularly. At some point almost every week my assistant Christine will hand me a new case. But we don't get convicted," Kassem said, shaking his head. One of the three reporters in the recent case had been convicted on a technicality over his identity papers, but not for libel or slander.

"The government hates the idea of a free press and is not committed, whatever it says. But it's ultrastupid for Mubarak not to leave a reasonable margin for the press. On satellite television, twenty or thirty million people can watch Kefaya condemning Mubarak personally. And it's not feasible for the government to try to control [telephone] text messages.

"No," Kassem told me, "closing Al-Masri al-Youm would be a big mistake. We've now come too far."

I had also asked Zeiny if she was concerned about the repercussions—losing her job and source of income as a single woman, getting summoned by the government to testify, or being ostracized.

She thought a minute. "I can't say I'm afraid—or not afraid," she offered. "I suspect I will have to testify someday, and there may be other consequences. But in the end, I felt I had to say that the election was rigged. And, for once, there was a place to do it."

The forces of change can take circuitous routes.

Nasser Amin is a forty-something lawyer who is a cross between the Marlboro Man—he steadily smokes the brand—and a campus intellectual. When we met, he was wearing well-fitted jeans, and the sleeves of his crisp, open-necked white shirt were rolled up to his elbows. The first thing a normally serious Egyptian friend told me about Amin is that his eyes twinkle and, behind a pair of wire-rimmed glasses, they actually did. He seemed perpetually bemused.

Amin is the director of the Arab Center for the Independence of the Judiciary and the Legal Profession. It is a lofty idea housed in a modest office with dated equipment. Its whitewashed walls are decorated, sparsely, with posters. One near Amin's desk declares, "Same blood, same rights."

On the day I visited, a Khamsin storm had engulfed Cairo. All we could see from the windows of Amin's eleventh-floor office was a sky of sand. Khamsins whip sands from the Sahara Desert across North Africa in late winter and can consume the horizon as completely as a dense fog. Rain clears it away after a few days, although falling drops pick up the fine grains, leaving everything in already dust-encrusted Cairo splattered with little circles of more dust. As we talked, the outside shutters flapped noisily from the storm.

I went to see Amin to hear about the hottest political conflict in Egypt. Emboldened opposition may have redefined the races for president and parliament, produced some fresh political faces, and expanded the parameters of activism. But a real rebellion was erupting among an unlikely force—Egypt's judges.

Unlike newer Arab countries, Egypt's judiciary has a history of independence dating back to the nineteenth century. It has long been the most respected branch of government, whether Egypt was ruled by monarchs, nationalists, or autocrats. For most of its history, however, it had been a largely passive force.

"Judicial tradition in this country prevented judges from getting involved in almost anything," Amin explained. "They wouldn't go to places where there might be a problem. They wouldn't even go to a café and join debates. Their position was that they'd wait until the issues came to them. It was a tradition that kept the judiciary very neutral in Egypt. They had a real aura of being the highest and most noble elite in this country.

"But," he continued, "it also left the judges so isolated among themselves that sometimes you felt they were sitting in a temple. Things around them could be burning, but they wouldn't do anything about it."

The judges also had diminishing power.

After Egypt's 1952 revolution, judicial authority steadily eroded under a sequence of strong presidents. Attempts by the judges to reassert themselves—and the law—were repeatedly beaten back. Capitalizing on the mood of crisis after the humiliating 1967 war with Israel, the Judges Club in Cairo called for greater freedoms to be protected by a stronger judiciary.[21] President Nasser responded in 1969 by firing more than 100 senior judges, in what is still widely remembered as the "massacre of the judiciary." In 1972, a new law then gave the executive branch wide powers over the judicial branch.[22]

The Judges Club offered proposals again in 1986 and 1991 to reform the nation's laws and ensure the judges' ability to uphold them. But the government balked at putting the drafts to a vote in parliament. It also increasingly meddled, either directly or through surrogates, in promotions, assignments, and salaries. And it tried to co-opt poorly paid judges with the carrot of bonuses or the stick of threats.[23]

"The government knows the judiciary is held in high regard in this country, so it tried to use the judges to carry out its own policies and crimes—and then claim that it happened under the judiciary so people would accept it," Amin told me.

But the tide began to turn in April 2005, Amin explained, after the case of the bounced check.

"It was a very ordinary case on a very ordinary day in an Alexandria courtroom," he began. "It's almost a funny story. But it reignited something very serious in this country."

The case centered on a bounced check in the amount of roughly

$500 written by one Ayman al Jazzar. The tale—which I subsequently also heard from parties to the case—began rather simply: The judge asked Jazzar's lawyer if the signature on the bad check was his client's or a forgery.[24]

The lawyer asked to see the check. He looked it over. He then handed it to a man behind him.

The lawyer had originally informed the judge that Jazzar would not be in court and that he had a power of attorney to act on his client's behalf. So the judge, now curious, asked the identity of the man holding the bounced check. It was, of course, Jazzar, who proceeded to admit that the signature was indeed his—effectively acknowledging his guilt.

The court session then erupted into an angry free-for-all: The lawyer loudly insisted that the statement was inadmissible, charging that the judge didn't know the law and was too young to be in the court in the first place. The furious judge countered that the defendant was in court and had willingly volunteered the information.

"Shut up," the lawyer shouted at the judge. And the judge replied to the lawyer, "No, you shut up." Others in the courtroom joined in the shouting. The judge then cited the lawyer for contempt.

I heard plenty of other juicy details of the raucous court session—some of them involving assaults on the judge rather than just insults—although accounts varied too widely to settle on one version. But the bottom line, on which all agreed, is that the case of the bounced check quickly became a cause célèbre for both sides.

Like a hero, the lawyer was carried on the shoulders of his colleagues from the courthouse onto the streets of Alexandria. The Alexandria lawyers' union then went on strike, forcing local courts to be temporarily suspended.

The Judges Club in Alexandria rallied its own, calling an emergency session to discuss the flap. It was the latest of several similar confrontations, and the judges wanted to stem the tide, Amin told me.

"This story represents a lot of what is happening in this country in the crisis over authority," he said.

In the midst of the Judges Club meeting, a senior judge stood up and said the core issue was not really the lawyers' challenge, but the judges' general loss of credibility.

"So they started discussing how their standing had sunk so low," Amin explained, "and they decided on the following: They were discredited when they supervised tainted elections in 2000 and had said nothing. When the government settled its accounts with opponents and political prisoners through the courts, they had not taken a stand. When the government kept emergency law in place for over twenty years, they did nothing to challenge it. And when the government refused to implement the judges' rulings, they did not follow through."

"And so they started to look beyond the lawyers to the body that was really insulting the judiciary—which was the government," Amin added.

The Judges Club in Alexandria ended up calling for broad new legislation to ensure judicial independence—and for a gathering of all 8,000 Egyptian judges to take a joint national stand.[25] Their summit convened in Cairo on May 13, 2005, in a massive tent put up on an empty lot across the street from the national Judges Club, a stately structure with chandeliers, marble floors, and imperial columns that was built during the last days of Britain's colonial presence.

The session was stormy. But Egypt's judges agreed to issue a direct challenge to Mubarak's regime. They called for major reforms to foster the rule of law. They demanded full independence from the executive branch. And they voted to put the government on notice that they would no longer provide cover for its behavior—from election fraud to prolonged emergency law.

Egypt's press dubbed it the Judges' intifada, or uprising.[26]

"This was an important turning point," Amin explained.

To avoid scandals or constitutional crises in the past, judges had usually taken their concerns to the Ministry of Justice. "But now the majority of judges have changed their basic philosophy," he said. "They have come to the conclusion that they are part of this society—and that they must act rather than defer to other authorities." In other words, the judges' summit set the stage for a confrontation with the government.

Judge Hesham Bastawisi, a widely respected member of Egypt's highest court, was one of its first victims.

I visited Bastawisi at his home in Cairo's Nasser City, a remote suburb of high-rise concrete apartment buildings, to hear this part of the story. Bastawisi is a slightly balding man with white hair and rimless glasses. He was wearing a gray pinstripe suit, and he smoked nervously. We sat on faux-French settees with embroidered pictures of musicians serenading comely courtesans. A framed verse from the Koran on black velvet hung on the wall next to a bookcase neatly filled with a set of encyclopedias and law books. His daughter, who wore the pink *hejab* now popular in Cairo, sat with us.

The government had just stripped Bastawisi of his judicial immunity and referred him to the government's chief prosecutor for investigation. The problem went back to Egypt's troubled parliamentary elections.

After Noha al Zeiny's bold testimonial, Bastawisi had gone one big step further: He filed formal complaints demanding an investigation into the vote-rigging. He also charged that some of his brethren had been involved in election fraud.[27] And then he took the case to the media.

Bastawisi spoke with authority. He was one of fifteen senior judges—selected secretly by his peers at the Judges Club—in charge of receiving complaints from colleagues deployed at polling stations. Egypt's Ministry of Interior organizes the mechanics of an election, but the judges officially oversee it, basically acting as supervisors on voting day, monitoring the count, and then certifying the results.

Fraud during the election, Bastawisi told me, had been insidious nationwide. "By the end of the election, I had three bags of complaints—big bags, like big grocery bags," he said, holding out his arms to approximate the size.

"There was one particularly horrifying story about a group of judges who had to escape with the ballot boxes because the police refused to protect them from the thugs," he said. "They ended up hiding under the stairs to protect the votes."

Unlike past elections, the Judges Club this time was not keeping quiet—even under threat.

"When we started exposing the problems and saying some judges of ill repute who work closely with the government were involved in fraud, we were dismissed as a minority of renegades and transferred to the prosecutor's office for investigation," Bastawisi told me.

He was not alone. When I saw Bastawisi, three of the fifteen on the Judges Club election committee had been stripped of their immunity. Over the next month, the list grew to eight judges. Egyptians began talking about a second "massacre of the judiciary."

The crackdown was not just to get the judges to withdraw their complaints, Bastawisi explained. It was also to prevent the Judges Club from releasing a final report, after a five-month investigation, which could challenge the election results—particularly in districts where the ruling party had won.

Noha al Zeiny's revelation about Damanhur had been shocking. But she was only one voice. And while she was a lawyer who worked for the Ministry of Justice, she was not a judge. The Judges Club, on the other hand, had the clout to legally challenge the legitimacy of the entire election process. And unlike past elections when the judges had avoided confrontation, this time they stood firm.

On March 17, 2006, Egypt's judges assembled again in Cairo to hold an unprecedented public demonstration. Wearing the green or red fringed sashes of their profession draped across their suits, nearly 1,000 judges from across the country packed the street in front of Cairo's Judges Club to demand change.

"The independence of the judges is the battle of the whole nation, and we all have to defend it," Judges Club chief Zakaria Abdel Aziz told the crowd.[28]

The judges then stood in the spring sunshine for almost an hour in silent protest.

Hundreds of prodemocracy demonstrators cheered them on. "Judges, judges, save us from tyranny," some shouted in unison.[29] One older male demonstrator, with a zipper taped over his mouth, held up a red pillow with "I ♥ judges" inscribed on it.[30]

The judges' uprising seriously altered the political dynamics in Egypt.

Baheyya, Egypt's leading blogger and a legal expert herself, opined,

Judges in this country have long been held in high esteem, but always at a certain remove. Charisma was anathema, unseemly and downright frowned upon. Now, judges are at the center of public politics and it

wouldn't be an exaggeration to claim that a handful have attained the stature of beloved public personalities, purveyors of a certain mystique.[31]

Egypt's judges, she concluded, had taken on "the public leadership roles usually assumed by politicians."

I asked Nasser Amin what the judges' uprising meant for Egypt's future. "The drama," he replied, "is just beginning. They hold the legitimacy of Egypt in their hands."

Before leaving, almost as an afterthought, I asked Amin about the origins of his unusual center.

It had been launched to work with Egypt's judges. But the center had quickly expanded to broader rule-of-law issues throughout the Arab world. It started drafting bill-of-rights amendments. It investigated torture cases. It provided legal aid to human-rights activists facing prosecution. It consulted on how to make a judicial branch independent. It visited prisons. And it was the only Arab group invited to help monitor Iraq's first elections. Amin led the delegation.

After the May 25 protest in Cairo, the center also kept track of what happened to victims and eyewitnesses of the attack on the women. It filed a complaint with Egypt's Attorney General as well as the World Organization Against Torture, citing State Security for continuing to threaten the molested women for weeks after the event.[32]

"Lazoghly is Egypt's Bastille, and it has to go," Amin told the Egyptian press at the time.[33]

"The center opened in 1997," Amin told me. "But it was originally the idea of a law student who was in his final year at Cairo University ten years earlier. He was a leftist, a Nasserite, and he took some critical stands against the government.

"Well," he continued, "one day, he and fifteen of his friends were arrested."

Amin stopped to light another Marlboro. "They were picked up under emergency law provisions and transferred to the high State Security court. Its rulings are final, and there's no appeal. They were forced to stand in a cage in the courtroom, where they were charged with plotting to overthrow the government, inciting society, and insulting the constitution."

Amnesty International mentioned Amin's trial in its annual report about cases in 1988. The government charges, it noted, also included sabotage and collaboration with Libya.[34]

"Well," Amin continued, "State Security tortured them, as well as members of their families, and forced confessions that were not true—including that they had weapons. None of it was true. But based on the charges, the prosecution asked for the death penalty or life imprisonment. The defendants couldn't believe this was happening to them."

State Security had also hauled the law student's brother and father into Lazoghly Square. Both were tortured, Amin said. "They stripped them naked and tortured them in front of each other. They used electric shock, and then forced the brother to beat the father. They were held for several weeks."

Amnesty International noted that some of the accused produced forensic medical reports in court, which appeared to corroborate allegations of physical and psychological torture while they were held incommunicado before the trial.[35]

The judge in the case was Said el Ashmawy, one of the real characters in Egypt's judiciary, I later learned. Ashmawy was occasionally hassled too.

A prolific author, he has written more than thirty books. But five of them were banned by Al Azhar, Egypt's state-controlled religious university.[36] Ashmawy countered by taking the ban to court.

"Without freedom of speech, you have only a culture of rumor," Ashmawy liked to say.[37] The ban was eventually lifted.[38]

I telephoned Ashmawy, now retired, to ask if he remembered the old case of the leftists.

"Of course. It was very famous," said the chatty judge. "The government had no evidence of anything—not of trying to overthrow the government or ties to Libya. The government thought the court should be convinced just because it was saying so, but it didn't offer any evidence.

"The first defendant gave a full confession, but I was sure he was tortured. Later he denied his confession, and I realized that all of them had been tortured."

During the case, the government pressured Ashmawy behind the scenes. "The general prosecutor visited my office at the court," the judge told me. "He didn't ask for anything *specifically,* but it was quite clear that he came to say that this case was important to him and to the government."

Despite the confessions, Ashmawy found all sixteen innocent.

The verdict was a turning point in the law student's life, Amin explained to me.

"The student realized what would have happened if the judge had not been independent—if the judge had instead accepted the government's case and done what it wanted him to do," he continued. "All of them could have been executed or spent the rest of their lives in prison.

"The student," Amin added, "concluded that the government could do whatever it wanted—oppress, detain, torture, whatever—but if the judiciary was independent, then freedom had a chance in Egypt. Without these independent judges, there was no hope of protecting human rights."

After the center was opened, one of the judges it honored was Ashmawy.

I asked Amin what had happened to the law student.

"Well," Amin replied, "he decided from that point on, whatever remained of his life, he was going to spend working on the independence of the judiciary and human rights."

Amin finished the story and smiled, with that little twinkle in his eyes. Then I realized something.

"You were that student, weren't you?" I said

"Yes," he replied.

THREE

EGYPT

The Players

Freedom is what you do with what's been done to you.

—French philosopher Jean-Paul Sartre

As long as we are suffering economically and politically in the Muslim world, God will be the solution.

—Egyptian analyst Ahmed Fakhr

In the early decades of the twenty-first century, the political forces in the Middle East can be divided into three broad categories. The brave Egyptian activist Saad Eddin Ibrahim—an academic who was among the first to study the jihadists in the 1980s and then went on to found a democracy center, for which he was imprisoned three times, ironically sometimes with the jihadists—calls them the three "crats": theocrats, democrats, and autocrats. I went to see representatives of all three in Egypt to discuss their visions of the future and how they planned to achieve them.

I started with the Muslim Brotherhood, because the theocrats are the most energetic political force in Egypt.

The Brotherhood's neatly efficient headquarters is in a residential apartment that overlooks a row of leafy palm trees along the banks of the Nile. The movement was outlawed in 1954. It was still illegal more than a half century later, so the only signpost was a small white board with blue letters that had been attached to the frame of the door. Even it, I was told, was a fairly recent addition.

Visitors are asked to take off their shoes at the door. "We pray on this rug," explained a greeter, politely. He was wearing natty suspenders but no tie. Like almost everyone in the bustling office, he had a bruiselike mark on his forehead, the sign of a devout Muslim who prays several times a day by getting down on his knees, bending over, and pressing his head against the floor in a sign of submission. Islam, literally, means submission, as in to God.

The headquarters is one of the few smoke-free environments in Cairo, a city where people still puff away in elevators, public transportation, shops, movie houses, and government offices. Members of the Brotherhood do not smoke or drink alcohol because they harm the body—"God's gift," the greeter explained.

The apartment-office is a deceptively modest facility for the most organized political movement in the Middle East and, almost certainly, in the wider Islamic world.[1] It was founded in 1928 by Hassan al Banna, a disillusioned twenty-two-year-old schoolteacher, whose first followers were six disgruntled workers in the Suez Canal Company. Eight decades later, the Brotherhood had spawned eighty-six branches and affiliates in Asia, Europe, and Africa. Most Islamic political groups are a by-product, directly or indirectly, of Banna's unlikely little band.

Hamas originally emerged in 1987 as the militant Palestinian wing of the Brotherhood, whose branch in Syria had become so strong by 1982 that former President Hafez al Assad launched a military crackdown against its stronghold in Hama, killing tens of thousands of people and leveling whole sectors of the city.

Given the Brotherhood's controversial history, some affiliates have taken different names. The Islamic Action Front became Jordan's largest opposition group during the kingdom's first elections for parliament, after a twenty-two year hiatus, in 1989. The Iraqi Islamic Party was the most significant Sunni political group to run in Iraq's 2005 elections.

Prominent Arab politicians as well as notorious extremists got their feet wet politically in Egypt's Brotherhood before moving on to lead their own groups. Yasser Arafat joined when he was an engineering student at Cairo University in the 1950s, before he founded Fatah and took over the Palestine Liberation Organization. Al Qaeda's chief ideologue, Ayman al Zawahiri, was a teenager when he signed up, but he left in the late 1970s to join the more militant Islamic Jihad and then, in the 1990s, to merge forces with Osama bin Laden. Fathi Shikaki joined during his years as a medical student in Egypt in the 1970s, but reportedly left out of frustration at its limited action agenda and founded the Palestinian Islamic Jihad in the 1980s.

The Muslim Brotherhood—or *Ikhwan,* as it is known in Arabic—is still strongest, however, in Egypt, its birthplace.

In Cairo, appointments often happen on Middle East time, meaning late, but I was ushered into the office of Mohammed Habib precisely at the appointed hour.

Habib is the second in command to the Brotherhood's Supreme Guide. His life is a microcosm of the recent Brotherhood experience. He served in parliament; he also served three stints in prison.

A tall man, Habib was wearing a blue and white pinstripe shirt and had a short, well-groomed beard. His glasses had rims at the top but not along the bottom. Habib started out as a geology professor who specialized in detecting geological data from satellite images. He still occasionally lectures.

"No, no, I'm not a cleric," he said, laughing. "Most of us here now are professionals—doctors or engineers or professors." He volunteered that he had done geological research at the University of Missouri at Rolla in the late 1970s.

Although his hair is white and thinning at the top, Habib represents the young guard or more moderate wing of the religious movement. He is middle-class, educated, courteous, articulate, and passionately devout while also experienced with the outside world.

The Brotherhood first moved into mainstream politics through men like Habib. In the early 1980s, Brothers who were doctors, lawyers, journalists, engineers, and other white-collar professionals started winning elections to lead Egypt's unions. Unions are called syndicates in Egypt; they had traditionally been dominated by secular leftist, nationalist, or liberal activists. The movement made the formal leap in 1984. Under cover of a legal centrist party, the Brotherhood ran its first candidates for parliament and won a token presence of eight seats. It ran again, in an alliance with liberal and labor parties, in 1987 and won thirty-six seats. Habib was one of the big winners.

The Brotherhood's presence in mainstream politics has been growing ever since, in fits and starts.

In 2005, although still illegal, the Brotherhood ran again. This time, it exceeded all projections. Eighty-eight of its candidates, running as independents, won twenty percent of the seats in the People's Assembly. It was the largest victory by any group against the ruling party since Egypt became a republic in 1952. The Ikhwan had redefined Egypt's political spectrum.

The Muslim Brotherhood was suddenly the main duly elected opposition party.

And the numbers were misleading: The Brotherhood actually won more than one half of the seats it contested. It put up only 161 candidates for the 444-seat assembly, and it stayed away from many races with high-profile politicians from the ruling National Democratic Party.

The Ikhwan's real strength is one of the most debated topics in Egypt.

The Brotherhood clearly has a critical advantage over all other opposition parties. "President Mubarak has closed down so much that there are only two platforms left for political activism—his National Democratic Party and the mosque," said Hisham Kassem, the editor of Egypt's first independent daily newspaper, who lost as a secular candidate for parliament in 2000. "And he can't close the mosques, so the Muslim Brotherhood effectively has thousands of general assemblies once a week."

Egyptians are a deeply religious people, both Muslims and Coptic Christians. Faith provides a sense of reason and a comfortable rhythm in difficult Egyptian life.

It is visible in Cairo taxis, in the miniature shrines built on the dashboards, or the "I rely on God" bumper stickers, or the lists of "The Ninety-nine Names of God" dangling from the rearview mirrors. It is audible in the lilting Muslim call to prayer chanted from thousands of mosque muezzins or interrupting programs on state-controlled television five times a day. It is evident in the standard response to statements on virtually anything from the weather and marriage prospects to politics—inshallah, or "God willing."

For almost 1,000 years, Cairo has been the world's largest Muslim city and its most important center of Islamic learning at Al Azhar, the oldest university in the Islamic world. Egypt has also produced the two most famous (and rival) new Muslim televangelists—the charismatic young modernist Amr Khaled on Iqra satellite television and the older and fierier Sheikh Mohammed al Qaradawi on al Jazeera.

More important to the shift in Egypt's political winds was the economic crisis of the 1990s, which produced what Egyptians dubbed their "Gulf-ization" period. Between 1989 and 1996, up to seven million Egyptians were driven to find work in conservative Persian Gulf countries. Egyptian officials told me they realized what was going on when the government could not keep teachers; some three million left Egypt.[2] Most Egyptians eventually came back, with new money but also often with conservative Gulf ways that were best reflected at home by the Muslim Brotherhood. The experience left a particularly deep impact on Egypt's middle class, the cornerstone of any society's political system.

The tide had turned so much that Habib predicted his movement could win sixty percent of the seats in a free election—if the Muslim Brotherhood could fairly compete for every seat.

Several Egyptian analysts disagreed. They countered that the highly organized Brotherhood mobilized all the votes it could get in the 2005 election and still did not attract the silent majority—more than seventy-five percent of Egyptian voters—who were not motivated enough to go to the polls to cast ballots for anyone.

Some cynics also argued that the movement put up only 161 candidates for the 2005 election because it had no other viable nominees.

The election proved the movement's weakness rather than its strength, Kassem, the editor of *The Egyptian Today,* told me. "Look, in 2005, it had been trying to get to power for almost eighty years," he said. "I would have trouble hiring someone who took that long to make an impact."

But Habib claimed that the number of candidates was a calculated decision. The Brotherhood's go-slow strategy, he said, sought to produce gradual change rather than radical upheaval.

"Our approach, our plan, our vision has adopted the slogan: participation, not overpowering," Habib explained, sitting at a desk covered with neat stacks of books and papers. "We know the Egyptian regime does not want us, and they are holding on tight to their seats of power. No one wants to provoke or confront the regime on that point."

In the early twenty-first century, the Brotherhood has evolved in its discourse and strategy, if not its goals. The Ikhwan's original creed projected radical transformation. "God is our purpose, the Prophet our leader, the Koran our constitution, jihad our way, and dying for God's cause our supreme objective."[3]

The motto is still in its official literature. But a simplified and vaguer version—"Islam is the solution"—has been used for public consumption in recent years. The movement talks less about jihad and theocratic rule, too.

Indeed, when the new class of Brotherhood members showed up for parliament in 2006, its early focus was not on stereotypical issues associated with Islamic rule, such as banning alcohol or imposing Islamic dress on women. They instead went after a government decision to let a retired French aircraft carrier loaded with tons of asbestos sail through the Suez Canal en route to India, where it was to be disassembled for scrap metal. A Brotherhood politician angrily warned of the environmental hazards to Egypt.[4]

To call for a chance to speak in the People's Assembly, legislators have to wave a copy of Egypt's constitution at the parliamentary speaker. With eighty-eight members, the Brotherhood delegation literally began a wave of challenges about reform issues that secular parties had been unable or unwilling to tackle. Persistently and sometimes noisily, they demanded answers on the use of torture. They called for a status report on more than 15,000 political prisoners. They pressed for an end to emergency law. They urged judicial independence and freedom of speech for journalists reporting on government corruption. They called for term limits on the presidency. They appealed for the rights to assemble and associate.[5]

In one session, Brotherhood parliamentarian Hussein Ibrahim scolded the regime for its human-rights record, noting "horror stories about torture in police stations, cases in which prisoners have disappeared from jails, and innocent citizens have been forced to admit to crimes they didn't commit."[6]

The disciplined movement also prodded parliament's work ethic, notably its high absenteeism. All eighty-eight Brotherhood members attended all sessions, all the time, Egyptian analysts told me. Votes can be called at any time, without a quorum, so ruling-party legislators were suddenly forced to attend more often for fear of what laws might get passed without them.

During my visit to Brotherhood headquarters, Habib insisted that the Brotherhood understood the pragmatic realities of twenty-first-century politics. The Ikhwan had made a full commitment to work within the system, he said.

"We can now say that for decades we have accepted democracy," he told me. "We approve multiple parties on the political arena, and this reflects a change or an evolution in our way of thinking about political life.

"We approve the peaceful transfer of power. And we declare as well that the people are the source of authority, that people have the right to choose their leader, and that people are the ones to choose their candidates. The people are the ones who have the right to choose the program that they see fit for them, politically, economically, and socially."

The source of authority is a central issue as Middle East societies begin the process of change, particularly as Islamist groups reconfigure the political spectrum. Is it God? Or is it the people? The answer will define the next stage of political development.

When pressed, Brotherhood officials still fudge the answer.

"We need to make a distinction between Western-style democracy and the kind of democracy we believe in," Habib said. "We believe that ballot boxes must be transparent. And we believe in state institutions with real separation of authority between the executive, legislative, and judicial branches.

"But democracies can look different from place to place," he added. "For us, we want whatever laws are passed to be in keeping with Islamic Sharia."

Like many Muslim countries, Egypt already requires laws to be compatible with Sharia. The Brotherhood has done little to specify how strict it wants those laws to be. But it has indicated some limits. In a press conference after the 2005 election, Habib argued that Egyptians should have the right to vote for presidential candidates from parties other than the ruling National Democratic Party. But he also declared that all presidential candidates had to be Muslim—in a country where ten percent of the population is Coptic Christian and Muslim-Christian suspicions run deep. "If we are to apply the Islamic rule, which says that non-Muslims cannot have guardianship over Muslims, then a Christian may not be president," he told reporters.[7]

For now, the movement emphasizes peaceful transformation. Its public literature warns, "Ruling a totally corrupt society through a militant government overthrow is a great risk."[8]

"We are against revolutions in general and definitely against chaos," Habib told me. "We are also against using armed struggle for change and military coups. No, no, we prefer peaceful change through constitutional and legal channels. There's no violence in our ideology."

That was not always true. The Brotherhood has evolved through at least three phases since 1928. Launched in the Suez Canal port of Ismailya, it was initially a grassroots religious and social reform movement with small but ambitious outreach programs. It spent the first decade penetrating Suez cities and then Cairo. In a precise formula, each new branch established an identical set of institutions that included an office, a mosque, a school, a workshop, and a sporting club.

The utopian goal was to create Muslim societies, the seeds for creation of a different kind of state. Founder Hassan al-Banna invoked Islam as a way both to lead one's life and to rule a nation, as in the faith's early days. "My brothers," Banna told his new followers, "you are a new soul in the heart of this nation to give it life by means of the Koran."[9]

But in the 1940s and 1950s, the Brotherhood entered a militant second phase. Angered by the monarchy, heavy British influence in Egypt, and Banna's thwarted attempts to run for parliament, the movement bred an extremist wing known as the "the specialists" or "the secret apparatus," which launched sporadic waves of attacks on both domestic and foreign targets. After four hits on British occupation forces in 1946, Brotherhood gunmen then assassinated the Egyptian judge who convicted their brethren for the violence. Its most brazen act was the assassination of Egyptian Prime Minister Mahmoud Nokrashi after he charged the movement was plotting to topple the monarchy and ordered it to dissolve.[10]

Three months later, Banna was gunned down on a Cairo street, in apparent retaliation.

In 1954, two years after the monarchy was toppled, President Nasser charged the Brotherhood was trying to assassinate him, too. He jailed thousands of Muslim Brothers.

The Brotherhood now tries to distance itself from past violence and its extremist offshoots across the Middle East. "The two incidents that happened during Banna's time—Nokrashi and the judge—were two individual acts conducted by members of the Muslim Brotherhood, but they were carried out without the knowledge of Banna and condemned by Banna at the time," Habib said, dismissing his organization's responsibility.

"As for the attempt to assassinate Nasser," he added, "this was a play, an act, which was orchestrated by Nasser himself to get rid of the leaders of the Ikhwan and to detain tens of thousands of them so that he was alone in power."

Yet that period of militancy has had an enduring impact well into the twenty-first century and well beyond Egypt. Among those jailed in 1954 was Sayyid Qutb, arguably the most influential ideologue that the Brotherhood—or any modern Islamic group—has ever produced. Decades later, al Qaeda's first angry treatise in 1998 against the United States and its Arab allies borrowed heavily from Qutb's work.

Ironically, Qutb had been radicalized in the United States. A mid-level Ministry of Education official in Cairo, he had been dispatched to do graduate work from 1948 to 1950 at a small teachers' training college that later became the University of Northern Colorado. But the American experience had repelled Qutb because of what he viewed as excesses and materialism.

In a 1951 essay he wrote upon his return to Cairo, "The America I have Seen," Qutb expressed disgust at everything from racism to the water wasted on big American lawns, from the sexuality expressed on the dance floor to the physicality of sports matches.

America's primitiveness, he wrote, "can be seen in the spectacle of the fans as they follow a game of football... or watch boxing matches or bloody, monstrous wrestling matches.... This spectacle leaves no room for doubt as to the primitiveness of the feelings of those who are enamored with muscular strength and desire it."

Qutb lived in Greeley, Colorado. Named after newspaper editor and Republican presidential candidate Horace Greeley, the conservative community was founded by an agriculture editor on Greeley's *New York Tribune* who wanted to set up a utopian society in America and carefully sorted through applications to decide who would be invited to settle in Greeley. The town was established in the nineteenth century on the principles of temperance, religion, and family values.[11] Even in the mid-twentieth century, when Qutb attended college in Greeley, alcohol was banned, and public entertainment was limited largely to church socials.

But the Egyptian found decadence even in this reserved environment. He wrote,

> They danced to the tunes of the gramophone, and the dance floor was replete with tapping feet, enticing legs, arms wrapped around waists, lips pressed to lips, and chests pressed to chests. The atmosphere was full of desire.

He was scathing about American women.

> The American girl is well acquainted with her body's seductive capacity. She knows it lies in the face, and in expressive eyes, and thirsty lips. She knows seductiveness lies in the round breasts, the full buttocks, and in the shapely thighs, sleek legs—and she shows all this and does not hide it.[12]

Of his American experience, Qutb concluded, "Humanity makes the gravest of errors and risks losing its account of morals if it makes America its example."

After Qutb returned to Egypt, he joined the Brotherhood and quickly became its most prominent author. He continued to write even after he was imprisoned in 1954, raging at the illegitimacy of modern societies, American and Arab alike, for barbarous ignorance comparable to the uncivilized period before Islam.

In his book *Milestones,* Qutb called on the faithful to topple illegitimate regimes and create pure Islamic states to free mankind "from every authority except that of God."[13]

Qutb was released in 1964 after a decade in prison, only to be arrested again eight months later for preaching the same radical doctrine. This time, he was sentenced to death.

The government offered clemency if he recanted his call for a militant jihad to topple the Egyptian regime. Colleagues urged him to accept, and many at the time thought he would. But in the end, he refused to back down. In 1966, Qutb was hanged for treason.

Qutb's influence proved even greater after his death. His writing inspired young activist Ayman al Zawahiri as well as a new generation of Egyptian militants in groups such as Islamic Jihad. His appeal crossed sectarian and ethnic lines as well as national borders. His thinking influenced Iran's Ayatollah Ruhollah Khomeini in the 1960s and 1970s in the run-up to Iran's Shiite revolution. Like Qutb, Khomeini warned against what he called "Westoxication," or poisoning of the spirit by lax Western morality.

After Qutb's execution, his brother Mohammed left Egypt to teach in the more hospitable climate of Saudi Arabia. Among his students at King Abdul Azziz University in the 1970s was Osama bin Laden.[14]

Qutb's ideas have since been adopted by militants as far afield as Afghanistan, Pakistan, Malaysia, and the Philippines. They remain popular in the twenty-first century. When I travel in the Middle East, one of the things I always do is stop in local bookstores or libraries to see if Qutb's works are available. Usually they are.

The Brotherhood's third phase began in the 1970s, after President Sadat released many of the thousands who had been imprisoned along with Qutb. "History evolves gradually, but I can say 1974 and 1975, when Sadat allowed a greater climate of freedom on the campuses and around Egypt," Habib told me, "that was the turning point of our Islamic work."

The Brothers gradually—and somewhat reluctantly, at first—began to absorb a younger generation. The movement was reenergized by student activists who ran for leadership roles on university councils and by professionals like Habib. The movement also began to emphasize again the kind of social outreach programs initiated by founder Hassan al-Banna.

The Brotherhood, in effect, tried to build a state within a state.

In the late 1980s, I visited a complex built around a Cairo mosque by a Brotherhood sympathizer. The three-story stone building in the al-Duqqi neighborhood included a clinic, an elementary school, a small library, and a rooftop observatory to explore the heavens. The classrooms were full. A long line waited to see a doctor; the basic charge was fifty cents a visit. Medical staff at the clinic told me they treated more than 200,000 patients a year.

Egypt soon had hundreds of clinics and schools operated by Islamic groups or individual sympathizers.[15] The Brotherhood does not discuss specific numbers, since any facility with a formal connection to an outlawed movement can be closed down by the state. And some have been.

"Schools are under a lot of scrutiny," Habib told me. "Many of the education organizations have been dissolved because of regime harassment. But you could say we still have tens of thousands of students and many Islamic health organizations."

In a country with seventy-six million people, most of whom live on a narrow strip of fertile land along the meandering Nile River, the Brotherhood's social services reach only a small minority of Egyptians, analysts in Cairo told me. Yet the Ikhwan's services are reliable, they conceded, and even Egyptians who did not vote for them believe the movement sincerely intends to help people.

After a devastating Cairo earthquake in 1992, the Brotherhood and other Islamist groups were the first to respond with food, blankets, and welfare for thousands of victims left homeless. Engineers put up temporary shelter; medical staff treated the injured. The Ikhwan also gave a thousand dollars to each family to rebuild. The government's reaction was belated and limited.[16]

In 2006, I again visited facilities unofficially linked to the Brotherhood. The Islamic Medical Organization operated a three-story hospital with an outdoor staircase in Talbeye, a poor area near the Pyramids that has dusty, garbage-strewn streets traveled mainly by donkey carts and battered old taxis. There was no other government or private facility anywhere nearby.

In the whitewashed emergency room, a clean but bare-bones facility, a large sign printed on pink paper read, "The idea of the organization is to get closer to God through medical work. The organization facilitates the means of diagnosis for every patient who needs it, regardless of his financial ability, social status, or medical condition, without discrimination because of color, gender or faith."

A calendar on the wall nearby sounded a less ambiguous note: "Islam is the solution."

The hospital staff included gynecologists, pediatricians, cardiologists, ophthalmologists, general surgeons, dentists, and others. The basic fees were all under three dollars. Once a week, a sign on the bulletin board next to the reception desk advertised, the facility offered free diabetes testing.

The state within the state continued to grow. And tensions between the Brotherhood and the Egyptian government deepened.

Habib's first stint in prison was not long after he returned from studying in the United States. In 1981, facing internal opposition to his peace treaty with Israel, President Sadat ordered a sweep of more than 1,500 religious activists, both Muslims and minority Coptic Christians.[17]

"I am dealing with fanaticism," Sadat said in an angry three-hour speech to justify the controversial crackdown. "This is not religion. This is obscenity." He charged that a sophisticated conspiracy was trying to destroy his authority.[18]

"Don't fear that we will have a Khomeini here," Sadat announced at a press conference, referring to the father of Iran's revolution two years earlier.[19] Less than a month later, Sadat was gunned down by extremists from Islamic Jihad.

Habib was not charged with anything. He was released five months later. Six years later, he won a seat in parliament.

The Brotherhood leader's second arrest was at the hands of President Mubarak in 1995, when he was charged with belonging to a banned organization that called for the overthrow of the state. Habib was tried by a military court under provisions of emergency law. He served the full five-year sentence.

"The real reason for my arrest was that I was going to be nominated again for parliament. So," Habib said, with an ironic little laugh, "the government eliminated my opportunity to run again, because now I've been convicted of a crime."

His third stint was fourteen months, from 2001 to 2002. Again, Habib was not charged. Egyptian dissidents jokingly refer to open-ended imprisonment without trial as preemptive "just-in-case detentions."

Habib was still in prison on September 11, 2001, when al Qaeda pilots flew suicide missions into the World Trade Center and the Pentagon. During our conversation, I noted that al Qaeda's ideological chief was Ayman al Zawahiri, another Egyptian, whose early training was with the Brotherhood. And the mastermind of the attacks was Mohammed Atta, an Egyptian.

"I was very saddened and upset," Habib replied. "I couldn't imagine that human beings who have a brain could carry out such acts, regardless of the extent of enmity they felt. Immediately, I thought we should stand against these actions, no matter who did them. They contradict Islam."

The Brotherhood's deepening involvement in politics has exposed cracks among Islamist groups—and fierce condemnation from militants.

Zawahiri lashed out at the group that first attracted him to politics—for being "duped, provoked and used." In one of the periodic videotapes delivered from his place in hiding, he warned,

> *My Muslim nation, you will not enjoy free elections, protected sanctity, accountable governments and a respectable judiciary unless you are free from the crusader-Zionist occupation and corrupted regimes. This will not be fulfilled by any means other than Jihad.*[20]

Yet the Brotherhood's position on the use of violence remained two-faced. Its leaders still supported what they call "acts of resistance" by Hamas against Israel and by Iraqi insurgents against American troops.

I asked Habib if the Brotherhood now accepts Israel's right to exist, given Egypt's 1979 peace treaty with Israel and the Palestinian Liberation Organization's recognition of Israel's right to exist in 1988. Every Brotherhood official I spoke to refused to use the word Israel and instead referred to the Jewish state as "the Zionist entity."

"We should leave this up to the people. If the people say it stays, it stays, no problem," he replied. "We don't want to impose anything on the Palestinian or Egyptian people.

"But, personally," he added, "I consider the Zionist entity as an occupier of Muslim land. There has to be a formula where people live in peace. I don't know what the formula is now. But, no, for us, they live in our country."

Habib was particularly bitter about what happened after Hamas's election in 2006. "The United States and Western countries are known for their double standards in evaluating democracy," he said. "Domestically, they practice true democracy. But abroad, they practice it only to the extent that it serves their interests. That's why they are doing their best to undermine Hamas's victory. These countries will continue to support corrupt regimes as long as their interests are served."

He was even more scathing about America's intervention in Iraq. In a 2004 interview with the television station run by Lebanon's Hezbollah, Habib had said suicide bombings "redeem self-confidence and hope, because a nation that does not excel at the industry of death does not deserve life."[21]

When he spoke to me, an American journalist, in 2006, he was more restrained, but just as angry.

"The United States has violated international laws and returned the world to the laws of the jungle," he said, jabbing his finger in the air as two deep scowl lines creased his forehead.

"We know that the United States is not a charity organization. It has its interests, but instead of attempting to truly spread democracy, look what it did to Iraq!" he said, getting angrier. "What happened at Abu Ghraib and Guantanamo Bay is a mark of shame."

In a view widely shared in Egypt, Habib reflected, "The United States after 9/11 has adopted a new strategy to establish an empire. It wants to control the Middle East. It's working on redrawing the Middle East map."

I asked Habib about the Brotherhood's own strategy for the future. The movement's literature lists six broad objectives, each one building on the previous step. Leaders deny that they want to convert Egypt into a theocracy led by clerics. Yet its platform is ambitiously theocratic.

The Brotherhood's first goal is to build the Muslim individual—"the brother or sister with a strong body, high manners, cultured thought, ability to earn, strong faith, correct worship, conscious of time, of benefit to others."

The second is to foster practicing Muslim families.

The third is to create an Islamic society.

The fourth is to build an Islamic state.

The fifth is to create a caliphate, "basically a shape of unity between Islamic states."

The last one is "mastering the world with Islam."

In the twenty-first century, the Brotherhood appears to be about halfway down its list.

I asked Habib what a twenty-first century caliphate, or a government representing God's will on earth, would eventually look like. Ironically, on this issue, the United States is something of a model.

"We hope that one day there are states like the United States. Each will have its own laws and leaders and army and everything," he responded. "But there should be a common constitution and character and border. A federal government like the United States is a very nice example, or what the European Union wants to achieve, where its member countries have their own parliaments and laws but with binding overall policies."

I asked him what the United States of the Islamic world would include and how big it would be. He took off his glasses and put them on his desk.

"Look," he said, "The world is moving toward large bodies. It's like the United States trying to create a larger body in a transatlantic alliance. There's the G-8 group of industrialized nations. There are the Asian tigers.

"So why shouldn't there be another big body created here, too, to complement the others?" he said.

"Of course, the Arab world is one phase," he added. "The Islamic world is a bigger and more comprehensive phase. We know this project will take time."

Among the three "crats," the democrats are the weakest—and at the greatest disadvantage. Unlike the theocrats and the autocrats, they are having to build from scratch.

On International Students Day, February 21, 2006, I took a taxi to Cairo University to watch a demonstration organized by Kefaya, the new democracy movement whose name means "Enough." I could hear it blocks away, and when I arrived, the scene outside the campus entrance had combustible potential.

A tight ring of shoulder-to-shoulder riot police with body shields, face masks, and batons encircled the unarmed protesters. There were at least ten police for every demonstrator. Two dozen large armored vans with little grill-covered windows were positioned nearby, in case of mass arrests. Plainclothed security officials, some with conspicuous cameras, were on the perimeter.

To the rhythm of a pulsating drum, the Kefaya protesters shouted one provocative chant after another, in unison, under the direction of white-haired Kamal Khalil. He and his battery-operated loudspeaker had become fixtures at many rallies.

"Down, down with Hosni Mubarak," they yelled.

"State Security, you're the dogs of the state," they shouted. "Why the security? Are we in prison?"

To the police, they turned and taunted, "What are you afraid of? Come join us."

"Open up. Open up. Freedom of thought, freedom for the nation!" they cried.

Inside the tall iron campus gates, a second demonstration was underway, creating a clashing cacophony of chants.

Three weeks earlier, an aging and packed Egyptian ferry had sunk in the Red Sea. More than 1,000 Egyptians had drowned with it. It was the worst maritime disaster in the country's history. Many of the victims were poor laborers coming home from jobs in Saudi Arabia. The government was still scrambling to explain what happened, why its reaction was slow and the rescue slower, why responsibility had not been assigned, and why bodies had not been found, death certificates not issued, and compensation not distributed. Meanwhile, the owner of the ferry company, who also happened to be a member of parliament's upper house, had gone abroad—amid press speculation that he was trying to dodge investigation or recriminations.

The students had plenty of gripes, but the tragedy was a recurrent theme of their protest.

"Officials travel in limousines and airplanes, but the people take buses and die on ferries," the students shouted.

"Why put students in prison? Put the ferry's killers on trial!" they yelled.

"Oh Egypt, oh Egypt, we won't get scared," the protesters cried. "And we won't back down."

"*Hor-i-yya. . . . Hor-i-yya. . . . Hor-i-yya*," they chanted, in accented syllables.

"Free-dom. . . . Free-dom. . . . Free-dom."

Since the first Kefaya rally in 2004, Egypt's democrats had clearly found their voice. Illegal street protests became a common feature in Cairo. Kefaya's democrats were the pioneers for a new type of movement, adding energy to stale Egyptian politics and spurring others into action too.

But by 2006, the new democrats had still not found their political mass. Hundreds had dared to show up for the two rallies in blatant violation of emergency law—but not the tens or hundreds of thousands needed to nudge, prod, pressure, or politically force the government's hand on major reforms.

As the dramas unfolded inside and outside Cairo University's front gate, I talked to two young women in their mid-twenties. There were at least as many Egyptians watching as participating. Both women wore modest but colorful *hejab* scarves; one scarf was striped and the other was a spring floral pattern.

"If these people would do something, I'd be with them all the way," said Rebab, who wore the striped scarf. She asked that I not use her last name; as a university employee, she received a government paycheck.

"But this is all they do," she said. "I'm divorced, and I have a six-year-old son. More than three years ago, I applied for an apartment, and still I don't have one. I sleep on the sofa with my son in a one-bedroom apartment with my grandparents. Now, the price of sugar is going up, and our chicken is diseased," she added, referring to the spate of avian flu chicken deaths in Egypt. "We don't know what to eat. We can't afford meat. It's now forty pounds (about seven dollars) a kilo.

"I know people with apartments who applied years after I did. They have connections with the NDP," she continued angrily, referring to the ruling party. "That's how things get done in this country. All these people are doing," she said pointing to the noisy protest, "is demonstrating."

The day after the rally, I visited George Ishak, the head of Kefaya, to discuss Egypt's new democratic movements. Ishak is a retired high school history teacher and a Coptic Christian who has snowy white hair and wire-rimmed glasses that rest on a wide nose.

Kefaya's headquarters is a two-room office on a scruffy hall with what looked like large black skid marks along the wall. The entrance door said "Center for Egyptian Studies," which is a cover name, because Kefaya had not been able to register as a legal group. One room had inexpensive meeting chairs that were still covered with plastic and piled on top of each other; the second room contained Ishak's well-used desk, a single old computer, and a fax machine covered with many fingerprints. The door in between the two rooms had half of a broken pane of glass, the remaining section shaped in a menacingly sharp pointed peak.

Kefaya's full name is the Popular Campaign for Change. It emerged, Ishak explained, in 2003 when friends with disparate political views met over a holiday meal to discuss the future and then agreed to continue talking.

"Marxists, Nasserites, liberals, Islamists—they were all in these meetings," Ishak added. "We agreed that our country is in miserable condition and that the regime is despotic. But, after that, we had some very difficult discussions because we are not all on the same wavelength. Every week, we tried to come up with part of a statement that was acceptable to all of us. Those first seven months were very hard."

In the end, the Kefaya "declaration to the nation" was sparse, just over one page. It was signed by 300 prominent Egyptians, including a senior Muslim Brotherhood official who had twice served in parliament.

To address its disparate membership, the manifesto had two parts. One section lambasted the "odious assault" on Iraq, the "Zionist devastation" of the Palestinians, and American designs "to recast the fate of the Arab region." It called for mass political efforts "to ward off this peril to the survival of the Arab peoples."[22]

The second section addressed the route to democracy for Egypt. It called for the rule of law. It demanded an end to the political monopoly by the president's party. It urged a two-term limit on the presidency. And it appealed for separation of the legislative, judicial, and executive branches.

The twelve-person leadership then decided Kefaya was ready to take its campaign to the streets in defiance of martial law.

"Before, talking about change was like talking to a comatose person, because the Egyptian people were basically dead," Ishak told me, sitting behind an old desk with nothing on it. "They hadn't talked about political issues, real issues, in more than fifty years, since the days before the republic. All they cared about was how to feed their babies and stay with their families in a safe way.

"So, we had to start a political revival—on the streets," he said, smiling broadly. "I loved this idea. I *needed* to go to the streets. We *all* needed to go to the streets."

The first demonstration, on December 12, 2004, was held in total silence. Over their mouths, Egyptian protesters taped yellow stickers with Kefaya, or "Enough," written in red.

Over the next year, Kefaya's protests expanded the political boundaries wider than at any time since the 1952 revolution. Its demonstration on May 25, 2005, to coincide with the referendum, spawned new waves of participation and new activists. Even the Muslim Brotherhood scrambled to keep up with what initially looked like a popular movement that might rival or even surpass it. For the first time, the Brotherhood also began mobilizing followers for its own demonstrations.

"We opened the doors," Ishak said. "The barrier of fear no longer seemed so high anymore."

Egypt's leading blogger, Baheyya, credited Kefaya as a catalyst.

It jolted the Ikhwan behemoth out of its satisfied complacency as the prime opposition force. It infuriated police chiefs and their superiors and threatened the gerontocracy running the 'opposition parties.' . . . Like the

Judges Club, Kefaya confounded all its interlocutors while compelling
them to radically reorder their plans.

Yet unlike the Brotherhood, Kefaya did not come up with a concrete program of action or candidates for either the presidential or parliamentary elections. Internal divisions were too deep. The movement
instead urged supporters to boycott both elections in 2005—a decision
that backfired.

Kefaya was unable to take the critical step from a protest movement
to a political alternative or even a strong lobbying group, whether legal
or not.

The movement inspired a host of offshoots: Youth for Change. Journalists for Change. Teachers for Change. Doctors for Change. Artists
for Change. Lawyers for Change. And several others for change. But
Kefaya itself remained something of a shell and a loose umbrella.

Kefaya reflected the core problem for nascent democratic movements throughout the region. It did not have a professional political
elite. Its members were well intentioned but untrained. It had limited
infrastructure—no office manager, no communications chief or equipment, no real staff. Ishak took all calls on his own cell phone. Funding
depended on scanty donations. Protests relied on people who could
afford—or dared—to get off work or go to jail, which was why the
demonstrations usually involved the same group of people meeting up
at diverse venues. And many of its most enthusiastic members were the
idealistic young, who had limited clout.

"You call the Muslim Brotherhood at seven A.M., and someone
answers the phone," Ishak admitted. "You talk to the younger generation in our organization, and they don't answer the telephone until
one in the afternoon because they don't go to sleep until after the first
prayers of the day. They talk to the girls all night."

Wael Khalil, a forty-year-old information technology specialist
with short curly hair and big round eyes, was among the early Kefaya
activists. He went to its first protest. I met up with him at the annual
conference of Egyptian socialists, where he was an organizer. He was
wearing jeans and a deep-red polo shirt.

Khalil was candid about Kefaya's impact. "The movement is still an infant," he told me. "We have to be patient."

But he conceded that Kefaya was stuck. "The success of that first year is gone. Kefaya has to reinvent itself. It has to be able to say, 'OK, Mubarak won reelection and is still in power. What role can this network of forces play now?' If someone wants to join Kefaya, the movement has to be able to tell him what he can do.

"The problem," Khalil said, pulling his hand through his curls, "is that Kefaya doesn't have an answer. Kefaya hasn't had more success because people who are unemployed don't see it as their beacon."

During parliamentary elections, Khalil ended up voting for a Muslim Brotherhood candidate—partly as a protest but also because Egyptian politics offered limited alternatives.

Most of the region's traditional opposition groups are spent forces or are losing constituents.

Egypt's oldest opposition group is the Wafd Party. But it, too, had begun to implode politically. Its presidential candidate, Noman Gomaa, received less than three percent of the vote when he ran against Mubarak in 2005. And Wafd won only six seats in parliament.

Wafd means "delegation." The party emerged in 1919 among liberal activists who challenged both British colonial rule and Egypt's monarchy. It was widely popular until it was forced to disband, along with other parties, after the 1952 revolution. The New Wafd was revived in the late 1970s and, again, became the main legal opposition party. Its power brokers were merchants, middle-class professionals, landowners, and the bourgeoisie marginalized after the revolution. But it never regained its earlier standing.

In a political soap opera, the party dumped Gomaa after his humiliating defeat in the 2005 elections. Gomaa, a former dean of Cairo University's Faculty of Law then in his seventies, refused to go quietly, however. Backed by some fifty well-armed thugs, he stormed the party headquarters in an elegant old Cairo villa to reassert his control in April 2006. The group welded the front gates shut and overwhelmed staff and journalists putting out the party newspaper. Gomaa locked himself in his old office.

For the next ten hours, the two wings of Wafd had it out. The new leadership mobilized some 500 party faithful to confront Gomaa and retake the building. His thugs responded with gunfire and Molotov cocktails, according to local press accounts. In the end, Gomaa and his accomplices surrendered. They were charged with attempted murder, possession of firearms, instigating a riot, and a host of minor offenses.[23]

Wafd had never sunk so low.

One new democrat did emerge from Cairo's turbulent elections in 2005, however. Ayman Nour is a baby-faced lawyer with a full head of dark hair and oversize glasses. He first made a name as a student activist in the 1980s. He won a seat in parliament in 1995, as the youngest member in the opposition, and again in 2000, both times for the Wafd Party.

Nour had a reputation as a feisty politician with a flair for show-manship. A champion of political prisoners, he often harangued the government about their treatment and demanded their release. During one of Egypt's periodic bread shortages, he challenged the prime minister publicly to sample the rock-hard bread doled out to the poor.[24] He regularly lambasted Mubarak as an old man, isolated from voters, and ineffective in office.

But after a falling-out with Gomaa, Nour broke away and founded al Ghad, or the Tomorrow Party. After a three-year battle, Tomorrow was finally allowed to register as a legal party in 2004. Nour then began a meteoric rise as the most prominent liberal democrat in Egypt.

I did not get to see him, however. He was in prison when I was in Cairo. It was his second stint in jail. He was first picked up in January 2005 and charged with forging names on petitions required to register a political party. He recounted what happened in a column he wrote for *Newsweek* entitled "Letter from Prison: Did I Take Democracy Too Seriously?"

Egyptian security forces snatched me as I was leaving my seat in Parliament amid the cries of my political allies and the suspicious indifference of my opponents. I was dragged away and assigned to a new seat, at Tora prison south of Cairo. Now I sit writing by candlelight, trying to make sense of what is happening to me, my country and the Middle East.

Only 89 days before my arrest, I had celebrated the birth of my "liberal" dream: the Tomorrow Party. This project to form a new opposition group in Egypt had suffered governmental rejection for three years, and we won our license to operate only after four legal battles in court. It was a momentous achievement: ours was the first liberal party to be licensed in Egypt since the military coup of 1952. Now a white, rectangular placard is posted at Tora prison carrying my photo and the number 1387.[25]

Nour's arrest came shortly before President Mubarak proposed a constitutional amendment allowing multiparty elections for president. Nour's wife, Gameela Ismail, remembered the day of the announcement—and Nour's reaction.

"Ayman was on a hunger strike, and I went to visit him, to try to convince him to stop, when he heard on the radio about the proposed amendment," she told me. "So he immediately wrote a letter and said, 'Give this to the party and have them approve it, and then give it to the media.'"

Nour had decided to run for president.

"I thought he was really going crazy," she told me. "He was in prison!"

Under mounting pressure both at home and abroad, the government soon released Nour on bail—shortly after Condoleezza Rice canceled her first trip to Egypt as secretary of state to signal displeasure over the arrest.

Nour ran a quixotic campaign under the slogan "hope and change." His platform offered Egyptians a two-year transition period. It would include an end to emergency law, release of political detainees, press freedom, an anticorruption campaign, education reform, and new laws to convert Egypt into a parliamentary republic.

Nour often spoke emotionally, occasionally breaking down from a combination of exhaustion, excitement, and behind-the-scenes harassment. Crass stories were leaked to the press, including one that his father had falsified Nour's birth certificate to cover an illegitimate birth, a sensitive issue in Egypt. Another widespread rumor alleged that his two teenage sons played "satanic" music in a band, another sensitive issue in a deeply religious society.

"At the heart of frustration is oppression and the loss of hope," Nour said on the day he opened his campaign. "The worst thing they stole from us is hope."[26]

Nour came in second out of ten candidates, at a distance, with almost eight percent of the vote.

Defiant and still facing charges, Nour then ran again for parliament. This time, he lost the seat he had held for a decade in his stronghold. His supporters charged fraud.

A month later, in December 2005, Nour was convicted on the charges of forging names on his petition to register the party. He was sentenced to five years in prison. The verdict was condemned by governments and human rights groups worldwide. The White House said it was "deeply troubled" by the trial and called on Mubarak's government to act "in the spirit of its professed desire for increased political openness and dialogue" and release Nour.

As usual on human rights issues, Cairo had no public reply.

Nour had been in prison again two months when I arrived in Egypt, so I called on his wife. A few hours beforehand, however, I received an urgent text message from her to go instead to a Cairo district court. Ismail had just been informed that her husband was being brought from prison to face seventeen new charges.

When she arrived, however, Ismail was also told she was going to be charged with two offenses.

The court proceedings were over by the time I got there. Getting anywhere in Cairo takes a long time. But Ismail, the family lawyers, and a small crowd of supporters were standing out on the curb of the courthouse with banners. She had a bullhorn in her hand and she was shouting as loud as she could, "Down, down Hosni Mubarak. Shame on the regime! End tyranny. Freedom for all!"

Police milled around on the outskirts, and I saw a line of young thugs with truncheons walk by single-file and deploy beyond the police. Ismail continued her one-woman protest until she was almost hoarse, and then it broke up.

Nour and Ismail met when she was an editorial assistant for *Newsweek* in Cairo. It was a love marriage. Her first assignment for the magazine had been to profile a young opposition figure under fire. He had recently launched a campaign against torture in prison and then been roughed up. During the interview, she asked his marital status—for the article. He took it as a sign she was interested and later asked her out. They were married two years later.

Since then, they have had an unusual political partnership.

Nour and Ismail live in a large apartment in the trendy Cairo suburb of Zamalek. The living room wall has an enormous picture, in oils, at least ten feet long, of Nour talking with a handful of colleagues in the courtyard of Egypt's parliament. There is a pool on the large rooftop terrace and, as we talked, a large fluffy cat kept circling it.

Ismail has dark hair that falls in wavy curls. She has a creamy-soft face; she once was a television presenter on a government-controlled station. But she was also edgy and drained from the courthouse experience. Suddenly she was dealing with her own legal crisis.

"You know," she said, "I remember one of the incidents they're now charging me with. It was two months ago, and I was beaten on the head by a policeman at a demonstration. I told Ayman I wanted to file a report, but the policeman asked Ayman not to do it. Ayman told me this man is too poor, so we didn't do anything. And then he files a report against us!

"These are the dogs of the regime," she said. "We should have filed a report just to protect ourselves."

Ismail was exhausted from threatening telephone calls. "They call late at night and say, 'If you keep talking, he will never let him out of prison. Shut up. Stay home.'

"I got a call once at midnight," she continued. "He said, 'If you don't shut up, you will have a case of vice—he meant prostitution—against you.' My parents are willing to have their daughter face any charge, but not this one. I have children. What would this do to them?

"Then there were the threats of kidnapping the kids, stopping my brother's business. They got women on the phone who said that they had had relations with my husband, that they had a baby with him. Another time they would call and say, we know what you are doing, what you are wearing, where you are sitting.

"They do everything they can think of," she added, "to plant fear in the hearts."

After Nour's election losses and arrest, the Tomorrow Party fell into disarray. It split into two factions, after one side tried to remove Nour from the leadership.

For all their problems, however, the democrats remain determined.

I asked Ismail how she could hold out any hope for political change in Egypt, given her husband's defeat in two critical elections, his imprisonment, the collapse of the party, and the personal harassment.

"Oh, definitely, there will be change," she said. "This culture of fear, of hidden anger, of hidden torture, of hidden suffering, of hidden everything is being shaken.

"For so long, this country was closed. People didn't have a voice," she said. "We may not be winning elections, but now we can challenge the system and the president in public, and be heard. We have suffered a lot, and we will suffer a lot more. But we have done a lot too.

"Nothing," she added, "is as eternal as they once thought."

A year later, however, her husband languished in prison, largely forgotten by the outside world and unable to connect with Egyptians. Ismail held a Tomorrow Party summit to try to rally support. Five police trucks with police in riot gear assembled outside the meeting. But only fifty people showed up.[27]

Of the three "crats," the autocrats are both the toughest and most vulnerable.

Many now recognize the new political undercurrents. They feel the pressure of satellite television, the Internet, and public opinion they can no longer easily control. For them, politics is now a game of calculating two factors—what token changes they can risk, and how much repression they can use—in the quest to hold on to power.

Before my final trip to Cairo, I made arrangements, through the Egyptian Embassy in Washington, to see Gamal Mubarak, the son of the Egyptian president. The younger Mubarak had emerged in 2000 as the young face of the regime. I wanted to talk to him about whether Egypt's autocrats could change and, if so, how much.

A tall man in his early forties, Mubarak has a trim, athletic build.

He is noted for his well-tailored suits, and he wears his dark, slightly receding hair slicked back. He is a stark contrast with his bulkier father in other ways, too. While the president was born in a village—a fact still reflected in his speech—Gamal Mubarak grew up in the presidential palace. His father worked his way through Egypt's military academy, while Gamal Mubarak earned undergraduate and graduate degrees in business from the American University of Cairo. The president did part of his pilot's training in the Soviet Union, while Gamal Mubarak worked six years at the Bank of America branch in London and started a private equity firm before returning to take up politics.

Since Gamal Mubarak's political debut in 2000, Egypt's notorious political grapevine has frequently reported that he is his father's favored political heir.[28]

One of the major reasons the Egyptian regime appeared so brittle for so long was because President Mubarak refused to appoint a vice president—the route to the top job for all but one of Egypt's presidents since the 1952 revolution. Mubarak balked after inheriting the presidency when Anwar Sadat was murdered in 1981. And he did not change his mind after an assassination attempt on his own life during a 1995 trip to Ethiopia or when he collapsed from illness during a nationally televised speech to parliament in 2003. He was not willing to designate a deputy or a running mate when he opened the presidency to popular elections in 2005. Nor did he budge when his health, at age seventy-eight, became the buzz of Cairo because of his frail appearance at the televised All-Africa Cup soccer championship in 2006. By then, Mubarak had become the third longest ruler in Egypt's 6,000-year history.[29]

Only half jokingly, Egyptians often referred to President Mubarak as "the last pharaoh" for his failure to share power or name a deputy. Many believed he was holding the position open to avoid the emergence of a rival to his son. Cairenes whispered that First Lady Suzanne Mubarak was particularly anxious to see her second son succeed her husband.

The president denied that he wanted to create a new political dynasty. "It's nonsense," he once huffed.[30] Gamal Mubarak—sometimes called Jimmy by friends—also claimed to have no presidential ambitions. "I am neither seeking nor do I wish to nominate myself," he told Egyptian television in 2006.[31]

But almost everyone I talked to in Egypt, including government officials speaking in private, did not believe the denials. The issue had become a regular feature of the new protest rallies. Kefaya demonstrators had a sequence of rhythmic chants: "Wanted, wanted, a new president—with conditions: Not corrupt. Not a dictator. And no kids!"

"No to Hosni, No to Gamal," they would cry.

The demise of monarchies was one of the dominant themes of the twentieth century worldwide. The Middle East's biggest upheavals, after gaining independence from European powers, were also revolutions that toppled kings in the name of social justice. But in the twenty-first century, several Arab countries began moving to establish new dynasties: President Mubarak created prominent political space for son Gamal. Libya's Col. Moammar Qaddafi ceded power increasingly at home and abroad to son Saif. Before his ouster, Iraq's Saddam Hussein was grooming sons Uday and Qusay. When he died in 2000, Syrian President Hafez al Assad left son Bashar in power; the originally designated heir and older son, Basil, had died earlier in a car crash. Yemeni President Ali Abdullah Saleh put son Ahmed in charge of the most powerful branch of the military.

For the regimes, the issues were ostensibly stability and continuity. But the trend emerged at a time when the systems in each capital were failing, and change was the more popular public theme.

Gamal Mubarak made his formal political debut after the 2000 parliamentary elections, in which the ruling party had the poorest showing in its history. His father brought him in as chairman of a new Policy Secretariat designed to reform and reinvigorate the National Democratic Party.

The Egyptian leader told the press it took a week of coaxing to get his son to take the job. "They told me he could help upgrade the party," the president said. "I hope there will be forty or 100 people as active as him, so that I have a broad base of young leaders to choose from."[32]

Over the next six years, the younger Mubarak became assistant secretary-general of the ruling party. His peers took key party positions, replacing his father's old guard. He made choreographed trips to Washington for talks with top White House, State Department and Pentagon officials. At home, he was widely photographed for the state-controlled media. And he held "Meet Gamal" town-hall meetings across the country with targeted groups, notably students and business leaders.

He struck themes of change at every stop.

"I think it's time we stop viewing reform as something which is always imposed from outside," he told 600 faculty and alumni at his alma mater in 2003. "We cannot claim to have achieved all our objectives, or that we are nearing the conclusion of the reform process. Much still needs to be done."[33]

A government reshuffle in 2004 led to the nickname "Gamal's cabinet," because the executive branch now included so many of his associates. During the 2004 party conference, his picture was emblazoned along with Egypt's Olympic heroes on a four-sided billboard in downtown Cairo.[34]

In 2004, a new book entitled *Gamal Mubarak: Restoration of Liberal Nationalism* described him as the most qualified person to be Egypt's next leader. It was written by a university professor—and a senior member of the ruling party.[35]

But the dead giveaway was shortly after the volatile 2005 elections, when the regime postponed city council elections for two years. The issue was not just local power; the move also made it more difficult to run for the presidency. Under the amendment proposed by President Mubarak and passed in the troubled May 25, 2005 referendum, independent presidential candidates had to have the written endorsement of at least 140 elected members of local councils as well as ninety members of the People's Assembly—just to run. Without a new round of local elections, only the ruling party qualified.[36]

Opposition movements quickly charged that the move was to foil any real competition to Gamal Mubarak. Even analysts on the government payroll told me they believed the often relentless government campaign against Ayman Nour was an attempt to derail a future rival to the younger Mubarak. The two men were the same age.

Nour referred to the rivalry after he lost the presidency. "I dared to challenge the pharaoh," Nour said afterward. "And the pharaohs used to kill all the possible male heirs except their own. Mubarak wants to hand Egypt over to his own son, Gamal, and Gamal could never beat me in a free election."[37]

When I made the request to talk to the younger Mubarak several weeks before my trip, Egyptian officials assured me that he was quite eager to answer questions about his reform agenda. I had interviewed his father several times in Cairo and Washington over a twenty-year period, so it seemed straightforward. But as soon as I arrived in Egypt, a foreign ministry official whom I had known for two decades traveled through tortuous Cairo traffic just to tell me that, unfortunately, Gamal Mubarak was "in retreat"—no specifics, just that he would be unavailable during my entire trip.

I was instead invited to call on Osama al Baz, the longtime chief presidential adviser who studied law at Harvard, worked in the Arab-Israeli peace process dating back to the 1970s, and had become the old-guard mentor to the younger Mubarak. Baz had chaperoned him on his Washington visits.

Baz is a slight, wiry man with a thin face, graying hair, age spots, and eyebrows that arch at the very end rather than in the middle. We met in his cavernous, paneled office at the Foreign Ministry; it was decorated with fading brocade couches and a tired philodendron in a brass pot. He was dressed informally in a white shirt with rolled-up sleeves and no tie.

Baz promised that he would work immediately—"yes, immediately!"—to get the promised meeting back on track. But in the meantime he offered his own reflections about Gamal Mubarak and the first family's reform agenda. He speaks with a congenial but little-tough-guy insistence that reminded me of Edward G. Robinson.

"Egypt is already in a state of transition," Baz told me, waving his hand as if it was old news. "But you have to do it within the realm of political stability. There are peculiar conditions here. A political system depends on a country's past, and the political and social factors at play, and a nation's needs.

"For that reason," he continued, "Gamal believes there's no formula that can fit all countries at all times. You also can't do reform overnight, in a way that will result in massive unemployment."

Like many Arab regimes, Egypt invokes the China model, with economic reform to precede political openings, in the name of avoiding instability.

The younger Mubarak was particularly focused on issues that most affect Egypt's youth, Baz said, such as education and employment.

Egypt's education system was so broken in the first decade of the twenty-first century that most public schools had abridged double shifts, and some planned triple shifts to accommodate a burgeoning young population. Egypt needed to build at least 30,000 schools within the next five years just to provide enough classrooms for a single eight-hour shift, a senior official at the government's largest think tank told me in deep frustration.

The mediocrity of Egyptian education was reflected by Cairo University, the official added. The once-noted university had dropped to twenty-eighth place in Africa, the continent with the world's worst education system. The Cairo campus was also no longer among the top 500 universities in the world.[38]

Egypt's troubled economy also had to accommodate at least 800,000 new young job seekers every year—complicated by the regime's pledge that all college graduates could get a government job. As a result, the government spent most of its revenues on security, a bloated bureaucracy to keep people employed, and subsidies for gasoline, wheat, and sugar—leaving little to invest in infrastructure, much less Egypt's future.

Baz described Mubarak as a practical person in responding to these challenges. "He has never been a government employee; he's not an ideologue. He doesn't like bureaucratic formulas and ideas," the presidential adviser explained. "He thinks bureaucrats are limited by nature, because they want to protect themselves."

Ironically, bureaucrats were also big obstacles to Gamal Mubarak's future. The old guard grumbled about the young Mubarak, several analysts told me, because they believed it was their turn next at the top. Key military officials felt the president should emerge from within their tradition.

Baz insisted that Gamal Mubarak was not running for the presidency, although he did leave the door quite noticeably ajar. The caveat became a common refrain in comments from other Egyptian officials, too.

"Gamal Mubarak wants only the rights of *any* Egyptian," Baz said, "and that includes the right to run for parliament, or office, or to be active within the National Democratic Party." As if Gamal Mubarak were just *any* Egyptian.

As I waited to hear about the Mubarak interview, the Foreign Ministry urged me to talk to Mohammed Kamal, a young political scientist on Mubarak's new policy committee. Kamal's office is in a new building at Cairo University constructed out of the side of an old one. It was an Alice-in-Wonderland experience finding it. I walked down the hall of the old building, opening one classroom door after another, until I found one that instead opened up into a hallway with a whole new set of classroom doors. Then I had to find Kamal's door. Finding my way out was just as tricky. Every door looked the same.

Kamal did his graduate work at Johns Hopkins University; his dissertation was on the role of the United States Congress in crafting foreign policy. He had a simultaneous fellowship on Capitol Hill, where he said he did work for the House International Relations Committee and Democratic congressmen Tom Sawyer of Ohio and Sam Gejdenson of Connecticut.

"I liked the Democrats," he told me, sitting behind his desk in a white, freshly painted office. "The experience taught me a lot and helped me fine-tune my dissertation."

Kamal, who looks a bit like the younger Mubarak but with rounder cheeks, joined the ruling party in high school. When it won only thirty-eight percent of the seats in parliament in 2000, he was one of nine young Egyptians summoned to form Gamal Mubarak's new policy committee.

"That election was a real wake-up call," he explained. The little group, made up of young experts who had all been educated or lived in the West, drafted a new platform for the National Democratic Party.

"The old platform places the party in the socialist camp. It contained elements of a one-party state. It identified the party as a big tent—for all ideological orientations and for all classes, rich, poor, and middle class," Kamal explained. The revised platform redefined it as center-left and largely of the middle class.

"We're talking free enterprise but also government that has a social responsibility towards the people, like the thinking of Bill Clinton or Tony Blair," Kamal said.

During the process of defining a new direction for the leadership, he added, the younger Mubarak had created political space and helped to empower his generation.

"Before, the process of legislation had been dominated by old-fashioned legal scholars who lost touch with the modern world a long time ago," Kamal explained. "Today, if you look at different departments in government, you will see people in their late thirties and early forties who are involved in key executive committees. And the influence of this group is expanding. I'm now responsible for educating members of the party politically. I am forty. I credit Gamal with doing that."

Kamal had also been appointed to Egypt's Shura, which translates as "consultative council"; it is the upper house of parliament. He was its youngest member.

Looking ahead, Kamal explained, Mubarak's advisory group was working on a new antiterrorist act to replace emergency law. It was also crafting reforms to foster a multiparty system and empowerment of women. He specifically cited talk about a quota for women in parliament, a practice adopted in Iraq and the Palestinian territories and increasingly popular in dozens of developing countries.

When I asked him what kind of numbers, he suggested thirty or forty seats—or less than two percent. It was a telling sign of how little the autocrats want to change.

To get a sense of how open the ruling party would be with its rivals, I asked Kamal about the Muslim Brotherhood.

"We don't consider the Ikhwan a terrorist organization," he said, even though the group was outlawed. "There is a big debate about this issue, not just in Egypt, but all over the Arab and Muslim worlds. Everywhere they are moving forward and, as a political scientist, I feel it is the key to democracy development. The question is how to regulate the relationship between Islam and politics, and this debate is healthy."

The ruling party was divided into three schools, Kamal explained. One argued that all religious parties should be banned, on grounds that they ultimately will not share power. "It's Iran all over again. It's one man, one vote, one time," he said.

The second school argued that the Brotherhood was a reality and had to be recognized. "This school argues: If it walks and talks like a party, it's a party," Kamal explained.

"I'm somewhere in the middle, in the third camp," he said. "Society is not ripe for creation of a party because Egypt is a conservative society—and because more people are becoming religious every day. If you allow the Islamists to establish a political party, they will undermine the development of democracy because they will dominate the discourse with their religious ideas.

"You cannot compete with the words of God or the sayings of the Prophet," he continued. "The Islamists will try to present you as against God—and this resonates very well with people."

Kamal then told me the story of the blue cheese. He had recently been to his local grocer in an upscale neighborhood to buy Danish blue cheese, but the grocer told him he no longer carried it. As it happened, the refrigerator door was open behind the grocer and Kamal clearly saw the cheese on a shelf. The grocer then confessed that he still had some but quickly added, in front of other shoppers, that he was preparing to return it.

The grocery encounter happened shortly after a Danish newspaper published caricatures of the prophet Mohammad that triggered riots in dozens of countries on three continents. More than 100 people had died and more than 800 had been injured in protests. The Muslim grocer could not afford to be carrying anything Danish.

"This is the danger I'm talking about," Kamal said.

"So, you can't exclude the Islamists from the political process. The fact is, they're there already. They need to be part of this formula but to evolve as the political system evolves—into a conservative party that believes in family values and prayers and references to religion, like the Republicans in the United States," he said. "But the way they are today, they want a state based on religion."

Kamal is on the most liberal fringe of the National Democratic Party and, he conceded, the younger generation faced uphill battles of its own. "Our influence is exaggerated because we are working with the president's son. Change is not easy. There are many others in both the party and the government who have vested interests in the status quo. For them, it's not a battle for reform, but a turf war."

Before I left, Kamal promised that he, too, would put in an urgent call to help me get in to see Mubarak.

As I continued to wait, I went around to talk to Hala Mustafa, the glamorous editor of *Democracy Review,* a journal published by the government's leading think tank. She had also been recruited to assist the new Policy Secretariat, although at the second of three levels. The inner circle had only nine members. The second had some 130 prominent younger Egyptians. And the third had around 400 people to advise Gamal Mubarak.

Mustafa is an intense woman who speaks quickly and does several things at once. She was wearing a smart gray suit with a designer scarf in bright red, yellow, and green. Her jewelry included a heart-shaped pendant and earrings, both encrusted with diamonds. She had manicured French nails, and her two-toned hair was softy coifed. She is in her midforties but looks a decade younger. On her desk was a large photograph of an attractive young woman who I initially took to be her daughter; there were six other pictures of the same person in various sizes and poses arrayed on bookshelves behind her desk. Looking closer, I realized they were all of Mustafa.

Mustafa, who did her graduate degree on Islamist movements, considers herself to be a secular, open-minded liberal. *Democracy Review* gives voice to a range of ideas—in Arabic and English—on the steps to democracy, press freedoms, women's rights, grassroots movements, the role of opposition parties, and both Christian and Muslim cultures. She was never a member of the ruling party, although she received a government paycheck. And she was initially enthusiastic about Gamal Mubarak's reform initiative.

"I eagerly embraced this whole idea of liberalizing the regime or the party from within," she told me.

But like others I talked to, she soon became frustrated. "The first year, there was real discussion. I felt there was new space to express my pro-reform ideas. But then things began to change," she said. Economic reform got priority, while political change was put on hold. Gradually, the most outspoken reformers were marginalized or excluded.

"The government, instead of going forward, took a step back to defend itself," she said. "When the moment came to make a choice, the panic began.

"Then," she added, "It became worthless to participate. It became clear that this process was only a vehicle for Gamal Mubarak's succession."

As she began to criticize Mubarak's reform efforts in public and in the domestic and foreign press, Mustafa also began to receive threats. One was made in a face-to-face meeting with a representative of Egypt's State Security. "They told me that what I was saying endangered the regime and the policy-planning project," she recounted.

The harassment made her reluctant to openly quit Gamal Mubarak's policy group for fear of the consequences.

"I was really worried for a period of time in 2005 about both my job security and my physical safety. Frankly, I felt hopeless," she said. "Now, things are a bit better. But I'll tell you this: If they try to ride the same old political horse, they won't get anyplace.

"That old horse," she said, "is finished."

The autocrats' attempts at something new increasingly appeared to be just more of the old, as notable figures began to turn on the younger Mubarak and the reform bodies that he had launched.

The National Council for Human Rights was one offshoot of the new policy committee. It was established in 2004. It was supposed to show that the government was working harder to improve human rights.

But in the spring of 2006, the council issued a report charging that the number of detainees held without trial was instead growing— and that they were being held for longer periods of time. The regime, it added, was blatantly ignoring court orders to set many of them free. Besides the thousands in more recent detention, at least a dozen people had been held without being formally charged or tried for twelve years—since 1994. The council called the trends dangerous for the political health of the nation.[39]

The same month, a prominent Egyptian writer did finally dare to quit Gamal Mubarak's reform committee. Osama Harb, editor of the moderate foreign-policy journal *International Politics,* publicly blasted Egypt's reform efforts as "a sham."[40]

"I fear for the future of this country," Harb declared, "And many others share this fear."[41]

Like Mustafa, Harb came under a sudden deluge of criticism in the state-controlled press. Officials suggested that he was disgruntled only because his personal political ambitions had gone unfulfilled.

Harb countered that his journal could publish criticism of governments throughout the Middle East—but not about Egypt. He could speak critically of President George W. Bush or Russian President Vladimir Putin—but not Gamal Mubarak. He could not even extricate himself from the inner circle without risk.

"It should be easy to resign, to say no," he said. "But not here. This is Egypt."[42]

Over the next eighteen months, the Mubarak regime steadily tightened its squeeze against the disparate array of groups that had spawned, haphazardly, the Arab world's most ambitious democracy movement. It also ran another round of tainted elections. Thousands were harassed or detained in the run-up to a poll for Egypt's upper house of parliament, the Shoura Council. More than seven hundred Muslim Brotherhood members were among the many activists and dissidents locked up. Charges of using religious slogans—a new offense—were filed against seventeen of the nineteen candidates from the Muslim Brotherhood. Judges were kept away from monitoring the election.

Ghada Shahbender of "We're Watching You" again dispatched volunteers to monitor the election. Afterward, she reported widespread ballot stuffing and bribery—even attempts to bribe her monitors. Many voters had been turned away, she reported.

"The government has reestablished the fact that elections are fraudulent," she told reporters. "Our monitors were offered money ... to go in and vote," she said. "Outside Cairo, we had reports of very, very low participation but then full ballot boxes." The government claimed more than 30 percent of eligible voters turned out. "We're Watching You" estimated the turnout at only three percent.[43]

Not surprising, President Mubarak's ruling party won—overwhelmingly.

But a total monopoly of government apparently was not enough. In August 2007, Saad Eddin Ibrahim—the aged and ailing democratic activist who was the first to publicly criticize the meteoric rise of Gamal Mubarak—was warned not to return to Egypt for fear of once again going to jail. "Or worse," he wrote.

In a clever legal scheme, the regime's supporters filed more than a half dozen civil lawsuits and criminal complaints, accusing Ibrahim of everything from treason to undermining Egypt's economic interests. One dared to charge him with harming national interests by persuading the U.S. Congress to cut back on aid to Egypt.[44]

"My real crime is speaking out in defense of the democratic governance Egyptians deserve," he wrote in an op-ed in *The Washington Post*. "Sadly, this regime has strayed so far from the rule of law that, for my own safety, I have been warned not to return to Egypt. My family is worried, knowing that Egypt's jails contain some 80,000 political prisoners and that disappearances are routinely ignored or chalked up to accidents. My fear is that these abuses will spread if Egypt's allies and friends continue to stand by silently while this regime suppresses the country's democratic reformers."[45]

The silence was indeed deafening. And the way was increasingly clear for the Mubarak dynasty.

FOUR

LEBANON

The Dreamers

Ideologies separate us.

Dreams and anguish bring us together.

—French-Romanian playwright Eugene Ionesco

They say that time changes things, but you actually

have to change them yourself.

—American artist Andy Warhol

Two dynamics will define political change in the Middle East for years to come. The first is the oldest force in politics—identity, the accumulative package of family, faith, race, traditions, and ties to a specific piece of land. Few regions have a more complex or competing set of identities, long before factoring in Israel. The clash of cultures begins *within* the Middle East.

The second dynamic is the newest force in the Middle East—youth and an emerging generation of younger leaders. The young have never been so important: More than seventy percent of the people living in the region stretching from Tehran to Rabat are under thirty years old.

The young will have more influence than any previous generation because, for the first time, the majority of them are literate. They are also connected enough to the outside world to be deeply dissatisfied with the status quo at home. They are the dreamers.

Both dynamics play out in Lebanon with spectacular passion.

No country in the Middle East has more legally recognized identities than Lebanon—seventeen, to be precise. All are religious. The range is vast and unusual. Lebanon is home to the Maronites, an eastern wing of the Catholic Church that emerged around a Christian hermit named St. Maron in the fifth century. Their priests are allowed to marry. Lebanon also has the largest concentration of the secretive Druze, an eleventh-century offshoot of Shiite Islam with tenets influenced by Greek philosophy, Gnosticism, and Christianity—and known fully, after "initiation," only to its elders. They believe in reincarnation, do not accept converts, and are not considered to be Muslim by other Muslims. Lebanon also has Orthodox, Alawites, Sunni, Chaldeans, Shiites, Protestants, Melkites, Copts, and two types of Armenian Christians, among many others. Each of Lebanon's seventeen sects has an official role in government, claim to jobs, and a share of the military.

All seventeen are also crammed into the Arab world's second smallest country. Think twenty percent smaller than Connecticut.

On my first day back in Beirut, it took less than ten minutes to get from the Shiite stronghold of Hezbollah, conspicuous by the posters of martyrs and turbaned mullahs, to a Christian suburb where a van with a fifteen-foot dying Christ on a crucifix drove solemnly through the streets, religious hymns echoing through a megaphone, in the run-up to Easter.

That disparate identities coexist in a confined space is a virtual miracle in the turbulent Middle East. "If you understand Lebanon, it's because someone hasn't explained it to you," reflected Paul Salem, the head of one of only two independent think tanks in the Arab world and son of Lebanon's former foreign minister.

A T-shirt I found for sale at the glitzy new Virgin Megastore, which is housed in the former Beirut Opera House, summed it up: WE ARE DIFFERENT. WE ARE LEBANESE.

But Lebanon has always been a fragile miracle. Its future now depends on what an array of younger actors do about sectarian divisions. Since 2005, Lebanon has witnessed breathtaking moments of hope as well as events that generated crushing despair. Lebanon is rarely a country of moderation.

Saad Hariri is one of the young faces in Lebanese politics. Born in 1970, he was elected to parliament in 2005. He also heads Lebanon's new Future Movement. Among Lebanese, he is considered something of an Arab heartthrob. He wears his wavy black hair gelled back and just long enough to curl up a little on the nape of his neck. He has a mustache and cropped goatee that curve around his mouth, a style now widely emulated by his peers, a Lebanese hairdresser told me.

Hariri's goal is to eliminate the role of religious sects in politics— completely. "Most people are fed up with the rhetoric of confessionalism," Hariri reflected, when I visited him at Qoreitem Palace in the Muslim-dominated sector of West Beirut. Hariri is a Sunni Muslim, one of Lebanon's three most numerous sects.

"The problem is: How do we strengthen our sense of belonging to this country, rather than to just our religion?" he said. "Over the past year, as we've talked about reconciliation and unity, the sense of confessional loyalties has actually grown."

The underlying conundrum is that Lebanon exists only because of its sectarian identities.

After World War I and the Ottoman Empire's collapse, France took control of the Levant region along the Mediterranean, while Britain took the inland area that became Iraq and Jordan. Each power drew up borders as it saw fit. To protect the Maronites, France decided to create a separate nation. It carved a slim strip of land, from the mountains to the Mediterranean coast, out of Syria. Lebanon comes from *laban,* a word in Aramaic, the language of Christ, meaning "white" and referring to the snow-capped Mount Lebanon range that was for centuries a Christian refuge in the Muslim region. European Crusaders built strongholds among the Maronites more than 800 years ago.

Before departing in the 1940s, France brokered an unwritten gentleman's agreement, known as the National Covenant. It stipulated that Christian sects would abandon any claim to European protection, and Muslim sects would abandon any pan-Arab aspirations, including a return to Syria's fold. Based on a 1932 census, which showed that Christians were fifty-four percent of the population, the covenant also gave Maronite Christians permanent right to Lebanon's presidency. The premiership went to Sunni Muslims. And parliament's speaker went to Shiite Muslims.

All seats in parliament and all government jobs—from the top judge and army general down to kindergarten teachers and traffic cops—were then divided up in a permanent ratio: six Christians for every five Muslims. Within each category, Christians and Muslims then divided up slots among their own diverse sects. It was the ultimate quota system.

Ever since then, religion has always trumped merit in Lebanon. In elections, all candidates have to run as members of their faith. And all voters cast ballots only for candidates in the town where their ancestors first registered to vote—often connected to one of the seventeen sects—even if the family has not lived there for generations.

In everyday life, Lebanon also practices a version of sectarian apartheid, or segregation, which affects everything from the way people are married to where they are buried. To wed someone from a different sect, Lebanese have to find a civil authority in another country to officiate. Cyprus is the most common destination. Marriage is only performed—and recognized—within a sect. Every Lebanese identity card lists religion, so there is no getting around the rules.

"Our system doesn't allow us to be just Lebanese," sighed Lebanese political scientist Nawaf Salam, a friend from my days covering the civil war who was appointed to Lebanon's electoral commission in 2005 to reform the law. "We have to have a declared religion, whether we practice it or not."

The arrangement did, however, produce the Middle East's first fledgling if flawed democracy, way back in the 1940s. In 2005 and 2006, Lebanon still ranked the highest of any Arab country on an international freedom index.[1]

Ironically, Lebanon is also strictly secular. It has no Islamic law and no Christian law. Its constitution borrows heavily from that of France, the former colonial power. Article Nine of the constitution stipulates: "There shall be absolute freedom of conscience. The state in rendering homage to the Almighty shall respect all religions and creeds and guarantees, under its protection, the free exercise of all religious rites." And it does.

The result is a maelstrom of diversity that has made Lebanon the political laboratory for the Middle East since its independence in 1943. The Lebanese embrace East and West, Christianity and Islam, post-modernism and traditions dating back millennia to their seafaring Phoenician forefathers—and both decadence and piety.

A Hedonist's Guide to Beirut describes the Lebanese capital as "party central" in the Middle East "highlighted by extravagant dining, drinking, and decadent partying" at some of the chicest nightclubs in the world.[2] Casino du Liban is also the region's most infamous gambling joint. Lebanon makes the best wine in the Middle East; its Kasara label was once (although only once) internationally rated. Beirut's racetrack, which runs only purebred Arabian steeds, is packed with rowdy bettors on Sundays. The Mediterranean beaches are awash with men in the barest swimming briefs and women in skimpy bikinis, while billboards are plastered with lovely young things, alluringly posed, legs spread, lips glistening, in ads for jeans. Singers from all over the Middle East come to compete in *Superstar,* the wildly popular Arabic version of *American Idol.* Radio stations play punk, rap, heavy metal, hip-hop, and the new electronic music. And when I was there in 2006, the most sought-after theater ticket was for a local variation of *The Vagina Monologues.*

Another local T-shirt succinctly frames the country's laissez-faire attitude: TALK ARABIC. THINK ARABIC. FEEL ARABIC. LIVE LEBANESE.

Yet Lebanon is also a place where people cling to the practices and allegiances of both Christian and Muslim faiths.

It is the only Arab country where thousands of men turn out annually with chains or whips for the self-flagellation ceremony of Ashura, when Shiites commemorate the martyrdom of Hussein in the seventh century. Both the book and movie versions of *The Da Vinci Code* were banned after an insistent appeal by the Christian Maronite patriarch. Police once seized hundreds of DVDs—including *Some Like It Hot, Rush Hour, Key Largo, Jesus of Nazareth, The Nutty Professor,* and all of Stanley Kubrick's films—from the Virgin Megastore on grounds that they "undermined religions and contravened good morals."[3] Conservative

Islamic dress and headscarves are as common in some areas as barely butt-covering skirts and tight tank tops are in others. The main beer available in conservative southern Lebanon is nonalcoholic, imported from Iran. Competing with *Superstar* for the biggest audience share on television and radio are the sermons of Hezbollah leader Sheikh Hassan Nasrallah. And the most unusual interview I did in Beirut was with a gynecologist who performs hymen reconstruction—on both Christian and Muslim females—so grooms will not know their brides have already had sex with someone else.

But the formula for coexistence—to make sure everyone feels included—has also made Lebanon a battlefield.

The covenant designed to avert sectarian tension became a nightmare as demographics shifted in favor of Muslims. Shiites particularly had higher birth rates; tens of thousands of Maronites emigrated. Unlike Iraq, where one sect has the largest representation because it has the votes, Lebanon's seventeen sects have permanently allocated seats in parliament—even though their shares have not reflected their numbers for decades. The Lebanese have been both unwilling and unable to carry out a new census since 1932, for fear of what it will show. So the system has no elasticity; the political pendulum can not swing. Battles over the imbalance of power almost undid Lebanon during a civil war that raged for fifteen years.

I arrived back in Beirut on April 13, 2006—the thirty-first anniversary of the day the war erupted. I lived in Lebanon for five years of the worst fighting. The conflict ended in 1990, but almost a generation later many buildings still had gaping holes from artillery or deep pockmarks from rockets, grenades, and sustained gunfire. The Murr Tower, the unfinished shell of a high-rise where militias used to post snipers and execute rivals by pushing them off upper stories, still stands empty in the middle of town. I went to dinner at a fancy refurbished restaurant but parked around the corner in front of a gutted building with broken glass on the ground that had probably been there since I left in the mid-1980s.

The Lebanese did most of it to themselves. Many sectarian leaders had their own militias, armed with vast arsenals. The truest believers—Christians and Muslims—were among the most brutal. An array of regional players, from Israel to Iran and often featuring the Palestinians, exploited the divide, armed allies, and dispatched their own forces into the militia melee. At least four percent of Lebanon's population was killed between 1975 and 1990—the equivalent of twelve million Americans.[4] Iraq's insurgency may be nastier, but no other Middle East country has been so traumatically riven for so long by people who worship the same God, only in different ways or on different days.

Politics in labyrinthine little Lebanon are complicated by the clans. They are more like political mafias with bosses—*zaim* in Arabic—who function with a modern version of feudal patronage. Many of the faces of the twenty-first century are from the same families—including the Gemayels, Jumblatts, Chamouns, Franjiehs, Karamis, Murrs, and Salams—that have dominated politics as far back as the 1930s.

Saad Hariri is no exception. He inherited his political position from his father Rafiq Hariri, a man of epic wealth, wide girth, and Groucho Marx eyebrows. The difference is that the elder Hariri was trying to change the face of Lebanon both politically and physically. He founded the Future Movement.

Born in 1944, Rafiq Hariri was the son of a greengrocer. He went to Saudi Arabia as a young math teacher but turned to construction and amassed billions from putting up office blocks, palaces, and conference centers during the boom oil years. He grew close to the royal family; the king eventually made him a Saudi citizen. With holdings all over the world, including Houston and Boston, Paris and Monaco, Forbes ranked him among the world's wealthiest men.

But Hariri never lost ties to Lebanon. During cease-fires in the 1980s, he spent millions to clean up Beirut. He even paid to have new palm trees planted on the long seafront corniche. I remember the big orange trucks that came in to clear away rubble; they were one of the few signs of hope in the midst of anarchy. But it was always for naught, as the fighting soon started again. He also built a new university and a hospital in his hometown of Sidon. And his Hariri Foundation funded more than 20,000 scholarships for Lebanese youth, both in Lebanon and abroad.

In 1989, Hariri was pivotal in organizing and bankrolling a reconciliation conference hosted by Saudi Arabia in Taif, a mountain retreat near Mecca. The meeting brought all the warlords together and finally ended Lebanon's grisly conflict.

The Lebanese celebrate that turning point in a T-shirt too. It says: THE GREAT LEBANESE WAR 1975–1990. GAME OVER!

The Taif Accord radically overhauled Lebanon's National Covenant. It stipulated an end to politics based on religions. It called for a transition, in phases, to full democracy. Terms were to be worked out in a new commission—with equal representation of Christians and Muslims. It also required all government jobs to be based on capability rather than sect. And it mandated the disarming of all Lebanon's militias.

During the interim, it changed the ratio of Christians and Muslims in government to parity—fifty-fifty in everything, even though that still did not fairly represent their shares. Muslims by then outnumbered Christians by at least three to two, which effectively meant that a Christian vote counted more than a Muslim vote.

In 1992, after Lebanon held its first elections in two decades, Rafiq Hariri ended up as prime minister. He approached the post-war era with the same swashbuckling ambition he did business. He lacked charisma. He did not come from one of Lebanon's clans and did not have a militia to enforce his will, so he used the leverage of his wealth as a tool.

"I want to go down in the history books," he said, "as the man who resurrected Beirut."[5] He boasted that Beirut would become the Singapore of the Middle East.

"Rebuilding the country," he added, "is the revenge of honest people on war as an idea and the miseries arising from this choice, including all the savagery, destruction, and catastrophes. It is revenge on the idea of resorting to weapons to resolve problems."[6] His big ideas, wealth, plain talk, and political aspirations occasionally led to comparisons with Ross Perot.

Some Lebanese saw Hariri as a savior, others as an exploiter—and many saw him as a bit of both. He ran Lebanon's reconstruction like a personal business, reaping profit along the way. He was the largest shareholder in the company that rebuilt Beirut. His government borrowed heavily from his banks at steep interest rates, in what even allies

admitted was a gross conflict of interest. He reportedly used government contracts and his profits to curry favor with the traditional political elite and the warlords.[7] His plan put Lebanon into exorbitant debt
for expensive infrastructure—a new international airport and new
roads—while the poor felt few immediate benefits.

Yet Rafiq Hariri did have a vision, however controversial. He was
particularly devoted to renovating the commercial district of pic-
turesque old French buildings along the notorious Green Line that
divided Christian and Muslim militias during the war. The ravaged
area reemerged as an architectural jewel in the center of Beirut, bringing in high-end businesses, charming outdoor bistros, classy boutiques,
bustling city life, and revenue-generating tourists. If Hariri had not run
reconstruction the way he ran his businesses, given Lebanon's squabbling warlords and tendency to implode, it might not have happened.

"I was afraid that if I did not contribute, confidence in the project
would be lost," he once explained, "and many people would in turn
not contribute, which could lead to the failure of the project." All profits, he claimed, went into the Hariri Foundation for charities.[8]

In the end, Hariri did what virtually no other Lebanese politician could do—restore confidence that Lebanon was a viable country.
Lebanon's beleaguered currency soared by thirty percent after he took
office; the famed black market disappeared.[9] Since he had no role in the
war, Hariri could also credibly reach out to all of Lebanon's sects. He
eventually won grudging respect even from those who did not like or
trust him. He became known as Mr. Lebanon. Political analysts wrote
about "Hariri-ism."[10]

But to be Lebanon's prime minister, Hariri also had to make a devil's
bargain with Damascus. More than a half century after they had been
separated into two states, Syria was not over losing Lebanon. Damascus
still dominated its little neighbor. It intimidated politicians. It harassed
newspaper editors. It threatened religious leaders. Its intelligence services were widely linked to assassinations of anyone who dared to defy
it.[11] After the civil war erupted, Syria was one of a handful of nations
that dispatched troops to Lebanon under an Arab League mandate
to try and end the war. They failed. In 1979, the other nations left;
Syria stayed—and stayed and stayed—in defiance of Arab and United

Nations requests to leave. Lebanon once again fell under almost total Syrian control. And every leader had in some way to do its bidding.

Hariri was no different. He acquiesced on appointments, security, foreign policy, and working with Syria's hand-picked candidates for president of Lebanon.[12] *Baksheesh* is the Arabic word for bribe; it is an integral part of life in the Middle East. Hariri reportedly paid plenty of *baksheesh* to Syria, including construction of a new presidential palace in Damascus.[13]

Asked once about the ubiquitous pictures of Syrian President Hafez al Assad in Lebanon's international airport, Hariri told *The Boston Globe* with unusual candor, "It's not a problem to put them up. It's a problem to take them down."[14]

Hariri calculated that restoring Beirut's old splendor and strengthening its economy would, in time, create leverage to counter Syria's pull.[15] In the meantime, however, the relationship was a roller coaster. Hariri resigned once after Assad handpicked an army general and ally, Emile Lahoud, to be Lebanon's president in 1998. Lebanon's president is elected by parliament, and Syria then controlled the majority by graft, intimidation, and manipulating the political system of a country its troops had occupied for decades.

Hariri returned to the job after new Lebanese parliamentary elections in 2000—and Assad's death. But in 2004, relations ruptured permanently when Syria pressured Lebanon to pass a constitutional amendment extending Lahoud's term for three years. Lebanon's president is limited to a single term of six years.

Hariri opposed the extension. Behind the scenes, he appealed to French President Jacques Chirac to help stop the erosion of Lebanese sovereignty. Chirac took the appeal to President Bush. In 2004, Paris and Washington were still deeply at odds over Iraq. But Lebanon was one issue on which they could agree—and which they could use to rebuild their own relations. Together, they agreed to go to the United Nations to propose an unusual resolution. It called for presidential elections in Lebanon as scheduled, "without foreign interference or influence." It also called for all foreign forces to withdraw from Lebanon, an even bigger affront to Damascus. Without its heavy military presence, Syria would have limited leverage.

The resolution was a direct slap at Syria. It also had rippling consequences.

A week before Lebanon's parliament was to vote on August 26, 2004, as momentum was building at the United Nations behind the new resolution, Hariri was summoned to Damascus. The session with Syrian President Bashar al Assad, who had taken over after his father's death, was stormy. It lasted less than fifteen minutes.

Hariri later told his son that Assad put it bluntly, "This extension is to happen, or else I will break Lebanon over your head."[16]

On September 2, the United Nations passed resolution 1559.

On September 3, Lebanon's parliament went ahead and voted to extend the president's term. In the end, Hariri also voted with the majority to keep Syria's man in power, even though he had rallied an international effort to defy Damascus.

Six weeks later, however, he resigned.

Over the next four months, Hariri increasingly struck out on his own with the new Future Movement. It was more of an idea than a party. But it reflected a shift in his focus, from rebuilding Lebanon physically to reshaping the nation politically. Lebanon was due to hold elections for parliament in May 2005. They would serve as the test, pitting Hariri's new coalition against Syria's candidates.

Hariri knew he was being closely watched. After Lebanese analysts began predicting his alliance would sweep the vote, he received another warning from Damascus. Syrian security services had him "cornered," a senior official told him bluntly. Hariri should not "take things lightly."[17]

The St. George Hotel has long been a landmark on Beirut's scenic corniche, a symbol of Lebanon's riches and its woes. The four-story luxury hotel was named after the Christian martyr who allegedly slew a dragon somewhere nearby in the fourth century. When Beirut became the Middle East's center for banking, education, culture, and espionage in the 1960s, kings, foreign film stars, and spies stayed at the hotel. Its bar overlooking the Mediterranean was the place deals were brokered, secrets exchanged. The St. George became a victim itself shortly after the civil war erupted in 1975. It was left a haunted shell, its pink facade charred. But the pool and an outdoor bar famed for its Bloody Marys remained open. During the five years I lived in Lebanon in the 1980s, Beirutis flocked there during cease-fires, however brief. Whenever the rat-a-tat-tat of rifles or ka-boom of artillery started again, men packed up their backgammon sets, and women grabbed their towels, and we all scurried home—until the next cease-fire. It became a symbol of Lebanese resilience.

On Valentine's Day, 2005, Rafiq Hariri held talks about the upcoming election with colleagues in parliament. At lunchtime, he headed back to Qoreitem Palace. Hariri always took precautions. His limousines were armored-plated; they also had jamming equipment to block any remote-control device that might set off a bomb. But it was not enough. Just as his five-car motorcade rounded the corner in front of the St. George, then in the final throes of reconstruction, a bomb with over 1,000 pounds of explosives went off. It tore apart the armored cars and the bodies inside. Hariri was killed instantly. Twenty others also died; more than 100 in the area were wounded. The facades of the St. George and buildings in all directions were ripped off. Windows more than one-quarter mile away were blown out. The sound rippled for miles. A black cloud of smoke rising from the bomb site could be seen beyond the city limits.

The crater left in the road in front of the St. George was more than thirty feet wide and six feet deep.

Hariri's murder was the most traumatic event in the fifteen years since the civil war ended—and perhaps even longer. The assassination was another of the seminal events in the early twenty-first century—like the Palestinian elections and Egypt's May 25 crackdown—that provoked people in the Middle East to engage in ways they had never done before. It mobilized Lebanese like no single event since the nation was created.

It also launched a new generation of activists. Saad Hariri inherited his father's mantle, after consultations within the family. "We decided that what my father wanted to achieve had not been achieved," he said, "and that we had to continue."

But the assassination also spurred people well outside clan politics.

Asma-Maria Andraos was one of them. She heard the massive blast on the Christian side of the old Green Line. It blew open the windows of her office, whooshed a sliding glass door down its track, and then blasted open the inside doors—all in the flash of a second.

"Everything moved. It was like an earthquake," she recalled, when I visited her office in Christian-dominated East Beirut. "You think you've forgotten those noises from the war, but it came back instantly. I ran to the balcony and saw the black cloud of smoke. Then we switched on the television and those horrible pictures of burnt corpses and burning cars and people crying and ambulances."

Andraos, a tall woman with a long face, throaty voice, and brown hair that falls down her back, had been highly critical of Hariri's policies. "He was a ruthless businessman, and I believed you can't be both prime minister and the biggest businessman in the country," she explained.

"But he also had a dream, and I admired that," she said. "And when I heard it was Hariri who was killed I went quite mad, and I wondered: What was going to happen to us? Who was going to hold us down? Who else was doing to fight for us at the superpower level? As long as he was around, we could stick it out.

"I became scared, physically scared," she said.

Andraos was born in 1971 and was only four years old when the civil war broke out. She is an event planner for product launches, everything from mobile telephones and sport clothing to hygiene products. She had been typical of the young in Lebanon—disillusioned with or disinterested in politics.

But on the day of Hariri's funeral, Andraos was one of more than 150,000 who turned out on the streets of Beirut. Maronites, Sunnis, Catholics, Druze, Orthodox, Shiites, Armenians, and others—some bitter rivals during the war—followed the ambulance carrying Hariri's body to the district he had restored. People threw rice from balconies as the cortege passed. Hariri and his bodyguards were laid to rest near Martyr's Square, in a special burial site in the former parking lot of the Virgin Megastore that was converted into a tented shrine. Christian church bells rang amid the Islamic incantations and calls to prayer from mosque muezzins.

"Brothers, we must all grieve together," a Muslim imam told mourners.[18]

Beirut's Maronite Bishop, Boulos Matar, declaimed, "This was a man of moderation and unity."[19]

Many in Lebanon assumed Syria was ultimately responsible for Hariri's murder, but no one dared to say it. Saad Hariri came the closest. Asked by a British television correspondent who assassinated his father, he had responded simply, "It's obvious, no?"

So Andraos and a group of friends brought two banners to the funeral. In big letters, they had written, IT's OBVIOUS, NO?

"We didn't know how free we were to say what we wanted to say," she told me. "The Syrians were still running the show. They were everywhere in Lebanon. We could not have had this conversation back then without them knowing about it. The Syrians killed him, and it had to be said in some way for everyone to see."

A threshold was crossed the day of Hariri's funeral. As the mourners marched, they began to shout: "Syria out! Syria out!"

And that was only the beginning.

The next morning, Andraos went back to Hariri's grave site and began calling friends and asking them to join her—and to call their friends and neighbors too. "A lot of people said it was back to business as usual," she recalled. "But I said, 'No way.' This was way too big."

On an impulse, Andraos also organized a petition to generate a sense of doing something besides mourning the past. She had no pen, so she used lipstick. She wrote only one word on a piece of cloth: "Resignation." The focus was broadening—now to the Lebanese government, too.

"I realized we had to kick the bastards out," she said.

As word spread about a sit-in, people poured into the area. They signed the petition too. Within three days, the petition was 1,200 feet long with thousands of signatures.

"It was that spontaneous," Andraos said, looking back. "We didn't really fully realize what we were doing."

The sit-in vigil grew into a full-time protest, and the call for the Lebanese government to quit became its rallying cry. Most of the protesters were students. Two young men set up individual tents and vowed to stay until the government stepped down. Hundreds of other youths soon joined them. Most were students who had never been involved in politics. They came from all sects. Most had never met before; they just showed up.

"Suddenly, I was leader of a group that had no existence a few days earlier," Andraos said. "We realized the opposition was confused. We assumed they had a plan but they didn't. They were lost. So ten of us met—we were from multiple confessions and none belonged to any party—and came up with a piece of paper in which we said simple things, all around 'Let's unify.'"

Andraos became the mother superior of the protest—mobilizing a task force of about 100 people, both Christians and Muslims, to assemble supplies, food, literally tons of water, portable toilets, hundreds of mattresses and blankets, gas lamps, and a big tent for the 500 young people who by then had pledged to sleep near Hariri's grave site until their demands were met. She raised $200,000—in a country with a per capita income of only $6,000 dollars—through word-of-mouth requests, refusing all funding from political parties or foreign donors. In the evenings, when thousands more came down to Martyr's Square after school or work to join the protest, she organized a dialogue among the students.

"This is the first time in Lebanon that the politicians followed the people," Andraos said. "The heartbeat was the youth. They dropped out of jobs or didn't go to university to carry the message through to the end. Young people in this country have not been active like that before. They had always deferred to the politicians. The other part of the movement was civil society, which some had thought was dead."

The crowds became so large that a giant screen was set up around Martyr's Square to let everyone see and hear speakers at the evening rallies.

Exactly two weeks after the assassination, on February 28, the prime minister who had replaced Hariri stepped down. His government collapsed. Tens of thousands watched it happen live on the screen set up at Martyr's Square.

The protest had won the first round.

Encouraged, the demonstrators pressed on. They pledged nationwide strikes until four demands were met: Syria's withdrawal from Lebanon. The resignation of Lebanon's security chiefs. Elections on schedule, with no delays or outside interference. And a thorough international investigation into Hariri's death.

President Lahoud, Syria's ally and Hariri's old nemesis, tried to ban the protests, to no avail. Every Monday—the day of the week when Hariri had died—the nation all but closed down as tens of thousands of workers, businessmen, and teachers either did not go to work or showed up to join the running demonstration. En masse, lawyers dressed in their black robes and doctors in their white coats appeared at Martyr's Square.

A big banner scrawled on the wall next to Hariri's grave summed up the public mood: ENOUGH.

Syria was stubborn. On March 8, its allies, led by Hezbollah, staged a counter-rally to support Damascus. Hundreds of thousands turned out. But, for a change, there were no pictures of the Syrian leader, no Syrian flags, not even Hezbollah banners. There were new limits that even Syria's allies would not cross.

Infuriated by Syria's attempt to hold on to Lebanon, Saad Hariri and Andraos were among dozens who called on the Lebanese to turn out on March 14, the one-month anniversary of Hariri's death, to support a rival protest. And they did. More than one million Lebanese—about one quarter of the entire population, the proportionate equivalent of seventy-five million Americans—poured into Beirut from all over the country. Despite the cold, windswept day, the throngs were so thick that many had to abandon their cars on the outskirts and walk all the way to the seafront grave site. In a pointed jab at Syria, they waved tens of thousands of red-and-white Lebanese flags emblazoned with the cedar, a symbol of the fragrant trees on Mount Lebanon. Some of the young painted their faces with both a crescent and a cross—the symbols of Islam and Christianity.

It was the largest protest ever assembled in a modern Arab country. Mass outpourings in the Middle East tend to be rent-a-crowds mobilized and transported by the government. The Lebanese surprised even themselves.

"It was shocking in a positive way—the students and the children, the people in wheelchairs, the turbans, the old hags, they all came in to say, 'We want our country,'" said Jamil Mrowe, a Lebanese Shiite and publisher of *The Daily Star,* the largest English-language paper in the Middle East. "The Syrians made the mistake of killing someone who would not have been an icon, but in their killing he became an icon who represented the entire Lebanese ethos. The shrapnel that killed him hit every Lebanese. I can't take it from my mind—that cold, dry anger you saw after he was killed."

In stark contrast to Lebanon's tense civil war, when people shot at each other just to break up traffic jams, the people-power confrontation with government unfolded peacefully. Demonstrators passed around flowers and sweets to security forces and police deployed around the capital.

The March 14 Movement, as it came to be known, achieved all four of its goals: By the end of April, only seventy-two days after Hariri's death and the protest began, Syria pulled out its last troops. Its twenty-nine-year occupation was over.

Lebanon's top security officials were sacked; some were later arrested for complicity in Hariri's murder.

In an unusual step, the United Nations then voted on a second resolution to conduct an investigation into Hariri's murder. It also warned Syria to cooperate—or face punitive action.

And finally, elections were held on time, in May and June 2005. A coalition led by Saad Hariri, who had taken over his father's Future Movement, won seventy-two of the 128 seats in parliament.

"Today, Lebanon is united in you," the younger Hariri told supporters who massed outside Qoreitem Palace after the vote.[20]

The State Department dubbed the mass protest the Cedar Revolution, after the country's famed tree. The name was picked up around the world—except in Lebanon.

Lebanon's outpouring was never a revolution, like Ukraine's Orange Revolution, Georgia's Rose Revolution, or Czechoslovakia's Velvet Revolution. It was instead a cry for sovereignty, for a formal divorce from Damascus, for a Lebanese identity, and for justice. And it made stunning progress. In the Arab world, it was the first broad popular movement to demand sweeping change and get it.

But it was only the opening round of a much longer political battle. When Lebanon settled down, as it did quickly after the election, it was stuck with the same sectarian system. None of the reforms to eliminate the sectarian quotas, as mandated in the 1989 Taif Accord, had been implemented—or seemed imminent. And President Lahoud was still the head of state.

When I visited Lebanon the next year, the specter of unfinished business hung over Beirut. Massive posters of Rafiq Hariri were still plastered throughout the capital fourteen months later. The most striking was a giant black billboard at the entrance to Hamra Street, the city's main drag. At the top was a red electronic ticker counting the days that had passed between the assassination and the ongoing investigation to determine, officially, who was responsible. THE TRUTH FOR THE SAKE OF LEBANON, the billboard said.

After the election, many Lebanese had expected Saad Hariri to become prime minister, in part to signal Lebanon's commitment to his father's agenda. "I don't have a magic wand," he had warned, acknowledging his total lack of experience. "I would have to grow pretty fast. A month ago, I was a businessman."[21]

But President Lahoud refused to step down. Syria still had one powerful ally in place. Hariri would get no traction on reforms as long as Lahoud was still there. Syria's motive was to sustain the status quo—and ties that might provide future openings—to ensure its own survival. Full democracy in Lebanon might infect neighboring Syrians.

When I visited Hariri, he had become a virtual prisoner in his father's palace in downtown Beirut. The whole area was cordoned off to traffic. Security inside was at least as tight as any American airport, including metal detectors and screening equipment for bags. Cell phones had to be left with the flock of well-armed security guards at the entrance.

Like many Lebanese politicians, Hariri admitted that he feared more car bombs. The elder Hariri's assassination had not been the last.

"We have a neighbor that wants to control Lebanon, like Saddam Hussein wanted to control Kuwait," he told me. "They want to prevent the wave of democracy from crossing the border into Syria."

Hariri had preserved his father's plush office in Qoreitem Palace as it was when he died. The fortified family mansion was filled with Phoenician artifacts, Persian carpets, antiques, and chandeliers. But most striking were the six-foot-tall posters of Rafiq Hariri on walls, tables, and easels throughout the palace. One of the biggest was perched on his chair behind his old desk. I sat with his son in oversize dark green leather furniture across from it.

When we spoke in 2006, he was one of fourteen politicians in a wobbly new national dialogue. Assembling them all at the table was the dialogue's only real success; it had avoided the issue of eliminating Lebanon's sectarian divide in government. Underscoring the problem, one half of its members were the same geriatrics who had dominated Lebanese politics since Hariri was a toddler—and torn the country apart during its civil war.

Hariri argued that a process had at least begun. The March 14 movement had demonstrated for the first time that change was possible. "This is the first time the Lebanese have empowered themselves," he said. "In the past, Lebanese couldn't talk among themselves without a foreign chaperone. The National Dialogue is the first time Muslims and Christians have come together and are doing it by themselves."

He had become sanguine, however, about the prospects for progress.

"This is like a boxing match," he reflected. "Some rounds you win, and some you lose. Sometimes you will bleed, fall, break a rib, or lose a tooth. Sometimes the allies of Syria seem to be making a comeback. I assure you it's not something we didn't know would happen. In politics, nobody just fades away. But we're determined to see it through all twelve rounds."

Beirut's Virgin Megastore carried another T-shirt made for the moment. DEMOCRACY: THE LEBANESE TRIAL VERSION.

Andraos, however, was anything but a prisoner. On April 30, 2005, she and her friends organized one last dinner for the student protesters to celebrate Syria's departure. They packed up the tent and went home. Then they got even busier.

"I was hooked. I had to keep going," Andraos told me, in her deep, throaty voice. "We started calling each other, and we all said the same thing: There has to be more. For us, we knew there was no way we could count on the warlords and the mafia that destroyed postwar Lebanon to do anything for us. They are the problems. Fairy tales don't exist in politics.

"People know they have power now. We just have to figure out what to do with it. Half the people in this country don't belong to a political party, and a lot of those in sectarian groups would like to get out if there was an alternative. We wanted to help give them a voice. But we didn't want to form a political party—yet. We decided we needed to do more basic things."

They instead founded Amam 05—an acronym for an Arabic phrase meaning "to the front," and '05 was for the year that changed Lebanon.

Andraos, who is an Orthodox Christian, was busy organizing three projects when I visited her office. Amam 05 had mobilized more than sixty nongovernment organizations to form a common lobby to sustain pressure on all Lebanon's politicians. It had also just received a World Bank grant to set up a municipal council in one of Lebanon's poorest areas, near the Syrian border. The project was investing power and funds in the young. It included municipal elections—just for youth—to select a council, identify the region's needs, develop projects, and then implement them. For the summer, Amam 05 had also designed a traveling exhibition with games to teach the concept of citizenship to the young; it was scheduled to hit every Lebanese city.

"March 14 petered out because there was no structure," Andraos said. "We are trying to build institutions and generate different ideas and educate."

The fledgling civil-society groups are no match for the warlords and entrenched clans. Yet they had begun to grab some of the new space created since Hariri's assassination. They represented a radical departure from traditional and deferential Lebanese politics.

"I've undergone a total transformation," Andraos said. "I went from someone who was disinterested in Lebanon's politics, sort of sleepwalking and living in a bubble. I was awakened at Hariri's death. I've become obsessed. And I'm not alone. There are others like me."

In 2005, *Time* magazine named Andraos one of thirty-seven heroes—"extraordinary people who illuminate and inspire, persevere and provoke. They take on challenges the rest of the world often prefers to avoid, reminding us all of just how much a single person, even in the face of adversity, can accomplish."[22]

I asked Andraos if she was disappointed at the difficulty in achieving enduring change in Lebanon.

"People forget how much has changed. More has happened in the past year than in the past thirty-five years," she responded. "Why should we feel disappointed? It will take fifteen years if we all start working now. But fifteen years is OK. We've wasted the last thirty years doing nothing."

FIVE

LEBANON

The Shadows

There is no law of progress. Our future is in our own hands, to make or to mar. It will be an uphill fight to the end, and would we have it otherwise? Let no one suppose that evolution will ever exempt us from struggles. "You forget," said the Devil, with a chuckle, "that I have been evolving too."

—BRITISH THEOLOGIAN WILLIAM RALPH INGE

There is no doubt that giving a chance to major political forces to take part in decision making burdens them with larger political responsibilities and affects their decision making to a large extent.

—HEZBOLLAH LEADER SHEIKH HASSAN NASRALLAH[1]

In the process of change, poverty and political disadvantage are the wild cards. They spawn the unpredictable and the unconventional.

The outskirts of Beirut are known as the *dahiya,* Arabic for "suburb." It is a generic term, but *dahiya* has come to mean the poor, dense, and sometimes dangerous maze of slums on the capital's southern fringe. Its dirty alleys are crammed with concrete-block shanties and shabby apartment buildings packed together. Its chaotic streets are clogged by decrepit old cars with bad mufflers. Laundry hangs from windows; gnarled masses of wires dangle from one building across to the next, illegally tapping into electricity, phone, and television lines.

While lights burn brightly in trendy downtown Beirut, the *dahiya* is often eerily dark more than two decades after electricity became sporadic, a casualty of Lebanon's civil war, Israel's three interventions, and government neglect. The *dahiya* is ignored or avoided by anyone who does not live there.

The *dahiya* is separate politically too. The scruffy suburbs are the stronghold of Hezbollah, the Party of God. Since the 1980s, the Shiite movement has evolved into the most powerful actor in Lebanon. It was almost as if the country had two political stages—one for Hezbollah and then one for all the rest.

I went to the *dahiya* one evening in April 2006 to see Sheikh Hassan Nasrallah, the secretary-general of Hezbollah and the most controversial leader in the Middle East.

Nasrallah is a man of God, gun, and government, a cross between Iranian revolutionary leader Ayatollah Khomeini and Latin America's Che Guevera, a mix of charismatic Islamic populist and a wily guerilla tactician. He took over the Shiite movement in 1992. He was thirty-one at the time, a virtual kid by the standards of either senior clergy or Lebanon's aging warlords.

But he soon built the widest following of any politician in Lebanon. Although he is only a midranking religious leader, Nasrallah became a local cult icon, a rock-star cleric. Lines from his speeches were popular ring tones on cellular phones. His face was a popular computer screen saver, too. I met youth in both Lebanon and Syria—many not religious, some not even Shiite—who gathered friends for parties to watch broadcasts of his passionate oratory. Wall posters, key rings, T-shirts, and phone cards all carried his picture. Shops sold CDs and DVDs of his speeches. Taxis played them instead of music.

Even Christians and Sunnis opposed to Hezbollah acknowledged Nasrallah's impact and style.

"I think Hezbollah is the biggest threat to the stability of the Lebanese system. It was created by Iran, and for years Syria served up whatever it needed on a silver platter," Michael Young, a political analyst and columnist for *The Daily Star,* told me over tea at a café in Christian East Beirut.

"But everyone thinks Nasrallah is a remarkable figure," he added. "He is impressive as a populist leader and quite charismatic."

Israeli officials reluctantly concurred. "He is the shrewdest leader in the Arab world—and the most dangerous," the Israeli Ambassador to the United States, Daniel Ayalon, told me.

Running Hezbollah from the *dahiya,* Nasrallah straddled the often blurred line between religious and secular authority. He was trained, briefly, at seminaries in both Iraq and Iran. He rose to power in Lebanon's last private army—the only Arab force that has ever made Israel retreat. In a popular photograph, he is thrusting a Kalashnikov assault rifle into the air, surrounded by cheering Hezbollah fighters.

Yet Hezbollah also won fourteen seats in parliament in 2005, one of the larger blocs.[2] And Nasrallah held one of the coveted few seats at Lebanon's national dialogue of top Christian and Muslim leaders.

In one breath, the Hezbollah chief could sound like a prototypical militant, only to defy the stereotype in the next breath. A few weeks before I saw him, he gave a speech coinciding with the Danish newspaper publication of cartoons mocking the Prophet Mohammed, which triggered rioting in Europe, Asia, and the Middle East that led to more than one hundred deaths. Nasrallah condemned "those fools who did wrong to our prophet." But he also criticized the attack on the Danish Embassy in Beirut as a serious mistake, said the perpetrators should be punished, and urged a "disciplined" response.

"Let us stop this nonsense," he said. "As Muslims and Christians, we should continue to cooperate and unite in order to reject the offense to our prophets and our holy belongings."

In the same speech, however, he extolled suicide bombings. "As long as there are fighters who are ready for martyrdom, this country will remain safe."[3] The *dahiya* was plastered with posters of young men who had died as human bombs under his command.

Nasrallah's headquarters was behind a tall, well-guarded gate in an area of the *dahiya* that Hezbollah cordoned off as a security zone. As stipulated, I arrived in the car of a Hezbollah official. But a guard still thoroughly inspected the trunk, peered under the hood, and ran a long pole with a mirror under the car to check for bombs. The steel gate then slid open. Inside, I went through a metal detector, a meticulous bag search, and still had to leave my cell phone and metal pens behind. Several bearded bodyguards stood in the hall; they all wore dark shirts, dark suits, and no ties—Iranian style. They also had the same type of communication devices that the White House Secret Service uses—an earpiece attached to a wire that runs under a shirt to a mouthpiece at the wrist.

Nasrallah has one of the riskiest jobs in the Middle East. Ten days before we met in 2006, a cell of al Qaeda, which had recently begun to take root in Lebanon, had tried to assassinate him. The Sunni purists of al Qaeda loathe Shiites as heretics. Three months later, Israeli officials admitted that they had hoped to eliminate Nasrallah during their bombardment of Beirut. It would not have been the first hit. In 1992, an ambush by Israeli helicopter gunships assassinated Nasrallah's predecessor, along with his wife and child, as they drove in a motorcade through southern Lebanon.

The United States has also long sought to hold Hezbollah's leadership accountable for attacks on American targets during the 1980s. In 2002, a senior State Department official called its followers "the A-Team of terrorism" and pledged "their time will come."[4]

Inside the headquarters, I was ushered into a reception hall, a long room ringed with faux-French brocade couches. I was led to one of two chairs at the far end. A few minutes later, Nasrallah's guards opened the door and glanced around. Then the Hezbollah chief walked in.

Nasrallah has a commanding presence. He has a full beard, a pudgy, full figure, and large glasses. He wore a stone ring on his pinky. His dark robes, like a military uniform, implied authority; they swayed rhythmically as he walked across the room. As with many devout Muslims, he does not shake hands with women to whom he is not related. Nasrallah speaks with a slight speech impediment, a lisp particularly noticeable in words with r's. But he does not seem self-conscious about it.

Nasrallah had always wanted to lead Lebanon's Shiites. It was the first thing he told me. He told the tale with a touch of self-deprecating humor, a note he often injects into his speeches, to great public effect.

"Ever since I was nine years old, I had plans for the day when I would start doing this," he explained, smiling and pulling his robes around him.

"When I was ten or eleven, my grandmother had a scarf. It was black, but a long one. I used to wrap it around my head and say to them, 'I'm a cleric. You need to pray behind me.'"

Nasrallah's name carries religious meaning. "Nasser" means victory, "Allah" means God—thus "God's victory." He did not come from a religious family, however. He was born on August 31, 1960 in a Christian suburb of Beirut, the first of nine children. His father was a fruit and vegetable vendor who later opened a small grocery. The family fled back to their ancestral village in the Shiite-dominated south after the civil war erupted.

That's when he got religion, Nasrallah explained. He was the first in his family to become a cleric.

Nasrallah's story is a microcosm of the rise of Lebanon's Shiites. Until their influx into the *dahiya,* Shiites were concentrated in the farming towns of the south and the verdant plains of the eastern Bekaa Valley; Maronites, Sunnis, and Druze dominated the cosmopolitan cities and scenic mountains. For most Shiites, life was still feudal until the 1960s. Most were poorly educated. Most worked in agriculture—in apple, citrus, fig, and peach orchards, corn fields, banana groves, or vineyards spread out on the rocky hills. Many families had worked the same small pieces of land for generations. Back then, the government allocated less than one percent of the state budget for public works and health care in Shiite areas.[5] Few Shiites engaged in politics. Activists tended toward the small Communist Party, one of the few multisectarian movements, and long led by a Christian.

Two events originally mobilized the Shiites. The first was creation of the Movement for the Disinherited in 1974 by Imam Musa al Sadr, an intense, charismatic cleric who wore a black turban denoting descent from the Prophet Mohammed. He gave poor Shiites a political identity, built a network of small schools, vocational centers, and clinics not provided by the state, and cautioned other sects about hogging power.

"The deprived are, unfortunately, the time-bomb for conflicts," Sadr warned.[6]

Sadr accepted Lebanon's ecumenical essence. He cofounded Lebanon's Social Movement with the Greek Catholic Archbishop, lectured in Christian churches, and formed an alliance with Christian spiritual leaders in southern Lebanon. But he also protected his own. On the eve of Lebanon's civil war, he formed an armed wing called the Lebanese Resistance Battalions. Its acronym was Amal, the Arabic word for "hope." It was the first Shiite militia.

Nasrallah was captivated by Sadr. "I always dreamed of becoming like him and doing what he did," he told me. He put up Sadr's picture in his father's small grocery. Then he joined Amal. At age fifteen, about the time the civil war started, Nasrallah also enrolled in a seminary.

Sadr was of Lebanese descent, but he was born in Iran and trained in its seminaries. He was typical of the cross-fertilization of Shiites in Lebanon and Iran, dating back almost five centuries. Clerics from Lebanon had helped Persia's monarchy convert from Sunni to Shiite Islam in the sixteenth century. The conversion was largely for political reasons. Persia wanted to differentiate itself and distance its people from the rival Ottoman Empire, ruled by a Sunni caliph, by breeding a separate identity.[7]

The Shiite connection deepened over the centuries. As the largest minority in the Islamic world—roughly fifteen percent of the world's 1.4 billion Muslims—Shiites share a common sense of persecution. The Iran-Lebanon link endured through religion, politics, and marriage. Sadr's niece married Mohammed Khatami, a cleric who went on to become Iran's president in 1997.

Sadr mysteriously disappeared in 1978. He was on a trip to Libya with two aides. Their next stop was supposed to be Italy. Their luggage showed up in Rome, but they were never heard from again. Sadr's fate—whether murdered or still imprisoned in Libya—has never been determined. It remains a source of obsessive anger among the Shiites. I once interviewed a young Amal commander who had hijacked seven planes in the early 1980s just to demand Sadr's release.

Amal was eventually taken over by Nabih Berri, a bland and suited lawyer who had an American green card and a family in Dearborn, Michigan. Berri used traditional patronage and political favors to stay in power. Amal gradually became just another Lebanese political party, losing much of the passion central to its early appeal and to traditions of the Shiite faith.

The second event that mobilized the Shiites was Israel's invasion in 1982 to roust the Palestine Liberation Organization.[8] Ironically, many Shiites initially welcomed the Israelis—with traditional rosewater and rice—in gratitude for liberating them. For more than a decade, Yasser Arafat's guerrillas had usurped large chunks of the south to wage war against Israel. The local economy was hard hit; Shiites had also come under fire during Israel's counterattacks. In less than three months, the invasion forced the Palestinians to leave Lebanon. And no group was happier than the Shiites to see them go.

But then the Israelis stayed—and stayed. The invasion turned into a long-term occupation. And Lebanon's Shiites then turned on the Israelis.

Most of the Arab world paid only lip service to protesting Israel's invasion. But Iran's zealous new revolutionary regime eagerly stepped in. Although the mullahs were in the midst of their own grisly war with Iraq, Tehran dispatched more than 1,000 Iranian Revolutionary Guards to Lebanon—and tapped into Shiite rage. From secret camps, Iran mobilized young men into the new Party of God and then provided them with arms, funds, training, and explosives.

Many in Amal, including Nasrallah, switched to Hezbollah.

"The attempt by Israel to control our country left a deep impact on me and others like me. I was then twenty-two years old," Nasrallah told me.

"We used to discuss issues among ourselves," he added. "If we are to expel the Israeli occupation from our country, how do we do this? We noticed what happened in Palestine, in the West Bank, in the Gaza

Strip, in the Golan, in the Sinai. We reached a conclusion that we cannot rely on the Arab League States nor on the United Nations. The UN Security Council adopts resolutions, but Israel does not implement these resolutions.

"If we were to wait, Lebanon would become another Palestine," Nasrallah said. "So I, just like many thousands of Lebanese youth, had to leave schools and classes, and we had to take up arms to liberate our land from Israeli occupation, because we had no other way."

Hezbollah thus took root.

Most political movements in the Middle East carry huge baggage from history. Some are now tapping into centuries-old traditions in the quest for future rights.

Sheikh Nasrallah had three brothers and five sisters, all younger. His next younger brother remained in Amal's militia. His nom de guerre was Jihad al Husseini—or "holy war of Hussein." The name reflected the essence of Shiism.

Among Shiites, a parable from the origins of the faith, in the seventh century, still guides dozens of movements in the Middle East 1,400 years later. It grew out of a political dispute, but it sparked enduring and divisive passions over the issue of injustice.

Shiite means "follower of Ali." In the greatest schism ever within Islam, the Shiites broke away within thirty years of the Prophet Mohammed's death. At the time, as in many parts of the world, leadership descended through a family. The prophet had no sons, so many in the family believed that the next leader of the new Islamic faith should be his cousin Ali, who had married the Prophet's daughter Fatima. (Marriage among cousins remains a common practice to this day in the Middle East—in Lebanon, among Christians as well as Muslims. Some countries, such as Iran, now provide genetic testing for cousins.) Ali, who is famously portrayed among Shiites in pictures, posters, tapestries, and even silk carpets as a handsome young man with penetrating eyes, had been an early convert to the new faith that emerged from the sands of the Arabian Peninsula.

But the Prophet had left no instructions. And many of his early advisers believed that the caliph of the new Omayyad Dynasty—a position deemed to be God's representative on earth—should instead be selected from among them. The Prophet's circle of advisers was the nucleus of what became the mainstream Sunni.

Ali did eventually become the fourth caliph, briefly. But after his murder in 661, the issue of political succession came up once again: The emerging Shiites wanted the new leader to be Ali's son and the Prophet's grandson, Hussein. The more numerous Sunnis again wanted to pick from outside the family—and again they did. The breach has never been healed.

What happened next set the stage for the Shiite tradition of resistance still practiced in the twenty-first century.

Hussein believed that the new faith had been usurped, that its fate was at stake. So he challenged the new rulers. The battle played out in Karbala, in today's Iraq. The odds were overwhelmingly against the Shiites. The Omayyad dynasty had thousands of troops; Hussein had less than 100 fighters and a handful of women and children. The showdown was the Shiite version of David and Goliath, but Goliath won. The prophet's grandson was willing to take the risk because he believed that it was more honorable to die for belief than to live with injustice. Hussein and his followers were all slaughtered.

Hussein's ultimate protest left an enduring legacy. He became the supreme martyr. Each year since his death, for fourteen centuries, Shiites have reenacted his struggle during the ten days of Ashura. Street parades in Lebanon's crowded *dahiya* and in many Iranian cities include long lines of men rhythmically flagellating themselves with chains, knives, or swords, replicating the act of self-sacrifice. Most Sunni governments ban the commemoration—with its themes of victimization of minorities and their resistance—among their own Shiites.

Ashura climaxes with the "passion play" of Hussein's death. It is not unlike the Christian reenactment of Jesus's stations of the cross and the agony among his followers on Good Friday. Ashura is the most important holy period of the year for devout Shiites—a constant reminder of the duty to resist injustice and tyranny in the name of God. Martyrdom has also remained the most honored defense of the faith.

Nasrallah often invoked Hussein. Among his fighters and his followers, he trumpeted "the weapon of martyrdom" as the only edge over the major powers' military superiority. In a 2002 speech aired on Hezbollah TV, he told a crowd,

> *Hussein, may peace be upon him, rose up and fought with the very few members of his family and his companions. He was protecting Islam, the values of Islam, and the existence of this religion, in order to prevent its termination, transformation, vanishing, or the manipulation of its teachings to send people back to the early days of ignorance.*
>
> *From Hussein, we learn that we may have to pay a high price in order to triumph and may not live to see victory. We learn that the true sacrificing people are those who offer their blood in order for others to live afterwards with dignity and freedom. . . . Our present generation should . . . teach this type of culture to the next generation so that it would find the ability to transform confrontation into victory.*[9]

Since Nasrallah and his Shiite peers mobilized under Hezbollah's umbrella in 1982, the movement has evolved through four phases—each heavily influenced by Shiite origins. The first phase was the pure extremist era, from 1982 through 1991.

Nasrallah's first major job was as chief of operations against Israel at the new Iranian-run camps.

"After the invasion in June 1982, we started establishing camps in Bekaa, near the city of Baalbek, to take volunteers from the Lebanese youth, to train them, to mobilize them," Nasrallah told me. "During the first stage, my role was to receive these young men, to study their files, to give my OK, so that they can join the training camps. After that, we organized them as cells within the framework of the resistance, and then they returned to their occupied cities or towns."

"I didn't have the role of a militant, meaning to bear arms and shoot," he added. "I didn't have the honor of taking part in direct combat. But I shouldered different leadership posts. I commanded combat operations."

Hezbollah transformed the landscape, literally.

Lebanon's ancient city of Baalbek—or City of the Sun—became

one of the most feared places on earth. Two thousand years earlier, Julius Caesar had constructed the largest temple in the Roman Empire to the god Jupiter in Baalbek. Its colossal walls and columns still stand. Baalbek's temple to Bacchus, which was larger than the Parthenon in Greece, was the most beautifully decorated temple in the Roman world. Finished in 150 A.D., much of it is preserved today. In the mid-1950s, Lebanon launched the Baalbek Festival, which drew the likes of Miles Davis, Rudolf Nureyev, and Ella Fitzgerald to perform amid the mammoth ruins in the Middle East's finest summer arts series.

But in 1982, Iran set up training camps in Baalbek and the surrounding Bekaa Valley, a fertile plain near the Syrian border. The area became off-limits.

I witnessed the birth of Shiite militancy in the 1980s. It emerged in extremist spectaculars that were an extension of Iran's revolution, mixed with the pent-up anger of Lebanon's poorest sect, spurred by the inherited Shiite sense of persecution, and inflamed by Israel's lingering occupation of Shiite land.

The rage was compounded by the deployment of American and European troops in Lebanon. They originally arrived in 1982 as peacekeepers to oversee the exodus of Palestinian guerrillas. But within a year, they ended up as participants in the local strife, especially after American warships opened fire on a Muslim faction. The American Marines and their French, Italian, and British counterparts came to be seen as part of a larger package—foreign intervention in Lebanon. Hezbollah's early targets were all foreigners.

The new Shiite radicalism literally exploded on the scene in 1983. Its tactics and impact were startling even in the context of Lebanon's vicious civil war.

In one day alone, on a sultry Sunday morning in October 1983, a suicide bomber in a yellow Mercedes truck set off the largest non-nuclear explosion since World War II at Beirut's International Airport. The four-story airport building housing American peacekeepers collapsed into a grotesque pile of concrete and twisted steel. Most of the Marines were crushed in their beds. The final death toll was 241, the largest American loss in a single attack since Iwo Jima in 1945.[10]

Twenty seconds later and four miles down the road, a second truck rammed into an eight-story building used by French paratroopers. The entire structure blew over on its side, killing fifty-eight. It was the worst death toll for France since the Algerian war twenty-two years earlier.

The blasts stunned me out of bed many miles away. The explosions were so close together that they sounded like a single long roar bellowing through Beirut. I was down at the Marine compound for days reporting on the attack—and watching rescuers pull out the dead and wounded from under tons of rubble.

"We are the soldiers of God," an anonymous caller from Islamic Jihad told Agence France Presse. The same group had claimed the attack on the United States Embassy six months earlier, when sixty-three had been killed. "We said after that [embassy bombing] that we would strike more violently still. Now they understand what they are dealing with," he added. "Violence will remain our way."[11]

Ten days later, another bomb-laden truck plowed its way into an Israeli command center in southern Lebanon. It killed twenty-nine Israeli troops, as well as thirty Palestinian and Lebanese prisoners. Islamic Jihad again claimed credit. It was the first of dozens of suicide attacks against Israeli targets.

The strategy produced the desired effect.

In February 1984, four months after the Marines were attacked, the world's mightiest power withdrew its most elite fighting force from tiny Lebanon. French troops pulled out a month later. Their mission was unaccomplished.

In June 1985, Israel withdrew most of its troops to a protected buffer zone in southern Lebanon. Hezbollah had forced its hand.

Yitzhak Rabin, Israel's defense minister at the time and later prime minister, reflected,

> *I believe that among the many surprises, and most of them not for the good, that came out of the war in Lebanon, the most dangerous is that the war let the Shiites out of the bottle. No one predicted it; I couldn't find it in any intelligence report. . . .*
>
> *If as a result of the war in Lebanon, we replace PLO terrorism in southern Lebanon with Shiite terrorism, we have done the worst [thing] in our*

struggle against terrorism. In twenty years of PLO terrorism, no one PLO terrorist made himself a live bomb. . . . In my opinion, the Shiites have the potential for a kind of terrorism that we have not yet experienced.[12]

Indeed. The Shiite movement from little Lebanon redefined modern extremist tactics. Its terrorist trademarks—including the human bomb and simultaneous attacks for multiple impact—were later copied with deadly effect by Palestinian nationalists, Iraqi insurgents, Saudi dissidents, Egyptian extremists, Moroccan militants, Algerian rebels, Jordanian renegades, Kuwaiti fanatics, Yemeni zealots, and, in the most spectacular schemes, by Osama bin Laden's multinational movement, al Qaeda.

For the first time, small unconventional groups could effectively challenge their own well-armed governments, occupation forces, regional powerhouses, and even a global superpower. The trend soon spread well beyond the Middle East, from Pakistan to the Philippines and from Chechnya to Indonesia.

The Shiite movement's use of the first Islamic suicide bombers in modern times can be traced to the eleventh century. The practice was perfected by a Shiite offshoot sect that dispatched young soldiers on a single fatal mission against Christian Crusaders and Sunni opponents. According to legend and the Oxford English Dictionary, the word "assassin" comes from *hashashin*, the name for young devotees administered hashish to induce a state of euphoria before those missions. By the thirteenth century, courtesy of terrified Crusaders, the word "assassin" had entered the Western vernacular.

In a rare visit, Marco Polo toured the Hashashins' fortress near the Caspian Sea.[13] He wrote of an early leader,

He kept at his court a number of youths of the country, from twelve to twenty years of age, such as had a taste for soldiering, and to these he used to tell tales about paradise . . . then he would introduce them into his garden, some four or six or ten at a time, having first made them drink a certain potion which cast them into a deep sleep, and then causing them to be lifted and carried in, so when they awoke, they found themselves in the garden . . . so charming, they deemed that it was paradise. . . .

So when the Old Man would have any prince slain, he would say to such a youth: "Go thou and slay so and so; and when thou returnst my angels shall bear thee into paradise. And shouldst thou die, nevertheless even so will I send my angels to carry thee back into paradise. So he caused them to believe; and thus there was no order of his that they would not affront any peril to execute, for the great desire they had to get into that paradise of his. And in this manner the Old One got his people to murder anyone whom he desired to get rid of.[14]

Nasrallah once used a similar description to explain the appeal of becoming a modern martyr—or *shahid* in Arabic. In the *dahiya,* many streets and Hezbollah facilities have been named after specific martyrs, with *shahid* added, as if a conferred title.

"The best metaphor for a Westerner to try to understand this truth," Nasrallah told a British journalist, "is to think of a person being in a sauna bath for a long time.

"This person is very thirsty and tired and hot, and he is suffering from the effects of the high temperature. Then he is told that if he opens the door, he can go into a quiet, comfortable room, drink a nice cocktail, and hear beautiful classical music," Nasrallah continued. "Then he will open the door and go through without hesitation, knowing that what he leaves behind is not a high price to pay—and that what awaits him is of much greater value."[15]

The early militants were also the first to seize civilian hostages— more than 100 foreigners over a seven-year period—as leverage for political or military concessions. Among the hostages were Associated Press correspondent Terry Anderson and American University of Beirut Dean Tom Sutherland. Some were held in the *dahiya,* Baalbek, or southern Lebanon for as long as seven years. Not all survived. CIA station chief William Buckley and Colonel William Higgins, a Marine who was assigned to the UN Truce Supervisory Organization in southern Lebanon, died in captivity; both were brutally tortured.

The tactic had enormous impact. In the mid-1980s, Hezbollah's hostages enabled patron Iran to do a secret swap with the United States. Engrossed in its own eight-year war with Iraq, Tehran needed weaponry. So Washington secretly provided missiles in exchange for Tehran's

intervention to free three American captives. The scandal later rocked
the Reagan Administration. Top White House officials were forced to
resign; some faced trials. It proved to be Reagan's worst blunder.

And the swap did not end the problem. Shortly after the three
Americans were released, three more Americans were kidnapped off
Beirut's rough streets.

A common theme in the hostage dramas was Shiite prisoners.[16]
Hezbollah's close-knit adherents hatched daring schemes to free their
brethren.

The most notorious member of Hezbollah in the early days was a
thug named Imad Mughniyah. A surprisingly slight man at five foot
seven and about 150 pounds, he had a short beard that arched around
the angular jawline of his face. Mughniyah was widely tied to the
deadliest acts of terrorism against American targets until September 11, 2001. He was often linked to the Marine bombing; he was
also implicated in many of the early kidnappings. President George H.
W. Bush dubbed him America's Enemy No. 1. He remains on the FBI's
list of most wanted terrorists—with a five-million-dollar reward for
information leading to his capture.

Mughniyah was connected to hostage seizures in part because of
a Shiite prisoner. Mustafa Badreddin was Mughniyah's cousin and
brother-in-law. He was arrested and tried for a stunning 1983 series of
six bombings in Kuwait that simultaneously targeted the United States
Embassy, the French Embassy, Kuwait's main oil refinery and airport,
and the Raytheon Corporation compound. It was the deadliest violence
ever in the little oil-rich Gulf country. Badreddin—who was linked to
a Shiite group called Dawa, or the Call—was convicted, along with
sixteen others, and sentenced to death. They became known as the
Kuwait Seventeen.

Between 1984 and 1991, the hostage takers repeatedly demanded
freedom for the Kuwait Seventeen as their condition for releasing the
American and other Western hostages seized in Beirut.

Prisoners were also the motive behind the extraordinary saga of
TWA 847, which was hijacked by Hezbollah supporters in 1985. The
plane was forced to shuttle for days between Lebanon and Algeria. Dur-

ing one stop in Beirut, the hijackers murdered American Navy diver Robert Dean Stethem; his body was dumped onto the airport tarmac. The drama unfolded over sixteen days. In what became known as the "no-deal deal," the TWA passengers and crew were eventually driven to Syria and freed. Israel soon freed 766 prisoners, mainly Shiites—but denied that the release had anything to do with the hijackers' demands. The FBI eventually charged Mughniyah, in a sealed indictment, with the TWA hijacking.

In the early years, the new militants were an amalgam of clandestine and often overlapping little groups. Leaders were unknown. Titles varied. They phoned in claims under the names of the Revolutionary Justice Organization, the Followers of the Prophet Mohammed, the Organization of the Oppressed on Earth, Islamic Jihad, and the Organization of Right Against Wrong.

Hezbollah's leadership later denied the most violent bombings and hostage seizures of the 1980s. Those acts, they insisted, were conducted by cells outside the party structure.

But the early activists were basically the embryo of what became Hezbollah. They all had the same Iranian tutelage, training and funding, as well as Syrian support. Years later, during a trip to Tehran, an Iranian cabinet minister boasted to me that Iran had trained the bomber who attacked the Israeli headquarters in Lebanon in 1983—and gave me his name.

Hezbollah—which should technically be written Hizb 'Allah, or Party of God—took its name from the last verse of the fifty-eighth chapter in the Koran: "Verily the party of God shall be victorious." The verse, in dark green, runs atop a logo on the movement's bright yellow flag. The logo consists of the party's name written in thick, artistic calligraphy. An arm thrusting a Kalashnikov assault rifle into the air extends from the first Arabic letter in Allah. To the side is a globe.

The implications are obvious—worldwide Islamic revolution.

During the movement's early years in the 1980s, I wangled the first Hezbollah press pass from one of its cells; it may still be the only one ever issued. As I spent more and more time in the *dahiya,* I wanted some kind of credential to avoid being detained, harassed, or taken hostage, especially as an American. Most other militias issued press passes to use at their checkpoints. Since Lebanon had many armed groups—almost forty at the height of the civil war, including foreign troops—journalists carried a wallet full of passes.

The trick was pulling out the right pass at constantly shifting checkpoints. Several journalists who guessed wrong were detained or beaten; at least two were killed.

In those days, Hezbollah had no headquarters, much less public officials. But one day when I was in the *dahiya,* heading to the office of a Shiite cleric, I saw an unfinished building nearby with a black, spray-painted stencil of the new Hezbollah logo; it had begun to appear on walls all over Beirut. I ducked inside. Several gunmen with beards and Kalashnikov rifles were in a ground-floor room that was plastered with Hezbollah posters.

I explained who I was, described an earlier book I was writing, and then said that I wanted a press pass. One of the gunmen, who did not introduce himself, told me that the group did not issue press passes. When I persisted, he shrugged, walked over to one of the posters, ripped off a corner with the logo, and handed it to me.

"Can't you date it, or write your name on it, or something to make it look a bit more official?" I asked.

"Just show it," he replied, "and you won't have any problems."

I assumed he was trying to get rid of me. But when I was stopped at a Hezbollah checkpoint a few days later, I pulled out the little piece of Hezbollah's poster. The gunmen waved me through. I used it for years.

The Party of God finally emerged from the underground—and as a single unit—in 1985 in an open letter addressed "to all the oppressed in Lebanon and the world." It was read at a Beirut mosque and published in a Lebanese newspaper. Its tone was militant, its goals absolute. It called for an Islamic society in Lebanon and blasted Lebanon's Christian Maronites.

We don't want to impose Islam upon anybody, as much as we don't want others to impose upon us their convictions and their political systems. We don't want Islam to reign in Lebanon by force as is the case with the

Maronites today. . . . [But] we call upon you to embrace Islam so that you can be happy in this world and the next. . . . Only an Islamic regime can stop any further imperialist infiltration into our country. . . .

In more aggressive language, it also demanded the destruction of Israel.

The Zionist entity is aggressive from its inception and built on lands wrested from their owners, at the expense of the rights of the Muslim people. Therefore our struggle will end only when this entity is obliterated.[17]

The Party of God defiantly pledged that it would never compromise with the Jewish state. "We recognize no treaty with it, no cease-fire, and no peace agreements," Hezbollah announced.

The open letter also warned, "No one can imagine our military potential."[18]

Hezbollah's first phase ended with Lebanon's civil war in 1990 and the brief 1991 Gulf War to liberate Kuwait after Iraq's invasion. Both events altered dynamics throughout the Middle East.

The Iraqi invasion also, inadvertently, eliminated the prisoner issue. In one of those accidents of history, the Iraqis had opened Kuwait's prisons—and unwittingly released Mughniyah's cousin and other members of the Kuwait Seventeen, thus ending a key reason for the hostage abductions.

The early era symbolically came to a close, after Iran's intervention, when Hezbollah then freed its last foreign hostage, Associated Press correspondent Terry Anderson, in 1991. Anderson was a friend; we had offices in the same building. A former Marine, he was nabbed after he came back from a tennis game in Beirut in 1985. He had been bundled into the trunk of a getaway car and held for the next seven years, much of it chained to a radiator or a bed.

Hezbollah's tactics shifted after that—at least in practice, if not in policy.

Anderson returned to Lebanon five years later to purge the ghosts of his captivity. Among his stops was the Hezbollah headquarters to see Nasrallah, who had since assumed leadership of the movement.

Anderson asked Nasrallah, who is often called sayyid as a man of religious learning, what he thought of kidnapping foreigners.

"I'm not saying whether their methods were good or not, right or wrong," Nasrallah told him. "These actions were short-term, with short-term objectives, and I hope that they will not happen again."

"Can you say, sayyid, flatly, that this was wrong or a mistake?" Anderson pressed him.

"I can't make such an absolute judgment," Nasrallah replied.[19]

Transitions from militancy into mainstream politics depend on a confluence of factors.

Hezbollah began to evolve as it moved into a second phase in 1992. It coincided with Nasrallah's sudden rise to the leadership, after Israel assassinated the movement's secretary-general. The specific turning point was the most controversial decision Hezbollah had yet taken—to enter politics. It was Nasrallah's first major act. And it was a major reversal.

During its first decade, Hezbollah had rejected any role in Lebanon's convoluted confessional system. The Shiite movement had considered itself above other parties, militias, clans, and the Lebanese government generally. The Party of God believed it was a bigger actor. It played on a regional stage, engaging with an outside enemy rather than in domestic squabbles.[20] It had largely avoided the civil war, except for turf battles with Amal, the other Shiite militia. In politics, Hezbollah was the odd man out.

But after a heated internal debate, and at Iran's urging, the movement opted to run candidates for parliament in the first elections after Lebanon's fifteen-year civil war ended. Under pictures of its martyrs, its campaign posters appealed, THEY RESIST WITH THEIR BLOOD. RESIST WITH YOUR VOTE.[21] At a rally for thousands assembled in a *dahiya* stadium on election eve, Nasrallah sounded like a conventional politician talking about Hezbollah representing Shiite interests in parliament.

"We will seek to serve you in our new positions to end this area's deprivation and oppression," he said, exhorting a large crowd and pumping his arm in the air. "Tomorrow, God willing, our candidates will stand in the Chamber of Deputies to remind those who have forgotten that there is a deprived area in Lebanon called the southern suburb. . . . We refuse to let anyone deal with it as if it were foreign to Lebanon."[22]

The Party of God won twelve seats in the 128-seat parliament. Overnight, it became one the biggest of Lebanon's seventeen political blocs. Former clandestine leaders in an extremist movement were suddenly elected officials. Hezbollah soon became engrossed in politics as an opposition party. It criticized government for corruption, ineptitude, and allocating inadequate funds for Shiites. It pushed for no-confidence votes. It was politically engaged.

"We've taken the decisions that suit each stage," Hezbollah external relations chief Nawaf al Musawi, an intense and portly man with a dark beard, told me during one of several interviews with Hezbollah officials in offices scattered around the *dahiya*.

"I always remember a saying by the Greek philosopher Herodotus," he continued. " 'You do not swim in the same river twice.'[23] He meant, if you swim the river, the second time it will not be the same because the water will not be the same as it was the first time.

"Politics," Musawi pronounced, as his left hand flipped through a set of white worry beads, "is the same."

The shift was not universally popular. "When we took the decision to engage in the parliamentary process, not everyone wanted to participate," he conceded. "There was one who opposed it, and he left."

Hezbollah experienced its first split over the 1992 elections. Sheikh Sobhi Tufayli—the movement's fiery first secretary-general, who was controversial even within Hezbollah—had bolted. He went off and later formed the rival Revolution of the Hungry.

During the eight years of its second phase, Hezbollah also began to transform its strongholds in the *dahiya* and southern Lebanon. It built a major hospital, complete with the latest CAT scan and MRI technology, as well as several clinics, schools, discount pharmacies, groceries, and an orphanage. It built reservoirs in districts where water lines had collapsed or wells had failed; tanker trucks circulated weekly to keep them filled. It started a garbage service for the *dahiya,* where debris once simply piled up. It ran a reconstruction program for homes damaged during Israel's 1982 invasion. It supplied school fees and college scholarships. It paid for emergency operations and health insurance stipends. It set up loan funds for small businesses. It ran farms, factories, and cooperatives. It eventually became one of Lebanon's largest employers.

In most Shiite strongholds, Hezbollah outperformed the state. Unlike many government agencies, it had a reputation for being frugal, uncorrupt, and organized. Members even bragged that the movement was so disciplined that the Hezbollah soccer team almost never chalked up penalties—in a country where games are notoriously rowdy.[24]

Iran propped up Hezbollah, providing most of its initial funds—at least ten million dollars each month in arms, humanitarian goods, and cash, according to many estimates. "Iran stands by Lebanon on all the major issues, the government, the people, the army, the resistance," Nasrallah told me, although he would not talk specific sums.

"There are institutions, foundations in Iran that present aid of a social nature, and we run the branches in Lebanon, such as the foundations that take interest in the families of martyrs, and the refugee aid foundations, such as for the needy," he said. "Iran presents aid and grants at a good level for farmers and for the projects that the farmers do."

In the 1990s, Hezbollah also increasingly raised its own funds, reportedly off both legal and illicit activities. Shiites are supposed to pay khums, an Islamic tax equal to one-fifth of their annual income, to their religious leaders for charitable causes. The Shiite Diaspora from Africa to Australia and both the Americas supplied remittances too. At home, "charity boxes" wrapped in bright yellow Hezbollah flags were strategically placed in shops, public facilities, and even at traffic stops.[25] Hezbollah's financial operations were run through the Bayt al-Mal, or House of Money, which in the Arab world was historically the caliph's royal treasury or a financial institution for distributing taxes for public works. In 2006, the United States charged that the House of Money in Lebanon served as the bank, creditor, and investment arm of Hezbollah. Washington charged that it was under Nasrallah's direct control, headed by one of his advisers, and used to fund Hezbollah's services and companies.[26]

Hezbollah supporters were also widely reported to be contributing cash off their own criminal activities, such as smuggling—diamonds in Africa, drugs and pirated compact disks in Latin America. Some Lebanese businesses abroad were also reportedly "taxed" by Hezbollah agents to help pay for its charity operations and public services.[27] Fundraising was run by the Islamic Resistance Support Organization, the United States charged.

Its new public services were an enormous boost to the Shiite movement's local legitimacy. As its focus shifted, so did its language. By 1998, a new "statement of purpose" contrasted with Hezbollah's inaugural proclamation in 1985.

> *If Islam becomes the choice of the majority, then we will apply it. If not, we will continue to coexist.... We hereby affirm that our Islam rejects violence as a method to gain power, and this should be the formula for the non-Islamists as well.*

During its second phase in the 1990s, Hezbollah's tone about the outside world changed as well. Nasrallah's new gripe was that the United States provided only paltry foreign aid to Lebanon.

"It is both ridiculous and ironic for the U.S. ambassador to donate $10,000 to a humanitarian institution or to come to the Bekaa Valley to distribute cows to farmers when the United States is giving Israel three billion dollars annually," he groused at a 1997 rally in the Bekaa Valley.[28]

The atmospherics in Hezbollah's realm changed too. Baalbek was still a stronghold. Posters of Hezbollah martyrs were still plastered on public sites. But the military presence became less conspicuous. In 1997, the Baalbek Festival resumed after a twenty-two-year break. World-renowned cellist Mstislav Rostropovich played Dvořák under the floodlit Corinthian columns of the world's largest remaining Roman ruins. Sting, Andrew Lloyd Webber's *Cats*, and Michael Flatley's *Lord of the Dance* were highlighted in subsequent years.

Hezbollah's shifts should not be mistaken for moderation. As for all Islamist groups in the Middle East, change has always been about survival of both cause and constituents, about reassessing and revising strategy in response to events around them. Hezbollah adapted because it had to.

The end of Lebanon's fifteen-year civil war altered the environment. When wartime Lebanon had no system, it had not mattered that Hezbollah operated outside the state. When a system emerged in peacetime, however, Hezbollah needed to be part of it to convince others of its special role. All militias were supposed to dismantle, according to terms of the final cease-fire. Hezbollah engaged in Lebanese politics in part to win approval to keep its weapons—on grounds that it was the only force capable of challenging Israel's ongoing occupation. The Party of God's participation in politics was also part of a joint strategy with Syria and Iran.

And on Israel, Hezbollah's raison d'être, Nasrallah's rhetoric remained venomous.

In 1998, Ashura commemorations of Hussein's martyrdom coincided with Israel's fiftieth anniversary. Nasrallah used the occasion to lambaste Israelis as "the descendants of apes and pigs.

"A few million vagabonds from all over the world, brought together by their Talmud and Jewish fanaticism, are celebrating their victory over the nation of 1.4 billion Muslims," he said, in a speech broadcast on television. "It is a tragic, painful, and bitter thing that a small number of people gather in Palestine, dancing and holding celebrations in the Al-Aqsa Mosque and the holy city [of Jerusalem] to celebrate their great victory over the nation of Mohammed."[29]

Hezbollah launched a small media empire in the 1990s to propagate its vitriolic message. Its new magazine was entitled *The Fist of God*. Its radio station was called God's Light. Its modern television station was named al Manar, the Beacon. Most of its programming—news, game shows, kids programs, and docudramas—carried biting and sometimes bizarre propaganda against Israel and the United States.

Hezbollah TV recruited suicide bombers, aired footage of their attacks, and then ran their pretaped last testaments. Programs appealed to mothers to surrender their sons "knowing that their blood will mix with the soil." Martial music, Koranic verses, and flag-burnings were staples. Airtime between programs was filled with gruesome graphics. One set of pictures purported to show Jews killing Christian children to use their blood for Passover bread. The Statue of Liberty was re-created as an angry ghoul, her face a skull, a dagger rather than a torch in her hand, her gown dripping with blood.[30]

By 2000, Hezbollah TV was beaming worldwide by satellite. Its audience expanded to an estimated ten million viewers daily. It soon ranked as one of the five most popular stations in the Middle East. Besides Arabic, it aired programs in English and French—and Hebrew.

Hezbollah's military attacks against Israeli troops in Lebanon also intensified between 1992 and 2000. The battlefield widened; Hezbollah's strategy diversified.

To suicide bombings and guerrilla attacks, the Shiite guerrillas added conventional tactics, including the famed Katyusha rocket. Katyusha is a Russian name equivalent to "Katie." Russian troops named the inaccurate and inexpensive rocket during World War II after a song about young Katyusha pining for her beloved at war. Katyushas are fired individually or in multiple launchers, sometimes on the backs of trucks that can be quickly driven to another location. With deadly impact, the short-range rockets were also widely used in Vietnam, Afghanistan, and Iraq. In the 1990s, Iranian cargo flights flew thousands of short-range Katyushas into Damascus to be trucked into Lebanon.[31]

In 1993, Hezbollah fired the first Katyusha into northern Israel, broadening the arena of conflict after weeks of tension and provocations by both sides along the border. The fighting became so intense across the border that the United States twice intervened to broker cease-fires, in 1993 and 1996.[32]

Hundreds also died in clashes between Hezbollah and Israeli troops in the rocky hills and fields of southern Lebanon in the 1990s. Among the Lebanese casualties in a 1997 clash was Nasrallah's eighteen-year-old son Hadi. Israel kept his body, as Hezbollah kept the bodies of Israeli troops, to be used in prisoner swaps. Nasrallah's reaction to news of his oldest son's death was still noted a decade later by Lebanese from all sects and Arabs of many nations. At a Hezbollah rally that evening in the *dahiya,* he paused only briefly from his speech to mention it.

"We in the leadership of Hezbollah do not spare our children and save them for the future," Nasrallah told a large crowd. "We pride ourselves when our sons reach the front line, and we stand heads held high when they fall as martyrs."

Iraq's deputy prime minister, Barham Salih, a British-educated Kurd and a Sunni whose children were raised in America, brought it up out of the blue in a conversation in 2006. "This impressed me deeply," Salih told me, shaking his head. "It was a lesson to us all. Nasrallah keeps his word. This is why he has such impact."

The arena for resistance also moved beyond the Middle East for the first time. Hezbollah and Iran were linked to two bombings in Argentina: In 1992, an attack on the Israeli Embassy in Buenos Aires killed twenty-nine. The strike followed Israel's assassination of Nasrallah's predecessor; the two events were widely linked. In 1994, a second bombing at an Israeli cultural center killed eighty-five. The cultural center's library was largely destroyed, including records that had been preserved through the Holocaust.

Hezbollah denied responsibility for the bombings outside Lebanon just as absolutely as the Argentine government held it responsible. After a twelve-year investigation, Argentine prosecutors ordered the arrest of former Iranian President Ali Akbar Hashemi Rafsanjani as well as the former Iranian foreign ministers and intelligence chiefs, two Revolutionary Guard commanders, two Iranian diplomats and a former Hezbollah security chief.

At a press conference, the Argentine prosecutors said they suspected Hezbollah launched attacks outside Lebanon only "under orders directly emanating from the regime in Tehran."[33]

The second phase ended in 2000, when Hezbollah's relentless campaign of attacks wore the Israelis down. The costs to Israel of occupying Lebanon heavily outweighed the benefits. The war was increasingly unpopular at home. More than 900 Israeli troops had been killed, proportionately the equivalent of 42,000 Americans—not far off what the United States had lost in Vietnam.

Israeli Prime Minister Ehud Barak, a former army chief of staff, won election on a peace platform to pull out of Lebanon. When he took office, he followed through on his pledge. On May 23, 2000, the last Israeli tank rumbled across the dusty border. The famed Fatima Gate on the security fence was locked.

"This tragedy is over," Barak pronounced.

Hezbollah's armed wing at the time was estimated at only between 500 and 1,000 full-time troops, with up to five times as many "weekend warriors" who could be called away from their day jobs to fight. Yet a small militia had managed to accomplish what tens of thousands of soldiers in the mightier and better armed militaries of Egypt, Syria, and Jordan had failed to do for a half century: make Israel abandon Arab land with neither a formal agreement nor an informal understanding to end hostilities—or to guarantee future security. Israel left with virtually nothing to show for a costly occupation that spanned a generation.

And it had unleashed an even more potent rival.

Within hours, Hezbollah fighters waving their bright yellow flag swept across southern Lebanon to fill the space that for years had been Israel's "security zone." Some clustered along the border to taunt Israeli troops on the other side. Most brandished Kalashnikov rifles; many waved portraits of Nasrallah.

"You lost. You lost," one group of fighters shouted across a former border post.[34]

Israel's retreat was a second pivotal turning point. At home, Hezbollah's image was transformed—from a scorned terrorist group to a legitimate resistance movement.

"There is only one headline in Lebanon tonight," pronounced an anchorwoman, beaming, on Lebanese state television. "The liberation of the land. The slinking, servile withdrawal by Israel."[35] Lebanon declared May 25 an annual public holiday to commemorate its liberation.

Hezbollah's third phase, which began after Israel's withdrawal in mid-2000, marked the movement's political evolution. It lasted for six years.

Within days of Israel's withdrawal, Nasrallah went to the border and gave a speech that was still quoted years later. "This first victory lays the foundation for a new era," he said in Bint Jbeil, a charming mountain town three miles from the Israeli frontier. "People of the Arab and Islamic world, defeat, humiliation, and shame are things of the past."

Nasrallah then laid out Hezbollah's ten military and political goals. In contrast to the rhetorical ramblings of many Arab leaders, Nasrallah's speeches tended to be tightly structured, with neat sections and numbered points. The Shiite movement is technically led by a handful of clerics in a council called the Majlis al-Shura, or Consultative Council. Nasrallah was its secretary-general. But by 2000, Hezbollah had clearly become his movement. And each point in his address reflected the discipline with which he ran it.

The conflict with Israel was not over, he told thousands of followers assembled on a hot May day. First, Hezbollah had to work to "consolidate and protect" its position along the Israeli border, free for the first time since the early 1970s from both Palestinian and Israeli domination.

Second, the Muslims and Christians of the south had to demonstrate real coexistence. Although Shiites were far more numerous, several southern villages were Christian or had strong Christian populations. "When a trivial incident occurs, if we handle it as a small problem, we can solve it," he said. "If we exaggerate it, this will mean that it is we who are wasting the chance and undermining coexistence. Keep things in proper perspective. . . .

"Heal the wounds in every town, every village, and among all families," he said.

Third and fourth, collaborators—a reference mainly to the South Lebanese Army that had collaborated with Israel for two decades—should be a lesson to all Lebanese. But they should be punished only "by the law," not vigilante justice, he said.

Fifth, Hezbollah did not plan to assume political control of the south. "We are not power seekers. . . . We are not a security authority, nor do we plan to become one. The state is the party that is in charge," Nasrallah said. "It is the state that decides who it plans to send here and what to do."

Sixth, the state also had responsibility for reconstructing the south in an "urgent and exceptional manner," although he pledged that Hezbollah would "economize every bread that the fighters eat" to extend its own aid.

Seventh, the Hezbollah chief reached out to Lebanon's other

communities—and urged his followers to do so as well. "This is not the victory of one party, one movement, one organization. It is not the victory of one sect and the defeat of another," Nasrallah said. "Anyone who thinks so is wrong and ignorant. This is a victory for Lebanon."

Nasrallah admonished his followers to show "greater humility than ever before."

Eighth, Hezbollah would not accept peace along the border as long as Israel detained Lebanese prisoners—and Nasrallah named some of them—and as long as it occupied Shebaa Farms. Shebaa Farms was a disputed area that abutted the Lebanese, Syrian, and Israeli borders. Disputes over the small territory—less than ten square miles—dated back to the French mandate; they were not settled when Israel captured the area in the 1967 war. Some who lived around Shebaa Farms considered themselves Lebanese, even though a United Nations commission ruled that it was Syrian territory.

Nasrallah's claim surprised both Lebanese and Israelis. It was widely interpreted as Hezbollah's pretext to keep its arms—as if it still had to finish "liberation."

"The resistance has been the strength of the homeland—and will remain so," he said.

Ninth, he called for harmony between the resistance and the government to foster a "sense of national responsibility." "The new Lebanon is a homeland of adversity when facing invaders, but a homeland of mercy in the dealings of its sons and sects with each other," he said.

Finally, Nasrallah said he presented the Lebanese "victory" as a model for the Palestinians.

"This Israel, which possesses nuclear weapons and the most powerful air force in the region, by God, it is weaker than a spider web," Nasrallah railed. "But if you want to depend on the former Soviet Union, you will get nowhere. If you are waiting for the international community to act, you will not get results. But if you side with God...then nobody can defeat you."[36]

Israel's retreat had elevated Hezbollah overnight to national stature. Nasrallah's speech was broadcast on state-run television as well as Hezbollah TV. Even Christian leaders lauded Nasrallah for liberating Lebanon. The government arranged a meeting between the Hezbollah chief and United Nations Secretary-General Kofi Annan a month later. In an event unthinkable just weeks earlier, they were photographed shaking hands at Beirut's presidential palace.

After 2000, Hezbollah became increasingly Lebanon-ized, literally domesticated.

"We are now a full-fledged political party, we have ministers, we have members of parliament, we have municipal council members, leaders of unions," Nasrallah told me.

"If we have kept our arms until now, it is because the need is still there, because of the permanent, or constant, Israeli threats against Lebanon. And this is a different issue," he said. "Whether we keep on with the resistance or stop the resistance, we are effectively now a full-fledged political party."

The postwar period—and economic realities—spurred some of the changes.

Israel's withdrawal opened the way for Lebanon to again become a tourist haven. By 2003, more than one million foreign tourists poured into little Lebanon annually for its ski slopes and beaches, Roman ruins, and culture. They came from the West as well as from Middle East countries. Many Arabs were no longer comfortable traveling to the West after the September 11 terrorist attacks. Before the wars, Lebanon was known as the Switzerland of the Middle East because it was neutral ground for both East and West. By 2003, it was again. And for a country with the highest per capita debt ratio in the world, struggling to rebuild from both a civil war and an invasion, tourists meant revenue and jobs.

Peace was good, indirectly, for Hezbollah's constituents. In 2002, Nasrallah was candid about the movement's stake in peace.

Once, in a discussion of resistance operations, I told certain officials that "we are concerned about the nation, the state, and the future more than you think." Why is this so? Because when, Heaven forbid, the country is menaced by security, military, and political dangers or economic collapse, then those people who have capital, bankrolls, companies, children, luxury homes, and houses abroad, flee. They have a second citizenship. It is very simple. They collect the rest of their family and leave the country.

[However], our houses, graves, life, death, honor, and mortification—
they are all here.

Where else can we go?[37]

Hezbollah also became the main agent of recovery in Shiite areas, particularly in the southern third of the country. The state failed to move in and provide meaningful resources, personnel, or programs to rebuild the country's poorest and most vulnerable territory after more than twenty years of strife. So despite Nasrallah's promise to step aside for the government after Israeli's withdrawal, the Shiite movement remained in charge. And, in the process, Hezbollah became an even more powerful state within a state.

In 2004, Nasrallah again endorsed holy war against Israel. But he also warned that "this does not mean all is permitted and that we can do whatever we like—while abandoning the blood, money, and property of the people—and perpetrate serious crimes under the banner of jihad and war against the enemy."[38]

The shifting balance of military and political power in Lebanon, and the withdrawal of Hezbollah's allies between 2000 and 2005, also contributed to the movement's domestication.

In 2000, after Israel's withdrawal, Iran withdrew most of its Revolutionary Guards. Fewer than fifty officers remained, most attached to Tehran's Embassy in Beirut.[39] Hezbollah fighters went to Iran for advanced training, and the Islamic republic remained the primary source of funds and arms. But the conspicuous Bekaa Valley camps were closed.

In 2004, Syria also came under pressure to remove its 14,000 troops. The fury after the assassination of former Prime Minister Rafiq Hariri on Valentine's Day 2005 then forced a showdown. Hezbollah was the largest faction to side with Syria, and Nasrallah tried to mobilize support for Damascus. Three weeks after the bombing, he summoned hundreds of thousands to a rally that was not in the *dahiya* but, for the first time, took Hezbollah politics to downtown Beirut.

But Nasrallah's March 8 rally backfired. It instead unified the rest of Lebanon. On March 14, on the one-month anniversary of Hariri's murder, the largest public demonstration in Lebanon's history assembled near Hariri's grave. More than one million Lebanese took to the streets to demand that Syria leave. Six weeks later, Damascus withdrew. The twenty-nine-year Syrian military occupation of Lebanon was over.

Hezbollah no longer had an ally and protector at its fingertips.

Weeks later, Lebanon held its first free elections in over three decades. All the foreign armies that had controlled Lebanese turf were gone. And Syria no longer ran the political show with the intimidating help of its army. Capping the Cedar Revolution, the new March 14 coalition won the largest share of votes.

And Nasrallah reversed policy again.

For the first time, Hezbollah joined a coalition government—led by March 14 politicians. Hezbollah was no longer the opposition. One of its top officials became minister of energy. A sympathizer became minister of labor.

Hezbollah also launched outreach to other sects and even a bit to the outside world. In 2005, Nasrallah went to a conference in France attended by many sectarian leaders—as well as the American ambassador. He was photographed shaking hands with the Maronite patriarch.[40] In 2006, Nasrallah made an unusual alliance with a former Maronite army general, Michel Aoun. They issued a detailed political agreement. Again, Hezbollah's language mellowed—at least on Lebanese issues.

The Shiite movement had a greater stake in a pure democratic vote—and ending confessional quotas—than any other party because of the surging Shiite numbers. For years, its platform reflected that preference. The Party of God had originally criticized the 1989 Taif Accord, which ended the civil war, for entrenching society's divisions in a revised quota system. Its 1996 election platform advocated abolishing sectarianism altogether, calling it Lebanon's "essential flaw."[41]

Yet a decade later, when I met him in the *dahiya,* Nasrallah sounded almost protective of the Christians and Lebanon's old confessional system.

"People have talked about abolishing political sectarianism and the confessional distribution of the three senior posts—president, prime minister and speaker of parliament—and also the number of ministries or parliamentary seats," he told me.

"This proposal frightens Christians because the numbers of Muslims are on the rise, and this means that the majority in parliament will then become Muslim—and will influence [parliament's] election of the president, the formation of the cabinet, and the speaker," he said. "And then perhaps Christians will feel that they don't have guarantees."

"In a nutshell," he added, "we are not working to abolish political sectarianism, not because we refuse the idea, but because it worries our partners in the homeland, the Christians."

Hezbollah had edged away from the idea of an Islamic republic.

In person, Nasrallah speaks calmly, not with the vibrancy of his public speeches. He holds steady eye contact, smiles slightly when he completes a thought, listens intently to translations, occasionally corrects his English interpreter, and seems at ease, engaging, even with an American. But when I asked Nasrallah if he hoped the Lebanese would someday, down the road, embrace Islam, adopt Sharia, or imitate Iran's theocracy, he shook his head and waved his hand dismissively.

"In Iran, ninety percent of the people are Muslims, the overwhelming majority of them Shiite—in spite of the fact that they come from different ethnic groups," he said. "So Iran has the basis and ability to have an Islamic regime or system.

"The situation in Lebanon is completely different, because it is made of different sects. So we believe the viable formula in our country is the democratic system—provided that it enables everybody to participate.

"In Lebanon," he added later, "there won't be an Islamic government."

Hezbollah's alliance with a Christian leader may not last. Lebanese politics is a kaleidoscope of constantly moving pieces that retain their colors and shapes but form totally different pictures with the tiniest motion. Yet in making its first alliance, the Party of God was immersed in Lebanon's distinctly unholy politics—and some realpolitik.

"When you are in the streets, you have certain calculations," Nasrallah had said in the same speech addressing the Danish cartoons. "And when you are in the state you should have different responsibilities, and that is why you should have different calculations."[42]

When we spoke, Nasrallah acknowledged the potential limitations of merging political agendas with a Christian party—or any other group.

"I admit that partnership would mean things move a little bit slowly. But any single-handedness could lead to injustice and the destruction of the country," he reflected, pulling his hands together from the sides of his robes over his chest.

"In other words," he said, "to move slowly is better than creating a national problem or putting an important part of the Lebanese population outside the government."

The reality of governing may have influenced Hezbollah's shifts. In its first year, the one ministry Hezbollah controlled was not performing well. Electricity shortages still continued for up to ten hours a day in some areas. The state agency ran a whopping 800-million-dollar deficit. And hundreds of its workers went on strike over health insurance. The luster of a victorious resistance movement was wearing off.

Hezbollah was proving to be no government of God.[43]

The Daily Star, the popular Beirut newspaper, warned in 2006 that Hezbollah risked "joining the ranks of those described in Lebanese parlance as 'cheese-eaters,' those who scavenge on the state with the sole aim of carving out a piece of the pie for their sectarian communities."[44]

Yet Hezbollah had become integrated. It had a fully developed political wing, and it had taken a place in Lebanon's fragile democracy. The evolution, however, was far from complete. Its policies were tortuously two-faced. Hezbollah was both part of the state and outside it. It retained its own private army, and it crafted its own defiant foreign policy.

Nasrallah once admitted reading the memoirs of two Israeli prime ministers—Ariel Sharon's *Warrior: An Autobiography* and Benjamin Netanyahu's *A Place Under the Sun.* But in his public language, he still treated Israel as a historic hiccup, a temporary aberration.

"We face an entity that conquered the land of another people, drove them out of their land, and committed horrendous massacres," Nasrallah told Egyptian television two weeks after Israel's withdrawal in 2000. "As we see it, this is an illegal state. It is a cancerous entity and the root of all crises and wars and cannot be a factor in bringing about a true and just peace in this region."[45]

A few months later, he boasted, "We have liberated the south. Next we'll liberate Jerusalem."

Hezbollah's jihadist cult continued to recruit potential suicide bombers. Shops in the *dahiya* sold Hezbollah videos of previous attacks, while T-shirts were imprinted with martyrs' faces. Little boys marched in Hezbollah parades wearing bands around their heads—in green, black, or red, each inscribed with a Koranic verse—as potential future martyrs. Toy stores sold miniature tanks and guns with the Hezbollah logo.

After two Israeli invasions, Nasrallah claimed that his militia provided a defense capability that no other force could provide. "The Israeli Air Force could destroy the Lebanese army within hours, or within days, but it cannot do this with us," Nasrallah told me. "We don't have a classical presence. We exercise guerilla warfare....Lebanon still needs the formula of popular resistance."

Along the fifty-mile border, tensions remained high after 2000. Hezbollah launched sporadic attacks against Israeli troops, mainly around Shebaa Farms. It fired at Israeli overflights as their sonic booms cracked the sound barrier. And twice, Hezbollah launched unmanned drone spy planes over Israel's northern Galilee. To beef up Hezbollah's military capabilities, Iran secretly shipped even more potent arms, including missiles with a much longer range than the old Katyushas.

I asked Nasrallah about Iran's arms supplies, noting international alarm about Hezbollah's deadly arsenal. He smiled coyly.

"At the military level, there is an expression: 'The pen broke,' meaning this issue is not open for discussion," he told me. "Because if I say there is no military cooperation, they are not going to believe me. But if I say there is military cooperation, this will be harmful. Therefore I leave this issue. It is possible we can talk about it in the future."

I told Nasrallah I was leaving Lebanon in a couple of days.

He smiled again. "By the future," he said, "I mean, maybe, in twenty years."

Yet Hezbollah operations during the third phase were noticeably limited—defying predictions of a hot new guerrilla war along the border, the kind the Palestinians had fought.[46] An Israeli think-tank assessment concluded that Hezbollah seemed in no rush to liberate Jerusalem, that it had deliberately "circumscribed" operations to avoid massive Israeli retaliation, and that it had even blocked plans by Palestinian cells still operating from refugee camps in Lebanon to fire across the border. Hezbollah's focus was primarily deterring Israel, it concluded, not destroying the Jewish state.[47]

Nawaf al Musawi, Hezbollah's burly external-relations chief, put it a different way. "This is the new Cold War."

Hezbollah's strategy was partially produced by the international reaction to the 2001 terrorist attacks on the World Trade Center and the Pentagon. Osama bin Laden's operation forced the Lebanese movement for the first time to publicly define itself on terrorism—and to differentiate itself from al Qaeda.

Hezbollah TV initially reported that the suicide hijackings were the work of Israeli agents, not al Qaeda. The story, based on widespread rumor in the region, alleged that Israel had tipped off some four thousand Jews employed at the World Trade Center, so they would not report to work on September 11.

But Nasrallah soon shifted gears. He issued a communiqué condemning the attack on the World Trade Center. He publicly called it a "barbarity" that contradicted the teachings of Islam.[48]

Shortly after September 11, he also assembled a group of Lebanese not in his movement. Among them was Jamil Mrowe, publisher of *The Daily Star,* a former Nieman Fellow at Harvard, and a Shiite. Mrowe is a handsome man with a full head of silvering hair who likes a good scotch or two, can talk a blue streak, and has been my friend for more than two decades. He recounted the meeting called to analyze the impact of September 11 and what it meant for Hezbollah.

Mrowe was blunt with the leadership about its rhetoric and mission.

"I told them that no one starts a restaurant in order for it to close. Everyone wants to succeed, including their endeavor," he told me over dinner at a renovated café on the old Green Line that once divided Christian and Muslim militias. "I told them: 'Let us imagine you win your war with Israel. You will have millions of Jews on your hands. What do you do with them? Kill them?'

"Two people sprang up and said, 'Do you not know our religion? How can you even say that? These [Jews] are people of the Book!'" Mrowe recalled, shaking his head.

"If they want to play that game, they have to take that responsibility," he added. "And that kind of recognition of religion was not reflected in their political positions."

During our meeting a few days later at his headquarters, I also asked Nasrallah about Hezbollah's attitude about September 11—and what circumstances or causes justified violence.

"To give a very clear answer, in any war or ongoing battle, you need to distinguish between those who are partners in the war against me and those who have nothing to do with this war," he replied. "There is the division criterion—partner, accomplice, or innocent."

On September 11, he applied the distinction. "What do the people who worked in those two towers, thousands of employees, women and men, have to do with war that is taking place in the Middle East? Or the war that Mr. George Bush may wage on people in the Islamic world?" Nasrallah said. "Therefore we condemned this act—and any similar act we condemn."

"But not the attack on the Pentagon?" I asked him.

Nasrallah paused. "I said nothing about the Pentagon, meaning we remain silent. We neither favored nor opposed that act," he said.

In the West, al Qaeda and Hezbollah are often lumped together as violent Islamist groups. Both were put on the State Department's list of terrorist groups—Hezbollah in 1997, al Qaeda in 1999. Both have ideological roots in religion, use identical terrorist tactics, and hate the United States and Israel. But they are hardly identical. The Sunni-Shiite divide also runs deep between the two movements, igniting public friction.

The al Qaeda leader in Iraq, Abu Musab al Zarqawi, condemned Hezbollah as the "enemy of the Sunnis" in a videotape message released just days before he was killed in an American air strike in 2006. Zarqawi accused the Shiite movement of protecting Israel from Palestinian attacks—which in fact, and ironically, it did. Hezbollah wanted to control the conflict on its own border on its own terms. It sent aid and arms to Hamas for operations in the Palestinian territories. One major weapons shipment was discovered in transit via Jordan, Hezbollah officials told me. But the militia did not want Palestinians operating again from Lebanese soil. Underneath the common enemy were different national loyalties. So Hezbollah restrained militant cells in Lebanon's Palestinian refugee camps.

Nasrallah also loathed Osama bin Laden.

The Hezbollah leader needed no prompting to talk about al Qaeda and its Afghan allies, the Taliban. "We do not endorse the method of bin Laden, and many of the operations that al Qaeda carried out we condemned very clearly," he told me. "We disagree with bin Laden at the intellectual level, theoretical level, practical level, and also on priorities.... We are two completely different movements.

"That's why since the beginning of Hezbollah and the beginning of al Qaeda there has never been any contact between us and them," he said.

And the Taliban, Nasrallah continued at a determined clip, was "the worst, the most dangerous thing that this Islamic revival has encountered. The Taliban presented a very hideous example of an Islamic state."

I asked Nasrallah how his criterion on violence applied to Iraq. The Hezbollah leader did not always take stereotypical positions.

Iraq's breakup into sectarian pieces, he said, would create a new model of collapse, internecine fighting, sedition, and divisions for the entire Middle East. "The most popular project today in Iraq, unfortunately, is federalism or separation," he had lamented in a speech broadcast on Hezbollah TV. "Everyone wants to live alone and to stay away from his brother in the Iraqi homeland."[49] Yet when we spoke, he also did not want American troops to remain to hold Iraq together. Any foreign presence on Muslim land was wrong—and justified violent resistance.

"The Iraqis have the right to fight any occupation force, American or non-American. But should they fight or should they not fight? This is something to be decided by the Iraqis themselves," Nasrallah said.

At the same time, he pronounced, doing harm to the innocent was forbidden.

"To have Iraqis confronting the occupation army, this is natural. But if there are American tourists, or intellectuals, doctors, or professors, people who have nothing to do with this war, they are innocent, even though they are Americans," he told me. "It is not acceptable to harm them."

In 2004, Hezbollah issued a communiqué condemning the beheading of American contractor Nicholas Berg by al Qaeda in Iraq as a "despicable act" that did "grave damage to Islam and the Muslims."[50]

The day before we spoke in 2006, a suicide bomber had detonated himself at the entrance of a Tel Aviv fast-food restaurant during the busy lunch hour, killing eleven and wounding more than sixty innocent civilians. The bomb was laced with nails and other projectiles; the injuries were particularly gruesome. Islamic Jihad, an Iranian-backed group, claimed credit.

I asked Nasrallah how he applied his metric on civilians to Israelis. He replied that the issue was "complicated."

"It is our opinion that in Palestine, women and children need to be avoided in any case," he said. "But it came after more than two months of daily Israeli killing of Palestinians, and the destruction of houses and schools, and the siege that is imposed on the Palestinians.

"There is no other means for the Palestinians to defend themselves," he said. "That is why I cannot condemn this type of operation in occupied Palestine."

Nasrallah's aides tried to end the interview several times. Each time one of two aides interjected or pointed to their watches, he nodded, and then he continued. He had spoken for almost two hours, and it was almost ten P.M.

Nasrallah had one last issue he wanted to talk about—America's push for democracy in the Islamic world. He brought it up. For the first time, he ruminated, at length. To talk about democracy and freedoms for the Arab world was "lovely," he began. But then he asked, rhetorically, if Washington understood the long-term damage when it did not recognize the results—or tried to undermine the parties elected if they were not American allies.

"Your administration says it is assisting the democratic process in our countries, but it has to respect the results of this process," he said.

"After the Palestinian elections, in my opinion, the American administration made a historic mistake. The Palestinian people have chosen Hamas, and the American administration is punishing all the Palestinian people because they elected Hamas," he said. "Now the Palestinian people are being starved, besieged, and subjected to huge pressures.

"What will the result be?" he said. Almost certainly, he answered, even greater support for Hamas.

"In the longer run, the real democratic process in our countries will often produce, will bring into being, governments that will be Islamist," he said. "But you can have mutual respect and ties with them."

And then he was ready to go. He offered to answer further questions at another time, but he said he still had work to do. Then he got up, offered a polite nod instead of a handshake, and walked across the long room past all the faux-brocade couches, his robes swaying. His security detail asked that I stay until Nasrallah had left.

When I drove out of the *dahiya* that night, most of the lights were out for blocks in all directions. A few generators rumbled noisily in the distance.

During political transitions, vacuums are often filled, at least initially, by those who get there first.

Hezbollah's fourth phase began on July 12, 2006, a scorching hot summer day along the dusty Lebanese-Israeli border. At 9:05 A.M., as Hezbollah fired rockets in other directions to divert attention, a band of Shiite guerrillas scrambled across the fortified security fence into Israel's northern farmland. The militants found their target on a secluded stretch of road near a peach orchard. In a lightning strike on the small Israeli border patrol, they fired rockets that blew up two Israeli military Humvees, killed three Israeli troops, and wounded two other soldiers.

The Hezbollahis then nabbed the two injured Israelis—Ehud Goldwasser and Eldad Regev, both army reservists on their last day of duty—and fled back across the border. Once on Lebanese soil, the Shiite militants shed their fatigues, bundled the wounded Israelis into cars, and sped off.[51]

The raid changed Hezbollah—and the Middle East.

The attack should not have come as a total surprise. Five months earlier, Nasrallah had publicly promised to free prisoners held by Israel in 2006—a vow made at the annual Ashura commemoration of Hussein's death.[52] The issue of prisoners and long-term detainees—whose offenses ranged from murdering Israeli children to being in the wrong place at the wrong time when Israel carried out its own abductions inside Lebanon—was always wrapped up in the Shiite sense of injustice.

A few hours after the raid, Nasrallah appeared at a hastily organized press conference in the *dahiya*. "This is the only way to shed light on the suffering of ten thousand Lebanese, Palestinian, and Arab detainees in Israeli prisons... after diplomatic means, political discussions, the international community's interventions, and organizations failed to release them."

Operation Faithful Promise—hatched a year earlier, planned for five months—was not the first scheme to force a prisoner swap. Hezbollah had done it before.

In 1998, Israel had turned over sixty Lebanese prisoners and the corpses of forty Hezbollah fighters—including Nasrallah's son, nine months after his death—in exchange for the remains of one Israeli soldier.

In 2000, another Hezbollah cross-border raid had seized three Israeli soldiers, who all died during the operation. In 2004, Nasrallah had swapped their bodies, along with an Israeli businessman who had been in Lebanon under questionable circumstances, in return for 400 Palestinian prisoners, twenty-nine prisoners from other Arab nations, and the bodies of sixty Lebanese guerrillas.

But Israel still held more than 9,000 Palestinians and an unknown number of Lebanese, including three prisoners that Hezbollah particularly wanted.[53] So the Shiite movement organized another raid for another big swap.

Hezbollah claimed that it did not want to fight Israel. "That is not our intention," Nasrallah told reporters. "We committed to calm all this time, despite all the circumstances. The only exception—and I told some political leaders about it—is imprisonment. We will not forget, ignore, or postpone this suffering.... [But] if the Israelis are considering any military action to bring the hostages home, they are delusional, delusional, delusional."

Nasrallah miscalculated—grossly.

Israel struck back, instantly and ferociously. It unleashed the most punishing artillery, air and naval assault on Lebanon in almost a quarter century. On the first day alone, its warplanes hit Hezbollah missile launchers and military sites in southern Lebanon. It bombed roads and bridges across the nation, along borders, and in between cities to cut off Hezbollah's fighters and resupply attempts. It struck power stations, television transmission centers, and Beirut International Airport. Within hours, Lebanon was cut off from the outside world. Israel also sent troops back into Lebanon for the first time since 2000.

Israel wanted more than its two soldiers. The government of Prime Minister Ehud Olmert, in office only three months, decided to use Nasrallah's mistake to eliminate his militia as a threat—and perhaps eliminate it altogether. Preferably, that included Nasrallah. Since 1997, Israel had kept a small DNA sample from Nasrallah's son—in case it was ever needed to identify his father's body.[54]

"It seems like we will go to the end now," Israeli Ambassador Daniel Ayalon told me. "We will not go part way and be held hostage again. We'll have to go for the kill—Hezbollah neutralization."

Nasrallah went into hiding. Two days later, the Hezbollah chief abandoned his offer of calm. "The battle today is no longer one of prisoners," Nasrallah said in a recorded audio message that was relayed across a crackling telephone line to a Beirut television station. "You wanted an open war, let it be an open war. Your government wanted to change the rules of the game, let the rules of the game change."

The sixth modern Middle East conflict had erupted.

The dynamics of this war were different than any other in the Middle East, especially Israel's previous thrusts into Lebanon. Its 1978 and 1982 invasions had targeted a secular Palestinian guerrilla movement made up of outsiders no longer welcome in much of Lebanon. Yasser Arafat's troops were predominantly Sunni, with a smattering of Christians. The fight had its roots in the creation of Israel in 1948 and the conquest of Arab territory in 1967. The battle was between rival nationalisms over a piece of land.

The 2006 conflict, in contrast, played into fourteen centuries of Shiite history and their sense of minority persecution. Israel this time was targeting the most popular Lebanese political and military force on its own turf. The fight pitted one religion against another. And the issues were existential.

"You don't know who you're fighting today," Nasrallah warned.

"You're fighting the children of the Prophet Mohammed, Ali and Hussein and all the Prophet's household. You're fighting people who have faith.

"The surprises I promised," he added, "will begin, from now."

And then Hezbollah launched its own punishing counterstrikes with missiles and rockets from the vast arsenal Iran and Syria had supplied over the previous six years. Nasrallah had at least 12,000 missiles at his disposal.

For the first time, Israeli civilians bore the brunt of an Israeli war. The entire northern quarter of Israel was vulnerable. Haifa came under irregular missile attack. Hundreds of thousands of Israelis were under fire. Many fled; others spent days in shelters. Hezbollah even hit an Israeli warship, deployed off Lebanon's coast as part of a naval blockade, with a sophisticated radar-guided missile.

Just as surprising, however, were Hezbollah's ground forces.

"We are not a regular army, and we will not fight like a regular army," Nasrallah said in another of his periodic broadcasts during the war.

Yet Hezbollah was also no longer a ragtag group of suicide bombers and individual cells based around neighborhoods and extended families. The Shiite force was well trained, well organized and surprisingly well stocked.

Hezbollah fighters had Russian antitank weapons to pierce Israel's most advanced tanks. They had body armor, night-vision gear, mortars, and rocket-propelled grenades. They had satellite communications to coordinate attacks and command scattered forces. They drove mobile Katyusha rocket-launching platforms from place to place on the back of GMC trucks. They had teams of scouts with walkie-talkies who zipped around on motorbikes. They had "listening rooms" with equipment to eavesdrop on Israeli communications. They even had Israeli uniforms, complete with Hebrew lettering, for decoys.

Hezbollah troops had trained from purloined American and Israeli military manuals, with particular attention paid to the Vietnam War. They constructed a network of bunkers and tunnels to hide themselves and their missiles. One bunker, near the border town of Maroun al-Ras, was more than twenty-five feet deep. It was connected to a network of tunnels complete with a camera at the entrance, several storage rooms, and many emergency exits.[55]

Elusive Hezbollah proved hard to find, much less defeat. To the surprise even of the Lebanese, it had become the most effective guerrilla force in the world.

"If you're waiting for a white flag coming out of the Hezbollah bunker, I can assure you it won't come," Israeli Brigadier General Ido Nehushtan told reporters during a wartime briefing. "They will go all the way."

Israel's overwhelming air superiority—a full array of warplanes, bombers, helicopter gunships, and unmanned drones—had been key to every earlier victory against the Arabs. In the 1967 war, Israel defeated three conventional armies, which had well over 100,000 troops and sophisticated armor and artillery, in a mere six days. In 1973, air power pushed back the Arabs' initial gains on the ground. In 1982, Israeli air power gutted Syria's air force, while Palestinian guerrillas simply abandoned positions under air attack. One of the many tongue-in-cheek T-shirts that appeared in Beirut during that summer war launched by Israeli Prime Minister Menachem Begin read, BEGIN AND THE JETS, APPEARING NIGHTLY, IN SUPER-SONIC SOUND. Protected by air power, Israeli troops blitzed to within ten miles of Beirut in less than two days, surrounding the capital and laying siege for ten weeks, until Arafat finally agreed to put his troops on ships that took them to new places in distant exile.

In 2006, Israeli air power was again impressive. Over thirty-four days, Israel hit more than 7,000 targets in little Lebanon. Air strikes left Lebanon's infrastructure tattered. More than 15,000 housing units were destroyed. Dozens of southern villages were scarred, charred, and left without electricity and water. Damage was estimated by the United Nations at up to ten billion dollars.

The *dahiya* was particularly ravaged. Satellite photographs of the area before the war showed a dense labyrinth of tall buildings. A week later, whole blocks had been flattened into vacant patches. The Hezbollah headquarters where I had met Nasrallah three months earlier—and the entire security zone around it—were reduced to heaping piles of concrete rubble.

"We've decided to put an end to this saga," said Israeli cabinet minister Isaac Herzog.

Yet in 2006, Israeli air power failed to scare Hezbollah or stop its missiles. For thirty-four days, Hezbollah did more than survive. It returned fire, pounding northern Israel with almost 4,000 missiles—an average of more than 100 per day. And the number did not diminish. The last day of the war was the heaviest—almost 250 Hezbollah missiles slammed into the biblical Galilee.

Israeli ground troops, who outnumbered Hezbollahis by at least ten to one inside Lebanon, had mixed results as well. They were stuck fighting in towns only a few miles inside the border. Rather than advance deeper, units often retreated after blowing up or clearing out suspected military sites. And it was often slow going. CNN correspondent Anderson Cooper went embedded on one mission that was supposed to take three hours, but lasted fourteen. "We moved inch by inch," he told me.

It was the longest war Israel ever fought. Israel had to constantly adjust its military strategy—and lower its expectations. And, in the end, Israel's tank-led assault was unable to gain control over a border buffer zone.

In the sixth war, Israel was not invincible. Israel's aura as the Middle East's lone impregnable power was shattered.

Rubbing propaganda salt in the military wound was Hezbollah TV. Its headquarters was leveled. Its mountaintop relay towers were felled. Yet the station remained on the air throughout the war, broadcasting Nasrallah's stream of speeches to his supporters and the outside world over and over again.

At best, Israel fought to a draw. At worst, it achieved few of its goals. Israel lost almost 120 soldiers in only five weeks—a staggering loss compared with 900 troops killed in the eighteen years of its Lebanon occupation. Hezbollah was weakened, but hardly eliminated or disarmed. It still had at least one half of its missile arsenal.

"I say this to the Israelis, there is no point of your blockade on the borders, ports, and airport, because our conduct throughout the war was based on our assumption that we are headed for a destructive, tough, and long battle, so what we have used is only a minute percentage of what we had assembled," Nasrallah said shortly after the war ended.

"Some people like to categorize this as a psychological war, and I admit that I engage in them," he said. "But even during psychological wars, I don't throw out lies."[56]

Israel also did not win immediate release of its two captured soldiers. A year later, they were still in Hezbollah's hands.

Politically, Prime Minister Olmert's new government paid a huge price. The initial overwhelming enthusiasm for the war slipped steadily. In a sharp public rebuke, a survey one week after the war found sixty-three percent of Israelis wanted Olmert to resign.[57] A year later, Olmert's support had plummeted to less than three percent.

For Hezbollah, the standard of success was much lower. Without an air force, naval fleet, or tank corps, Nasrallah never claimed that Hezbollah could defeat Israel.

"I don't want to raise expectations," he said in the early days of the war. "I never said that the Israelis cannot reach any place in southern Lebanon. Our dogma and strategy is that when the Israelis come, they must pay a high price. This is what we promise, and this is what we will achieve, God willing."

To survive, in some ways, was to come out ahead. Wars in the Middle East are often good for extremists.

Despite public fury over the destruction of a country only recently rebuilt, the vast majority of Lebanese said they supported the Shiite movement. A survey by the Beirut Center for Research & Information during the war found a staggering eighty-seven percent supported Hezbollah's attacks on northern Israel.[58] In a banner front-page headline, *An Nahar* declared the fighting to be "The War of All Lebanon." A front-page editorial concluded, "It has united the Lebanese in position and word, instead of dividing them and sowing dissent among them, as some may have hoped."[59]

During the war, Lebanese Prime Minister Fuad Siniora publicly thanked Hezbollah for its "sacrifices." He specifically praised Nasrallah. "We are in a strong position, and I thank the sayyid for his effort," said Siniora, a Sunni.

After the war, Defense Minister Elias Murr, a Christian, said on national television that the Lebanese Army would not disarm "the resistance," as Hezbollah prefers to be called. Despite the conflict's huge costs, another survey found only one half of the Lebanese wanted Hezbollah to disarm.

Yet for Lebanon, Hezbollah's daring raid into Israel also produced mass ruin and endangered a fragile internal peace. One million people—one quarter of the entire population—were forced to flee. Some 1,200 died, with thousands injured and maimed. The vast majority were civilians, including many children. Tourists disappeared, and the already troubled economy withered.

For Hezbollah, its miscalculation carried huge costs. Operation Faithful Promise basically sacrificed the movement's long-term military strategy. Its secret arsenal and troop capabilities were exposed. The element of tactical surprise was lost. Its deterrent capability was weakened. Most important, it was also a war that Hezbollah could only fight once without losing serious support at home—and this had not been the moment of its choosing. The Party of God lost an important edge it might have had, or needed, down the road.

The Hezbollah chief also became a permanently wanted man, permanently in hiding. "There is only one solution for Nasrallah," a senior Israeli military official told *The New York Times:* "This man must die."[60] The Hezbollah chief dropped out of the national dialogue, he announced, so as not to endanger Lebanon's other leaders. When United Nations Secretary-General Kofi Annan visited Beirut to shore up the cease-fire, Nasrallah was nowhere in sight.

In the end, Nasrallah had to admit the raid had been a mistake.

"We did not think, even one percent, that the capture would lead to a war at this time and of this magnitude," he said two weeks after the war ended. "You ask me, if I had known on July 12...that the operation would lead to such a war, would I do it? I say no, absolutely not."[61]

The 2006 war marked the beginning of a new phase because it forced Hezbollah's hand. The Shiite movement still had many, maybe even most, of its weapons, but it was compelled to shift focus to the war's consequences; it had to try to dodge any lingering blame as the dust settled. To retain legitimacy in the postwar period, the movement became even more immersed in the conventional political and economic life of Lebanon. Its ambitions and hubris had to be checked.

The shift started even before the war ended. Under pressure from his mistake, Nasrallah took four decisions to end the war. In each, he had to defer to the Lebanese state, a marked change after two decades of often arrogant independence as a state within a state.

First, Hezbollah accepted the government's seven-point plan—including the principle of dismantling militias—as the basis for long-term peace. The movement still had plenty of pretexts to keep its arms. But it had to publicly embrace the idea of eventual disarmament, a principle to which at some point it could be held accountable.

Second, Hezbollah agreed to let the Lebanese Army deploy throughout its southern strongholds. Although Hezbollah's bright yellow flags still flew in many of the old stone villages in the south, Shiite fighters donned civilian clothes and moved their weapons out of sight. The atmospherics changed out of the wartime mode.

Third, Hezbollah accepted a United Nations resolution deploying 15,000 foreign troops to back up the Lebanese Army. It was the largest new deployment of foreign peacekeepers since American, French, Italian, and British troops were scared off by Hezbollah's bombings in 1984. And for the first time, the expanded United Nations mission would have the armament to fight any force that threatened it, including Hezbollah.

And finally, to avoid renewed warfare, Nasrallah held back Hezbollah fighters from attacking Israeli troops who remained in Lebanon. The quiet in Israel's encampments was a striking contrast to the violence during Israel's occupation.

Unannounced, Hezbollah also shut down fourteen positions around Shebaa Farms. Bulldozers moved in to seal entrances to tunnels and bunkers, while fighters removed missiles and artillery. Then they dismantled checkpoints.[62]

The turning point was apparent the day the war ended, at eight A.M. on August 14, just as abruptly as it had begun. Just hours after the United Nations cease-fire took hold, Nasrallah appeared on television to give the last and perhaps the most important of his nine wartime speeches. With meticulous precision, he detailed Hezbollah's plan to reconstruct Lebanon.

"You will not have to ask for anyone's help. You will not have to stand in lines or go anywhere," he promised people stranded in the cutoff south. "Today is the day to keep up our promises. All our brothers will be in your service starting tomorrow."

In a telling signal to his movement, Nasrallah added, "Completing the victory can come with reconstruction."

Within twenty-four hours, Hezbollah bulldozers were roaring down streets of the *dahiya* and southern towns, clearing away rubble. Trucks delivered crates of food—peppers and peaches, sardines and cheese, as well as "victory sweets." Trucks ferried in water.

Within two days, Hezbollah teams with clipboards were dispersed in southern towns doing house-to-house assessments, cataloging damage, knocking on doors to check on what people needed. In the *dahiya*, a high school was converted into a reconstruction center. Signs on the wall directed Lebanese who had lost their homes. One line was marked DAMAGED; the other, DESTROYED.

Within four days, Hezbollah was doling out $12,000—in crisp American bills—per household to pay for one year's rent and to buy what Nasrallah called "decent and suitable" furniture. With 15,000 destroyed housing units, the total was well over $150 million dollars just for compensation, before rebuilding even began. Lebanese officials rightly grumbled that Iranian largesse had provided the instant funds. Iranians rightly grumbled that they might get more attention to their own problems if they were living in Lebanon.

By the end of two weeks, Hezbollah had divided the *dahiya* into eighty-six zones. Each zone had a four-person engineering team assigned to develop plans for rebuilding.

Hezbollah's public-relations prowess was on full display. Massive piles of debris from bombed buildings were cordoned off with yellow crime-scene tape. Propped atop the ruins were big signs proclaiming DIVINE VICTORY—NO TRESPASSING and MADE IN THE USA. In a play on Nasrallah's name, a billboard proclaimed the war A VICTORY FROM GOD.

Meanwhile, the Lebanese government and the international community were still trying to get organized.

The imagery of military prowess and postwar political street smarts proved a powerful combination at home. Because of its postwar efficiency, Hezbollah's profile evolved yet again.

Even Israel and the United States had to accept, reluctantly, that Hezbollah would remain a political player in Lebanon. The United States backed Israel's right to defend itself with punishing air strikes, but Secretary of State Condoleezza Rice told me and other reporters traveling with her in the Middle East during the war that Washington acknowledged Hezbollah would remain a legitimate political force in Lebanon.

"To the extent that it remains a political group, it will be acceptable to Israel," Israeli ambassador Daniel Ayalon also told me during the war. "A political group means a party that is engaged in the political system in Lebanon, but without terrorism capabilities and fighting capabilities. That will be acceptable to Israel."

The impact of Hezbollah's war may have been even greater outside Lebanon. The party—whose members came from Islam's often-scorned second sect, and from one of the region's smallest countries—vaulted into a position unimaginable a few weeks earlier.

In 2000, after an eighteen-year war against Israeli occupation, Hezbollah had emerged as a legitimate player inside Lebanon. In 2006, after a thirty-four-day war against Israel, Hezbollah became a legitimate player in the wider Middle East. The Lebanon conflict jolted public thinking about the broader issues of contemporary leaders and political systems.

Nasrallah emerged as an unlikely regional champion. In newspaper editorials, political commentaries, and blogs, he was compared with almost mystical reverence to Egypt's Gamal Abdel Nasser and Iran's Ayatollah Khomeini, the two leaders who had redefined the region's political direction.

"Israel has just set Nasrallah on a trajectory to become the hero of the Arab world," said my friend Jamil Mrowe, the Shiite editor opposed to Hezbollah.

The Lebanon war came at a critical juncture in the Middle East. It erupted during a summer of discontent—as Iraq crumbled, Syria cracked down, Egypt increasingly inched toward dynastic rule, the Palestinians remained politically deadlocked and under virtual siege, and democracy regionwide seemed to be ever more elusive.

Posters of Nasrallah, many of them wall-size, went up all over the

Middle East. Men and women were photographed kissing them. More than 120 babies in the Egyptian port city of Alexandria were named Nasrallah during the war.[63] Young women on blog sites pined about marrying the Shiite cleric's sons. On the West Bank, pendant necklaces with little Nasrallah pictures became the new fashion chic. And in several countries, Nasrallah T-shirts became the new political chic.

The Hezbollah chief was the subject of instant odes and ballads. In Egypt, satellite music channels played the new hit tribute by Shaaban Abdul Rahim: "O Hassan! O Nasrallah! We are behind you and will not leave you." A Palestinian band, once limited largely to the wedding circuit, gained instant fame off its song in praise of Nasrallah, entitled "The Hawk of Lebanon."

"The last thing I expected is to fall in love with a turbaned cleric," Howeida Taha, a Sunni, an Egyptian, and a secular columnist, wrote in the *Al-Quds al Arabi* newspaper about the leader of Lebanon's Shiite movement. "I don't like them, and of course they will never like somebody like me.... [But] I feel I've been searching for Nasrallah with my eyes, heart, and mind. I feel Nasrallah lives within me."[64]

Across the Sunni world, the Shiite leader was feted—at least temporarily uniting Islam's two rival sects like little else in their fourteen centuries. Sunni protesters from Tunisia to Pakistan, Nigeria to Kuwait, took to the streets waving Nasrallah's photograph. It was far from a unanimous sentiment, particularly in conservative Sunni sheikhdoms like Saudi Arabia. Yet some powerful Sunni clerics issued fatwas endorsing Hezbollah. In Egypt, Grand Mufti Ali Gomaa's edict defended its fight, and the popular scholar Sheikh Yousef al Qaradawi called support of Hezbollah forces "a religious duty of every Muslim."[65]

Even al Qaeda tried to jump on the bandwagon. Just a few months after its Iraq branch had condemned Hezbollah, Osama bin Laden's deputy praised the Shiite movement in a videotape broadcast on al Jazeera. He may have sensed a shifting tide. Al Qaeda had accomplished nothing useful for the Arab world. Indeed, bin Laden had cost the Arabs politically, financially, socially—with no gains for the one cause at the heart of Arab despair.

In contrast, Nasrallah had been able to punish if not defeat Israel. And he had nourished a hungry loneliness. Hezbollah filled a void.

"The reason is not ideology but psychology—a basic human need for self-respect and affirmation," said Rami Khouri, the columnist for Beirut's *The Daily Star* newspaper. "Three generations of Arabs have endured painful humiliation at the combined hand of Israel and the West. Five major wars all ended in defeat. The false and cruel promise of peace talks withered just as regularly."

Khouri is no Hezbollah sympathizer. He is Christian Palestinian. He graduated from Syracuse University and is a sports fanatic so devout that, in the middle of the Lebanon war, he e-mailed me his bet that the Yankees would beat the Mets in the 2006 World Series by four games to two.

Yet in the same e-mail, he also predicted that the outcome of the Lebanon war would have a bigger impact than the 1967 conflict—when Israel redrew the region's map by capturing big chunks of Egypt, Syria, and Jordan.

The 2006 war again had redefined political patterns in the Middle East, Khouri warned. "Almost overnight, Nasrallah produced what three generations of ordinary Arabs have yearned for: military effectiveness instead of haplessness, political empowerment instead of marginalization, and resistance instead of forced submission to Israeli and American threats. A new man, indeed, responding to a stubborn need among all Arab societies."

Every Middle East war has had its political casualties—toppling kings and producing coups. Following the pattern, the chasm between rulers and the ruled clearly deepened during the Lebanon war. The leaders of Egypt, Saudi Arabia, and Jordan initially criticized Hezbollah for provoking a conflict, but then their own streets turned on them.

Egypt witnessed almost daily protests. In Cairo, where a public gathering of more than five people requires a permit, more than 1,000 demonstrators carried a large banner warning, ARAB MAJESTIES, EXCELLENCIES, AND HIGHNESSES, WE SPIT ON YOU. Most rallies condemned President Mubarak. In an overwhelmingly Sunni country, Egyptians carried posters of Lebanon's Shiite leader—and took off their shoes to shake at their own government. Another protest featured a large poster of the Egyptian leader with a Star of David drawn on his forehead. THE ENEMY OF THE EGYPTIAN PEOPLE, it read underneath.[66]

Regimes soon changed their tunes. "The Arab people see now in Hezbollah a hero facing Israel's aggression and defending their land," said Jordan's young King Abdullah. "This is a fact that the United States and Israel must realize: As long as there is aggression, there's resistance, and there's popular support for resistance."

Beyond the twenty-two Arab nations, the fifty-three countries in the Islamic bloc also felt the impact. An emergency meeting of Muslim leaders issued a joint statement calling for an immediate cease-fire. "This war must stop, or it will radicalize the Muslim world, even those of us who are moderate today," warned Indonesian President Bambang Yudhoyono. "From there, it will be just one step away to that ultimate nightmare: a clash of civilizations."

Every Middle East war has also produced unintended consequences. In one of his curious, rambling videotapes to al Jazeera, Osama bin Laden said in 2004 that he had originally been inspired to attack the United States because of Israel's 1982 invasion of Lebanon with American arms.

"When I saw those destroyed towers in Lebanon," he said, "it sparked in my mind that the oppressors should be punished in the same way and that we should destroy towers in America—so they can taste what we tasted and so they stop killing our women and children.... I could not forget those moving scenes, blood and severed limbs, women and children sprawling everywhere. Buildings were demolished over their residents' heads, rockets were raining down on homes without mercy... and the entire world saw and heard, but it did nothing."[67]

The Hezbollah war will also be a catalyst, with the impact still years from being fully felt or understood. "This war was crucial," Nasrallah told al Jazeera a few weeks after the war ended. "It was not about the fate of Hezbollah, but about the fate of Lebanon, Palestine, the Arabs, and the whole region."[68]

At the very least, the 2006 war spurred two phenomena that moved the center of political gravity in the region.

First, the war increased the already rising Shiite tide that began with Iran's 1979 revolution, grew with Hezbollah in Lebanon, and expanded after Saddam Hussein's ouster in 2003 brought the long-repressed Shiite majority to power in Iraq. Disgruntled but emboldened Shiites in the oil-rich kingdoms of Saudi Arabia, Kuwait, and Bahrain were also shaking up local politics.

In a conversation in 2004, Jordan's King Abdullah fretted about the emergence of a "Shiite crescent." An arc of Shiite-controlled regimes stretching across a strategic and oil-rich area, the Sunni monarch told me, would alter the regional political balance, heighten sectarian tensions, and Lebanonize other countries.[69]

A new wave of pan-Shiism seemed highly unlikely. Yet, once relegated to the margins of Arab politics, Shiites were clearly in political ascendance throughout the region. They were often the agents of change—of disparate kinds. There was also talk of a new "Shiite swagger" in their new found self-confidence.[70]

"For Shiites and the wider Arab world, Hezbollah has come out of the war as a symbol of resistance and defiance. Hezbollah did what governments could not do," Barham Salih, Iraq's deputy prime minister and a non-Arab Kurd, told me. "What it did for its own country was a disaster. But a lot of people, out of disgust at their own governments, now look to Hezbollah.

"I hate his politics, but I watch every speech Nasrallah gives," the Iraqi leader, who is a Sunni and avowedly pro-American, told me. "He's true to his word. He's not a thief. And he's successful at what he promises to do. This war really gave him a platform. He's now the most important icon in the region—in our era."

Second, among both major Muslim sects, the Hezbollah war inspired a shift from Arabism to Islamism, from rallying around national ideologies and identities to mobilizing around faith. It was a natural progression.

The 1967 war, which was fought in the name of pan-Arab nationalism, was the Arab world's most sweeping humiliation. Arabism, the root of all major ideologies as the region gained independence from European powers in the mid-twentieth century, also universally produced corrupt and despotic rule.

Islamism gradually became the alternative. In 1973, the Arab offensive against Israel was fought under a banner of Islam. The operation was named after the Prophet Mohammed's sword. The rallying cry was "God is great." It was the first war in which the Arabs performed well, albeit briefly.

Iran's 1979 revolution exploited an Islamic identity as the force unifying rival political trends to bring down a dynasty that had ruled for twenty-five centuries. The Persian upheaval had a wide spillover on the Arab world, including the creation of Hezbollah.

Over the next generation, in every country where they have taken root, Islamic parties gained ground. In 2005 and 2006, Hezbollah, the Muslim Brotherhood, and Hamas became major political fixtures through elections—no longer on the margins.

The Hezbollah war will further fuel that dynamic.

"Since 2000, Hezbollah hasn't known what its identity is," Michael Young, the Lebanese Christian analyst and columnist, told me during my trip to Beirut shortly before the war. "Deep down, Nasrallah thinks he is better than Lebanese politics.... And to a certain extent, he's right. To have to go into the pit with the rest of Lebanon's politicians is not something he relishes. He's inexperienced in sectarian bargaining. He's still learning.

"But more fundamentally, he has to figure out: Is he just a local leader, or is he a regional Che Guevera?" Young said.

After the 2006 war, Nasrallah emerged as both.

SIX

SYRIA

The Outlaws

*We have to go forward; we can't go back. But I am
worried about the price we will pay along the way.
We know nothing will be for free.*

—Syrian human rights lawyer Anwar al Bunni

*Under a government which imprisons any unjustly,
the true place for a just man is also a prison.*

—American philosopher Henry David Thoreau

The human toll in the struggle for political change is the
Middle East's most inspiring tragedy. Tales of hardship and
loss are often passed around only in whispers. Over the
next decade or two, the pace of change in the Middle East will be
determined in part by the democratic opposition's strength, ideas, and
increasing defiance. A regime's response will in turn indicate whether
it can be salvaged.

As the struggle intensifies, the human costs are certain to grow, in some cases exorbitantly. Yet the fledgling agents of change are a stubborn lot. Syria is a wrenching example.

Shortly before leaving for Syria, I went to the Beirut home of a Syrian dissident to view a homemade documentary, filmed secretly in Damascus, about Riad al Turk. Turk is the Old Man of Syrian opposition. Syrians call him their Nelson Mandela because of his noisy and unwavering resistance to authoritarian rule and his long incarceration. Turk was imprisoned four times, the total a bit shorter than Mandela's twenty-seven years. But the conditions were significantly tougher. Mandela at least had a trial.

The subtle film is about Turk's third prison stint. It's a two-man show, a conversation between the filmmaker, as he holds the camera, and Syria's most famous political prisoner. The film is called "Cousin"—Turk's nickname on the Syrian street.

Turk begins with characteristic irreverence. Shouldn't this film at least be managed by a qualified director?" he asks the filmmaker.

Born in 1930, Turk is a short man with thick glasses that magnify his eyes and his age. His hairline begins at the pate; his hair is a dull gray. The furrow in his brow and the lines astride his mouth are deeply rutted. He has heart and kidney ailments.

Turk's entire life has been about dissent. He has opposed virtually every form of government in Syria since its independence from France in 1946. His tactics were never violent; they usually involved speaking out, rallying opposition, or membership in banned political movements.

Turk was first imprisoned in 1952, when he was only twenty-two, shortly after finishing law school. The first stint was for opposing a military regime that came to power in a coup d'état. He was held for five months, and tortured. He was never tried.

His next arrest was in 1958. The second stint was for opposing the merger between Syria and Egypt—under the banner of pan-Arab unity—in the short-lived United Arab Republic. He was held for sixteen months, and repeatedly tortured. He was never tried.

But Turk's most costly dissent came during the rule of Hafez al Assad.

Assad was the former Air Force general who squeezed out rivals to win Syria's powerful defense ministry in 1966. In a bloodless coup in 1970, Assad then ousted President Nureddin al Atassi, who was the leader of Assad's own Baath Party. It was a coup from within; coups were the way Syrians dealt with politics even *within* a party.

In his last meeting with Assad and Atassi shortly before Syria's coup and his own death, Egyptian President Gamal Abdel Nasser reportedly mused, "Ah, you Baathists. You're so harsh with each other."[1] The ousted Atassi spent the rest of his life in prison. He, too, was never tried. He was finally released and allowed to go for medical treatment, basically to die, in France.

I watched the film in the Beirut apartment of the former president's son, Mohammed Ali Atassi. He was the filmmaker.

The confrontation between Turk and Assad lasted a lifetime. Both were stubborn men. Both were dogmatic. It was also telling of the political times that the new Syrian president was of peasant stock, the first in his family to complete either primary school or high school.[2] Assad was a socialist. His leading opponent was a man orphaned at the age of seven because his father died and his mother could not afford to keep all her children. Turk was a Marxist. Yet they were rivals.

Turk was fifty when Assad's secret police came to arrest him the third time in 1980. This time, he was held for almost eighteen years. It was all in solitary confinement. He was locked away in a windowless underground cell, about the length of his body or the size of a small elevator compartment, at an intelligence headquarters. Syria has more than one dozen intelligence agencies, so there are several headquarters. He was never charged with a crime. He was never tried. He never knew when it was going to end.

The film shifts back and forth between Turk's reflections on politics and prison, and silent pictures of him carefully laying down tiny dark objects, like dots, on a sheet. In an opening sequence, there are only a few dots. There is no explanation.

The film then switches to Turk's gravelly voiced recollections. He responds to the filmmaker's questions with succinct answers, without drama, adjectives, or laments. He mentions beatings, almost in passing, and the months of healing that followed. He recounts sleeping on a concrete floor without a bed. For the first decade, he never saw the sun or the sky or the outdoors. He was never allowed out of his cell to exercise. Until the final months, he was not allowed a book, newspaper, mail, or anything else to keep his mind occupied.

"Any man rots, gets sick, and wears out. That's what they wanted—to make me give up," he told the filmmaker. "They frankly told me that: 'You are here as a surety for the presidential palace.'"

Turk's only activity was being allowed three times a day to go to a shared toilet, always when no one else was in it. He used the brief breaks to scrounge in the toilet bin for clothing thrown away by other prisoners as his own wore out and winters set in.

The film switches back, briefly, to Turk laying down more tiny dots. They are now forming a line.

Turk's wife, Asma, was arrested the same month he was. They left two young daughters behind. Asma was held for two years, also without charges or a trial. Turk was not told when she was released after two years or what happened to his children. For the first thirteen years, he received no communication from family or friends. He had no idea what had happened to any of them or what was going on in the outside world.

The scene again switches momentarily to Turk silently hovering over his dots. A pattern is emerging.

The filmmaker asks how Turk survived with his sanity. By forgetting, Turk says.

"You lose the world where you used to live, your family, your party, your neighborhood, your friends. This world is gone, as if you were dead," he said. "I could do nothing but suffer and groan, and I didn't want to suffer and groan...I cut the bonds with the outside world so I didn't carry its suffering.... The only position I took was to resist."

Turk limited his focus. "I had only one mission, a unique mission, not to give to the regime anything that it could use against my party. No information. No political positions. You must accept hell as a price to pay for remaining faithful to your convictions, and that's what I did."

The film switches back to the tiny dots. A geometric pattern comes into focus.

As years passed, Turk began to suffer ailments. During dizzy spells, he sometimes called out to a passing jailer to let him breathe for a moment outside his airless cell. "The air in the hallway is cleaner than the one in the cell, even though the air of the hallway also stinks," he tells the filmmaker.

Syrian officials claim that Turk was offered a chance to go home if he signed a statement supporting the regime.

Asked by the filmmaker if he feels remorse in his choice, which effectively meant abandoning his daughters, Turk is unflinching.

"No, I fulfilled my duties. I'm not at all responsible for what happened, except if you believe that I had to sign or do what the regime wanted in order to return home. If that was what needed to be done, then I consider myself criminal towards my daughters," he says.

"But that's not what needed to be done," he adds. "On the contrary, I don't like empty speeches. I will not keep anything for myself. No fortune. Nothing. At least I will leave to them the name of a father with a good reputation. And this is the best thing a father can leave to his children."

At the end, the film switches back to the little dots. They now form a grand geometric design, intricate in the style of Middle Eastern architecture and artisan woodcraft. Turk explains: After repeatedly searching the garbage in the prison toilet for something to do, unsuccessfully, he turned to his food. The evening meal was often a thin soup with dark grain that failed to soften when cooked. Turk calls them his "little gravel."

"I found them while I was eating my soup. The black grain is hard," he says. "I thought about the time I was in school, where I used to like drawing."

Turk began collecting them and, for the better part of eighteen years, spent every day in his silent world crafting large pictures from the tiny kernels. Over eighteen years, Turk collected thousands of grains.

"The big picture I composed used to take me more than a day," he recalls. "At noon, I used to hope they didn't bring lunch because that meant I had to ruin everything to have a place to eat. You must stand up very fast, and I had no glue to stick them. I had to ruin everything and then build everything again.

"I was like the guy with the rock—the Sisyphus myth, isn't it?"

Turk says. In the Greek myth, Sisyphus's punishment was to be blinded and to have to repeatedly roll a giant boulder up a mountain to the peak, only to have it perpetually roll back down to the bottom. The tale was grist for Albert Camus' 1942 essay exploring the absurdities and follies of life.

Turk was released in 1998. But in the 2001 documentary, Turk tells the filmmaker that he still feels stuck in a prison. "Prison represents oppression, and oppression is still practiced in my country. Destroying that prison is a major goal on which the country's liberty depends. Prison is also made to scare people. People do whatever they can to avoid it. They shut themselves up."

With uncharacteristic restraint, Turk also said nothing publicly for three years after his release. Then President Assad succumbed to longstanding heart disease in 2000 after ruling for thirty years. In less than an hour, Syria's parliament amended the constitution to bring down the minimum age for the presidency from forty to thirty-four, so Assad's second son, Bashar, could take over.

When the documentary was shot in 2001, Turk tells Atassi that he is growing restless. "Rebellion is still the same," he says, "as if it were marked in me."

In August 2001, as the filmmaker was editing his documentary, Turk reappeared in public. Political activity is restricted under Syria's open-ended state of emergency, which was first imposed in 1963 when the Baath Party came to power. So Turk gave his first speech at a private home. Nevertheless, hundreds were willing to take the risk, including arbitrary imprisonment, to hear him.

In his talk, Turk dared to say publicly that the Syrian regime "relied on terror" to stay in power. He condemned the new form of "hereditary" rule passed from one Assad to another as "illegitimate." He called on the regime to move "from despotism to democracy." And he appealed to all opposition groups to reconcile their differences and unite in a common front. Ten days later, he made the same statements on al Jazeera, which beamed his remarks across the Arab world.[3]

On August 31, Turk suffered an embolism that partially paralyzed his arm. The next day, he set off to get medical help. Then he disappeared.

A week later, the state-controlled media ran a brief government statement:

> *Turk and other malevolent people have recently spared no efforts in their campaign to slander and vilify all those who oppose their opinions by leveling false charges against them, in an exposed attempt to extinguish the flame of modernization and development in all spheres.*
>
> *In view of Turk's persistence in his tendentious onslaught against the state, in an attempt to block the march of freedom and democracy, he was arrested and referred to justice.*

For the first time, Turk actually had a trial. In June 2002, he was sentenced to three years for "attempting to change the constitution by illegal means."

Turk was back in prison.

Change in the Middle East requires confronting some of the most obstinate ideologies that still exist in the twenty-first century.

The morning after I saw the film, I drove from Beirut to Damascus. The trip winds from the sunny Mediterranean coast up into the cloud-shrouded Lebanon Mountain range, then down into the verdant plains of the Bekaa Valley to the border. Damascus is just twenty minutes beyond the frontier. The lonely stretch of road between the two border posts is broken up, incongruously, by a big pink-and-orange sign beckoning travelers to stop at a Dunkin' Donuts.

The distance is the shortest between any two capitals in the region. For decades after their independence in the 1940s, Lebanese and Syrians said they were one people split up into two nations. But by 2006, the two cities were in worlds apart. Beirut is raucously open. Damascus is rigidly repressed.

Damascus is the world's oldest capital. Among Arab countries, it is the city richest with history, the closest rival to Jerusalem. The main street of sprawling Souq Hamidiyeh, a bazaar filled with the smell of pungent spices, artisan stalls, and craft-your-own-perfume shops, dates back to Roman times. The old walled city is still bisected by the bibli-cal "Street Called Straight," which, in fact, is not straight at all. Saul of Tarsus was converted on the road to Damascus, took the name Paul, founded the first organized church at Antioch in ancient Syria, and spent the rest of his life proselytizing the new Christianity. After Islam's birth in the Arabian desert, Damascus was the first foreign conquest by the Prophet Mohammed's troops; it became the capital of the first Islamic dynasty. The armies of King David, Alexander the Great, the European Crusaders, Tamerlane, and the Ottoman Turks are among the many others that have either tried or succeeded at taking this strate-gic city and adding to its layers of history.

In *Innocents Abroad,* Mark Twain observed, "No recorded event has occurred in the world but Damascus was in existence to receive news of it. Go back as far as you will into the vague past, there was always a Damascus.... She has looked upon the dry bones of a thousand empires and will see the tombs of a thousand more before she dies."

Syria still has illusions of greatness. It wants all roads in the region—to the Arabs' final peace with Israel, Iraq's stability, Lebanon's future, regional security, Arab political unity, even the war on terrorism—to lead through Damascus. The problem of self-importance is pervasive in a region that gave birth to so many great civilizations. Based on bygone eras, the big countries—particularly Egypt, Iraq, and Syria—made lofty assumptions about their capabilities when they gained inde-pendence. But the pretensions affect Damascus the most because it has become so passé.

Damascus in the twenty-first century is stuck in time. Since a mod-ern state was carved out of the old Ottoman Empire in a deal between France and Britain that chopped up the Middle East into its current borders, modern Syria has never quite figured out how to effectively rule itself.

The Levantine country, about the size of North Dakota with a mix of mountain and bleak desert terrain, was so coup-prone between independence in 1946 and the Assad coup in 1970 that Damascus went through twenty governments and eleven presidents. In the decade from 1946 to 1956, disparate governments drafted four distinct constitutions.

Between 1958 and 1961, Syria merged with Egypt in a short-lived experiment as the United Arab Republic. Damascus did not like being the junior partner. It seceded, and then flirted with Iraq for a few months in 1963 about a possible merger. That was the year the Baath Party first took over in both countries, just a month apart.

Baath means "resurrection" or "renaissance." Its essence was captured in "On the Way of Resurrection," the five-volume work by party cofounder Michel Aflaq. Baathism blended socialism and intense nationalism with a determination to achieve broader Arab unity—and Arab power. The message initially had wide appeal, sprouting branches in Iraq, Jordan, Lebanon, Libya, and Yemen. Its Syrian founders, educated in Europe, wanted to craft a progressive and secular party, somewhat in the spirit of modernizer Kemal Ataturk in neighboring Turkey, except with an Arab bent. The Baathist constitution, passed in 1973, blended French, Turkish, and Islamic laws.

Hafez al Assad initially made a difference. He built highways and hospitals to give old Syria a new infrastructure. He improved access to education, focused on the plight of peasants, and used new oil money from Gulf countries to industrialize and subsidize basic commodities. The ambitious Euphrates Dam project was launched to bring electricity, irrigation, and development to the countryside. A building boom made Damascus an increasingly modern capital; its population quadrupled during the first two decades of Assad's rule.[4]

But Baathism fell short—chronically short.

Most of Assad's grand projects were haphazardly planned or poorly executed. The dam was a technical calamity. Modernization was exploited by corrupt middlemen, who gained far more than the people it was to help. Industrialization was not industrious enough to spur enduring economic growth. Syria had more schools, but education remained abysmal; books, reading, and the quest for knowledge did not become part of popular culture, as they were in Cairo and Baghdad. Society's growth was stunted; development stalled. Drought, the bills of war with Israel, and fluctuating oil prices did not help.

When I first went to Damascus in 1981, I was struck by the Mediterranean flavor of a developing city that was the western flank of the Orient. But by 2006, Damascus seemed drably outdated and in need of a coat of paint, exhaust emission standards, road crews, and an extreme makeover. It reminded me of a mix of three cities: Dirty Cairo, but without Egypt's charm and intellectual fervor; the planned capital of Brasilia, a city stamped of a now-dated era; and any medium-size East European capital after the Soviets got their hands on it.

Syria's ambitious goals in the region faced a similar fate.

Assad means "lion," and the Syrian leader always considered himself to be the conscience of the Arab world—the Lion of Damascus, as he was known. He wanted a deal with Israel that would ensure a long-term balance of power in the Middle East; he wanted no part of compromises that would give Israel an edge over the Arabs. Assad viewed Egypt's peace treaty as a selfish sellout, and he did not trust the Palestinians or Jordan to do more than look out for their own immediate interests.

Former Secretary of State Henry Kissinger called Assad the shrewdest Arab leader. But the taciturn Syrian president was also usually the most frustrating, arrogant, and querulous. He lectured Kissinger and anyone else who came through his palace for hours before hearing them out. I was on trips with other secretaries of state who were kept waiting for hours just to see Assad at his safe presidential retreat in the mountains overlooking Damascus.

In 1981, I also covered an Arab League summit in Fez, Morocco, when Saudi Arabia's Crown Prince Fahd was to debut his plan for a comprehensive peace with Israel to all twenty-two Arab leaders. The day before, Assad and Fahd had talked by telephone and Assad promised he would be there. Months of planning and lobbying had gone into the Fahd Plan. I was at the airport when a planeload of Syrian bodyguards and staff arrived. But Assad's plane never showed up. The summit eventually collapsed. Everyone went home.

The underhanded theatrics were so Assad. He was not one to defer to another's initiative. He did eventually attend a reassembled summit the next year, but only after hefty checkbook diplomacy by the Saudis and Israel's 1982 invasion of Lebanon forced Arab unity.

In the region, as at home, Syria's gains were often temporary and costly: Assad wrested a political principle—the still-elusive premise of land for peace—out of a huge military loss in the 1973 offensive against Israel. During Syria's military domination of Lebanon, Assad lost much of his prized air force, the channel of his own rise to power, when Israel invaded Lebanon in 1982. As the Arab world tired of the conflict and saw diminishing returns from war, Assad stuck it out, even squeezing little Lebanon to back out of its 1983 peace treaty with Israel.

The ends justified any means, no matter how bloody.

He both supported terrorists and resorted to terror himself. In a bizarre 1986 scheme, Syrian air force and intelligence officers, the Syrian airline, and the Syrian Embassy in London were all implicated during the trial of a Jordanian who had his unwitting and pregnant girlfriend tote a bomb aboard an El Al plane bound from Britain to Israel.

Assad offered refuge to hard-line groups that rejected peace. He provided virtual carte blanche to Iran when it deployed Revolutionary Guards in Lebanon, via Syria, and he cosponsored the creation of Hezbollah. He honored the deal made with Kissinger to maintain peace along his own border with Israel—but then, over the next quarter century, manipulated surrogates in Lebanon to harass Israel on Syria's behalf.

After the Soviet demise, Assad lost his backers, arms, and subsidies from Moscow. He was pressured into a new peace effort in the mid-1990s. In the end, however, he held out for all of the Golan Heights without meaningful security guarantees for Israel—and died having achieved nothing. Syria was more isolated, even in the Arab world, than when he took office.

Assad was just as uncompromising in keeping his hold on power at home. He built a cult around his presidency. Syria *was* Assad. Children wore semimilitary uniforms to school and were indoctrinated in the Baath Pioneers, similar to the youth groups in the Soviet Union and North Korea. His picture was everywhere—schoolrooms, billboards, shop walls, hotels, business offices, mosques and churches, hospitals, train stations, even in a giant stencil covering several floors of high-rise apartments en route into Damascus.

"I grew up thinking he was a god," said a young woman who had been a Pioneer and interpreted for me during a trip in 2006. "Really!"

No one was immune from suspicion or retribution if they dared to differ with Assad. Baath Party founder Aflaq fled the country; he ended up in Baghdad and never was able to go back to Damascus before his death in 1989. Assad even purged his own younger brother Rifaat, who was Assad's right hand in his rise to power, the commander of an elite military unit, and one of his three vice presidents. Rifaat was flown to Moscow and then to exile in Europe.

The primacy of survival and a legacy of tyranny were Assad's bequests to his son. Syria's political course will be determined by what Bashar al Assad does with them.

When I arrived in Damascus from Beirut, one of my early stops was to see Riad Seif, a two-term member of Syria's parliament. Seif spent most of his life as a prominent businessman, and he still dresses the part—tailored dark suit, crisp white shirt, navy tie with thin red stripes. Born in 1946, Seif has a thick frosting of white hair with traces of the original black underneath; his eyebrows are still black. He has a mole under his right eye.

For years, Seif had the lucrative Adidas franchise in Damascus; an Adidas logo was still showing on the sliding glass window of his apartment. His large living room is set up with couches against all four walls, like a *diwaniyeh,* or typical receiving room for Middle East politicos. He pulled a big, cushioned chair close to me as he has limited hearing; then he went to get a hearing aid, but the battery was dead.

Seif is a genial but nervous man. "I am walking in a minefield," he explained, lighting the first of a steady stream of long, thin, brown cigarettes.

"I have been forbidden to talk to the media. Last month, I promised not to give any interviews for two months—and I'm supposed to keep this promise for another four weeks. So I have to be very, very careful."

Seif first ran for parliament in 1994, as an independent, after being egged on by friends. He ended up receiving the largest number of votes of any independent candidate in Damascus. He easily won reelection in 1998.

Seif was very much a product of the Syrian system, however. He would not have been allowed to run unless the Baath Party and the government were willing to tolerate him. Assad's control was total. Seif was considered a safe candidate—and a safe politician once elected.

Syria's parliament is also almost toothless. It has no power to draft laws; it can only criticize or modify drafts put forward by the president.

Yet Seif crossed a threshold after the abrupt death of Hafez al Assad in June 2000, the first change in leadership in thirty years. Two weeks later, Seif assembled leading intellectuals and independent voices to discuss a longstanding taboo—how to open up Syria's oppressive political system. Once again, the issue of how Syrians ruled themselves was on the table. But this time, it centered on peaceful and public debate. No one was plotting a coup.

The beginning of transitions is often spurred by unplanned moments or events. This was the first one. It spurred talkers to become doers. And even people who had cooperated with the regime began to consider alternatives. The meetings continued week after week, on Wednesday evenings, in Seif's living room. They debated human rights, pluralism, press and academic freedoms, and how to build a civil society. Seif's group eventually dubbed itself the Forum for National Dialogue. It was the first of ten new political salons, or forums, launched in Damascus after Assad's death. The debate became contagious. Salons soon followed in Aleppo, Homs, and other major cities.[5]

Together, they marked the onset of what became known as the Damascus Spring.

"It was like drinking nice water, pure water," Seif told me. "Hundreds used to come into this room to discuss ideas and exchange opinions. It was all new for us and really very interesting.

"The Baath Party sent some professors from the university to discuss with us," Seif added. "Some people didn't want them, but I said we had to have them. This was for all Syrians. We gave them double time, just so the government knew we were trying to be fair."

All the new forums wanted change, but they were also willing to work within the system to get it.

The elevation of young Bashar al Assad had initially spurred a sense of movement. An ophthalmologist trained in London, he had been his father's second choice. His flamboyant older brother Basil, the designated heir, died in a 1994 car crash. His father, the Arab world's toughest leader, was reportedly bereft. For years, black-bordered pictures of Basil, often in his trademark aviator sunglasses, hung next to pictures of Hafez al Assad all over Syria. Although faded, a few were still visible a dozen years later.

A gangling man with a small head and long neck, middle son Bashar was reportedly a reluctant replacement when he was summoned back from London. His brother had been groomed through the military. Charismatic and well-connected, Basil had been deep into his father's Syria-centric agenda. Bashar, by contrast, had been a painfully shy child. As an adult, he trained in the sciences, lived in the West, and was into technology. His wife, whom he met in London and married after taking office, had lived in Manhattan, worked as a JPMorgan banker, and been accepted at Harvard Business School. His credentials created a different aura around the second Assad president.

Seif and others believed they could negotiate with the new leader. "When Bashar inherited the state, he introduced himself as a reformer," Seif explained. "He promised us a lot."

During his 2000 inaugural address to parliament, the new president used words little heard in Syria—democracy, free speech, a free press, and accountability. He talked about the "dire need" for "constructive criticism . . . from different points of view."

> *To what extent are we democratic? And what are the indications that refer to the existence or nonexistence of democracy? Is it in elections or in the free press or in the free speech or in other freedoms and rights? Democracy is not any of these because all these rights and others are not democracy, rather they are democratic practices and results of these practices which all depend on democratic thinking.*
>
> *This thinking is based on the principle of accepting the opinion of the other, and this is certainly a two-way street. It means that what is a right for me is a right for others, but when the road becomes a one-way road it will become selfish. This means that we do not say 'I have the right to this or that.' Rather, we should say that others have certain rights, and if others enjoy this particular right I have the same right. This means that democracy is our duty towards others before it becomes a right for us.*[6]

Assad began his presidency by releasing 600 political prisoners and closing a notorious prison. Big satellite dishes soon proliferated on

crowded rooftops. New Internet cafés competed with traditional cof-
feehouses, particularly for the young. Two mobile telephone networks
transformed communications in a country where faxes once had to be
registered with the government. A new satirical weekly, *The Lamplighter,* was the first independent paper in almost forty years to get a
license to publish. It dared to poke fun at Syrians and their system.

From June 2000 into the winter of 2001, Syria was almost vibrant.
Intellectuals published increasingly bold demands. The first was the
Manifesto of the Ninety-Nine, so called because that many writers,
academics, lawyers, doctors, and even a handful of cinematographers
were brave enough to sign it. Issued in September 2000, it called on
Assad to pardon all political prisoners, end censorship, establish the rule
of law, allow the freedom to assemble in new associations, and end the
pervasive surveillance.[7]

It was soon followed by the Manifesto of the One Thousand, which
reflected the burgeoning movement for reform and the growing number of people willing to publicly attach their names to it. The second
manifesto demanded even more: an end to emergency law, democratic
elections, no privileges for a "ruling front," judicial independence, and
human- and women's-rights guarantees.[8]

By January 2001, Seif was sufficiently emboldened to announce at
one of the Wednesday-night forums that he intended to create a new
political party to compete with the ruling Baath Party. He wanted to
call it the Movement for Social Peace.

"I was very naïve. I found that people took it very seriously and
immediately offered suggestions about how to build it," he told me,
laughing at the memory. "But the government also took it seriously.
And it saw a new movement as a big danger."

Syria's Mukhabarat secret police soon showed up. "First, they called.
Then they came here," Seif said. "They asked me to stop."

The tone of Syria's new president also shifted. In one of his first press
interviews, Assad warned the reformists against "any action threatening the country's stability."

The Forum for National Dialogue, the embryo for a new party, was
shut down in February 2001.

Seif continued to gnaw away at the system, however. In parliament, he pressed for an official probe into corruption, the other big taboo in Syria.

Bribes, kickbacks, and rip-offs affect most aspects of Syrian life, often blatantly. One of the first taxis I took in Damascus was ordered to pull over by a cop who appeared out of nowhere on a street corner. The taxi had done nothing wrong, but the driver had no recourse. He could pay off the policeman, face a trumped-up ticket for more, or even be arrested. "It happens every day," the cabbie shrugged. "Tomorrow the police will be on other corners doing the same thing."

The bigger problem is at the top, where corruption impacts Syria's deeply troubled economy. Most of it is tied to Syria's political families, prompting comparisons with the mafia—dynasty founder Hafez al Assad as the archetypal Don Corleone and his three sons as the impetuous Santino, hapless Fredo, and wily Michael Corleone.[9]

Seif specifically dared to question a monopoly on Syria's new cellular telephone system by the Makhloufs, the other half of the Assad empire. Hafez al Assad married Anissa Makhlouf. Her family—particularly Bashar al Assad's cousins—ended up running many of the most lucrative businesses and franchises throughout the country, reportedly including the Dunkin' Donuts.[10]

"As a member of parliament, I was very well-informed about the Makhlouf family deal with the mobile business. It was a big scandal that would cost Syria, an underdeveloped country, millions and millions of dollars," Seif told me. "I spoke against it loudly in parliament and forced them to investigate it. But when I realized it was only going to be a formality, I made a study and printed three 3,000 copies of it—I did this on my own—and I distributed it all over Syria.

"The minister of communication warned me that, if I didn't give up this matter, I was taking a big risk," he continued, agitated. "And the Makhloufs sent around someone who made very generous offers—a lot of money—to back off. I told them to go away."

Seif's situation came to a head in August 2001.

As the scrappy politician distributed his booklet on corruption, he also moved to relaunch the Forum for a National Dialogue. Earlier meetings had been informal. Invitations had been by word of mouth. Local intellectuals had begun the evenings with commentaries on some aspect of reform and then opened it up for discussion. The idea was to stay below the radar. The regime had not allowed the forum to register as a nongovernment organization, so the meetings could be considered a violation of emergency law.

But Seif decided to do it up big. He invited a prominent Syrian exile to fly in from Paris to give a formal lecture. And he printed up invitations.

"As a member of parliament, I insisted that this was my right," Seif recalled. "But the Mukhabarat contacted me three days before the event and told me not to hold it. They said it's not allowed. I told them I was doing it anyway—and they could do what they like.

"The lecture was held on September 5, 2001. More than 600 people came from all over Syria. They were sitting down the stairway and into the street," he continued, pointing beyond his living room. "We knew a lot of people would come, so we had loudspeakers for them. We talked from seven P.M. until one in the morning. People were really very energetic and courageous."

The next day, Seif was arrested.

The police came five days after the arrest of Riad Turk, the grandfather of Syria's opposition. Over the next few weeks—as the world was caught up in the al Qaeda attacks on the World Trade Center and the Pentagon—Syria arrested other increasingly vocal politicians, academics, writers, and journalists.

The Damascus Spring was over.

Seif was formally charged with defying the state and trying to change the constitution by illegal means.

"In court, I said, 'By force? With these muscles?'" Seif told me, laughing. He looks a little like actor Tom Bosley, the portly father from the television series *Happy Days*.

Seif was defiant when he faced the judge. There are no jury trials in Syria.

"I want an explanation as to why I am here. I am a deputy in the Syrian parliament. I performed my duties as a deputy, yet the existing regime in Syria does not accept any opposition or argument other than its own," he told the judge, in front of a courtroom that included diplomats from the United States, Germany, Switzerland, Norway, Belgium, and Holland.

"I did not violate the constitution. I am here because I demanded a breakup of the political, economic, social, and media monopoly in Syria."[11]

The legally elected and most popular independent politician in Syria, a leader of the Damascus Spring, was sentenced to five years in prison.

Seif was released in January 2006.

He emerged pledging to move ahead with his new party. To friends, colleagues, and well-wishers again filling his living room, Seif vowed to pick up where he had left off. With an eye on the future, Seif said, his new party sought a membership with a majority among the young.

"We have arrived at the point where we really have to change," Seif told them. "There is no way to continue as it is now. We want to build, as soon as possible, democracy in Syria, because that is the only way to save the country and to avoid catastrophe."[12]

But when I met him three months later, Seif told me his ordeal had not yet ended. Four weeks after he went home, the Mukhabarat showed up at his door at two A.M. He did not hear the bell because of his deafness, so the secret police went to the homes of his cousin and then his son.

"They came back at five A.M. I looked through the door and saw my son surrounded by secret police," Seif recalled. "As soon as they came in, they put handcuffs on me and a blindfold, then they took me to a Mukhabarat office. They talked to me, then beat me. They wanted me to sign a promise that I would not contact any diplomats or foreigners. If I didn't sign it, they said I'd be humiliated every day for the rest of my life.

"The same officers warned my son. They said if he said one word about his father, one member of his family would disappear or be killed," Seif added. "They said this without shame.

"Now, I have to report to the police every day from eleven until one," he continued. "I am followed by an intelligence patrol wherever I go, twenty-four hours, seven days a week. They have warned my family, friends, and associates not to deal with me. They register everyone who comes to my office. People are very afraid to be in touch with me."

Seif can not run for parliament again for five years—the time matching his prison sentence. "I have no business," he added. "The government long ago forced me into bankruptcy. It started when they cut off supplies for my factories."

"I am," he conceded, "a little broken. Not completely," he added hastily, "but a little."

I asked Seif about the future. Words had been pouring out of him all evening, but this time he paused for a moment.

"Look," he responded, leaning forward in his big chair. "The regime is very strong. Every farmer depends on the government. Maybe one quarter of all jobs are in the public sector, provided by the government.

"But the regime has also done many horrible things during its thirty-six years," he continued. "Corruption is hurting everybody. Unemployment is horrible. No one believes they have the even most basic rights. And then there are hundreds of thousands of Mukhabarat—and they warn everybody, not just me. So a very big majority of Syrians are dreaming of change, but they are also not yet ready to pay the price. They are what we call the silent opposition.

"Myself and the others, the activists in the opposition, are determined to go on. We're waiting and watching for opportunities to push," he said. "They've been taking people back to prison again lately, but it's backfiring. It makes us more committed.

"We've already paid a big price. But we're willing to pay more. The key for us is that we just have to be steady. We can't waver."

The shifting political winds in the Middle East are upending perceptions about who the allies of democracy are and who are its enemies.

During the Cold War, the West encouraged the emergence of Islamic movements to foil Communist influence in the Middle East. Islam seemed a natural ally against an atheist ideology.

But with Islamic parties now rising rapidly, the ultimate irony in the Middle East is that so many of the secular activists putting their necks on the line for democracy are Marxists. Or, as some insist, former Communists who are now just leftists seeking a democracy that gives them political space.

In fairness, many have evolved, in varying degrees, in both tactics and goals since the Cold War's end. The neo-Marxists are often taking the biggest risks, organizing the boldest demonstrations, penning the most scathing criticisms, and serving the longest prison stints. They are, in a delicious twist, becoming the best de facto allies of the West on democratic reform.

Nowhere is that truer than in Syria. Riad al Turk entered politics through Syria's Communist Party. His position began shifting in the 1970s, forcing a party split. His breakaway faction became critical of the Soviet Union, opposed its invasion of Afghanistan, and put forward a program for multiparty democracy in Syria. In 2005, the party abandoned its Communist moniker; it is now the Syrian Democratic Socialist Party. But Turk remains a Marxist, albeit one willing to share power.

The neo-Marxist democrats are small in number. For millennia, political life in the Middle East has centered around family, tribe, religion, or neighborhood, with decisions left to a band of elders—not unlike other parts of the world before their own transitions. In Syria, the rise of ideology that crossed those traditional boundaries is a mid-twentieth-century phenomenon. Aflaq's Baath Party movement, launched in the 1940s, was one of the first, and for more than a decade it was little more than a clique of intellectuals.

Modern ideology is also a luxury of the literate. And literacy is a phenomenon of the late twentieth century in both Syria and the wider Arab world. Literacy doubled from forty percent in 1970 to almost eighty percent in 2000 in Syria. Education politicizes, intentionally or not. Hafez al Assad's own experience was proof—and one of the reasons, as Syria opened up schools, that he ensured that teachers and university professors were all certifiable Baathists.

Since Assad's death, Syria's leftists have done the most to define a different future. They have established the parameters and rhythm of action. And, seasoned in Syrian prisons, they have been realistic about the long view.

Michel Kilo is a neo-Marxist democrat and one of Syria's leading opposition thinkers. We met late on Easter Sunday, after he returned from Easter dinner. Kilo is Greek Orthodox. Amid the hundreds of books squeezed onto shelves that line his living room and hallways are religious icons, including a picture of the Virgin Mary and baby Jesus. His wife offered me Easter cookies.

"I am a democrat, an Arab, and a leftist, in that order," Kilo said, when I asked him how he identified himself. Kilo is a man of imposing heft and height with Nixonesque jowls, and he speaks with a baritone certainty. "I have always been a Marxist," he added, "and I will always be a Marxist."

During the days of Hafez al Assad, Kilo was imprisoned once and harassed often for his opposition. He was jailed—without charges or a trial—for two-and-one-half years. He was released in 1982. Since then, he told me, he had been summoned frequently by Syrian intelligence for extended questioning, and his telephone and activities were heavily monitored. He and his wife said they could always tell when they were being tailed—by the cigarettes glowing in the dark across the street at night, or when cars with three men are parked nearby during the day.

I asked Kilo, who was educated in Germany, how he distinguished between Marxism and the socialism of the Baath Party.

He scowled, his big black eyebrows knitting. "There's a huge difference! Baathism is Stalinism. Neither includes the idea of the citizen or liberal freedoms. They don't talk about civil society. There is nothing of the ideas of the Renaissance or the Enlightenment. They just have the authority, the state, and the one class," he said. "Baathism and Stalinism are the opposite of Marxism."

After Hafez al Assad's death in 2000, Kilo became an engine for change in Syria. During the Damascus Spring, he mobilized the opposition behind the Manifesto of the Ninety-Nine; his signature is sixth on the list. In 2001, he was a sponsor of the Manifesto of One Thousand.

Kilo often negotiated with other dissidents at Café Rawda across from parliament in the modern business district of Damascus. It is a bustling, noisy place with a canopied courtyard where men smoke hubble-bubble waterpipes and play backgammon or chess. After the 2003 United States invasion of Iraq, Kilo also designed a petition imploring the government to avoid a similar "looming danger." It warned that "cumulative mistakes" had "exhausted" Syria and exposed the country "like never before."

On his own, Kilo also pressed the regime for specific reforms, including distinctly non-Marxist changes in banking and insurance to help jump-start Syria's troubled economy. "We have banks, but only to put your money into. They're not modern," he said, shaking his head.

"Whenever I think about this government, I think 'They are stupid.' Really," he added, then laughed derisively. "They're donkeys. When you have clothes that don't fit anymore, you buy new ones."

But Kilo launched his boldest initiative in 2005 when he set out to unify Syria's often querulous opposition, including the Muslim Brotherhood. He proposed a detailed statement of unity on all the major issues facing Syria and a common platform to tackle them. Kilo wrote the first draft.

The result was the Damascus Declaration.

Syria, the Declaration warned, was at a crossroads requiring an urgent "rescue mission." In blunt language, it said, the monopoly on power by an "authoritarian, totalitarian, and cliquish regime" had torn apart the country's social fabric, put it on the brink of economic collapse, and led to stifling isolation. Syria's foreign policy was "destructive, adventurous, and short-sighted," especially in Lebanon.

That's imprisonable language in Syria.

"The present moment calls for a courageous and responsible national stand," the Declaration added. The proclamation represented a huge leap for Syria's opposition. The Damascus Spring in 2001 had been about ideas of reform. The Damascus Declaration in 2005 was calling for regime change.

The five-page document, boldly unveiled at an unauthorized press conference in October 2005, laid out an alternative vision based on reform that would be "peaceful, gradual, founded on accord, and based on dialogue and recognition of the other." It acknowledged Islam as the "more prominent cultural component," but it stipulated that no party or trend could claim an exceptional position. The role of national minorities must be guaranteed, along with their cultural and linguistic rights.

The document was signed by more than 250 major opposition figures as well as parties both secular and religious, Arab and Kurdish. It was also the first time the opposition inside and outside the country came together in a national accord.

Kilo personally traveled to Morocco and Europe to meet exiled Muslim Brotherhood leaders and convince the Islamists to join their secular counterparts.

Riad Seif, the former parliamentarian, was the first name on the list. He had signed it while still in prison. The regime, Seif had told me, later tried to force him to withdraw his signature.

"They were crazy that I signed it," Seif had said. "They asked my son and my daughter to convince me to take my name off it. The chief of the prison came and talked to me many times. I told him the last time, 'You can hang me, but I won't make this announcement.'"

When I talked to Kilo, he was working with other dissidents on the next steps. The fathers of the Damascus Declaration were trying to establish a permanent leadership, with a general secretary, a media office, and an outreach program for the public. The goal was a national conference to bring all sides together to make decisions.

I told Kilo that the odds of success seemed pretty remote. The government had publicly ignored the Declaration. The Damascus Spring had been squelched after less than one year. And Kilo had admitted that he was increasingly being summoned for questioning by Syrian intelligence.

"The Damascus Declaration represents the coming together of ninety-five percent of the opposition—the democratic opposition, the Islamist opposition, and the Kurdish opposition," Kilo replied.

"The opposition is now strong enough to emerge as a new pole on the political spectrum. It is strong enough to develop a program of democratic change," he said. "For the first time since 1963, when the Baathists took over, it is strong enough to try to assemble its own system and leaders."

"Yes, the spring is over," he added. "But each step builds on the last one."

It is likely to be a long march, however.

Three weeks after I left, on May 14, Kilo was summoned by Syrian intelligence. He had just helped craft yet another defiant pronouncement. This one called on Syria to normalize diplomatic relations with Lebanon, define their borders, and open an embassy—a step that would have recognized the separation of the two countries, formally ended any Syrian claims to its little neighbor, and cost Damascus its one trump card in negotiating for the return of its own Golan Heights from Israel. The petition, signed by 500 prominent Syrians and Lebanese, was quickly dubbed the Damascus-Beirut Declaration.

This time, Kilo did not return home.

Three days later, he was charged with "weakening national sentiment" and "spreading false or exaggerated news that can affect the standing of the state." The crimes carried the potential for a sentence of decades, even life, in prison.

Kilo's arrest marked the beginning of the biggest crackdown since Bashar al Assad assumed power. The opposition was maturing, but Assad was proving to be little different from his father.

The neo-Marxists have taken a circuitous route to their current democratic agenda. They have assumed a leadership role largely by default; Syria has few Western-style liberals, while the Muslim activists are either in exile or underground. Most of the neo-Marxists have mellowed with time, their thinking shaped by the Soviet Union's collapse, Lebanon's sectarian civil war on one border, Iraq's bloody chaos on another, and the general triumph of Islamic movements in elections regionwide. Most now want to avoid both radical ideas and sudden upheavals.

Yassin Haj Saleh and his wife Samira al Khalil are both neo-Marxist democrats. To see them, I drove to one of the new Damascus suburbs, which are mostly blocks of sterile apartment buildings on the barren hills surrounding the capital. Their small apartment is on the sixth floor and, like many buildings in Syria, theirs did not have an elevator. The walls on the walk up were splattered with cement drippings, and on a windy day the stairwell was a cold wind tunnel.

Saleh and Khalil, who were both born in 1961, are former jailbirds. Both were arrested because they were members of one of Syria's

Communist Parties, although not the same one. (They did not meet until after they were released.) Saleh belonged to Turk's party; his wife was a member of the communist Labor Party. All communist parties were outlawed, even though Syria's Baath Party is socialist.

Saleh is a tall, handsome man with prematurely silver hair and the easy demeanor and attire of an academic. Khalil was wearing jeans and a denim jacket, and she wore her brown hair in a flip with big, curled bangs. Her pale lipstick was outlined by a darker lip pencil.

Saleh was a nineteen-year-old medical student at the University of Aleppo, in Syria's second largest city, when he was arrested in 1980. He was held for the next sixteen years. He told me the now familiar tale of detainee torture during interrogations—the floggings with electric cable that crush muscle and break bones, the infamous "wheel" that detainees are chained to for hours, and another wooden device to which the hands and legs are tied so tightly that it leaves hands paralyzed for months.

Saleh had no inkling of his fate until well into the eleventh year, when he was finally charged. The first count was opposition to the Baath Party goals of "unity, socialism, and progress"; the second was belonging to a group whose aim was to overthrow the regime. He was tried along with 600 others at the Supreme State Security Court—without lawyers, witnesses, or evidence. He was sentenced to nine years for the first offense and fifteen years for the second, both at hard labor, to serve concurrently.

At the end of fifteen years, Saleh was asked to cooperate with the regime, effectively to become an informant. "I said to them, 'It's not enough to jail me for fifteen years? It's now my right to be released,'" he recalled.

So Saleh was held for another year—"and fourteen days," he noted. "They don't even respect their own laws or their own courts." He was transferred to Syria's most notorious prison, in Tadmur, also known as Palmyra, which means "city of palms." It is an oasis in the eastern desert with Roman ruins dating back to the second century. It was once a caravan stop between the Persian Gulf and the Mediterranean. It is a city far from the fertile strip between the coastal mountains and the desert where most Syrians live.

"The extra year was the harshest and most atrocious," Saleh told me. "Tadmur is a place that literally eats men. It was worse than the 'house of the dead' described by Dostoyevsky. Fear is a way of life in Tadmur, where every day primitive and vengeful torture is carried out at the hands of heartless people," he added. "I was always hungry and always afraid." When he was released in 1996, he weighed 104 pounds.

His wife, Khalil, spent four years in jail. She and her sister were arrested for membership in the communist Labor Party. A bakery worker at the time, she was never charged, never tried, and never told how long she would be held.

"We just wait," she said. Khalil was freed in 1991 when Hafez al Assad pardoned female prisoners.

After his release, Saleh returned to medical school, since employment is difficult for former political prisoners. He graduated in 2000 but never practiced. He instead became one of Syria's most outspoken critics. The state-controlled press will not publish Saleh in Syria, so he writes opinion pieces in papers ranging from Lebanon's *An Nahar* to *The New York Times* to air his view on changes needed in Damascus. He now lives, somewhat precariously, as a freelance intellectual.

Saleh chuckled when I asked him why the Marxists of the twentieth century have evolved into the most outspoken Middle East democrats in the twenty-first century.

It was, he replied, largely a reaction. "We originally became Marxists because the first generation of liberals failed to solve the national problems that faced our countries after independence," he said.

"The majority of Syrians and Egyptians and Iraqis were poor farmers. In fact, they were more than poor, they were nearly slaves. But the old liberals of the Arab world, the people who led the struggle for independence against colonial rule, generally came from a class of urban notables—people who were rich and had big landholdings. They were not interested in agricultural reform."

"They collapsed completely in Syria in the 1960s. That's why the Baathists had an easy victory over them," he added.

The Baathists, led by Syria's Alawite minority, identified with the farmers. Hafez al Assad was of peasant stock from the northern mountains. He was born in a two-room house without electricity, the ninth of eleven children. As a child, he worked and played in the fields, and rode a donkey or walked for transport.[13] The majority of Alawites were poor, rural, and less educated.

Through the Baath Party, the Alawites got their revenge against Sunni Muslims and Christians who lived in the cities and owned much of the land. The Baathists squeezed out the traditional power brokers— and had their dominance entrenched in law. Article Fifty-three of Syria's constitution stipulates that at least one half of the members of the People's Assembly must be workers and peasants.

"So, since we don't have a liberal heritage in this region, rehabilitating liberalism and democracy will come mainly from people who were Marxists, people who are more aware of political modernism," Saleh said. "Many of us read about the French, British, Italian, and German experiences. We are historians and thinkers and economists.

"After the Cold War, many became liberals. Some are liberals today in the same way they were Marxists before," he added, a smile breaking across his face. "They would never have criticized the Soviet Union before. Now, they would never criticize the United States—or at least what it stands for."

Neither Saleh nor his wife is active in their respective Communist parties. And both now oppose radical political upheaval. "As we have seen in Iraq, 'regime change' is easy, but ensuring stability afterwards is very difficult," Saleh wrote for *The New York Times* in an article entitled "Don't Rush the Revolution."

> *Despite the authoritarian nature of the Syrian leadership, gradual change is preferable to abrupt change. A slower pace would not only provide a better chance at avoiding bloodshed, but would give a larger number of Syrians a chance to gain some experience in public affairs, as many have started doing recently by more openly criticizing the regime.*
>
> *True democracy requires a maturation process with respect to participation.[14]*

Despite the evolution in his thinking, Saleh still gets summoned occasionally by the Mukhabarat for lengthy questioning. Given the challenges of dissent, I asked Saleh if pressing for change in Syria was worth the costs.

"I think it is," he said. "We haven't been able to defeat the regime, but we have participated in saving the dignity of our people. This is the moral capital we need—that some of our people are saying no to dictatorship, no to tyranny.

"It is humiliating when you have such a regime," he added, "and no one says how bad it is."

The ultimate redline for politics in Damascus is religion. It is another of Syria's ironies.

On Easter weekend, I visited the Umayyad Mosque. It is one of the most magnificent settings in the Middle East. Built in the eighth century, it was named after the first dynasty to lead the new Islamic world, which ruled from Spain to India for almost a century. More than 10,000 stonemasons and artisans labored on the mosque for more than a decade. It is the first monumental work of architecture in the Islamic world. In 2001, Pope John Paul II chose it for the first visit by a pope to a mosque since Islam was founded. Like everyone else, he removed his shoes when he entered.[15]

The grandeur of the mosque's vast courtyard always reminds me of the great piazzas of Venice and Rome. It bustles: Children slide on stocking feet across the smooth white stone floor. Small groups of women sit and talk. Men stroll. Pigeons peck and flock. The courtyard is surrounded on three sides by an arched arcade; the fourth side is a facade of golden mosaics that leads to a huge prayer hall.

Three of the most influential characters in Middle East history are buried here. The sarcophagus of Saladin, the Sunni leader who died in Damascus in 1193 after forcing European Crusaders out of Jerusalem, is in a tranquil little garden. In a small room off the courtyard is a shrine with the head of Hussein, the grandson of the Prophet Mohammed. His battle against the Omayyad dynasty in 680 A.D. symbolized the greatest schism within Islam, dividing Sunni and Shiite. I got caught up in a crush of Shiite pilgrims from Iran trying to touch the shrine. Several chador-clad women brought their children's clothes to rub against its silver grill.

In the heart of the long prayer hall, the head of John the Baptist is reputedly buried in a domed sanctuary with unusual green glass windows. Muslims revere John as the prophet Yahya; he is mentioned four times in the Koran. Because of the story of his birth to a barren mother and aged father, devout Muslim women sometimes pray in front of his shrine if they are having trouble getting pregnant. On the day I visited, several Muslim women mingled with Christian tourists in front of the tomb.

Politically, Syria is arguably the Arab world's most secular country, particularly after the fall of Saddam Hussein in neighboring Iraq. Both Syria and Iraq were ruled by the socialist Baath Party, albeit by branches with rival interpretations. Yet underneath, Syria remains a conservative religious society.

"Spiritual wealth is ingrained in the Syrian character," Mohammed Habash told me when I stopped in to see him at the Islamic Studies Center. Habash, a diminutive but ebullient man, is both a Muslim sheikh and an independent member of parliament. He also hosts popular television shows on religion.

"We believe this land is a cradle of religions," he explained. "More than one half of the people in the world belong to a religion that has ties to Abraham, Jacob, Isaac, Moses, Jesus, John the Baptist, or the prophet Mohammed and his companions—people who came from Syria or came through Syria. That is why this country is known as Cham Sharif, or Noble Land."

Article Thirty-five of Syria's 1973 constitution stipulates that "freedom of faith is guaranteed. The state respects all religions." It also promises "freedom to hold any religious rites, provided they do not disturb the public order." Both provisions are selectively observed.

The Old City in Damascus still has a vibrant Christian quarter. During my visit, candy shops were selling big chocolate Easter eggs, while my hotel displayed baskets of pastel-dyed eggs and stuffed Easter bunnies. Because the Orthodox Easter is celebrated later than the Catholic Easter, Syria had two three-day national holidays on sequential weekends to observe both. Christmas is a national holiday too. Syria is still home to almost two million Christians, roughly ten percent of the population. The cofounder of the Baath Party, Michel Aflaq, was a Christian.

Freedom does not extend to Jews, however. For millennia, Damascus's labyrinthine Old City had a Jewish quarter. But almost all of the 30,000 Jews fled during periodic waves of persecution following Syria's independence in 1946, Israel's creation in 1948, and the 1956 and 1967 Arab-Israeli wars. Synagogues were attacked or burned down. Jewish businesses were ransacked. And special identity cards were issued with the word "Jew" in red stamped across them. The last large group of Jews left when Syria lifted the ban on travel during peace talks with Israel in the early 1990s.

Damascus instead became the refuge for Mohammed Oudeh, better known as Abu Daoud, the aging and unrepentant mastermind of the 1972 Munich Olympics massacre of eleven Israeli athletes.[16]

But no domestic issue rattles the regime more than what Muslims are doing—or thinking—given recent history and current public opinion.

"If you ask me about sentiment on the street, I can tell you that more than ninety percent of Syrians believe in God," Habash told me. "But if you ask me about the role of religion in political life, I can tell you that at least fifty percent of Syrians believe religion must play a role in our political life. That's almost ten million people."

As in Egypt, the most consistent challenge has come from the Muslim Brotherhood. Unlike Egypt, however, it was not always outlawed. Egypt's Ikhwan was founded by a disillusioned schoolteacher challenging the elite—and pitted Sunni against Sunni. Syria's movement was founded by Islamic scholars with ties to the powerful Sunni notables and landowners of Aleppo and Hama—and the clash eventually pitted Sunni against Alawite.[17]

The Syrian wing was founded in 1945, a year before independence from France. In the 1950s, it was initially part of the legal opposition. In the 1961 parliamentary elections, it won ten seats. It was outlawed after the 1963 coup that brought the Baath Party to power.[18]

Tensions played out most traumatically in the charming old city of Hama. Syria's fourth largest city was famed for its quaint labyrinthine streets and the creaking waterwheels along the meandering Orontes

River. Its roots date back to the Neolithic Age, several millennia before Christ. But after the 1970 coup that brought Hafez al Assad to power, Hama also epitomized the far end of Syria's political spectrum:

Hama was a stronghold for the Muslim Brotherhood as well as cells of militant guerrilla groups, like the Fighting Vanguard and Mohammed's Brigades. The government in Damascus was staunchly secular and socialist.

Hama was traditional; many women wore head scarves; many men, loose tunics. Damascus was a Westernized metropolis of suits and ties.

Hama was dominated by Sunni Muslims, who account for seventy-five percent of Syria's eighteen million people. The Assad regime was dominated by minority Alawites, an offshoot of Shiite Islam with secretive beliefs that account for eleven percent of the population.

The only common denominator was that both sides were willing to use brutal violence to achieve their goals. The result was a mini-civil war.

Muslim extremists were linked to an escalating series of kidnappings, bombings, grenade attacks, and assassinations in the late 1970s. On June 26, 1980, amid a hail of machine-gun fire and grenades, militants tried to assassinate Assad during an arrival ceremony for the visiting president of Mali. Assad reportedly kicked one of the grenades away himself.[19]

The next day, Syrian troops were dispatched to Tadmur Prison, where they opened fire on inmates. Some 500 prisoners were murdered.[20] Within days, the government also introduced Law No. Forty-nine. It made membership in the Muslim Brotherhood "group"—lumping the organization and guerilla cells together—a crime automatically punishable by death.

The confrontation climaxed during a three-week period in February 1982, when a full-scale military offensive by land and air pummeled Hama. People were rounded up in door-to-door searches of hospitals, schools, offices, mosques, shops, and homes. Some were executed on the spot. Amnesty International reported that others were taken to detention centers at the airport, city stadium, and military camps. It also cited local reports that the military flushed containers of cyanide gas into buildings where rebels were suspected of hiding.

To mark an anniversary more than twenty years later, the Syrian Human Rights Committee published a lengthy reconstruction. The Hama massacre, it said, targeted about one-fifth of the city's 180,000 inhabitants. It noted one particularly chilling account from an unnamed survivor who was among a group of residents driven off in eleven trucks.

> *I was among a huge number of people, so crowded that we almost could not breathe, and we were taken to Sriheen, where we were ordered to step out of the trucks, so we did as told. First thing we noticed was those hundreds of shoes scattered everywhere on the ground. It was then that we realized that it meant that hundreds of our fellow citizens were killed and we were next to face the same imminent death.*
>
> *We were searched afterwards and any cash or watches were taken off us. Then the elements of the Syrian authorities ordered us to move forward towards a deeply dug trench, which stretched long. Some of us were ordered to go to another nearby trench. When I stepped forward to my spot by the trench, I saw the pile of bodies in there still tainted by running blood, which horrified me so much that I had to close my eyes and I had to contain myself to avoid falling off. As expected, streams of bullets were fired towards us and everyone fell in their blood into the trenches, whilst the ones who were inside the other trench got shot inside the trench where they stood.*[21]

The unidentified Syrian was shot but survived, according to the account, by waiting until the military drove off and then sneaking away. But some of the injured, he recounted, died "under the weight of the other bodies."

The heart of Hama's old city was razed. Parts were bulldozed with bodies still in the rubble underneath.[22] To drive home the point, the government clamped down nationwide. Praying within the army was banned. Mosques and their services came under close surveillance.

The sweeping slaughter may have been the single deadliest act by any Arab government against its own people in the modern Middle East. Amnesty International initially estimated the death toll was between 10,000 and 25,000, the vast majority innocent civilians. Syrian human rights groups now claim the loss was between 30,000 and 40,000 people.[23] If true, the fatalities could exceed the death toll for each of the five Arab-Israeli wars.[24]

Yet the savagery did not end the challenge. In the twenty-first century, Syria is again struggling with the role of religion in politics—and religion is increasingly winning.

The Muslim Brotherhood is still widely considered Syria's most popular opposition, even after a quarter century underground or in exile. All other groups, even pooling their supporters, are comparatively weak—as most are willing to admit. The appeal of an Islamist alternative has also received a big boost from Baathism's failures over the intervening decades.

Ibrahim Hamidi grew up during the crackdown against the Brotherhood. Hamidi, who was born in 1969, is Syria's most respected independent journalist. A correspondent for the London-based *al Hayat* newspaper, he was jailed for six months in 2002 and 2003 for his political coverage. His family had no ties to the Brotherhood, but fear was so pervasive throughout Syria during the crackdown that his family hid their audio cassette of the Koran, which is played by observant Muslims for three days after a death.

"My brothers and I went out and buried the cassette in the field," he told me. It is still there. Over lemonade at a Damascus café, Hamidi explained the state of play between the regime and Islamists a generation after Hama.

"In the 1980s, the government started to promote moderate Islam. It wanted to show it was not against all Islam," he explained. "That was fine then, as the world was different. The Soviet Union still existed."

"But twenty-five years later, the internal, regional, and international dynamics are all different. The regime's ideology is not pervasive anymore," Hamidi said. "And for the first time, Syria is surrounded by Islamic regimes: Turkey, Iraq, Hamas in the Palestinian territories, and the Muslim Brotherhood in Egypt. Many expect the Muslim Brotherhood to win in Jordan in 2007. So now the regime is trying to adapt."

We met a few days after Syria marked two national holidays—the anniversary of the founding of the Baath Party and the birthday of the Prophet Mohammed. For the first time, the regime celebrated the

Prophet's birth with greater fanfare than the anniversary of the ruling party. Billboards once heralding "progressiveness and socialism" were also being replaced with new admonitions: PRAY TO THE PROPHET, and DO NOT FORGET TO MENTION GOD.[25] Assad had recently approved Syria's first Islamic university as well as three Islamic banks. And Mohammed Habash, the head of the Islamic Studies Center, had been invited to speak on Islam at Syria's military academy—where praying had been banned twenty-five years earlier.

"The Brotherhood is illegal, and it's forbidden to talk about it, so no one knows how strong it is," Hamidi told me. "But the street is definitely more Islamist. There are more scarves, more Islamist books in bookstores, and now more Islamic schools. They're government-built—but because people want them. That's also why they allowed Islamic banks, because they found people were reluctant to put their money in regular banks," he added. "The government is being forced to meet the demands of the people on Islam. Its version is a 'controlled' Islam."

As superficial as it may be, the headscarf is often a barometer of politics in a country that does not take public-opinion polls. In the early 1980s, a distinct minority of women in Damascus wore *hejab,* or modest Islamic dress. In 2006, a distinct majority in Syria's most modern city had put it on. They were not black or dreary gray; many were pastels and lively prints. But the fashion still sent a conspicuous signal.

The Brotherhood is the biggest unknown in Syrian politics. The leftists are small but increasingly active. Their agenda is detailed and public. The Brotherhood may have wider support but it is invisible at home. It has name recognition, lofty religious values, and a notorious past, but not much more. Its agenda is vague.

Since there are no known Brotherhood leaders to interview in Syria, I telephoned Ali Sadreddine Bayanouni in London, after I left Damascus. Pictures on the Brotherhood's Web site show him to be a trim man with short white hair and a short white beard.

Bayanouni was born in 1938 and grew up in a religious family. He joined the movement when he was eighteen. He was imprisoned from 1975 until 1977; one year was in solitary confinement. He left Syria for a conference in France in 1979, just as Damascus cracked down on the Brotherhood, and opted not to go back. He lived in neighboring Jordan for two decades, until he became unwelcome. Then he moved to London. He assumed leadership of the Brotherhood in 1996. But, he stressed, he was operating largely in the dark.

"You assume I know what's going on inside the country," he told me. "I don't."

The exiled wing calculates its strength largely by tallying the number of people the government admits it has detained for activities related to the Brotherhood—some 30,000 over the previous fifteen years, by Bayanouni's count.

Bayanouni is not a cleric. He studied law at the University of Damascus, where he played tennis. "Yes, with female college students," he told me, with some annoyance, when I asked. "Why not?" He prefers to be described, he added, as a "medal-winning Ping-Pong player."

Bayanouni has struggled to put a different face on the Brotherhood. He renounced any claim that the movement represented all Syrian Muslims. He issued a new national charter in 2002 and invited secular counterparts to meet to discuss it. He acknowledged "mistakes" in confronting the government in the past.[26] He met with Michel Kilo and signed the Damascus Declaration in 2005. He talked to al Jazeera, *The Washington Post,* National Public Radio, and other international media to make his case for democracy. In 2006, he even met long-serving former Syrian Vice President Abdul Halim Khaddam after he defected; the two agreed to collaborate in a new National Salvation Front.[27]

"The Brotherhood does not seek to run the country alone," Bayanouni told me. "After more than forty years of destruction, Syria needs a broad-based government with all the other political forces to rebuild the country. We are looking to share power, not to rule the country."

Even with godless Marxists? I asked.

"Yes," he replied, "just as they call in *their* political discourse for sharing power with all political communities."

What about freedoms for Christians? "We believe that all ethnic and religious parties in Syria should enjoy complete freedom," he said.

And Jews? "We don't differentiate on the basis of religion," he replied. "Citizenship is the basis of intercommunal relations."

The most sensitive issue is actually the Brotherhood's position on

other Muslims. The Sunni movement has shied away from acknowledging Alawites, the Shiite offshoot, as equal members in the community of Muslims. The issue is vital to democracy's viability and avoiding
sectarian strife.

Unlike Egypt's Muslim Brotherhood, which is involved in day-to-
day politics, the Syrian branch is now engaged only in talk. It is headquartered more than 2,000 miles from Damascus. Given the movement's
track record, it is impossible to know if Bayanouni's current spin on
policy will bear any resemblance to the Brotherhood's future practices.
Like leaders of the Palestinian and Iraqi diasporas, Syria's exiles may
eventually discover differences with constituents at home. Who knows
if Bayanouni would even be retained if the movement were legalized in
Syria. He was not elected by the party democratically.

The movement also already has competition from a new Islamic
group called Jund al Sham, or Soldiers of Greater Syria, which launched
small attacks in Syria in 2005. Its goal, according to pamphlets shown
on Syrian television, is to create an Islamic caliphate in the greater Syrian region. Greater Syria includes Syria, Jordan, Lebanon, Palestine,
and Iraq.

The name Jund al Sham is claimed by diverse cells trained in Afghanistan by al Qaeda; they were reportedly dispersed after the United States
intervention in 2001. They began reemerging in Syria, Lebanon, and
the Persian Gulf sheikhdoms in 2004. In 2005, a Jund al Sham cell
claimed credit for a suicide attack on a British school in Qatar.[28]

Bayanouni claimed the Brotherhood has disavowed all forms of
extremism. He alleged that breakaway guerrilla cells were responsible
for bloody attacks that led to the Hama showdown. "The Fighting
Vanguard claimed they were members, but there was no relationship,"
he told me. "We publicly renounced their tactics."

Those claims elicit mixed reactions even from secular counterparts
now willing to do business with the Brotherhood.

Unlike Jund al Sham, the Brotherhood advocates a civilian government, not an Islamic state, Bayanouni said. Authority would be vested
in the executive and legislature. The clergy would have no role in
political life. Its government would "champion" democratic tenets that
"do not conflict with Islamic values."

"I don't see a model in the world today for the kind of civilian government inspired by Islam that I'm talking about," Bayanouni noted. "I completely disagree with what is happening in Iran,"

And Hezbollah? I asked.

"No relations whatsoever," he replied. "On the contrary, we see Hezbollah as taking extreme positions against the Muslim Brotherhood because of its relationship with the [Syrian] regime."

And Egypt's Brotherhood? I asked.

"We frequently hold meetings in Amman and London," he said. "We belong to the same school. But each conducts its own politics in a local context."

And Hamas? I asked. Hamas was originally a wing of the Egyptian Muslim Brotherhood. Yet its headquarters was in Damascus, like Hezbollah, courtesy of the Assad government. Islamist politics can get complicated and sometimes even appear contradictory. Islamist parties are not automatically allies.

"Hamas is just like other Islamic movements," he said. "We've had some meetings outside Palestine with people who belonged to the Islamic movement, but we have no relationship with the resistance inside the territories."

And al Qaeda? I asked.

"Osama bin Laden demonizes the Muslim Brotherhood," he replied. Bayanouni was in Tampa, Florida, on September 11, 2001, visiting his daughter, he told me. Two of his children came to the United States as students, and both became citizens. His son, with whom I later spoke, lives in North Carolina. Ten of his grandchildren are American citizens.

One of the things that surprised me in Damascus was how many dissidents were talking—among themselves, if not in public—about bringing the Muslim Brotherhood back into the political fold. Part of it was necessity. Other groups have limited prospects without a broader opposition front. Part of it was also a strong Islamic wind blowing through the region. The secular opposition has to be realistic about public preferences.

Syria's religious leaders—clerics with government approval, including Sunnis who might view the Brotherhood as a rival—have also begun to urge détente. Habash, the parliamentarian, told me he had been urging his colleagues to rescind Law No. Forty-nine, which automatically sentences any Brotherhood member to death.

Other clerics went further. The Father of Light Mosque is a comparatively new facility. It is run by Sheikh Salah Kuftaro. His father, the previous grand mufti of Syria, had hosted Pope John Paul II. The grand mufti died in 2004. At the entrance to the mosque's administration offices are two giant portraits—one of the late mufti, the other of Bashar al Assad.

The mufti's son is a burly, confident man who is one of Syria's most-quoted Sunni clerics. Kuftaro speaks bluntly about politics—and Arab failings. "The nationalist movement has been the dominant force since the beginning of the 1970s, but it has only led to more weakness and backwardness and failure in the Arab world," he told me. Disillusioned youth—in a country where seventy percent of the population is under age twenty-five—had turned to religion as a substitute.

Kuftaro worried that a great religion should not be "dwarfed" in a political party. "When the Muslim Brotherhood says 'Islam is the solution,' here I have reservations," he said. "Islam is *one* of the solutions, not *the* solution. But the reality is that the Brotherhood is part of the spectrum. And today we have to hope for their return—not going back to the state we were in during the 1970s and 1980s in challenging the government.

"No," the sheikh said. "I wish for these people to come back to participate in rebuilding the country under the canopy of legality. It's time all parties should sit at the table and discuss reform and democracy."

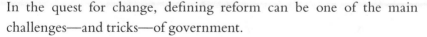

In the quest for change, defining reform can be one of the main challenges—and tricks—of government.

In the Middle East, the Arabic word for reform is *islah*. It is interpreted in different ways. It can mean "change," as in improving or overhauling. It can also mean, in a more technical sense, simply "repair." The difference is the abyss between most Arab governments and the agents of change.

Syrians debate it a lot. "If you talk about starting from scratch, you'll get nowhere here. But if you talk about repair, then you'll understand what the regime wants," said Sami Moubeyed, a savvy young political analyst who was engaged to Syria's most glamorous film star, told me.

"The conflict here," he said, "is that people want reform, while the government is thinking repair."

Syria will be one of the two most difficult regimes to democratize. The other is Saudi Arabia. Their governments' hold on power is absolute. People have the fewest rights or avenues of action. The secret police—and public fear—are the most pervasive. The two regimes have spawned sufficient support networks through family and corruption and by playing on cultural traditions.

To get a sense of the Syrian government's plans for reform, I went to see Bouthaina Shaaban. Born in 1953, she joined the Baath Party at the age of sixteen. In her forties, she became the regime's face to the outside world. She rose to power as an interpreter for the two Assad presidents. Her Web site, www.bouthainashaaban.com, features an array of her pictures—standing between Hafez al Assad and Bill Clinton, translating for Bashar al Assad with Tony Blair. Educated in Britain and a specialist on the poetry of Shelley, Shaaban speaks snappy English.

During the rule of Hafez al Assad, Shaaban became an adviser to the foreign ministry.

After Bashar al Assad inherited power, she ended up in the Syrian cabinet. She now embodies the second Assad regime—and an attempt to make up for lost time on issues that make the regime most vulnerable.

In 2003, Shaaban was named minister of expatriates. It was a new post created to try to lure wealthy Syrian expatriates abroad—or at least their resources—back home. Her office is in a building so new that contractor's paper was still on the elevator the day I visited in 2006. Her ministry has the reputation of being the one government office that reliably answers the phone and gets things done on time—or at all. Syrians can be engaging and hospitable, but the country lacks a sense of energy.

An old joke about poorly paid civil servants in Syria is that they go into work in the morning, put their suit jackets on the backs of their chairs, go out for coffee—and return at day's end to retrieve their jackets.[29]

Shaaban was running late, so I waited in a reception room. I was chatting with the young interpreter I used when her mobile telephone rang. I could hear the tone of the male voice on the other end. The caller did not identify himself. He wanted to know who I was seeing, what I had been told, and what I was saying during my visit, the interpreter told me.

Surely, she replied, he knew everything I was doing.

He asked if she wanted to come in to talk to him in person.

"No," she responded.

He kept pressing her. She explained that we were sitting in a government ministry. He said he would call back later.

"And he will," the interpreter said. "I'm surprised he didn't call earlier."

I had been particularly careful on this trip. I have been going to Syria since 1981; I can usually pick out the Mukhabarat goons in a hotel lobby, restaurant, shop, or office in seconds. I have been to Syria with three American secretaries of state, and it's always interesting to note the beefed up intelligence presence wherever we are staying. On this trip, I deliberately did not make telephone calls from my hotel room, even to the interpreter. I did not bring a cell phone. I did not plug my laptop computer into the Internet. I selectively checked e-mails at a business center and later changed passwords on the account. The intelligence officer's call was either clumsy, or they wanted me to know.

I raised the issue with Shaaban as soon as I was ushered into her office.

"No, no, this is wrong. This is silly. Really. This should not be happening anymore," she said. "I will make a telephone call later."

I asked Shaaban to call the interpreter in—she had asked that the young woman not join us—and tell her the same thing. She reluctantly did.

Shaaban is a precise and brusque woman. She was wearing a navy business suit, navy stockings and a string of pearls. She wears her thick brown hair short, combed behind her ears. She has a Crest smile. She is also a devout Baathist.

Shaaban again became the public face of the regime after the

Valentine's Day assassination of former Lebanese Prime Minister Rafiq Hariri in 2005, after Syria came under political siege from the outside world for what many Lebanese charged was its role in the murder. The United Nations launched an unprecedented investigation into the murder. Even traditional allies Egypt and Saudi Arabia demanded accountability by Damascus. The probe soon implicated top Syrian intelligence and military officials, including Assad's younger brother Maher and his brother-in-law Asef Shawkat. Shawkat married Assad's older sister Bushra, reportedly the most politically astute of the Assad children, against her father's wishes.[30] Bashar al Assad later named him head of military intelligence, tightening the family circle around him.

Shaaban was unleashed to defend the regime. She did slews of television interviews dismissing the international probe. She penned several op-ed pieces in the Arab and Western media pointing in other directions. She took on the kind of role that Tariq Azziz had performed for Saddam Hussein in Iraq as English-speaking front man.

Shaaban, who did a Fulbright Scholarship at Duke University, insisted that Israel and the United States were responsible for Hariri's murder. A week after the massive bombing of Hariri's motorcade, she wrote a rambling opinion piece alluding to former American intelligence operations as a precedent.

> We all know which countries can organize civil disturbance in Iran, Chile, Venezuela, and a long list of other countries where democracy was buried under tyrants appointed just because they were "friends."
>
> The parties who benefit most are those very same parties who benefited from the occupation of Palestine and Iraq, destabilizing Lebanon, targeting Syria, and severing the close ties that bind the Syrian and Lebanese people together. . . . Eliminating him in that criminal manner from the Lebanese equation paves the way for international and regional forces, well known to all in terms of capabilities, expertise, and incentives, to implement the scheme of taking over the Middle East.[31]

On the home front, however, Shaaban conceded her government had serious problems. "If the Baath Party wants to survive, it has to reform itself," she told me.

"The most important thing is that we are looking at ourselves in the mirror, really bravely, and trying to face whatever problems we have," she added. "I hope in the next two years, most people would feel changes in the way we are functioning."

But Syria's focus is on institutional efficiency, not individual freedoms, Shaaban made clear. Priority goes to the economy, not democracy.

Syria's four-point reform package began with strengthening and streamlining government. "For the first time in government, we meet every other week with the cabinet so we can discuss strategy," she explained. "Each ministry takes a turn and gives a report. And then we have one year to implement it and come back with the results."

Shaaban was a bit rushed because her report was due at a cabinet session the next day, and she was still working on it. The regime had also hired a Malaysian firm to assess each branch of government and propose changes.

The second goal was to tap into Syria's rich history and market the country as a tourist destination. "Syria could be a huge attraction," she said, and tourism could be a vital supplement to revenues centered largely around oil and agriculture. The government was building new hotels and roads to attract more tourists. Bashar al Assad had just attended the opening of the lavish Four Seasons Hotel, one of the few new buildings in Damascus.

The third priority was her project to get expatriates to invest—and to keep their Syrian citizenship. "Syrians abroad have done extremely well. Our estimates show that there are 50,000 Syrian doctors in the United States and Europe. We also have many Syrian businessmen abroad," she explained. "We encourage them to take the nationality they want but to keep their Syrian identity. There's no conflict between being loyal to the country you chose and still being proud of your origins and culture."

Finally, the government was trying to modernize its industry, in part for exports. "Most of the time," she acknowledged, "our trade balance is in the red."

When I pressed her on political reforms, Shaaban would not to go into specifics. Ideas floated after Bashar al Assad took office—about a more independent media and a new law on political parties—were no longer floating. Shaaban insisted, however, that new political space was opening because nongovernment groups were "springing up like mushrooms.

"In fact, we should be more careful," she told me. "You don't want to jump from one state to another without organizing how that move should happen. Society must remain stable."

Stability has been the political catchword for Syria since independence. Syria has fourteen diverse religious and ethnic identities. Besides Sunnis, Shiites, and Christians, they include a restive and non-Arab Kurdish community that makes up almost ten percent of the population—in a country officially named the Syrian *Arab* Republic.[32] If political parties were allowed to form freely, Syrian analysts warned me, many would be built around a religious or ethnic base.

Even his toughest critics credited Hafez al Assad with holding the country together—albeit through Soviet-style repression.

Under his son, stability was central again in the debate over reform. With chaotic Iraq on one frontier and troubled Lebanon on the other, Syrians both in and outside government were nervous about sectarian divisions erupting at home. The influx of more than one-half million Iraqis fleeing across the 450-mile border between 2003 and 2006 had driven home the potential dangers.[33]

On the day I strolled through the Old City's historic souq, one of several huge maroon banners strung across the roof declared in awkward English, WE ARE IN SYRIA THE COUNTRY OF SELF-ESTEEM. WE REFUSE YOUR DEMOCRACY AFTER WHAT WE HAVE SEEN HAPPEN IN IRAQ.

A sense of vulnerability over the unknown impact of real reform ran deep. The end of Iraq's Baath Party produced sectarian strife that killed dozens of Iraqis daily, worsened the economy and unemployment, increased crime, kidnappings, and rape, and brought with it a massive and prolonged foreign military presence. Many Syrians I talked to worried about what the end of their own Baath Party would mean.

The sense that Syria was fragile was visible in unusual ways.

The Middle East has its own version of *American Idol*—called *Superstar*—which runs on Lebanese television and is open to contestants throughout the Arab world. One of the strongest singers in the 2005 competition was Syria's Shahed Barmada. Many Syrians thought she did not stand a chance because the show was in Lebanon—in the midst of the crisis over Hariri's assassination and Syria's troop withdrawal. A young Syrian told me she and her friends did not bother to telephone in their votes; they had assumed she would lose.

When Barmada was named runner-up, her father astonished viewers by racing onstage and wrapping her in the Syrian flag. The young singer quickly became the second-most-recognizable face in Syria, after Bashar al Assad. I saw her picture all over Damascus on billboard advertisements for Ford, often decked out in a baseball cap with the blue-and-white Ford logo. She had marketability because she was one of the few symbols of Syrian success.

Yet patchwork repair is also unlikely to be enough to placate Syrians, perhaps for economic reasons even more than political discontent.

Syria has been living on borrowed time for quite a while. The Assads, father and son, may have kept the country tranquil, but neither was a good money manager. Syria's old-fashioned and incompetent socialist economy got a reprieve when oil was discovered in 1984. Exports began in the early 1990s. Reflecting the sorry state of the rest of the economy, Syria's modest oil production soon accounted for half of government revenues and two thirds of its foreign exchange.[34]

In violation of international sanctions against Saddam Hussein, Syria also got a huge boost from smuggling Iraqi oil through Syrian pipelines and land routes for almost a decade. Damascus netted up to one billion dollars a year off illegal oil trading.[35] The ouster of its brother Baath Party was costly, literally, to Damascus.

Syria's health is now dependent on its own oil. But production peaked in 2000—and the oil has already begun to run out.

"Between 2008 and 2010, Syria will become a net importer of oil," former World Bank economist Nabil Sukkar told me. "So our revenues are on the way to a major decline." The current fields are expected to run out around 2025.

Sukkar, an older man with a patrician nose and expensive suits, now runs a consulting firm in Damascus. He blamed the regime. "Oil removed the sense of crisis, so it slowed down reform by creating a sense of complacency," he continued. "We should have been renovating other sectors—agriculture, industry, and tourism as an alternative. But with oil, the attitude became 'Why bother?'

"If we had done our homework in the 1990s, we would not be facing this future," he added. "But there was no clarity of what the economy was going to be. Now, we face a crisis around the corner."

Since 2000, Bashar al Assad's renewed promise of economic liberalization has never been realized. As with political reforms, most ideas get no further than the proposal stage. In 2005, the Baath Party held its first national congress since the younger Assad took office. It declared that Syria was shifting to a "market social economy," although the government offered few specifics.

"Of course the government had in mind China, which in 1987 introduced the idea of a market *socialist* economy," Sukkar said. "In Syria, the idea is that we are to move to a market economy. But to alleviate the fears of the working class they added the word 'social'—in order to keep some faith in the old system.

"But frankly, if you ask what that means, I don't think anybody knows," he said. "Nothing has really changed."

With revenues already dwindling, Syria's looming new burdens will be tougher to address. The demographic baby bulge is expected to put growing and unattainable demands on the economy over the next two decades. The regime is already unable to absorb the 300,000 young people looking for jobs every year. During my visit, unemployment hovered uncomfortably at around twelve percent officially, but more like twenty-five percent in reality.

One of the toughest steps for the Syrian regime may be cutting back on public subsidies, from basic foodstuffs to petroleum products, which are pivotal to both the Baath Party's populist ideology and its constituency. Syria heavily subsidizes gasoline, for example. The cost to the consumer is only one third of the market price.

"The government has wanted to reduce the subsidies for over seven years but always hesitates," Sukkar explained. "Jordan and Yemen faced sporadic street demonstrations for months after the governments began a gradual rise in fuel costs.

"Governments," Sukkar noted pointedly, "are particularly reluctant to take those kinds of steps when they are already under siege politically."

Before leaving Damascus, I went to see two men. The first was Anwar al Bunni, a wiry, gregarious man with a big mustache.

Bunni was born in Hama in 1959. He was eleven when the first Assad came to power. He was twenty-two when he almost became a victim of the military's surprise crackdowns in Hama. He and a few friends often went out to check on older couples without children to fetch food, water, or medicines. As Christians, he told me, he and his friends felt less vulnerable to the military sweeps against Muslims. But during one roundup in 1981, Bunni was stopped by a Syrian army officer who asked what he was doing.

"We said we were going to help families without food," Bunni recounted.

The officer asked Bunni if he was Muslim or Christian.

"I told him, 'I've lived in Hama over twenty years and no one has ever asked me this question. Why do you have to know?'" Bunni recounted.

The officer butted Bunni's head with his bayoneted rifle, Bunni told me, then stabbed him. Bunni showed me what he said were the scars from that encounter, visible a quarter century later.

Bunni was saved when neighbors rushed out to tell the officer that he was a Christian and only trying to help them.

"He stopped trying to kill me, but he ordered his soldiers to handcuff me in the back, and then they set fire to my beard," Bunni recounted. Many personal accounts at the time and subsequent reconstructions detailed how the Syrian military set beards ablaze.[36] Bunni was comparatively fortunate. The military moved on, and neighbors brought out buckets of water to douse the flames. He is clean-shaven today.

Bunni left Hama before the slaughter in 1982. But since his own run-in with arbitrary justice, he has spent most of his life defending Syria's dissidents.

He was a lawyer when Riad al Turk finally had his day in court, the fourth time around. He defended Riad Seif and another member of parliament arrested at the end of the Damascus Spring. He was the attorney for the satirist whose popular independent newspaper, *The Lamplighter,* was shut down within months of its first issue. He defended a doctor imprisoned for criticizing corruption, minority Kurds arrested after a series of protests, and dozens of others.

Bunni jokingly told me that he also became a lawyer to defend his own family. He was the only child who had not served time in prison. Since 1977, his three brothers and one sister, plus two of their spouses, had spent a total of sixty years in Syria's dungeons. They were all leftists.

The Syrian lawyer defended most dissidents pro bono. To pay the bills, he began selling his belongings. Then he sold his car. In 2005, he sold his office.

Bunni acknowledged that much of his work was for naught. His clients rarely had even a remote chance of being acquitted, he told me when I visited his small and sparsely furnished apartment in Damascus.

"The charges and the verdict come to the judges in the same envelope, before the trial even starts," said Bunni, who has the crow's-feet of a continuous smoker, as he puffed on another Marlboro. "But our duty as lawyers is not just to help our clients; it's also to bring their cases to the public's attention."

Bunni had been on the defensive himself in recent years. Since 2002, he told me, the Syrian bar association had been trying to get him disbarred on six different counts. He had appealed and was awaiting the outcome. His activities and his telephone, he said, were routinely monitored by security police. He was also barred from leaving the country. Bunni had been invited to Germany to stand in for Riad Seif when his imprisoned client was unable to receive a human-rights award from the government in 2003. But one of the regime's favorite tricks is to ban its critics from traveling, as I heard frequently from opposition figures in Damascus. They are not informed. They find out at the airport or at the border when immigration refuses to let them leave. They are given no reason.

A prominent dissident had shown me the small slip of white paper given him in 2004 when he tried to fly to France to receive his own human-rights award. The paper said only that the recipient should report to the investigation branch of the office of political security. Few Syrians bother to report, I was told, because they know what it means. They have no effective recourse or appeal.

"We are like hostages in the hands of this regime," Bunni told me. But he quickly added that he was not seeking to oust the regime. "If this government, with all its crimes, starts to practice human rights, I will say 'Welcome.' But we also can't wait three or four generations to have our freedom."

In 2006, the European Union funded a project to open the Center for Legal Research and Studies. They tapped Bunni to head it. The goal was to write an assessment of Syria's legal system, particularly laws affecting the press, women's rights, the economy, the judiciary, and the penal code. The center would also provide training for civil society or nongovernment groups. The opening day was February 21, 2006.

The regime originally approved the project, then abruptly closed it nine days later, on March 1.

With a resilience that is often surprising in a police state like Syria, Bunni decided to fight back—peacefully. He drafted a new constitution. He spent months studying Arab and Western constitutions as well as earlier Syrian laws. He paid particular attention to Iraq's experience in writing a new constitution in 2005.

Syria's 1973 constitution actually stipulates, "Freedom is a sacred right." But laws subsequently passed by parliament have taken freedoms away or left the opposition and minorities vulnerable to bad practices.

Bunni's twenty-one-page constitution, widely available on the Internet in Arabic, French, and English, imposes two-term limits on the leadership, bans political monopolies, and provides guarantees of equality for all Syrians in a multiethnic, multireligious, and multiracial state. Arabic is the first language, but Kurdish is the second language, and other minorities can fully exercise their languages and cultures. It guarantees the right of defense in court, while arrests and searches are barred without legal warrants.

Bunni's proposal also safeguards the right to form political parties but stipulates that they must be based on democratic principles. It separates the branches of government and specifically limits the executive's ability to meddle beyond its duties. Even the Supreme Court would be elected by parliament based on a list of candidates put forward half by the president and half by a parliamentary committee. The top justices also would have a fifteen-year term limit.

Bunni's constitution is laden with layers of guarantees—and a provision that they can not be changed without ninety percent of a popular vote. The media may also not be shut down, censored, or confiscated.

"I wrote it for two reasons: The constitution must be the background of all politics and a place for people to meet and to act," Bunni told me. "When they made their new constitution, the Iraqi political parties had discussions, but each tried to get a larger space than the other for its interests. No one thought about those not represented by political parties. A constitution should be the foundation and protection for all people, whether represented by political parties or not.

"The second point," Bunni added," is that all activities in Syria come from a background in nondemocracy—communist or religious or Nasserist or nationalist. All of them now ask for democracy because they're in the opposition.

"I tried to draft a constitution," he said, with a smile, "to put them all to the test."

Two weeks after I left Damascus, Bunni was disbarred. A week later, he issued a statement condemning the arrest of Michel Kilo, another client. A few hours later, Bunni was leaving his house for an English class when he was stopped by two security officers. They asked him to get into their car, according to his brother. Bunni demanded to see an arrest warrant. When they refused, he struggled to get away and began shouting for help.[37]

The two men then shoved Bunni into the car and drove away, according to his brother. He, too, was hauled off to prison.

I ended my trip to Damascus the same way I had prepared for it—with Riad al Turk. We met for coffee on a cold, rainy spring day. He was dressed in a light gray suit, with a yellow shirt and a navy sweater underneath. He clung to a small umbrella.

Although he underwent major heart surgery after completing his fourth prison stint, Turk had resumed his political activities. He was still active on the central committee of the Syrian Communist Party. At age seventy-six, he remained noisy and defiant.

"I will never, ever make a truce with this government," he told me.

The looming question in Syria and other Arab autocracies, however, is not the government's power. In 2007, Syria held a presidential "referendum." Voters went to the polls to vote yea or nay for a second seven-year term for Bashar al Assad. There were no other candidates and no choices. Not surprisingly, he won ninety-seven percent of the vote. So change will depend on the opposition's muscle and endurance. Specifically, how effective can the dedicated but outlawed dissidents be in prodding autocrats to either change or share power? And how does the balance of power finally shift?

Dissatisfaction with the status quo in Syria is clearly growing, spurred by a confluence of demographics, economic realities, international pressure, access to information, and particularly what has transpired in neighboring states. The 2003 ouster of Saddam Hussein's own version of the Baath Party in Iraq and the forced withdrawal of Syrian forces in 2005 from Lebanon were the biggest blows to Damascus since the loss of the Golan Heights to Israel in 1967. The timing made them a double whammy that provoked strong nationalist feeling, but also a lot of soul-searching, among Syrians.

Bashar al Assad also has neither the intimidating aura nor the political leverage of his father. He has pushed aside most of his father's closest lackeys in favor of his own. But, at least for now, he still relies heavily on the Assad name, the family, the tribe, the minority Alawites, and the security police.

For the opposition, the Damascus Declaration was arguably the most important moment in more than thirty-five years. It moved beyond reform to regime change. It brought together the full range of dissidents—secular and religious, leftists and liberals, urban and rural— to enunciate a common and peaceful agenda of change.

"The opposition's position improved significantly after the Damascus Declaration. People started to look at the opposition more seriously," Turk told me.

"This declaration contained—in addition to all political parties— new faces and new democratic national figures," he said. "And it linked the parties that emigrated outside Syria, especially the Muslim Brotherhood, with those of us inside."

Dissidents have also emerged in increasingly diverse fields, among businessmen, in the new blogosphere, even among cartoonists and cinematographers. At the same time, because the vast majority of Syrians are silent or not yet politically educated, the opposition is almost as much of an elite minority as those in power. And Syrian activists remain so vulnerable to harassment, punishment, or banishment that their leverage is limited.

Despite the vaunted position he holds among the opposition, Turk comes under fire from colleagues for being too outspoken, even inflammatory. But he, in turn, is disdainful of fellow dissidents for not taking a bigger leap in challenging the regime.

"The opposition doesn't yet have a compass," Turk said, as he began sipping a small cup of espresso. "It's really bad that some in the opposition are afraid. When they express their opinions, they do it in a way that avoids angering officials.

"Unjust Arab regimes are living in their last stage," he added. "But I don't think this opposition will be able to change the system. And what the Damascus Declaration created is not an authority that can replace the regime."

If the current opposition is not an alternative, I asked Turk if he felt he had wasted his life in protest and in prison—and also how he could be so confident of transformation in the future.

"The regime will eventually collapse on its own, due to isolation internally and internationally. Its own forces will dissolve. That's what happened in the Soviet Union and Czechoslovakia," Turk explained. "That's what will happen here.

"And no, my life has been hard, but it has not been a wasted life," he added. "Having an opposition is important, but they're not necessarily the ones to be the ready alternative when the regime collapses. In Russia, there's still no real alternative to the Communist Party. Vladimir Putin is a former Communist, and he still rules like one. Look what's happened in Iraq," Turk said. "It takes time.

"Finding the real alternative," he said, "only begins with the collapse of the regime."

seven

IRAN

The Revolutionaries

Men fear thought as they fear nothing else on earth—
more than ruin, more even than death. . . . Thought
looks into the pit of hell and is not afraid. Thought
is great and swift and free, the light of the world,
and the chief glory of man.

—British philosopher Bertrand Russell

Those who dream by day are cognizant of many things
which escape those who dream only by night.

—American writer Edgar Allan Poe

Revolutions often eat themselves up. The turmoil, blood-letting, and failure to produce the promised utopia trigger a backlash. But in the reaction can lie the seeds of longer-term political change.

The French Revolution ended the Bourbon dynasty and introduced equality and civil liberty, but it imploded into a reign of terror. France then needed almost a century to establish a stable republican democracy.

The Russian Revolution toppled the Romanov czar and introduced classless egalitarianism, but the new Soviet Union also spawned totalitarian rule for the next seventy years, until its failure opened the way for the current still-tentative experiment with democracy.

The same process is underway in Iran, the launching pad for the Middle East's most zealous and novel revolution.

In 1979, Ayatollah Ruhollah Khomeini, a spindly cleric with forbidding black eyebrows and a long white beard, combined an old faith with new technology to unite liberals and traditionalists, democrats and communists, conservative merchants and rowdy student activists. Using tape cassettes and faxes from afar, he inspired more than a year of street protests, strikes, and rampages against the monarchy by his followers. Together, they forced the last shah, with the empress at his side and a small jar of Iranian soil in his hand, to depart on an "open-ended vacation." Mohammed Reza Shah Pahlavi's exit ended twenty-five centuries of dynastic rule.

Iran's Islamic upheaval is the only original revolution among the half-dozen uprisings that have rumbled across the Middle East over the past century, because it introduced a genuinely new political ideology that altered the world's political spectrum. It introduced a unique and aggressive form of political Islam.

Yet it has also spawned some of the boldest ideas about democracy in the Middle East from revolutionaries who soon soured on the new system and then turned against it.

Among them are two men I met a dozen years apart. They met each other in 1979 as ardent revolutionaries tasked with converting a kingdom ruled from the bejeweled Peacock Throne into a theocracy governed by turbaned clerics. They started out in the new Islamic republic's inner circle. But over the course of a decade, both became deeply disillusioned.

Together, they illustrate the physics of political change.

Abdolkarim Soroush is a slight man with a whisper of a voice and a neat soft-brown beard. He dresses casually in the neutral tones of an academic and would disappear in any crowd. He is a philosopher. He worked to redefine the political debate in Iran during the last decade of the twentieth century. Soroush was the teacher.

Akbar Ganji is a short and once-beefy man with soulful eyes, a winsome grin, and a perpetual six-day stubble. Ganji is a writer. He worked to expose the regime's failures and misadventures in the first decade of the twenty-first century. Ganji was the student.

Within Iranian society, both of their names became code words for defiance.

"They launched the most dynamic and novel debate about mosque and state, religion and politics, democracy and Islam in Iran in at least 100 years," Hadi Semati, an American-educated political scientist at the University of Tehran, explained to me. "In fact, probably no where in the region could you find a more vibrant or original debate. And that debate," Semati added, "is still going on."

I set out to find Soroush in 1994 because his name was increasingly coming up in coffee-shop conversations, classrooms, think tanks, and seminaries. Iranians talked excitedly about his new ideas of reform. I tracked him down at his Tehran University office, where his big oak desk was covered with neat stacks of books; classical music played in the background. We began a conversation that has continued ever since.

"I'm not such an important man," he told me in our first meeting, in a little voice that forced me to lean forward to hear him. "I'm just a writer and a thinker, and I'm just toying with ideas about religion."

Born in 1945, Soroush came from the kind of lower-middle-class family that formed the revolution's backbone. His mother, Batoul, was named after one of the Prophet Mohammed's daughters; she refused to abandon the enveloping black chador that covers all but a woman's face and hands, even when the shah banned it. His father, a grocer, refused to buy a radio because it meant listening to the shah's state-controlled news. Most of the homes in old Tehran where Soroush grew up were mud brick; most had only a couple of large rooms and often no bathroom.

Soroush came of age in the 1960s as Ayatollah Khomeini began his campaign against the monarchy's modernization plan—for failing the poor, deserting religious values, and corrupting a civilization dating back five millennia. Soroush grew up as sleepy Tehran was transformed into a cosmopolitan capital, complete with casinos and discos, *Peyton Place* on television and Kentucky Fried Chicken in restaurants, miniskirts and makeup, and shopping malls and supermarkets to rival traditional commercial powers in the Middle East's grandest old bazaar. Iran became a hub of foreign influence in the Middle East.

"You see nothing but . . . self-interest, lechery, immodesty, criminality, treachery, and thousands of associated vices," Khomeini railed in a little book called *Secrets Exposed*.[1]

The ayatollah, already in his sixties, was a rare voice willing to risk the dangers of speaking out. In 1963, after condemning the shah as a "miserable wretch," Khomeini was arrested and held for ten months. Soroush was only a high-school student at the time. But when the cleric was released, Soroush was among the thousands who traveled to the cleric's mud-brick home in Qom, the dusty religious center an hour's drive from Tehran, to celebrate his release.

The final confrontation between king and cleric unfolded in 1964, when Khomeini attacked a new law granting immunity to thousands of U.S. military personnel—and all their dependents—for any crimes committed in Iran. To followers assembled in front of his home, the ayatollah thundered that Iran's dignity had been destroyed. He linked the law to a $200-million loan from the United States.[2] The controversial legislation, Khomeini pronounced,

> *reduced the Iranian people to a level lower than that of an American dog. If someone runs over a dog belonging to an American, he will be prosecuted. Even if the shah himself were to run over a dog belonging to an American, he would be prosecuted. But if an American cook runs over the shah, the head of state, no one will have the right to interfere with him. . . . Are we to be trampled underfoot by the boots of America simply because we are a weak nation and have no dollars?*[3]

On November 4, 1964, the shah expelled the fiery ayatollah.*

Soroush kept up with the ayatollah's wandering exile—in Turkey for seven months, in Iraq for twelve years until he was deported by

---

*Khomeini never forgot that he was deported from his own country because of the shah's preference for strong ties to America. The date would also come back to haunt the United States. Exactly fifteen years later, in 1979, Iranian students protesting the U.S. decision to take in the exiled shah selected the date commemorating Khomeini's expulsion to attack the United States Embassy in Tehran. More than fifty were taken hostage. The drama dragged on for 444 days—an event that redefined America's relations with the Islamic world long before September 11, 2001.

Saddam Hussein, and the final four months in Paris. The first in his family to go to university and the first to go to the West, Soroush took a break from his studies in London to visit Khomeini in France in 1978, as the revolution was building up steam back home. The two men hit it off. When the ayatollah returned triumphantly to Tehran to install Islamic rule several weeks later, Soroush followed him home.

Soroush quickly became a prominent figure in revolutionary circles. He was the youngest of seven men named to the Committee of the Cultural Revolution. Before Iran's universities were allowed to reopen, the committee conformed curriculum to Khomeini's version of Islam and purged hundreds of intellectuals sympathetic to the shah.

But the turmoil of the revolution's first decade took a toll. Daily life was harder for the average Iranian, and many were forced to take second or third jobs. Despite oil wealth, Iran's economy was in trouble. The country was isolated diplomatically and under economic sanctions by major powers. It fought the longest war in modern Middle East history against Iraq, suffering hundreds of thousands of casualties. Corruption was worse, far worse, than during the monarchy. Squabbling among the theocrats forced them to disband their own revolutionary party.

By the late 1980s, Soroush was deeply disillusioned, even with Khomeini. The charismatic ayatollah, he told me, had proven to be only a function of the political transition, and not the symbol of its ultimate goal. Soroush gradually weaned himself from the inner circle and worked on his own political theories.

In the early 1990s, Soroush tapped into a debate that had been brewing for a century in the Islamic world about the scope of individual freedom. Islam literally means "submission"—to God's will. The concept is enshrined in Iran's constitution. Chapter One stipulates that government is based on faith in one God and that "man should submit to His will."

But Soroush began to argue that Islam and democracy are not only compatible but inevitably intertwined.

"To be religious necessitates being a democrat as well," he told me during our first meeting. "An ideal religious society can't have anything but a democratic government."

Soroush pulled off his wire-rimmed glasses and cleaned them with a handkerchief, as he often did when making an important point.

"You see, in order to be a true believer, one must be free," he continued. "True believers must embrace their faith of their own free will—not because it was imposed, or inherited, or part of the dominant local culture. To become a believer under pressure or coercion isn't true belief."

Thus freedom always precedes religion—a revolutionary idea in the Islamic world.

I thought of Soroush's argument a few months later when I walked the Tidal Basin in Washington, D.C., during the cherry-blossom festival and decided to duck into the Jefferson Memorial. I was struck by the four quotations carved into the stone walls around Jefferson's statue, and I took a picture of each. On a trip to Tehran later that year, I showed them to Soroush.

The first inscription from Jefferson reads,

Almighty God hath created the mind free. All attempts to influence it by temporal punishments or burdens . . . are a departure from the plan of the Holy Author of our religion.

Another is Jefferson's language from the Declaration of Independence:

We hold these truths to be self-evident: that all men are created equal, that they are endowed by their Creator with certain inalienable rights, that among these are life, liberty, and the pursuit of happiness, that to secure these rights governments are instituted among men.

Each of the four invoked God as the guarantor of freedom.

I laid the pictures out on Soroush's oak desk.

"Yes," Soroush replied, "Exactly."

Soroush provided the intellectual bridge that allowed Iranians to be, at the same time, authentically Muslim and authentically democratic.

He quickly built up a strong following in Iran. A magazine was founded largely to promote his ideas—and the debate about them.

Students and young clerics flocked to his lectures. A burgeoning reform movement grew up around his discourse—to the fury of Iran's theocrats.

"Way back before September 11, Iran started the war on ideas—among Muslims themselves," said Hadi Semati, the jovial Tehran University political scientist who has long been one of my guides to reform and politics in Iran.

"For almost a century, intellectuals had not produced anything of note. Mostly, they brought ideas from the West. But Soroush initiated new ideas on Islam. He changed the redlines of Islamic discourse. And he did it in our own political space. This made it genuine."

Soroush's emergence reflected the wider context of political change in the Middle East.

In the West, the timeline of democratic change was slow and sequential. The Reformation within Christianity gave birth to the Age of Enlightenment, which in turn paved the way for new political ideas about individual rights and democracy. The process unfolded over four centuries—and is still far from complete even in the world's most durable democracies.

The Middle East is confronted with the extraordinary challenge of reforming Islam and overhauling political systems at the same time.

Adapting Islam is a process known as *ijtihad,* or "interpretation." It is applying the essence of the faith—based on the Koran and the traditions of the Prophet Mohammed, known as the hadith—to new problems or a changing world. The word *ijtihad* derives from jihad.

Jihad is today easily the most misunderstood word in the world. It literally means "trying" or "struggle." For practicing Muslims, it means engaging in the daily struggle—with oneself—to be a good Muslim. Jihad only becomes a legitimate military struggle with outsiders when Islam is believed to be endangered, in defense of the faith.

In the twenty-first century, *ijtihad* is the key to Islam's own version of a reformation. It is also the key to political change. But no issue is more sensitive in the Islamic world today than *ijtihad.* Deciding just *how* to interpret and *who* has the right to interpret are hotly disputed. Outsiders beware.

The *ijtihad* camps fall into three categories. Think of them like three doors.

The first are the purists, such as Osama bin Laden's al Qaeda or the ultraconservative Salafi ideologues. They believe Islam was perfect and absolute in its original form. They see the early generations of Muslims, particularly the first three in the seventh century, as the model for all Islamic life in any age. They are literalists. Most are Sunnis.

For them, the door to *ijtihad* is sealed—forever. Opening it would compromise or corrupt the faith. Evil and heresy are on the other side.

The second category includes the majority of clerics and Islamic jurists, who do tolerate *ijtihad*. They straddle a wide middle ground. Most view interpretation through the prism of Islamic law, producing sometimes obtuse legal interpretations. Some like to draw on the Middle Ages, the golden age of Islamic scholarship, when the Middle East was the center of science, medicine, literature, and the arts—and Europe lived in intellectual darkness. Their perspective is narrowly confined and not conducive to independent thought or sweeping new ideas. Using modern reason is not encouraged. Most in this camp are Sunni, although the group includes many Shiite clerics, too.

For most, any movement on *ijtihad* is confined inside the room. Most do not notice the door, much less consider opening it.

Reformers or modernists are another minority. Some are clerics, but many are also academics, scientists, and philosophers. They believe in exploring the sacred text in search of new interpretations and applications for modern life. They argue that the understanding of Islam, like other religions, was not fixed for all time and all places when it was founded. They believe strongly in applying reason and science to enrich the faith and revitalize Islamic civilization.[4] They want to reform Islam to take it forward. They include Sunnis, mostly nonclerics. But because of their own struggle to survive and adapt over the centuries, Shiites tend to conduct the more enterprising or adventurous exercises in *ijtihad* for the twenty-first century.

For them, the door to *ijtihad* is open—although how far is still a matter of fierce debate.

Soroush is one of those reformers.

"The essence of religion will always be sacred, but its interpretation by fallible human beings is not sacred—and therefore it can be criticized, modified, refined, and redefined," he told me.

Human knowledge and experience evolve with time, he said. So, too, should interpretations of the religious texts.

"What single person can say what God meant?" he continued. "Any fixed version would effectively smother religion. It would block the rich exploration of the sacred texts. Interpretations are also influenced by the age you live in, by the conditions and mores of the era, and by other branches of knowledge. So there's no single, inflexible, infallible, or absolute interpretation of Islam for all time."

Soroush even finds freedom in submission.

"Since you're free to be a believer, you should be free to leave your previous faith or to change your religion or to convert to another religion," he explained. "So submission is still there. But if you want to surrender or submit to another faith, you should be free to do that, too.

"It's a contradiction to be free in order to believe—and then afterwards to abolish that freedom."

Soroush also challenges the core idea—on which Iran's Islamic government was based—that there is a single right path for the faithful to follow. Tehran's clerics believe they are the only ones who can define it.

Soroush argues, however, that there is no single right path in Islam—and no single right religion.

"Every day, Muslims recite a prayer ten times entreating God to guide us to the right path," he explained to me. "Some say the only right path is Islam, and the rest stray or are on a deviant path. But I argue that there are many right paths. I try to justify a pluralistic view of religions—the internal sects of Sunni, Shia, and others, and also the great religions, like Christianity, Judaism, and the rest.

"We think they go to hell, and they think we go to hell," he said, a smile crossing his face, as if the idea were amusing in its smallness.

"But I'm trying to say that Christians and members of other religions are well guided and good servants of God. All are equally rightful in what they believe. To some, this sounds like heresy," he said, the smile widening. "But this, too, has found listening ears in our society."

Not within the regime, however. From the mid-1990s, the ruling clerics increasingly cracked down on Soroush. After he was slowly squeezed out of his teaching posts at three universities, he established the Serat Institute. Serat means "path," as in "in the path of God."

The emergence of an Islamic reform movement in Iran is not surprising. Settled by an Aryan people, an Indo-European race from which Iran gets its modern name, the country of both snow-capped mountains and steamy deserts has historically been a crossroads for culture and ideas, commerce and religion. Iran bridges the Arab world to the west and Asia to the east, the former Soviet republics to the north and the Persian Gulf sheikhdoms to the south, Turkey in Europe in the northwest across to Pakistan and Afghanistan in the Asian subcontinent on the southeast. The great caravan routes of the old Silk Road cut through several Persian cities. The discovery of oil by British geologists in 1908 brought in many more outsiders from the West. Over the millennia, Iran has been a repository for souvenirs of disparate cultures.

Faith has also been a central part of Persian culture, long before Islam.

The Zoroastrians of ancient Persia founded one of the world's first monotheistic faiths and heavily influenced subsequent Judeo-Christian thought. Their core ideas—about the devil, hell, a future savior, the worldly struggle between good and evil ending with a day of judgment, the resurrection of the dead, and an afterlife—had an impact on all other monotheistic faiths, and even Buddhism. The use of hands in prayer is widely traced to Zoroastrians praying by pointing both forefingers to the light above; they worship light as the symbol of a good and omnipotent God.

Iran's constitution embraces Islam. But it also acknowledges some of Iran's other faiths with their own seats in parliament, proportionate to their numbers. Christians, Armenians, Zoroastrians, and Jews have their own seats.[5] Each is sworn in on their own holy book.

Jews have been in Iran from the early days of Persian civilization. The Bible recounts Cyrus the Great's conquest of neighboring Babylon, today's Iraq, in the sixth century B.C. He decreed that Jewish slaves be freed and then mandated reconstruction of their destroyed first temple. Many Jews opted to live in Persia rather than move to Israel after their liberation. So many settled in what is today Isfahan that it was once known as Yahudiyeh or Dar al Yahud, Farsi and Arabic titles both roughly meaning "haven of Jews." The majority have fled sporadic persecution since the revolution, although Isfahan remains the largest Jewish community in the Middle East outside Israel.

But Islam, today, defines the national identity. It serves as the most common denominator among otherwise widely diverse ethnicities. The Persian descendants of the Indo-European settlers make up about one half of the seventy million people spread across a country larger than Alaska and more than three times the size of France. The rest are a mix of Turkish-speaking Azeris in the north, Baluchis (or "wanderers") along the border with Pakistan, nomadic herding tribes in the south, Arabs along the Persian Gulf, plus Turkoman farmers and horse traders, mountain-dwelling Lors (an Arab-Persian mix), Armenians, Mongols, Afghans, Indians, and a smattering of several others.

Islam is the glue: Eighty-nine percent are Shiite; another nine percent are Sunni. Only two percent belong to other faiths.

Iran has also always been awash with ideas and science, of which reason played an important and early part.

In science, Avicenna—called Ibn Sina in the Muslim world—was an eleventh-century physician, scientist, and philosopher whose medical texts were taught in Europe until the seventeenth century. One of the moon's craters is named after him. Nasir al-Din Tusi, who lived in the thirteenth century, is widely considered the most eminent astronomer in the 1,400 years between Ptolemy and Copernicus; he charted a science of evolution six centuries before Charles Darwin. The moon's Nasireddin crater is named after him. Abu Bakr al Razi was one of the greatest physicians and philosophers of the Islamic world; his work had enormous influence on subsequent European science. He is credited with the discovery of sulfuric acid and alcohol in the tenth century. He was also an early rationalist. Iran still commemorates Razi Day (August 27), and both a university and institute are named after him. The list goes on and on.

Politically, the quest for empowerment also did not explode out of the blue with Ayatollah Khomeini in the 1960s. Twice before in the twentieth century, Iranians had tried to end dynastic rule—long before democracy was a word uttered in any neighboring state.

The Constitutional Rebellion of 1905–1911 forced the weak Qajar dynasty to agree to Iran's first constitution and parliament. Foreshadowing the 1979 revolution, the revolt was launched by the same powerful troika—the clergy, bazaar merchants, and the intelligentsia—that would come together again later in the century. Their goal was to curtail the monarchy's powers.

The rebellion was a reaction to the shah's huge economic and political concessions to Europeans, particularly Britain and Russia. The dynasty was, in the end, permanently weakened. The last Qajar king fled to France in 1923.

A self-educated army colonel named Reza Khan wrested power from an interim government in 1926. He added the name Pahlavi, meaning "heroic," and crowned himself king—launching the Pahlavi dynasty.[6] He also changed the country's name in the mid-1930s from Persia to Iran, reflecting its people's Aryan roots. He ruled for almost sixteen years, until he was forced to abdicate for his pro-Nazi sentiments during World War II. In a virtual replay of the Constitutional Rebellion, his son soon faced similar demands to limit the monarchy's power.

In 1953, a new coalition called the National Front, led by Prime Minister Mohammad Mossadeq, moved to curtail massive concessions—particularly in the oil industry—given by the shah to foreign powers. Mohammed Reza Shah Pahlavi tried to dismiss Mossadeq, but it backfired—and the shah ended up fleeing to Rome instead. The young king returned to the Peacock Throne after American and British intelligence orchestrated riots that forced the prime minister to resign. The foreign plot infuriates Iranians to this day. Many still want a formal apology from the United States and Britain. Mossadeq has since come to represent, in a single name, frustrated democratic aspirations—and how close Iran came to peaceful evolutionary change.

After the shah's return, the Pahlavi monarchy ruled for another quarter century. Iranians turned to revolution only after evolution twice failed.

Abdolkarim Soroush embodies Iranian passions and politics. He is pious and immersed in its religious traditions. But he also loves the sciences. He earned a degree in pharmacology. After compulsory duty in the shah's army and work at a Tehran laboratory, he went to London for graduate work in analytical chemistry and the philosophy of science. His first book on Islamic philosophy was *The Restless Nature of the World*.

During our conversations, he often mused about reconciling religion and modern reason.

"The ancient world was based on a single source of information: religion. The modern world has more than one source: reason, experience, science, logic," he told me in the late 1990s.

"Modernism was a successful attempt to free mankind from the dictatorship of religion. Postmodernism is a revolt against modernism— and against the dictatorship of reason. In the age of postmodernism, reason is humbler, and religion has become more acceptable.

"The reconciliation between the two," he said, "is now more viable."

Over the years, I watched Soroush's ideas grow in substance and influence. He became daringly outspoken, despite clerical criticism of his work. He also increasingly became the target of young vigilantes when he stepped into lecture halls. Several times he was injured.

Soroush is actually a pen name. Abdolkarim means "servant of God." Soroush means "angels of revelation." His real name is Hosein Dabbagh. Dabbagh means "tanner," the profession of his grandfather. Most Iranians only took last names—many arbitrarily based on where they lived or a father's profession—under orders from the first king in the 1920s. Khomeini came from the town of Khomein, but his brother ended up with a different last name, not all that uncommon from the time.

Soroush originally combined the names of his now-grown children as a pen name when he started writing poetry. He later began using it permanently to protect his family.

By 1999, Soroush crossed a political threshold. "This is totalitarian rule," he told me when I returned to Tehran. "And they are totalitarian rulers. That is a harsh thing to say, but it's the truth. The regime can't survive the way it is."

An Islamic state simply can not be imposed, he told me. It has to be embraced, accepted, and voted on by the majority of people. The use of religion in politics without full freedom is not only wrong, he added, it is dangerous. It will inevitably lead to totalitarianism.

"Governments can make people pay taxes, but they will never

be able to breathe faith in God and the Prophet into people's hearts," he said. "Faith is made of the same fabric as love, and love cannot be created by force."

He paused, reflecting for a moment. "You know, our revolution was a haphazard, chaotic, and theoryless revolution, in the sense that it really wasn't well thought out—not by the leader, not by the people.

"For the Imam [Khomeini], Islam was everything. He wanted everyone to topple the shah in order to apply Islam. But he didn't elaborate on any of these points," Soroush continued.

"So now it's the intellectuals' job to provide a theory for the revolution, to rethink it, and to offer a new logic for it. And the outcome will be not another revolution, but reform. Because—two revolutions in one generation? Well, really! It's too much!" And he chuckled.

As his public following grew, a follower began to organize free Thursday evening lectures for the public. They were held at private homes and at mosques on the eve of the Muslim weekend. I went to several of them and sat on the floor or outdoors with the overflow crowds, listening to him speak in that soft voice, often for hours.

Although I didn't know it at the time, Akbar Ganji was in the crowd too.

Ganji was a former Revolutionary Guard, a member of the elite unit created to protect the fragile new Islamic republic. In the early years, he provided ideological training for its officer corps. Among those he invited as a guest lecturer was Soroush. He was captivated by the philosopher. Students often describe Soroush's lectures in Persian as poetry. He can, in fact, recite from memory many of the long works of Iran's great poets, Rumi and Hafez.

Ganji, who was born in 1959 and also grew up in the shabby suburbs of south Tehran, became a friend and a kind of disciple of Soroush. After the Revolutionary Guards, he moved to the Ministry of Culture and Islamic Guidance, where he helped to churn out revolutionary propaganda. But the bonds with Soroush strengthened as he, too, grew disillusioned with the revolution.

"We wanted to create a heaven. We didn't want a shah, but we were not clear on what we desired," Ganji told me, when we finally met in 2006.

"The more we had repression, executions, as the revolution started swallowing its own children, I started to see this unbelievable reality, and from the other side I started to read about revolutions throughout history. And I ended up seeing one pattern—that all revolutions are the same, they follow the same rules, and they all deviate.

"I realized that repression is in the essence of revolution," he said, smiling, the crows'-feet around his eyes crinkling. "And I realized that we cannot produce democracy with revolution."

Soroush provided the inspiration and intellectual foundation for a burgeoning new reform movement. But Ganji became the practitioner of dissent.

Ganji started writing about Soroush's ideas in *Kiyan*, Iran's leading intellectual journal. *Kiyan* means "source" or "foundation." Soroush wrote for it too—until the government denied the magazine access to printing paper. It was a common trick the regime used to close down publications that relied on state-subsidized newsprint.

Ganji then shifted his focus and began investigating the ruling clerics.

He was brazen by the standards of a movement more comfortable with nuance, nudges, and intellectual debate. In a series of investigative articles for the new crop of reformist newspapers, many of them started by Soroush's followers, Ganji linked Iran's intelligence ministry to the killings of dozens of dissidents in the late 1990s. He charged that key clerics, whom he dubbed "gray eminences" and "red eminences," had issued fatwas approving the murders.

As the regime closed the reformist newspapers one after another to silence them, Ganji compiled his accusations in the *Dungeon of Ghosts*, the Iranian equivalent of Aleksandr Solzhenitsyn's *Gulag Archipelago*. Other books chronicled corruption by top—very top—clergy.

"Ganji was the down-to-earth rabble-rouser of the reform movement," Semati, the Tehran University political scientist, told me. "Despite his junior status, he became the symbol of fierce resistance to a dogmatic vision of Islam and a status quo that had not wanted to change for centuries."

In 2000, the ruling clerics struck back. Ganji was arrested and charged with defaming the regime and jeopardizing national security.

After a series of trials, he was sentenced to ten years in prison, followed
by five years of internal exile. The sentence was later modified to six
years in prison.

But Ganji was not cowed by the ayatollahs. At his trial, he tore open
his gray prison uniform to sit shirtless in court, showing what he said
were the wounds of torture. In prison, often in solitary confinement,
he secretly started writing again.

In 2002, Ganji managed to sneak out his book-length *Republican
Manifesto*. He began with a quote from Thomas Paine. He was brutal
about the Islamic republic.

Iran's revolution was born in circumstances that could never have led
to democracy, he wrote. Khomeini had sought to create a society that
lived perpetually in an "iron cage." The Islamic republic, he concluded,
had reached a dead end.

"A vast stratum of society is in a state of despair, hopelessness, dis-
illusion and dejection," he wrote. . . . "Therefore, only a break from
tyranny can make transition possible."[7]

As the regime increasingly smothered the voices of reform, Ganji's
missives from prison were the buzz of Tehran. They went out on the
Internet, were passed around among students, and were scrutinized in
Iran's political circles.

In 2005, Ganji sneaked out a sequel, a more strident second volume
to his manifesto. This time, he went after the reformers.

He lambasted the movement for timidity and selling out. "The
reformists' false idea that only through active participation in the government can one achieve anything has, in practice, only led them to
function as mere window-dressing for the system, both inside and outside the country," he charged.

Change from within, he concluded bluntly, was no longer possible.

The time had come to end theocratic rule through a new strategy
of mass civil disobedience. He called on Iranians to boycott all elections, which he charged had a long record of fraud, forged ballots, and
"orders given from above" to add votes to bolster turnout figures—and
the regime's legitimacy.

Invoking Mahatma Gandhi, he called on student activists and intellectuals to ignore court summonses for opposition activity that, under

Article 500 of Iran's penal code, made them automatically liable to three to twelve months in prison.

"Citizens must break this law," he wrote. "If this law is broken extensively, the regime will not be able to send many people to jail for expressing their opposition.... The uneven path to freedom will be opened by our efforts."

From his isolated cell in Tehran's notorious Evin Prison, Ganji acknowledged that most Iranians were wary of more revolution, warfare, turmoil, and uncertainty. After a quarter century of upheaval, most Iranians simply wanted to make it through the day. Ganji tried to egg on fledgling democrats.

> *The struggle for freedom is always initiated by a few people. Others will eventually join them. A political player cannot give up with the excuse that people aren't politically motivated or do not support the fight for justice and freedom. The dissidents in the second half of the twentieth century constituted a small minority in all nondemocratic societies. But that small minority opened up the difficult road to democracy by their steadfastness and bravery in the face of suffering. ...*
>
> *We must show them that running away from political struggle is not the remedy to their despair.... We shouldn't believe that democracy is impossible unless all the people become democratic-minded.[8]*

The regime repeatedly tried to force Ganji to recant his treatises. When he fell ill, he later told me, the prosecutor refused to allow him medical treatment unless he repudiated his work. That's when Ganji heeded his own message.

Two weeks after the second manifesto was published, he went on a hunger strike. As the weeks passed, he dropped ten pounds, then twenty, then thirty. Pictures were sneaked out of prison showing his once beefy figure frail and gaunt, huge dark gullies encircling his eyes.

As he weakened, Ganji wrote two "Letters to the Free People of the World." Both were smuggled out of prison. In the second letter, he drew a parallel between his own struggle and Socrates' defiance of the state and his willingness to "invite death."

"Life in slavery is not worth a dime in my eyes," he wrote.[9]

On the forty-third day of his hunger strike, Ganji wrote Soroush. His mentor was among dozens of friends and fellow reformers—including Nobel Peace Prize laureate and human-rights activist Shirin Ebadi, who was one of Ganji's lawyers—who had appealed to him to end the hunger strike.

Ganji expressed the gratitude of his generation to their "beloved teacher" and was wistful about missing the freedom to have another long discussion with Soroush. But he had no choice, he wrote, because of the clerics' betrayal, hypocrisy, and deceptions.

"They are immersed in corruptions but claim to be innocents. Their other service is to defend killers and murderers," he wrote. "They know nothing but claim to be the holders of divine secrets. They are experts in breaking promises."

With scathing bitterness, he described the clerics' "machine" of terror and assassination. "It knew no limits, and every single dissident had to be eliminated," he told Soroush.

In his letter to Soroush, Ganji's transformation was complete. Ganji was not among the well-heeled in the villas and condos of North Tehran who had rejected the revolution from the early days. He was not among the thousands of the Western-educated elite embarrassed by the revolution's excesses and Iran's isolation. He was not among the businessmen who wanted to end economic sanctions as well as tensions with the outside world. He was not among the artists, writers, and filmmakers who felt confined by the Islamic republic's restrictions. He was not even among the prominent student leaders, many of whom were also jailed and tortured.

Once charged with protecting the clerical regime and teaching its virtues, the former Revolutionary Guard had become Iran's noisiest democratic activist and, some claimed, the most popular.

"No other dissident has emerged since the revolution who has the respect of all the disparate elements of Iranian society, from Revolutionary Guardsmen and Basij [volunteers], senior clergy and religious intellectuals, to the secular and religious middle class within Iran, and the strong Iranian exile communities in Europe and North America," Karim Sadjadpour, the Iran analyst for the International Crisis Group, told me.

"The fact that Ganji is held in such high esteem by all of these disparate actors is really quite remarkable."

Ganji held out for seventy-three days. By then, however, he was suffering severe kidney problems and other medical complications. He had lost over fifty-five pounds. In the end, he was lapsing in and out of consciousness. Pressured by family and friends, who argued that he would be more effective alive, he finally ended his hunger strike.

In March 2006, Ganji completed his prison term. Reformers and friends swamped his home to celebrate his release. International groups wanted to honor him; universities abroad wanted him to lecture.

The more important question, however, was how relevant he was at home. By the time he was freed, Iran's reform movement had faded into a whisper. The political environment had changed completely while he was in prison.

Parliamentary elections in 2004 and presidential elections in 2005 had put hard-liners in office. Even friends questioned his ability to effect change.

"Ganji probably represents the loudest and most courageous voice of dissent in Iran, but it's not necessarily a pragmatic or effective one," Semati told me. "His combative and aggressive ideas on reform may not be in tune with the broader popular mood. The economic situation and the problems of everyday life and people are their priorities."

But Ganji continued to speak out.

"The regime is driving Iran toward a catastrophe," he told me when we met several weeks after his release in 2006. "Iran is today an archipelago of prisons."

We met in Washington. He had always been in jail when I was in Tehran. He had come to pick up the 2006 International Freedom of the Press Award from the National Press Club. "There is perhaps no greater exemplar of journalistic heroism in the world today than Iranian investigative reporter and dissident Akbar Ganji," the club said in honoring him.

In his acceptance speech, Ganji said he became a journalist "in order to instigate protest." He cited Albert Camus' *The Plague,* a tale of a disease's devastating toll on society that is often interpreted as a metaphor for repression's deadly impact.

"I am with you here today in order to bear witness on behalf of the fallen victims of the plague of violence," he said. "It recognizes no boundaries. One day, incarnated as Stalin, it ran over the vast territories of Russia. One day, as Hitler, it tormented the people of Germany, the Jews, and other people.... One day, as Mussolini, it wreaked devastation on the beautiful landscape of Italy. And another day, as bin Laden, it wrought havoc on the United States."

As he traveled abroad, Ganji continued his protests. En route to Washington, he stopped in New York and held a symbolic three-day hunger strike in front of United Nations headquarters. Friends and supporters organized small simultaneous demonstrations in eighteen cities around the world to demand the release of Iranian political prisoners, particularly a philosopher, a bus-driving labor activist, and a male former legislator arrested during a women's-rights rally.

He also published a series of op-ed pieces in American newspapers condemning the clerics. "The official ideology of the ruling clerical regime considers all humans to be less than adult and says that without the supervision of the clergy, they will act like children, if not madmen," he wrote in *The Washington Post*. "According to this clerical theory, the people are most virtuous when they are most docile."

"We want the world to know that our rulers do not represent the Iranian people and that their religion is not the religion of the entire nation," he wrote, with almost reckless abandon.[10]

When we spoke, I asked Ganji if he wanted to return to Tehran—or dared to return. Soroush was under such pressure that he had left in 2000 to teach at a string of American universities, including Harvard, Yale, and Princeton, and then in Berlin. He went back to Tehran only occasionally. Soroush was writing, from outside Iran, about issues of justice and Islam. Again stirring huge controversy, he proffered that justice is the standard of what is Islamic—not the other way around.

When I saw Ganji, the two men had just had an emotional reunion, their first in seven years, in Germany.

The regime effectively encouraged its dissidents to leave—or face jail. Ganji's previous arrest in 2000 had come shortly after a trip to Europe for a conference. He had been warned that he would be arrested if he returned.

"I went back, was arrested, and I don't regret it," he told me.

"I told them from the beginning that it's a two-sided cost," he added. "They imprison me, and I pay the cost. But when I talk about them, they also pay a cost. And when they imprisoned me for six years, the cost was higher to them."

EIGHT

IRAN

The Reactionaries

If you cry "Forward!" you must without fail make plain

in what direction to go. Don't you see that if, without

doing so, you call out the word to both a monk and a

revolutionary, they will go in directions precisely opposite?

—RUSSIAN PLAYWRIGHT ANTON CHEKHOV

The most radical revolutionary will become a

conservative the day after the revolution.

—AMERICAN POLITICAL THEORIST HANNAH ARENDT

Islam's priests will wield enormous political influence during the Middle East's turbulent transitions. Many already do. They fill a void created by the imprisonment, exile, or execution of secular democrats and other opponents. Religion's utopian ideals define goals; its institutions offer instruments of action when other avenues are barred.

The phenomenon is not unique to Islam or the region. In their own different ways, popes, dalai lamas, reverends, and rabbis have played pivotal roles in earlier political changes elsewhere—some peaceful, some not.

Yet within Islam, the ayatollahs, imams, sheikhs, and sayyeds speak with many voices. The spectrum is as disparate among clerics as it is among the region's politicians, and in their own ways they are also competing—among themselves—for the future just as fiercely.

Nowhere is the disparity more conspicuous than in Iran. Among the clerical corps, rivalries have spawned opposing parties and led to political subterfuge, physical sabotage, house arrest or imprisonment, and even conflicting fatwas.

From his home in Tehran's foothills of the snow-capped Elburz Mountains, Ayatollah Khomeini regularly reprimanded the theocracy's squabbling clerics. "Stop biting one another like scorpions," he rebuked them in 1981.[1]

When the clerics' political party imploded from internal divisions in 1987, Khomeini again scolded them. "Sowing discord," he said, "is one of the worst sins."[2]

The Islamic Republic's raucous politics function much like Tehran's irreverent free-for-all traffic. Both are irreverent.

In a city with a sea of cars fueled on gasoline at twelve cents per gallon, the unwritten rules of the road are riotously counterintuitive: To turn left on one of the capital's leafy boulevards at busy rush hour, get in the far right lane—and vice versa. A red light means gun it. A green light means slow down and wait until the light turns red—and then gun it. Speed is limited only by what your car can do. See an ambulance or fire truck? Race it. If you pass your exit on a packed freeway, back up fast into oncoming cars. If you need to make a U-turn, wait until oncoming traffic is roaring toward you, and then veer wildly out in front of it. A two-lane road is actually three and possibly four—and, by all means, also feel free to move into a lane of oncoming cars. *The Lonely Planet* travel guide describes Tehran's roads as "lawlessly aggressive," even "homicidal."

In 2004, Tehran unleashed a new breed of traffic cops and meter men to restore order. Dressed in white broad-brimmed military hats and forest-green uniforms with gold epaulets, the traffic police acted like a brigade of generals let loose on street corners. Daringly deployed on busy streets and freeway entry ramps, they did not hesitate to order drivers to pull over for violating the dictate on new billboards, in Farsi and English: FASTENING THE SEAT BELT IS MANDATORY.

But at nine P.M., as the traffic generals retreated for the night, the chaos would resume.

It is much the same in politics. The theocracy has a plethora of forces charged with policing ideas in government, mosques, universities, the military, the press, and the professions. Yet after-hours, Iran bursts with a noisy, honking, chaotic cacophony of political notions.

"If you live in Iran, you have to deal with politics from seven in the morning until eleven at night," University of Tehran political scientist Hadi Semati told me. "It's like our traffic. It can be really frustrating—and really exhausting."

Khomeini's heirs reflect the competing array of visions—even on the theocracy itself.

The most powerful cleric in the Middle East is arguably Ayatollah Ali Khamenei, the supreme leader of Iran. He is only the second person to have the job; he has already held it twice as long as the revolution's founder.

To the great confusion of Westerners, Khamenei (with an *a*) was selected after Ayatollah Khomeini (with an *o*) died abruptly in 1989. The similarity in names was misleading; they were quite different men. The revolution's founder was popularly known as the Imam, an honorific denoting someone considered by the faithful to be capable of leading them in all aspects of life; his successor was a midlevel mullah with marginal credentials, scholarly or otherise, who had to be hastily elevated to ayatollah over the objections of many peers. It was roughly equivalent to picking a pope from among archbishops or monsignors and quickly elevating him to cardinal in the process.

Born in 1939, Ayatollah Khamenei is a tall, lean man with full white whiskers and square, oversized glasses. He wears the black turban of a descendant of the Prophet Mohammed. A student of the Imam's, he was jailed six times by the Shah. His most unusual physical trait is a limp right hand and thin, atrophied fingers that dangle at his side. He suffered serious chest and arm injuries in 1981, when a tape-recorder bomb went off as he was delivering a speech. The regime dubbed him a "living martyr."

I met Khamenei in 1987. He was the first Iranian leader to speak at the United Nations since the revolution. He was president at the time. His debut at the world body, in full clerical garb and turban, reflected the revolution's early hubris. Speaking in the cavernous General Assembly hall, Khamenei blithely dismissed the world body as "a paper factory that issued worthless orders."

He then portrayed Iran's revolution as a contribution to global order because it had toppled a monarchy that had been in "the service of imperial powers, particularly the United States." Washington, he angrily proclaimed, with no sense of the normal diplomatic politesse used at the United Nations, was the "arch Satan."

With a handful of journalists, I was invited to a small breakfast for him the next day at the Waldorf-Astoria. Given his speech, it was a slightly bizarre scene. A collection of clean-shaven U.S. Secret Service agents—who provide security for all visiting heads of state, even for countries with which the United States has no diplomatic relations— were working with a detail of bearded Iranian Revolutionary Guards to protect the Iranian leader. They coordinated and kibitzed like fellow professionals.

At breakfast, Khamenei came across as a dour and distant man, unable to go beyond tired rhetoric and devoid of the kind of mysterious charisma that originally attracted millions of Iranians to the Imam. A Revolutionary Guard stood next to the disabled president's chair and cut up his breakfast foods. It seemed symbolic. Widely considered a weak politician, he was dependent on others to achieve political office.

Yet Khamenei has emerged as the revolution's most enduring constant during its first three decades. The two big turning points in his career symbolize the two pivotal debates that have dominated politics since 1979.

The first big debate was about who should lead the revolution. The answer took two and one half years to sort out. It was the revolution's bloodiest phase.

The Imam—and many of the people who took to the streets to topple the shah—initially did not intend to create a theocracy or to see clerics rule. "Our intention is not that religious leaders should themselves administer the state," Imam Khomeini told *Le Monde* shortly before returning to Iran from exile in Paris.[3] After a wild welcome in Tehran, he moved back to his modest home on a muddy side street in Qom. The first revolutionary government was led by secular technocrats. The Imam was consulted mainly to settle disputes.

But when Iran got down to the business of writing a new constitution—the instrument to define the new state—the process began to look like Tehran's traffic.

In some frenzied politicking, sixty-two drafts were introduced, more than 4,000 constitutional proposals put forward. Many called for technocrats to continue; they opposed clerical rule. Others favored a strong parliament to prevent a president from becoming another autocrat. Some wanted an elected judiciary rather than appointees. Ethnic minorities wanted autonomy from Tehran.[4] The many versions were boiled down, with difficulty after heated disagreements, to two formal drafts. Both constitutions called for a strong president. Both outlined a secular structure for the new state. Both borrowed heavily from Europe's Napoleonic law. Neither allocated special roles for the clergy. And neither proposed a position of supreme leader.

The Imam accepted the second draft, but several parties balked at both. Controversy raged. Rivalries deepened. To end the political gridlock, Iran's Revolutionary Council called for election of an Assembly of Experts to write a final draft. The vote, however, only deepened the divide. When twenty political groups boycotted the poll, the unlikely coalition that had ousted the shah—including communists and clerics, radical students and conservative businessmen, nationalists and ethnic movements—formally collapsed.

The election, held six months after the Imam's return, marked the day the revolution was hijacked by the clergy.

With most secular parties staying away, clerics won two thirds of the Assembly of Experts seats. They then crafted a constitution steeped in Islam. Article Four stipulates, "All laws and regulations, including civil, criminal, financial, economic, administrative, cultural, military, political or otherwise, shall be based on Islamic principles."

The new constitution created a unique political system—with two parallel governments. The first layer is secular, based on Western models. It includes separation of the executive, legislative, and judicial branches, with elections by universal suffrage from the age of sixteen.

The parallel layer is religious. Every branch of government is mirrored by an Islamic institution led by clerics, most of whom are appointed. One body is elected, but the candidates emerge from a clergy whose members basically promote each other to religious positions behind closed doors, with lifetime standing and virtually no accountability.

The religious bodies were designed to be watchdogs. But in every case they have ended up more powerful.

At the top, the Islamic Republic's president is elected every four years and is limited to two terms. His powers are checked by parliament and the judiciary.

But the president is mirrored by the supreme leader, or *velayat-e faqih*. The concept emerged from the Imam's fascination with Plato's *Republic* and the idea of a philosopher-king, adapted to the Islamic world.

The supreme leader is charged with the oversight of all branches of government. He is infallible in all affairs of faith and state, with ultimate veto power over every issue in a country with the world's fourth-largest oil reserves and the region's second-most-powerful military. He also appoints the chiefs of the judiciary and military. And he controls the internal security and intelligence services. There is no appeal from any of his decisions.

The supreme leader runs the most powerful political papacy in the world.

The role is a radical departure in Shiite doctrine. For fourteen centuries, Shiites had been suspicious of political power. The state was viewed as imperfect, corruptible, and a source of persecution and injustice. Shiites had never before accepted temporal rule. It was anathema. So the Imam's decision to put clerics in charge of a modern government was a revolution within Shiism as well as in Iranian politics. It also went against the will of the majority of Shiite clergy, both in and outside Iran.

Other branches of government also have mirror images.

Iran's unicameral parliament has 290 members elected every four years. It is mirrored by the twelve-member Council of Guardians appointed on an open-ended basis. The guardians can reject both candidates and legislation for not being Islamic enough. And they often do.

In the judiciary, Iran's civil and criminal courts are headed by secular judges usually with legal training. Most proceedings are open. They are mirrored by Islamic courts headed by clerics. The clerics can charge people, vaguely or vindictively, with un-Islamic activity. And they often do. Many proceedings are held in secret.

Iran's military has the conventional branches of army, navy, and air force, with a total of more than 400,000 troops. They are mirrored by the elite Revolutionary Guards of some 125,000 troops, plus the young paramilitary volunteers called the Basij, or Mobilization of the Oppressed. They were formed in the revolution's early days to protect the clerics, specifically to prevent the conventional military from trying to launch a coup. During Iran's eight-year war with Iraq, however, the Revolutionary Guards and Basij emerged as far more powerful. They were also put in charge of Iran's secret military procurement programs, including missiles and weapons of mass destruction.

Yet Iran's new constitution did not create a theocracy. Even after it passed, Iran's government was still distinctly split. Secular technocrats ran the traditional arms of government, while clerics dominated the religious institutions. The Imam even decreed that clerics could not run in the first presidential election, which took place a year after the revolution, in January 1980.

The winner was Abolhassan Bani-Sadr, a French-educated economist who had been twice imprisoned by the Shah. A tall man with black, wavy hair, he had a mustache that turned up at the ends, but he was otherwise notably clean-shaven—at a time when beards and stubble were in vogue, even de rigueur, politically. He was close to the Imam during exile in France. Before the revolution, he wrote extensively on how Islamic economics could replace either capitalism or communism.

But Iran's political transformation was still not complete. Neither a new constitution nor a new government ended the discord. Internal spats escalated as revolutionary factions turned on each other. Amid crackdowns, arrests, and executions, the government's secular technocrats and the clerics began to fall out too. Bani-Sadr took to writing a newspaper column called the *President's Diary* to air his troubles. He criticized the clergy for creating a climate of fear. He equated their tactics with Stalinism. He called publicly for "resistance to tyranny," while privately writing the Imam to caution that the regime was moving toward dictatorship. Once he dared to warn that the revolution was "committing suicide."

Clashes soon erupted between supporters and opponents of the president. Two dozen died in the bloodiest one-day showdown.

The tensions finally played out on the floor of Iran's parliament. In June 1981, seventeen months after taking office, parliament impeached Bani-Sadr. The next day, the Imam used his absolute power to remove Bani-Sadr from office and order his arrest. Dressed as a woman, the revolution's fist president went into hiding. He eventually fled to France.

The next sixteen months were even bloodier, as Iran's factions fought it out. Two massive bombs in June and August 1981 eliminated a second president, the prime minister, ten cabinet officials, and twenty-seven members of parliament. In a four-month period in 1981, more than 1,000 government officials—including clerics, judges, politicians, and aides to Khomeini—were killed.[5]

The assassinations forced Iran to hold three presidential elections in a twenty-one-month period in 1980 and 1981, the last two within ten weeks.

In the disarray, the Imam lifted his ban on clerics running for government office. He no longer trusted many secular politicians. In the third presidential election in October 1981, clerics were the only serious candidates.

The winner was Khamenei.

His election marked the moment that the theocrats took over both halves of the state. Iran officially had its "government of God."

Khamenei served as president until he became supreme leader after the Imam's death in 1989. Despite his powers on paper in both jobs, however, Khamenei has never achieved the same aura as the Imam. In his weakness, he has been more thin-skinned about challenges and more vindictive in response.

In 1995, I was in Tehran during the sixteenth anniversary of the

American embassy seizure, an event commemorated each year with lots of speeches and a parade to the old embassy compound. The supreme leader devoted more time berating Soroush, Iran's leading philosopher and reformer at the time, than condemning the United States or Israel.

"It makes me very sad when I see people who seem to be one of us...understanding truths in such a distorted way and publishing them," Khamenei railed in his comments on the anniversary.

"Interpreting religion isn't something that can be carried out by just anyone. Jurisprudence is the main science of the clergy," he warned. "If someone confronts the clergy, he gladdens the Zionists and the Americans more than anything else...because they've set their heart on the destruction of the clergy.

"Well, the Islamic system will slap these people hard in the face!"

The regime's thugs often did just that. Soroush kept a collection of ripped and bloodied shirts from attacks on him in classrooms as well as on the streets.

As a cleric, Khamenei has issued thousands of fatwas, or edicts, ensuring strict Islamic interpretations on everything from Islamic law to betting on basketball, student loans to children in day care with non-Muslims, women on motorcycles to staying in hotels used by Buddhists.[6] Unlike papal bulls, which are initiated by the Vatican, fatwas are issued as answers to questions from members of the flock. They were used by the regime to control everyday life.

Music, Khamenei ruled, can cause deviant behavior and moral corruption among the young that is not compatible with the goals of an Islamic order.

Foreign news, Khamenei ruled, is outlawed if it in any way "lessens trust in Islamic government."

When riding bicycles or motorcycles, he ruled, women must avoid actions that lead to the wrong kind of attention.

Clapping, he advised, is not forbidden on "joyful occasions" but must be avoided if religion is involved.

Nose piercing, he ruled, is not forbidden, although as an adornment it must be covered.

On clothing, he wrote, pictures or symbols from Western countries are a problem because they "promote the cultural aggression against

Muslims." Wearing ties is forbidden as it "imitates and propagates the cultural assault" on Muslims.

But new restrictions are not what many Iranians expected out of the revolution. And three decades later, Khamenei faced the same irrepressible irreverence that makes Tehran's streets so crazy. A lot of Iranians do exactly what they want, fatwa or not.

In 2004, I was in Tehran again during the twenty-fifth anniversary of the U.S. Embassy takeover. During the commemoration in front of the graffiti-covered wall around the American compound, supporters of the regime handed out little cards listing companies to boycott, such as Calvin Klein, because they do business with Israel. Yet throughout the capital, billboards once reserved for revolutionary slogans and Iranians killed in their Iraq war instead now advertised Calvin Klein—as well as Cartier watches, Nokia mobile phones, and Hummer, a cologne for men named after the American military vehicle.

Victoria's Secret had also arrived in Tehran. So had the Gap, Diesel, Benetton, and Black & Decker. They were not legal franchises. Economic sanctions forbid American companies from doing business with Iran. So Iranian entrepreneurs bought brand-name goods abroad and resold them in their own shops, often with the brand replacing the shop name on storefront signs. Victoria's Secret was a bit more discreet. It was marked only by a trademark pink-and-white-striped Victoria's Secret bag in the window.

Iran's young, who comprise seventy percent of the population, are particularly defiant, sometimes desperately so. When Iran beat Bahrain to qualify for the 2005 World Cup, tens of thousands of young males and females poured onto Tehran's streets to celebrate. More than 100 young females even defied police—and fatwas against women attending male sporting events—to get into the stadium to see the game.

The eruption of life is visible every Thursday evening, the eve of the Muslim Sabbath, on Africa Boulevard. Teenagers and twenty-somethings cruise up and down a street lined with boutiques and fast-food joints in their colorful Japanese and Korean compacts. Boys in one car, girls in another, they drive slowly back and forth for hours, their cars blaring Justin Timberlake, Ricky Martin, punk, rock, rap, heavy metal, pop, jazz, electronic, or disco. Everyone seems to be talking, either shouting to passengers in other cars or on cell phones after beaming numbers to each other. Some will hook up later in alleys near the pizza parlors that have proliferated throughout Tehran.

Police try to break up the car cavorting, but they, too, get stuck in the bumper-to-bumper traffic.

Dress codes are openly ignored by the imaginative young. One of my favorite images was a young woman whose version of Islamic dress was a black skirt and a baggy black sweatshirt emblazoned PLANET HOLLYWOOD LAS VEGAS. Pale pink has increasingly replaced black as the female fashion favorite, even among the devout. Many of the young dare to wear tight jeans under bust-stretching shirts or jackets. Colorful headscarves are perched precariously at the crown of the head to expose as much of a beautifully coifed hairdo as possible without falling off. Open-toed shoes expose toenails lacquered in red, purple, pink, or black. Faces are heavily made up. Among the young, plastic surgery—especially nose jobs—is common.

Many of Khamenei's other fatwas are also ignored. Satellite dishes beam in CNN and BBC, which are viewed even in government offices. Women ride on the back of motorcycles, their chadors flapping dangerously in the wind. And the double bill at a local movie house the same weekend as the commemoration of the American embassy takeover in 2004 featured *Kill Bill* and *Fahrenheit 9/11*. They played to sold-out audiences. Despite its theme of religious irreverence, *Bruce Almighty* drew big audiences a few months later.

Khamenei's powers are at the heart of the second big debate in Iran. It pits the clergy against itself—even within Khamenei's own family. And it has still not been resolved three decades after the revolution.

Since 1989, the symbol of dissent among Iran's clergy has been Ayatollah Ali Montazeri. The Imam, who once called him "the fruit of my life," appointed Montazeri as his successor. They had been lifelong colleagues.

But ten years into the revolution, the two men had a final and politically fatal falling-out when Montazeri dared to criticize the Islamic republic and its rulers. The theocracy, he said publicly, had failed to fulfill much of its early promise. He called on the government to "correct past mistakes."

"One does not fight a doctrine by killing, because no problem can be settled this way. One fights back with a fair doctrine," he wrote the warden of Tehran's Evin Prison after word circulated about several secret executions of dissidents.[7]

In an open letter to the Imam, he then plaintively appealed, "For what valid reasons...has our judiciary approved these executions, which can result in nothing but damaging the face of our revolution and the system?"[8]

If the government continued to ignore the voices of dissent, Montazeri warned seminary students, then "dissenting words will turn into bullets."[9]

Montazeri, who was born in 1922 to a peasant family, also challenged the Imam's fatwa condemning author Salman Rushdie to death for satirical treatment of the Prophet Mohammed in his book *The Satanic Verses*.[10]

"People in the world are getting the idea that our business in Iran is just murdering people," Montazeri warned his mentor.[11]

The Imam abruptly fired his protégé.

Three months later, Khomeini suddenly died, leaving no designated successor.

For his criticism and candor, Montazeri's popularity only increased. Iranians have been attracted to strong, charismatic leadership since the days of Cyrus the Great and Darius in the sixth century B.C.; less dynamic leaders have fared poorly in Iran. Khamenei's subsequent selection, for many in Iran, failed to inspire. He lacked adequate stature and credibility.

And the simmering dispute over the supreme leader's infallibility suddenly intensified into an existential challenge for the state. In the wake of Khomeini's death, the clerics increasingly took sides.

Mohsen Kadivar was one of the early rebels. I called on Kadivar at his modest, book-packed office in 2004. Born in 1959, he has a short salt-and-pepper beard, a small gap between his front teeth, and the easy smile of a Shirazi. People from Shiraz—a former Iranian capital in the south famed for its roses, poets, sunshine, and, before the revolution, its wine—are noted for their lively charm and sense of humor.

Kadivar was clearly comfortable with his candid irreverence.

"Iranians are so dissatisfied with the supreme leader," he told me with a chuckle, "that if they see him on TV, they change the channel."

In a series of essays and lectures since the mid-1990s, Kadivar has challenged the very concept of a *velayat-e faqih,* or supreme leader. His argument is based on both Islam and Iran's constitution.

"Every member of society and every member of government is subject to the law. No one can be above it. Everyone has the same rights," he explained. "Yet the root of the *faqih* is inequality. He assumes he is above it.

"It is time," he told me, "for the supreme leader to be subject to the constitution too. After all, the supreme leader doesn't come from God!"

The position's absolute power, he once daringly said, made the *faqih* as unjust and illegitimate as the shah. That went too far. In 1999, Iran's Special Court for the Clergy charged and tried Kadivar for "disseminating lies about Iran's sacred system," defaming Islam, and "helping the enemies of the revolution." He was sentenced to eighteen months in prison, virtually all of it in solitary. He quickly became a hero to young Iranians.

Kadivar was unrepentant when he was released. The time had come, he pronounced, for the clerics to pull out of government.

"Our job as religious people is not politics," he told me, sitting across a small conference table and sipping tea. "They are taking Iran backward, not toward the future.

"Most Iranians believe what I say but are afraid to say it," he added. The supreme leader may have increased his powers over the years, but his authority was actually in greater question. "Authority you can see in the street from the people. But power you get from soldiers and security forces. When you're on a bus, in a taxi, in the street, in shops, you hear everywhere the criticism of the people. They are not satisfied with him."

Kadivar was not a lone voice.

In 2006, dozens of Iranians were arrested for forming a human shield around the home of another rebel cleric, Ayatollah Hosein Kazemaini Boroujerdi. Many of his supporters had been there for more than ten weeks to offer protection. Buses rotated them in and out. Imprisoned for several months in 1995 and 2001, Boroujerdi had again been summoned by the special clerical court—the usual indication of new trouble and a potential new arrest.

But Boroujerdi had not been cowed. "The most afflicted victim of this theocracy has been God," he said in 2006.

"The regime is adamant that either people adhere to political Islam or be jailed, exiled, or killed. Its behavior is no different from that of Osama bin Laden or [Taliban leader] Mullah Omar."

In desperation, Boroujerdi wrote the United Nations, the European Union, and the Vatican for help. "I believe people are fed up with political religion and want traditional religion to return," he told the Islamic Labor News Agency.[12]

But the controversy among clerics was perhaps best reflected in Khamenei's own family. His younger brother Hadi was a most unusual rebel. When I visited his office in 1999, he helped to put a human face on the clergy for me. His turban had been unwound; the long piece of black cloth was draped on a corner coatrack, alongside his limp dangling robe and above his shoes. He was wearing an open-necked shirt with rolled-up sleeves and large aviator glasses on his long, leonine face.

The younger Khamenei had been lecturing at seminaries and universities across Iran against the idea of absolute religious rule—and a supreme leader. He also edited a newspaper critical of the hard-liners' politics. He had even registered as a candidate for the 1998 election for the Assembly of Experts, which selects the supreme leader and is supposed to monitor his performance.

He was, not surprisingly, disqualified from running by the Council of Guardians.

"The most important thing we're looking for today in Iran is the rule of law," he told me. "And that means no one, whatever his position, is above it.

"Unfortunately for the rest of us," he added, "there are still people at the top who don't accept that basic right."

But many clergy do. The majority of Iran's clergy are actually not in government—and do not want to be. Many oppose religious rule.

"At least ninety-five percent of the clergy have not been beneficiaries of the revolution," Hadi Semati, the Tehran University political scientist, told me. "Some got money and prestige, but the overwhelming majority are poor and have not been part of the power structure."

They have also felt the fallout of public resentment.

Three decades after the revolution, Iranians are increasingly derisive about the regime's clerics. Iranians love to point out how many mullahs settled into the posh northern suburb of Jamaran. The Imam's home and mosque were near the top of one of its scenic hills. Jamaran means "haven of snakes."

Tehran taxis often do not stop to pick up clerics. One cleric told me his tale of a taxi slowing in front of him, only to have the driver look at him and run his finger, like a knife, across his throat, and then speed away. An Iranian friend recounted his own ride in a group taxi on a particularly hot day. His taxi next pulled over to pick up a cleric who had been standing on a curb under the cooling cover of a leafy tree. Two blocks later, the cabbie stopped and told the cleric to get out. My friend asked the driver what he was doing.

"I didn't want him to have the benefit of the shade," the cabbie replied.

Iranians, who love their humor, can convert even the most unlikely news story into a joke about the clerics—usually implying their ignorance. In 2006, Iranian-born Anousheh Ansari became the first female tourist in space when she flew on a Russian shuttle to the International Space Station. Iranians laughed that the clerics, when asked if there was anything wrong with a Muslim woman in space not wearing proper Islamic dress, debated the issue and finally decreed that it was OK—as long as outer door of the space station was left open at all times so that no sex could take place.

The clerics have come under the scrutiny of Iran's imaginative film industry, too. *Under the Moonlight* is the politically incorrect story of young Hassan, who reluctantly agrees to give up what he loves to become a cleric to please his parents. On his way back from buying clerical robes for his induction ceremony, the garments are stolen by a young boy. Hassan eventually tracks down the lad, who agrees to return the robes that evening under one of Tehran's main bridges.

But under the moonlight of the bridge, Hassan finds a world unknown to clerics—of the homeless and prostitutes and the unemployed. He listens riveted to their stories. When the garments are finally turned over, Hassan decides to sell them and buy food for the bridge people—and not become a cleric.

The implicit message of *Under the Moonlight* is that the clerics know little about reality; they live in isolation and do little for those suffering the most.

The box-office hit *The Lizard,* released in 2004, tells the delicious story of a thief who steals the robes and turban of a mullah to escape prison—and then gets stuck as a cleric to elude capture. Reza Marmulak—a double entendre name meaning Reza the lizard—heads for the border, but stops in a remote village where he is mistaken for the new cleric expected to take over the local mosque. He quickly becomes popular, slithering past complex religious questions, and giving off-the-cuff and occasionally humorous sermons that lead villagers to flock back to the mosque.

The film has another double meaning: A criminal may be able to find redemption through God, but at the same time an ignorant criminal can masquerade as a cleric—and bring believers back to their faith. Its mockery of the clergy, bordering on subversion, ended up being too much. *The Lizard* was banned a month after it opened to around-the-block queues in Tehran.

As supreme leader, Khamenei has the tools to quash, banish, and imprison to force conformity. But he has never been able to evoke reverence or impose fealty. Iranians, like their traffic, are simply not controllable.

Even after he was cast aside, Montazeri continued to offer a different vision. "One cannot work in the world by wielding clubs any longer. The government of clubs will no longer work," he said in an address to his followers in Qom in 1997. "Nothing is accomplished when two or three people sit and make decisions for the country. 'Republic' means 'government of the people.'"

Iran's Islamic courts ordered Montazeri to be silenced. He was also placed under house arrest. Guards were deployed around his home to prevent any contact with other clerics, seminary students, or the public. Thugs smeared a sign across his office: "HERETIC OF THE AGE."

But when his house arrest ended in 2003, Montazeri again went public with his criticism. "Either officials change their methods and give freedom to the people and stop interfering in elections," he warned in 2004, "or the people will rise up with another revolution."

The longer Islamists compete in elections, the greater the diversity—and the divisions.

Iranians love to joke: Where there are three Shiites, there are four political parties. And tomorrow there may be five.

During the revolution's first decade, there was only one party. Three decades later, there are dozens. But divisions are not always easy to diagram. Iran's hard-liners reflect a bloc of some two dozen different parties, both isolationist and internationalist. Reformers are dispersed among some eighteen parties, both religious and secular. In between are many others, constantly reconfiguring. Some, like the Freedom Party, are not allowed to run; their members are regularly harassed, questioned, and detained.

And names often confuse, even mislead. The difference can be only a couple of letters. The Association of Combatant *Clergy,* or *Rouhaniyat,* is hard-line. But the Association of Combatant *Clerics,* or *Rouhaniyoun,* is reformist.

Labels are somewhat simplistic too. The Association of Combatant Clergy favors unchallenged power for the clergy. It wants limits on personal freedoms. It includes the most right-wing mullahs, Friday prayer leaders, judges of Islamic courts, and older clerics in their seventies and eighties—and the supreme leader.

Yet it is still diverse. Its younger members tend to be ideologically hard-line, while older members tend to be conservatives guided by traditional religious values.

On the other end of the political spectrum, the Association of Combatant Clerics wants limits on clerical power. It advocates individual freedoms, although within limits that will not lead to secularism or liberalism. It includes left-wing and midlevel theologians, aged mainly in their forties to sixties, and less traditional in their interpretation of Islam. But it also does not fit a stereotype. Among its members is the spiritual adviser to the students who seized the United States Embassy in 1979, Ayatollah Mohammed Khoeiniha.

And those are just two of the parties. Few societies are as complex or nuanced as Iran. But understanding the diversity within political Islam is understanding its future.

Two Iranian presidents illustrate the chasm. Both are devout Muslims. Both have impeccable revolutionary credentials. Both pledged full loyalty to the supreme leader and the Islamic republic. Both were dark-horse candidates. And both were elected, against stiff odds, because Iranians wanted change.

Yet they have little else in common.

In their differences, the two men—the first elected in 1997, the second in 2005—personify the dispute among Iran's revolutionaries over just what an Islamic republic should be. Their presidencies also address the question of whether Iran's Islamic system is flexible enough to survive.

The first president was Mohammed Khatami, a mild-mannered cleric distinguished by a barbered beard, elegant robes, a black turban, and elastically expressive eyebrows that bob up and down over his rimless glasses. He was born in 1943. His father was a cleric and close adviser to the Imam; his brother married the Imam's granddaughter. As a seminary student, Khatami drafted and distributed pamphlets during the Imam's confrontation with the shah in the 1960s. He was elected to the first revolutionary parliament. He was elected president in 1997.

Khatami is a midranking cleric. A religious intellectual, he is also referred to as sayyid, an honorific title meaning "master" or denoting descent through the Prophet Mohammed's family. In his case, it is both. He is among Iran's clerical elite.

On Iran's peculiar political spectrum, he is a reformer. Unlike Soroush, however, Khatami is still inside the system. Like Iran's parties, personal relationships among its leading players are rarely simple: Khatami and Soroush are friends. But Khatami's family has also gone on vacation with the supreme leader and his relatives.

Khatami's victory marked Iran's greatest political comeback. After a decade as minister of culture, he was forced out of office in 1992 for encouraging openings in the press, arts, and film. He was almost literally shelved, relegated to the obscurity of Iran's national library. The charges against him included "negligence" and "liberalism."

Urged on by peers five years later, Khatami reluctantly ran for the presidency to offer a symbolic alternative to several hard-line candidates. He was not disqualified, by most accounts, because he was such a long shot against the regime's favorite and front-runner, Speaker of Parliament Ali Akbar Nateq-Nouri. Many Iranians considered the election a foregone conclusion.

But during Iran's brief presidential campaign, a mere twelve days, Khatami caught fire. He attracted growing crowds as he talked about the rule of law, encouraging debate, tolerating dissent, and addressing the needs of youth and women. He had an easy charisma. He also did not glower or lecture like so many of the mullahs.

Tehran suddenly buzzed with excitement.

"People were enthusiastic because that election offered the biggest choice of candidates since the revolution," Hadi Semati, the political analyst, told me. "One was the candidate of the status quo, while the other was for change. He was like Bill Clinton—a new generation. People wanted a new face and new energy, and Khatami was full of energy."

The vote was a landslide upset. Everyone over the age of sixteen can vote in Iran, male and female. Khatami ran just as the youth bulge born after the revolution came of voting age. More than twenty million people voted for Khatami. He won seventy percent in a huge turnout.

Iranians sent a decisive message: They were rejecting a generation of conservatives who had dominated politics since the revolution.

In his inaugural address in parliament, Khatami struck a new tone.

An Islamic government is one that considers itself to be the servant of the people, not their master. A government's authority is not realized by coercion or arbitrariness, but by legal acts, by respect for rights, and by encouraging people's participation in decision making. People must believe that they have the right to determine their own destiny—and that there are limits to government. . . .

We must try not to impose our personal preferences on our society at all costs. The government should even protect the rights of its opponents.

The atmosphere in Iran changed quickly.

A wave of independent newspapers opened with irreverent editorials and lampooning cartoons. Books long held back by censors were published; critical movie scripts were approved. The works of Western artists—European masters like Van Gogh, Picasso, Chagall, Miró, and Monet, as well as the pop art of Andy Warhol—were taken out of storage and put back up in the Museum of Contemporary Art. Satellite dishes proliferated, bringing in everything from CNN and Oprah Winfrey to the soap opera *Santa Barbara* and Asia's equivalent of MTV. Social restrictions were relaxed.

As president, Khatami was outgoing compared with the regime's aloof ayatollahs. He doffed his clerical robes on national television to give blood. In one of the world's smoggiest cities, he took the bus to work to draw attention to Clean Air Day. He did a call-in radio talk show.

Khatami gave a whole new look to the clergy—politically and literally. For a man of the cloth, the chic cloth the president wore was much discussed in Tehran. He was even something of a dandy.

Clerical garb has become politically telling in Iran. Some tailors specialize in crafting clerical robes; the prophet Mohammed, they say, urged his representatives to look good and smell fragrant. The supreme leader prefers the simple *qabaa,* a white pajamalike tunic with loose white pants underneath. But Khatami favors the more fashionable *labbadeh* robe, which has a round collar and slits on the side that show matching tailored pants. They come in beige, blue, green, or gray. The *labbadeh* has up to eight pockets hidden inside. One of the disparaging jokes in Iran is that the clerics are always looking to fill them—with money.

Over his well-tailored robes, Khatami wears diaphanous cloaks of fine mohair in summer and thick wool in winter, in shades of black or rich brown. Iranians love nicknames, and Khatami was been variously dubbed the "cleric in the chocolate robe," for the color of his favored cloak, and the "Armani mullah."

The size of a turban can also be telling. Many of the traditional or conservative clerics wear bulky headpieces wrapped from cloth sixty feet long. Khatami wears the trendier tighter turban crafted from cloth as short as twelve feet.

Shoes are the other political indicator. Conservative clerics wear slippers, in part for fear the leather does not come from an animal killed according to Islamic ritual. Modern mullahs wear shoes; Khatami's always match his outer cloak. His vice president, Mohammed Abtahi, once explained that his own father, also a cleric, had recently approved of Abtahi's shoes, but only as long as he wore socks so that the leather did not touch his skin.[13]

In the same way, wearing a wristwatch is a telltale sign of a modern cleric. Conservatives carry pocket watches, if they have watches at all. Khatami wore a designer watch.

Politically, Khatami's style differed too.

When he came to office in 1997, a country with almost seventy million people had only 400 elected officials, all concentrated in the capital. His government moved quickly to hold long-delayed local elections. In 1999, Iranians elected almost 200,000 people to run towns, villages, and hamlets throughout the country. Power, hogged for two decades by the clerics, was finally being dispersed.

I first met Khatami in 1998 when he made his international debut at the opening session of the United Nations General Assembly. The Iranian mission in New York organized another informal press breakfast. In contrast to Khamenei, Khatami was engaging, inquisitive, and expansive on a range of subjects. His one wish, he told us, was to be able to get to know New York by walking its streets.

Over bagels, mushroom omelets, and hash browns, he explained why he had come to New York to call for a dialogue of civilizations.

"At the end of the twentieth century . . . what is the legacy of humanity? In his famous book *The Republic,* Plato says, 'What is justice?'" Khatami opined to a group of journalists who had all come to talk about issues a bit more pressing than ancient Greek philosophy.

"The Koran says that the aim of the prophethood was defense of justice and equality. One can interpret the same meaning from the Bible and the Torah. "But twenty-five hundred years after Plato, two thousand years after Jesus, and fourteen hundred years after Mohammed, we *still* ask: What is meant by justice? The very fact that humanity has not reached a united definition means we are still in a period of trial and error. We need to have a dialogue among civilizations about the issue of justice. We must make efforts to have greater equality and justice for all humanity."

Khatami's idea resonated at the United Nations. The world body designated 2001, by ironic coincidence a year that sparked the deepest tensions between the Islamic and Western worlds, the year for a dialogue of cultures. It followed up in 2005 by creating the Alliance of Civilizations, cochaired by the prime ministers of Spain and Turkey, to keep a dialogue going. The panel included Muslims, Jews, Catholics, Protestants, Hindus, and others, as well as Khatami.

At home, Khatami took his own steps to ease Iran's tensions with the outside world. He ended a standoff with the West over a death sentence imposed by Imam Khomeini on Salman Rushdie for his book *The Satanic Verses*. The Imam had issued the controversial fatwa, inconveniently, just before his death in 1989; it was difficult for his less powerful successors to lift. It soured Iran's foreign relations and hurt trade for almost a decade.

"We should think of the Salman Rushdie issue as completely finished," Khatami told us during his 1998 United Nations visit.

In an interview with CNN the same year, he also said that the time had come to bring down the "wall of mistrust" between the United States and Iran. He called for cultural exchanges to begin the process. The diplomatic overture was daring, given suspicion and skepticism among hard-liners.

But Khatami had some unusual supporters, reflecting Iran's often unpredictable political alliances.

Among the most ardent reformers were the former students who had seized the American embassy in 1979. A generation later, many had moved on to major political positions. I tracked some of them down in Tehran to talk about Khatami's outreach both at home and abroad.

Ibrahim Asgharzadeh was one of three engineering students who masterminded the embassy seizure. Asgharzadeh had been the students' primary spokesman throughout the hostage crisis, which lasted 444 days, introduced the yellow ribbon as a national symbol, cost eight American lives in a failed rescue attempt, ostracized one of the world's largest oil producers, redefined both diplomacy and terrorism, and ended the Carter presidency. He coined the term "den of spies" to describe the American embassy. The little nook at the corner of the old embassy compound was converted into the Den of Spies Bookshop, which sold copies of secret U.S. documents pieced together from shredders after the takeover.

I met Asgharzadeh in 1999 at the home of husband-and-wife professors we both knew. He was forty-four by then; he had changed in many ways in the two decades since I'd covered the hostage crisis. I had also been on the tarmac of the Algiers airport when the fifty-two hostages arrived from Tehran on their first stop to freedom in 1981. Asgharzadeh's hair back then had been a dark, messy mane; twenty years later, his silver locks were fashionably barbered.

Over dinner, Asgharzadeh recounted the elaborate planning before the embassy seizure, after students from several campuses decided to protest Washington's decision to take in the ailing shah. Iran for decades had been one of two pillars of American foreign policy in the Middle East; Israel had been the other. Even after the revolution, the United States maintained relations, bought Iran's oil, and continued to sell it weapons. The embassy seizure abruptly turned Iran from ally into enemy.

"The critical phase was getting three pieces of information," Asgharzadeh recalled. "The most important was an inside plan of the embassy. Two student apartments were across the street, so we used different rooms to draw maps. We also had to find out about the staff, so we kept a log on the personnel. Students were posted around the clock to watch how many there were, and who went in and out. We wanted all the Americans inside when we took it.

"Finally, we had to know the security situation inside. We had to do this all ourselves, and we were just students," he continued. "But, in the end, we had really good information on the Marine guards."

The original intent, Asghazadeh explained, was to hold the embassy for three to five days. It was supposed to be a repeat of the first brief seizure of the U.S. Embassy on Valentine's Day nine months earlier, just two weeks after the Imam returned from exile. The first takeover had been resolved peacefully, and diplomacy resumed after the students left.

The second time, however, the Imam stunned the students by endorsing the embassy takeover. Holding the Americans hostage suddenly became a government cause.

"The masses demanded that we continue, something we didn't anticipate," Asgharzadeh told me. "It became a very complicated situation, one that was out of our hands."

But two decades later, Asgharzadeh was much more interested in discussing other issues. When Iran held its first local elections earlier that year, he had run—and won one of fifteen seats on Tehran city council.

"Traffic, pollution, sewage—ninety-five percent of my time is now spent trying to solve the issues of ordinary people's lives," he told me. "I've learned that people's worldview is changed more by dealing with the small problems of life.

"And, unfortunately," he added, "ideology can't solve them."

In the two intervening decades, all three ringleaders and many of the student captors had become, by Iranian standards, reformers. The radicalism of their youth—demanding accountability from the United States for embracing the deposed shah in 1979 and orchestrating, with Britain, the 1953 coup in Iran—had been channeled into demanding accountability from their own troubled government.

The conversion was striking. I often timed my trips to Iran to coincide with the embassy takeover anniversaries. The commemorations are a good barometer of Iranian public sentiment about the United States—and their own government. The year before, in 1998, I had heard Asgharzadeh speak to students for the first time since the takeover. His message had changed.

"Our dealings with the hostages were not directed against the American people, and not even against the hostages themselves," he told the crowd, standing on a specially raised dais put up every year in front of the old embassy wall.

Asgharzadeh was repeatedly interrupted by a group of young vigilantes shouting *Marg bar Amrika,* or "Death to America"—the same slogan he had shouted twenty years earlier.

But Asgharzadeh yelled back through a loudspeaker, "Today, we invite all the hostages to return to Iran, as our guests. Regarding relations with America, we must look to the future and not to the past. We have a new language for the new world. We defend human rights. And we'll try to make Islam such that it won't contradict democracy."

In 2000, I tracked down another of the original ringleaders. Mohsen Mirdamadi is a short man with a trim salt-and-pepper beard who had shed student garb for a pinstripe suit. Once willing to take the law in his own hands, Mirdamadi ran for parliament in 2000 on the reformist platform of restoring the rule of law. He had just been named head of parliament's foreign relations committee.

"We've always wanted a country that had independence, freedoms, and was an Islamic republic, though our emphasis originally was on winning independence from foreign influence and creating an Islamic state," he told me when we met at the Islamic Participation Party's headquarters, just two blocks from the old American embassy compound.

"But today our emphasis is on freedoms," he said. "And now we want to be more of a republic. Our tactics have shifted too. Before, we carried out a revolution. Today we're trying evolution."

Iran's disparate reform movement pulled together those early radicals as well as lawyers and human-rights activists, young clerics as well as Westernized elites, students and private entrepreneurs, women and academics. They channeled their frustration with almost two decades of autocratic and abusive rule by rallying around Khatami.

As the reform movement picked up momentum, Khatami was nicknamed Ayatollah Gorbachev, after the Russian leader whose policies introduced change at home and outreach abroad.

Unlike Soroush and Ganji, however, Khatami was still an insider. He still believed in the Islamic republic. He just wanted to reverse the emphasis. In Iran's constitution, the mix of Islamic law and Western republican law, borrowed from France and Belgium, had always left an unanswered question: Is Iran first a modern republic that factors in Islamic values? Or is it foremost an Islamic state that selectively borrows from democratic ideals, but has no obligation to the principles of republicanism? Which does the state protect first: individual rights or Islam?

Khatami came to office having thought a lot about the answer. During his five years in political exile at the national library, he had published two books. One was a collection of essays about recent Shiite clerics engaged in *ijtihad,* reinterpreting Islam; the second was an exploration of Western political thought—Plato and Aristotle, Thomas Aquinas and St. Augustine, Machiavelli and Hobbes. It was entitled *From the World of the City to the City of the World.* In it, Khatami explored the conflict in Europe on the eve of the Christian Reformation. The Church, then endowed with absolute power from God while the faithful were trapped in feudalism, was pitted against new Christian reformers, sages of reason, and advocates of individual rights.[14]

The same struggle was playing out within contemporary Iran 400 years later.

Khatami was particularly fascinated with seventeen-century British philosopher John Locke, the son of Puritans who wanted to separate church and state—largely to protect religion. Locke did not want faith to be discredited by incompetent rule. The same issue resonated again in contemporary debate among Iran's clergy. Many fretted over the impact of the Islamic republic's shortcomings on Shiites' faith in their faith.

Khatami's speeches often echoed Locke. "We must use all our strength to avoid doing anything against the Islamic Sharia—God forbid that day. But we must also do our best so that no one would accuse Islam of not being able to resolve economic, social, political, and security problems," he said in his second inaugural address, after his reelection in 2001 by an even bigger margin.[15]

Khatami prodded political discourse toward the idea of Iran, first and foremost, as a modern republic with Islamic values—or what he called a "republic of virtue." Officials elected by the people—rather than the religious institutions run by the clerical elite—should have primary power in running the state, he argued.

"Iranian culture is religious," he told me at another meeting a few years later. "I have been pressing for a reading of religion that would allow us to achieve independence, freedom, and progress. If we can interpret religion in a way that conforms with democracy, both democracy and religion will benefit. If we see freedom and religion as opposing each other, both will suffer."

Unlike the conservative clerics, Khatami was not afraid of what the Imam called "Westoxification."

"Without a doubt, we will succeed in moving forward only if we have the capacity to reap the benefit of positive, scientific, and social accomplishments of Western civilization," he said at an Islamic summit the year he took office.

Two aspects of democracy scare even reformers: One is secularism, for fear it will rob society of its core values. The other is liberalism, for fear it will introduce pornography and other perceived social ills. Khatami did not embrace or accept either. But he understood something of the outside world.

"Liberalism is the world's religion," Khatami said in 2006. "We do not have the right to insult liberalism." He saw the Islamic republic fitting into the world as it is—albeit on terms comfortable to Tehran.

In the end, however, Khatami's vision of reform proved illusive. He failed to achieve most of what he set out to do. His fellow clerics made it impossible.

During his two terms, the Islamic judiciary was a constant challenge. Its courts closed down more than 100 independent publications that had opened since he took office and encouraged a more independent press. Several journalists bravely turned around and launched new ones with the same staff, same slant, and same look, but a different name. When the Islamic judiciary could not stop them, it began arresting editors and reporters.

In 1999, the banning of the popular reformist paper *Salam*—edited by Abbas Abdi, another former hostage taker—triggered the largest protest since the revolution. Students poured out by the thousands in Tehran to demonstrate. Paramilitary vigilantes soon stormed campuses to quash the revolt. Several students were beaten. Police then arrested more than 1,400 people. Many spent years in prison. Two of the jailed students died in mysterious circumstances in 2006.

Parliament also moved against Khatami by impeaching the most popular reformer in his cabinet, Abdollah Nouri. In Iran, government permits are required for public gatherings, and Nouri had granted them for student demonstrations and other meetings, effectively endorsing greater freedom of speech and assembly. The judiciary tried and imprisoned Nouri on charges of insulting Islamic values, even though he was a cleric.

Tehran's charismatic mayor Gholem Hossein Karbaschi, one of Khatami's campaign advisers and an innovator who had beautified war-ravaged Tehran, was also tried and imprisoned on charges of corruption.

The tension became deadly. Khatami's rivals within Iranian intelligence were widely tied to the serial murders of dissident writers. They were also suspected of the motorcycle drive-by shooting of the chief architect of Khatami's reform agenda, Saeed Hajjarian, who had been elected to Tehran's city council in the first local elections in 1997, along with Asgharzadeh. He was left paralyzed.

As Khatami failed to fight back, his constituency began to turn on him. In an open letter, Iran's students chastised their president. "Are you awake or asleep?" they demanded. "Why do you remain silent? What is the price of staying in power?"

Soroush sent his own letter to the president.

"The peaceful and democratic uprising of the Iranian people against religious dictatorship in 1997 was a sweet experience," he wrote, referring to Khatami's election. "But your failure to keep the vote and your wasting of opportunities put an end to it and disappointed the nation."[16]

And Montazeri, in the speech that led the Islamic courts to put him under house arrest for eight years, scolded the president. "He should have gone to the Leader and said, 'You have your position of respect. Twenty-two million voted for me. They have expectations of me, and if you want to interfere with my ministers...I can not work. Hence, I will thank the people and resign.'"

The small Council of Guardians dealt Khatami the fatal blows. The twelve-man board quashed twin pieces of legislation submitted to parliament that would have strengthened the president's powers and effectively curbed the Guardians' clout. For the 2004 elections, the council then disqualified more than 2,000 candidates for parliament, including eighty-seven reform incumbents. Among them was Khatami's younger brother, a popular physician who was the deputy speaker of parliament and married to the Imam's granddaughter. The former hostage takers, Asgharzadeh and Mirdamadi, were also disqualified. So was the sister of rebel cleric Mohsen Kadivar, who had been one of the ranking female members of parliament.

Several of Khatami's own cabinet ministers resigned to protest the ban on reformers running again. Tehran's theocracy had never been so widely split.

At a 2002 commemoration of the student protest over the newspaper closure three years earlier, Khatami compared his situation to Socrates. The Greek philosopher, he noted, had opted to drink poison in order to maintain respect for the principle of law and order.

"Forget Athens," the students shouted back. "Change this place first!"[17]

In the end, Khatami was an ivory-tower intellectual more comfortable with lofty ideas than with dirty day-to-day politics. He was a thinker and a talker, not a doer.

"Khatami feared instability in Iran, so he wanted to move slowly," Hadi Semati, the political analyst, reflected. "He was not a street fighter. He did not want to take on his own people. He wanted to talk them into this. He felt moving one step ahead was better than moving three steps ahead and then having to move four steps back."

Khatami's presidency withered. With most reformers ineligible to run, parliament was taken over by conservatives and hard-liners. The reform movement disintegrated into its diverse pieces. He left office in 2005.

In 2006, the United States granted Khatami a visa to give a series of lectures in five American cities, including an address at the National Cathedral in Washington. President Bush later acknowledged that he personally approved the unprecedented tour. Khatami was the highest-ranking revolutionary to tour the United States since the shah's ouster in 1979. I saw him twice during that visit. I asked him what had happened to his presidency.

"Reform is a gradual process," he reflected during a long conversation in New York. "To make it work, two things have to happen. First, people's expectations have to be brought in line with reality. Freedoms can't be achieved in one night. We couldn't solve the long-standing problems of unemployment or poverty quickly. So we have to convince Iranians to lower their expectations.

"At the same time, we have to increase the tolerance of government for reform. It is a distinctive feature of dictatorships," Khatami added, "that they are intolerant.

"I wasn't successful in the first part," he continued, his arm emerging from under his chocolate cloak to scoop up a handful of pistachios from a decorative coffee-table dish. "But I was more successful in the other. For the first time you saw a president at least trying to give people more rights."

The solution in Iran, he said, was to shake up the system and redistribute power—including term limits on the supreme leader. Ultimate power should rotate, he added. Iran's Islamic pope would, in effect, no longer be infallible. "Of course, in our constitution, this is not the case," he offered. "But if it were, I think it would be better."

I noted that the twelve men on the Council of Guardians had been more of a problem during his presidency, since they were the ones to disqualify candidates and shoot down more than 100 laws proposed by a president who had come to office with tens of millions of votes.

"Twelve?" Khatami said, his eyebrows arching up, his forehead rising. "All they needed was seven votes! Seven is *their* majority."

But the pendulum does swing in Islamist regimes.

Religious ideologies invoked in earthly politics are just as vulnerable as any other utopian ideology. They come up against the real world. They can fail to deliver what they promise. Publics can turn against them.

Whatever their powers, clerics depend on the public for their legitimacy. They can be rejected.

In 2005, Iranians went to the polls to elect a new president. As in 1997, the election appeared preordained. For two decades after the revolution, Iran's master wheeler-dealer was Ali Akbar Hashemi Rafsanjani, the cleric with the Cheshire-cat grin. Iranians called him the Shark, for both his smooth, beardless skin and his killer political instincts. A centrist who appeased conservatives and teased reformers, he was also known as the Teflon mullah because he got away without anything sticking to him—including the arms-for-hostage scandal he secretly orchestrated with the United States in the mid-1980s.

A popular joke in the 1980s had him driving in a car with the two other most powerful politicians at the time—then-President Khamenei, a conservative, and Prime Minister Mir Hussein Musavi, a leftist. When they came to a T-junction in the road, the driver asked which way he should turn.

"Right," Khamenei said.

"No, go left," the prime minister said.

Rafsanjani then instructed, "Signal left, but turn right."

Rafsanjani was speaker of parliament in the 1980s. The position belied his power. He was Iran's wiliest politician. He finagled his way into one position after another. During Iran's grisly eight-year war with Iraq, he even took over as commander of the Revolutionary Guards. Iranians began referring to him as "Akbar Shah," or King Akbar, using his first name to imply that he had the powers of a monarch.

After the Imam's sudden death in 1989 left the revolution without its father figure, Rafsanjani crafted the post-Khomeini era almost single-handedly. He engineered a succession that put Ali Khamenei into the job of supreme leader. He then had the constitution amended by parliament, which he led, to create a stronger executive presidency—a job he then ran for twice and held in the 1990s.

In 1997, he put out feelers about amending the constitution again so he could run for a third term. But public opinion overwhelmingly opposed it, and he backed down. That was the year Khatami won.

In 2005, Rafsanjani decided to throw his turban in the ring again for president. Although he still held several positions, it was to be his comeback at the top. More than 1,000 candidates, including several women, registered to compete. The Council of Guardians disqualified all but eight men; among the rivals allowed to run were two reformers and the little-known mayor of Tehran. But Rafsanjani was the clear front-runner, with one of the reformers expected to be his main competition.

Then something happened on the way to the polls.

Rafsanjani ran a slick and lavish campaign the likes of which Iran had never witnessed, complete with bumper stickers, huge banners strung across streets, and campaign tents with Western rock music. Dozens of girls on roller blades skated around the capital with his name—in Farsi and English—pinned on their backs. Two famed Iranian film directors produced his television spots.

He fudged the issues, always talking in vague terms so he could be every mullah to everybody. But his ticket implied better relations with the United States, privatization to spur the troubled economy, and greater social freedoms.

Rafsanjani had said in 2002 that exposing a single strand of a woman's hair was "a dagger drawn toward the heart of Islam." But in a campaign meeting with youth in 2005, he teasingly offered a different redline. "No nudity," he quipped.[18]

"There is no use imposing tastes, being strict, and going backward," he told reporters. "Whoever becomes president cannot work without considering the demands and conditions of society."

On Iran's political system, he came down on both sides at the same time. "I certainly believe in democracy," he said. "But I believe we have to take this course step by step."[19]

In the first round of elections, as expected, Rafsanjani came in first out of the eight candidates, but only narrowly, and not with the majority needed to win outright.

The runner-up was the shocker. He was not a reformer. The dark-horse mayor of Tehran, a political nobody who had never run for office before, came in a close second. Although city councils in Iran are elected, mayors are appointed. And Mahmoud Ahmadinejad had been mayor for only two years.

In the run-off election, the two men offered a stark contrast.

Rafsanjani, the son of a wealthy pistachio trader whose brother had attended a California university, had just turned seventy. He is a tall-ish man with a robust girth, smooth fleshy cheeks, an almost invisible white moustache, and a tuft of white hair protruding from under his white turban. Of all Iran's clerics, he most revels in the limelight and is famed for the way he cajoles and circuitously manipulates others to embrace his positions. He lived in a villa in the cool foothills of North Tehran. He was driven to campaign stops in an entourage of bullet-proof Mercedes limousines.

Ahmadinejad is a skinny man, small at only five foot four inches. His head is wide at the top but tapers to a narrow jaw that is covered with a close-cropped black beard. He has small, deep-set eyes. His short black hair spills a bit over his forehead, partially covering a deep mark from praying several times a day—a telltale sign not found on Rafsanjani, Khatami, Khamenei, or many other ranking clerics in Iran. It is all the more striking because Amadinejad is not a cleric.

Iranians called the race "the turban versus the hat." Ahmadinejad was the first noncleric to make the presidential final runoff election since passage of the Islamic republic's constitution.

Born in 1956, Ahmadinejad was more than twenty years younger than Rafsanjani. He came of age during the revolution. He trained as a civil engineer and had a doctorate in traffic management. He was a campus leader during the student takeover of the American embassy, although one of the masterminds told me that Ahmadinejad had opposed the plan because it did not include a simultaneous takeover of the Soviet Embassy. He was a Revolutionary Guard during the war with Iraq in the 1980s. In the 1990s, he was appointed a provincial governor. He then taught engineering at Tehran's technical university. In 2003, he was appointed mayor of Tehran by a city council elected with only a twelve-percent turnout.

As mayor, Amadinejad shunned the official manor and stayed in his small town house in a working-class neighborhood. His campaign was unsophisticated. He tapped into mosque networks and personal ties to the Revolutionary Guards and Basij. In his television spots, he was shown praying and, dressed in military fatigues, praising veterans for their sacrifices during the war with Iraq. Many men on his campaign dressed in black shirts; women always wore the full black chador.

On domestic issues, Ahmadinejad was disdainful of reform. "We did not have a revolution," he said, "in order to have democracy."[20]

On foreign policy, he was disdainful of rapprochement with the West, particularly the United States. "In the past, the Americans broke off relations with Iran to create pressure," he said. "If they want to reestablish them now, it is for the same reasons. We do not want to have imposed relations."[21]

Ahmadinejad was a master of earthy street politics. "I take pride," he said often, "in being the Iranian nation's little servant and street sweeper." During the campaign, he drove around Tehran in his 1977 Peugeot.

The final vote stunned the establishment. The little mayor beat the most cunning politician in Iran by a humiliating seven million votes. Rafsajani garnered only one third of the tally.

Iranians had again signaled that they wanted something different. Even Khamenei, who owed his job to Rafsanjani, talked of the need for "new political blood."

Rafsanjani was not a gracious loser. He lashed out at opponents who "spent billions from the public funds to ruin the reputation of me and my family in a vicious way." He warned that those who intervened in the election would "pay back in life and after death."[22]

But Amadinejad heralded the election as a turning point. "A new Islamic revolution has arisen," he said.

His surprise win marked the emergence of a younger generation of conservative and hard-line technocrats. They were not clerics. They had limited exposure to the outside world, particularly the West. They were young adults during the revolution and worked their way up through the Islamic system, often as its foot soldiers in the war with Iraq.

But the pendulum swung so dramatically for three other reasons that had little to do with Ahmadinejad's hard-line politics. Thirty-five to forty percent of Iran's voters tend to prefer the puritan politics of traditional, conservative, or hard-line candidates, three quite distinct categories in Iran. But the rest had different rationales.

First, Ahmadinejad was a grassroots politician from the working class, a newcomer, and largely untainted. His father, he boasted, was a "hard-bitten toiler blacksmith." He campaigned as Mr. Clean—and against the notoriously corrupt clerical oligarchs who had become a virtual mafia. During the monarchy, Iranians complained that everything in Iran was run by 1,000 families close to the shah. With cronyism rampant again, Iranians complained that the oil-rich country was run after the revolution by 1,000 families close to the clerics.

Rafsanjani's family empire embodied the new privileged class. His children held powerful or lucrative positions in everything from the oil industry to Iran's Olympic committee. His daughter had also been a member of parliament. Siblings, nephews, and cousins fared well too. A few months before the election, I interviewed Rafsanjani's brother, who had headed Iranian television and radio for years; his opulent office was in the shah's old palace compound.

So a huge part of Ahmadinejad's victory was a protest. It was an antielite vote. Iranians have become increasingly sophisticated politically. Even in a rigidly restricted political arena, they look for options. As with Khatami, they were rejecting the status quo.

"People's expectations have not been realized over the past eight years [of Khatami's presidency], so they are looking for something different," Mirdamadi, the former hostage taker and ex-parliamentarian, told me shortly before the election. "People still want change, and they will vote for anyone they think will be able to change something."

Second, Ahmadinejad's populist economic message appealed to Iranians made poorer since the revolution. He ran as a man of the people on a ticket of piety, price controls, and clean management. He pledged to put oil revenues on Iranians' dinner tables. He crafted an image as Iran's Robin Hood.

The timing was right. The Islamic republic had not produced heaven on earth, and Iranians were increasingly impatient. Unemployment was officially ten percent, but in reality at least twenty percent— and some economists claimed even higher. With at least one in four living below the poverty line in a country with inflation at sixteen percent, many Iranians had two or even three jobs to make ends meet. Women increasingly worked because they had no choice. Despite rigid social controls, prostitution had become rampant, even among women who wore the chador.

Many in the huge baby bulge of young students who had voted for Khatami eight years earlier had graduated and were out looking for jobs and housing. Iran struggled—usually unsuccessfully—to absorb 500,000 baby boomers added to the labor market every year. Deferred marriage had become a chronic problem because of housing shortages.

As mayor, Ahmadinejad had set up a marriage fund, granting loans to young people who could not afford to wed. Bread-and-butter issues explained his appeal. He won in part on a variation of "It's the economy, stupid."

Third, Ahmadinejad beat two reformers because Iranians were exhausted by the political infighting and inertia. They were looking for a man of action. "People were tired of the political bickering. Iran was consumed every day with arrests, closures, and infighting. It led to a stalemate," Hadi Semati, the political analyst, told me.

"People thought conservatives weren't going to allow the reformers to move on. And they were tired of the reformers' inability to fulfill their promises," he said. "So many people thought the conservatives might at least be able to do something economically."

Many Iranians did not initially take Ahmandinejad seriously. Some saw him as a bit of a bumpkin. As mayor, he had banned billboard ads featuring Western celebrities, such as British soccer star David Beckham. He closed down cultural centers that had performed the works of Arthur Miller, Anton Chekhov, and Victor Hugo and converted them into religious education centers.

Tehran's ever-frenzied grapevine speculated that he would segregate, by sex, all public elevators, parks, and even sidewalks. An Iranian friend recounted a joke that had Ahmadinejad standing in front of a mirror combing his hair and repeating, "OK, male lice to the left, female lice to the right."

Cell phones are ubiquitous in Tehran, and the text-message crowd frantically exchanged new "Mahmoud" jokes, irreverently referring to the new president by his first name.

Iranians were generally as surprised as the outside world by how his presidency unfolded. Ahmadinejad quickly proved to be Khatami's opposite. In contrast to the western-educated advisers and enlightened clerics who surrounded Khatami, Ahmadinejad brought in colleagues from the Revolutionary Guards and the Basij. His spiritual mentor, Ayatollah Mohammed Mesbah-Yazdi, was often referred to as Ayatollah Crocodile for both his prickly positions, sometimes to the right of the supreme leader, and his long bulbous nose. "Beware! Don't let them fool you," Mesbah-Yazdi once said at Friday prayers. "In legislation, Islam and democracy cannot in any way be reconciled."[23]

Amadinejad began to sweep the nation back in time.

In the first year alone, he purged professors by forcing early retirements, then called on students to report professors with liberal or secular tendencies. He named a cleric to head Tehran University, replacing an academic normally elected by the faculties. He ordered the confiscation of satellite dishes that brought in news and entertainment from the outside world. He banned Western music, including the classics, from radio and television. The sound tracks, without words, of the Eagles' hit "Hotel California" and Eric Clapton's "Rush" had often been used as background music on Iranian news.[24]

The new president changed the face of the Islamic republic, both at home and abroad. He brought home dozens of Iran's most experienced diplomats. He banned the Center for Protecting Human Rights, led by Nobel Peace Prize laureate Shirin Ebadi. And he closed the last reformist newspaper and three magazines.

Even as he launched his own blog, the government clamped down on others. After Israel, Iran has spawned the largest number of Web sites in the Middle East. Iranians love technology. Several ayatollahs have their own sites, on which they issue fatwas in answer to followers' questions. I once interviewed a senior cleric in the dusty religious city of Qom who had made his life's work putting all the writings of Islam, Christianity, and Judaism through the ages, and in several languages, on a single website. More than 140,000 Iranian Web sites sprang up between 2001 and 2005. Khatami's vice president was one of the early bloggers and encouraged others to engage.

Ahmadinejad instead shut down chat rooms, sites on local politics or international affairs, and anything that even hinted of sexual content. Dozens of bloggers were detained, some on charges of subversion. Thousands of foreign Web sites were also blocked by state-controlled servers.

Some of his most striking reversals were economic. With oil revenues at an all-time high, he crisscrossed the country pledging wider distribution of Iran's petro-wealth—sometimes to the horror of the ayatollahs and the Central Bank back in Tehran.

"National resources must be freed from the state and given to people to use them for the advancement of the country," he explained shortly after his election. "There must be justice and equal opportunities for all."[25]

The response was tumultuous. He promised low-interest housing loans—and ended up with two million applications. At each stop, he collected thousands of letters from the poor with their stories and pleas for help. A large staff in Tehran went through the missives and referred them to government ministries for action.

"I love you, too," he would often shout back over a crowd's cheering.[26]

Ahmadinejad's decisions often reflected naïveté and inexperience. The most glaring example centered on Iran's swelling population.

Shortly after the revolution, the clerics had called on Iranian women to breed an Islamic generation. They quickly complied. Iran had thirty-four million people when the monarchy ended in 1979: Over the next seven years, the population soared to over fifty million. By 1986, Iran's population growth rate hit 3.2 percent per year, among the world's highest. The average Iranian woman was bearing around seven children.

"We'd just had a revolution that faced threats from both internal and external enemies," Ayatollah Nasser Makaram-Shirazi told *The New York Times*. "We wanted to increase the number of people who believed in the revolution in order to preserve it."[27]

But the ruling clerics soon realized that—whatever their belief in God's will—the state did not have the resources to provide food, education, housing, or employment for the population at the rate it was growing. And the surging numbers would take generations to slow and come under any control.

So in 1989, the year the Imam died, the regime had an economic epiphany: To sustain the revolution, Iran itself had to survive—and that meant keeping a modern state afloat. The needs of the state and the hard realities of earthly existence suddenly superseded the dictates of Islam or the traditional practices of Muslims.

The turnaround was stunning. After years of banning it, the clerics suddenly put family planning high on the national agenda. All forms of birth control—from condoms and the pill to Norplant—were distributed free. The new supreme leader issued a *fatwa* legalizing vasectomies for men, and free clinics were opened to perform them. A big water tower near a Tehran clinic was painted with a sign, in Farsi and English, advertising its location. Billboards went up along Tehran boulevards proclaiming, DAUGHTERS OR SONS, TWO CHILDREN ARE ENOUGH."

Clerics countrywide pressed the message. During Iran's annual

Population Week, tied in to the United Nations Population Day in July, mosques and centers of religious study all over Iran focused on the importance of small families—and how to keep them that way. More than 30,000 women were recruited to go door-to-door to educate poor and illiterate women on family-planning choices.

In 1994, the government introduced mandatory premarital family-planning courses; marriage licenses were not granted until a couple had completed the one-day course. I once attended a class with several couples, many of whom had only recently met because their marriages had been arranged by their families. In a room full of blushing brides-and grooms-to-be, a thoroughly uninhibited doctor took out a flesh-colored condom and demonstrated how to pull it over the model of an erect phallus. With maps of the male and female anatomies on the wall, he provided a graphic but fatherly lecture on human sexuality, then demonstrated other birth-control devices. To emphasize that men had equal responsibility in family planning, he went around the room to ask what the men planned to do about it.

The population problem had been the first issue on which the clerics demonstrated real pragmatism.

By 1998, the number of children born to the average woman had dropped from 7 children to 2.7, a change in just twelve years so striking that the chief of the UN Population Fund urged other Muslim countries with unsustainable population growth to look at the Iranian model. "It's soundly planned, and it responds to people's needs," he said.[28]

A year later, Secretary-General Kofi Annan bestowed the world body's highest award on population issues to the Iranian health minister who had designed the innovative program. By the 2005 election, Iran's population had hit about seventy million, twice its size during the revolution a quarter century earlier. But the birth rate had slowed to 1.2 percent, a rate comparable to that of the United States.[29]

Ahmadinejad, however, wanted to reverse course. In 2006, he called for a new baby boom. It was vital, he said, as a tool to threaten the West.

"Westerners have problems because their population growth is negative. They are worried and fear that if our population increases, we will triumph over them," he told parliament. "So I'm saying two children are not enough. Our country has a lot of capacity for children to grow in it. It even has the capacity for 120 million people."[30]

His sentiment was not widely shared, particularly among women, the young, the educated, the middle class, many professionals and academics, and even senior clerics.

Despite government crackdowns on the press, the newspaper *Etemad-e Melli* dared to chastise Ahmadinejad for "ill-considered" comments.

"He stresses the necessity of population growth and the triumph of Iran over Western governments. He ignores the fact that what leads to such triumph is not population size, but knowledge, technology, wealth, welfare, and security."

Change throughout the Middle East will be complicated by tensions with the outside world, both past and present.

Iran is the angriest example. Its 1979 revolution was almost as much about shedding a legacy of foreign influence as it was about abolishing the monarchy. Since then, the regime has also exploited tensions—and frequently fueled them—to rally support when the revolution was losing steam.

In the early days, Iran's rulers prolonged the student takeover of the U.S. Embassy during internal clashes over a new constitution. Daily demonstrations by thousands of Iranians against the United States diverted attention from the unraveling of the revolutionary coalition and the opposition to an Islamic constitution. The clerics used the embassy seizure to consolidate their hold on power. The Imam even dubbed it "the second revolution."

Saddam Hussein's 1980 invasion, which sought to undermine the Islamist regime at a vulnerable early stage, again allowed the clerics to divert attention from their failings and mobilize domestic support.

Three decades later, the pattern had not changed. Iran had still not established equilibrium with the much of the world.

Ahmadinejad, a former Revolutionary Guard with no foreign

exposure before taking office, played to Iran's deep-seated fears of survival as well as Persian nationalism dating back millennia. Both resonated among proud Iranians—and united clerics of otherwise disparate views.

Since the fourth century B.C, legendary forces—from Alexander the Great to Joseph Stalin, from Genghis Khan's Mongols to Tamerlane—have tried to occupy Iran because of its strategic position. The Turks invaded in the eleventh, sixteenth, and eighteenth centuries. Britain and the Soviet Union occupied part of twentieth-century Iran. The Cold War had its origins in the Soviet Union's refusal to pull its troops out of Iran's northern provinces after World War II. President Harry S. Truman issued an ultimatum to Stalin to get out of Iran, and the standoff produced the first crisis of the then-new United Nations Security Council.

Ahmadinejad began his presidential Web site, "I was born fifteen years after Iran was invaded by foreign forces," a reference to the Soviet presence.[31]

Iran today is twice the size of either Turkey or Egypt, with more than three times the population of either Iraq or Saudi Arabia. Yet Iranians still feel vulnerable. They are the odd people out on every border. Not one of their seven neighbors has historically been a reliable ally. Their longest land and sea frontiers are with the Arabs, including six countries across the Persian Gulf that formed their own security pact—largely to counter Iran. Turkey is a member of NATO.

A Shiite-majority country, Iran has lived for centuries surrounded by a sea of Sunni-ruled regimes, empires, and emirates. (Ironically, Persia did not embrace Shiism as the official religion until the sixteenth century, and largely to distinguish itself from—and resist—the emerging Ottoman Empire.) Shiites today are only some fifteen percent of the Islamic world. Two neighboring states represent the most rigid Sunni rule: To the south, Saudi Arabia is the guardian of Islamic holy places and ruled by followers of strict Wahhabism. To the east, Afghanistan is home to the Taliban and al Qaeda, both anathema to the Shiite clergy.

After the revolution, Iraq's 1980 invasion—which sparked the longest and deadliest conflict in the modern Middle East—deepened the defensive mind-set. Iran suffered hundreds of thousands of casualties over eight years. The ghastliest deaths were from Saddam Hussein's chemical weapons. I covered the war on Iran's western border and interviewed blistered, rasping, and emaciated victims of chemical weapons who were dying horrid deaths. The one thing they all recalled was the unusually enticing smell—of roses, or newly mown grass, or garlic—produced by chemical weapons.[32]

The outside world did little when Tehran first reported Baghdad's use of the deadly gases in 1981. After United Nations experts verified the claims in 1983, 1984, 1985, and 1986, the world body imposed no punitive sanctions and offered no humanitarian medical assistance. Indeed, by 1986, the United States, France, and key Arab countries were instead training Iraqi troops, advising Saddam's army on strategy, or providing satellite intelligence about Iranian positions.

By the war's end, more than 50,000 Iranians were victims of Iraq's chemical weapons, according to the Central Intelligence Agency.[33]

During the conflict, I often went to Behesht-e Zahra, or Zahra's Paradise, the sprawling cemetery in Tehran named after one of the Prophet Mohammed's daughters. One of the world's biggest graveyards, it was a good place to judge public sentiment about the conflict. It stretched for miles and miles by the war's end. A huge fountain in front spewed red-colored water to symbolize the nation's martyrdom. One of my most enduring memories was traffic at the entrance to Zahra's Paradise. It was often so congested that policemen had to frantically whistle directions to waves of funeral corteges for Iranian soldiers.

The human costs and public backlash against the war were among the reasons the Imam finally agreed to a United Nations–brokered cease-fire with Iraq; he compared the difficult decision to drinking hemlock. The war ended in 1988.

The conflict had many lingering consequences, reportedly including Iran's biggest secret. In 1984, as the war raged into its fourth year, Iran allegedly revived a clandestine program to develop a nuclear weapon. The program was reportedly hatched by the shah but suspended after the revolution.[34] It was still in an embryonic stage, experts concluded.

The motive may have been far more than just the war with Iraq.

Tehran had not launched a war in more than 200 years. Yet Iran found itself in the late twentieth century smack in the middle of the world's largest nuclear zone. It was surrounded by five of the world's eight nuclear powers—neighboring Pakistan and the Soviet Union, with China, India, and Israel nearby. Saddam Hussein reportedly had his own nuclear weapons development program too.

For the next eighteen years, Iran reportedly worked on acquiring pieces and technology for a clandestine program. In 2002, however, it got caught. An exiled opposition group exposed research and development at two sites, Natanz and Arak. The sprawling desert facility in Natanz included preparations for uranium enrichment. Enriched at low levels, uranium can fuel reactors in a peaceful nuclear energy program. At high levels, it can be subverted for bomb-making.

The dual-purpose technology presented a special conundrum for the outside world, as Iran definitely had been on a longstanding and legal quest for nuclear energy—a goal dating back to the monarchy. In the 1970s, the United States had actually approved Iran's plans for twenty-two nuclear reactors. Germany began to build the first one in Bushehr.

"Petroleum is a noble material, much too valuable to burn," the shah had said in 1974. The last Pahlavi king envisioned producing 23,000 megawatts of electricity a day from nuclear power.

Thirty years later, Iran's population had doubled, putting a growing drain on utilities. But the Islamic republic was still struggling to open its first nuclear reactor—the Russians having taken over the German project—with a capacity of only 1,000 megawatts.

Whatever their differences on other issues, Iranians old and young, conservative and reformist, rich and poor, urban and rural, men and women, generally agreed on one thing: Iran needed nuclear energy. They have long seen it as key to moving out of the Third World club into the twenty-first century of modernizing, globalizing countries. It was inextricably wrapped up in self-image and the quest to be a great nation—through industry and development, not arms.

Nuclear energy was also becoming an economic necessity. By the mid-2000s, the world's fourth largest oil producer used almost half of its daily oil output—1.8 million of 4 million barrels per day—for domestic needs. It had to import more than forty percent of its refined oil, some from as far away as Venezuela; its own refineries could not meet domestic needs. With its population surge, Iran faced the possibility of needing its entire oil output just for domestic consumption by 2025—in a country dependent on oil exports for seventy percent of its budget.

"This is the worst way of using our oil, especially since we won't have oil forever," Ali Alehi, Iran's former representative to the International Atomic Energy Agency, told me in 2004. "If we did that, we'd be like the United States, which is the third largest producer of oil in the world, but also the first largest importer of oil."

The economic and psychological importance Iran tied to its nuclear program was reflected in a new bank note issued in 2007. On one side was Imam Khomeini. On the other side of the 50,000-rial note, worth just over five dollars, was the nuclear symbol—electrons orbiting a nucleus—atop a map of Iran. It was accompanied by a quote from the Prophet Mohammed: "Men from the land of Persia will attain scientific knowledge even if it is as far as the Pleiades," referring to the stars.[35]

Although attempts to enrich uranium were not technically a violation of the Nonproliferation Treaty, Iran's denials and secret acquisitions for almost two decades led to widespread suspicions that it also wanted to become the ninth country with earth's deadliest weapon. The outside world was willing to allow Iran to have nuclear power, but drew a red line at a nuclear bomb.

The tensions became an issue in Iran's 2005 presidential campaign. Rafsanjani implied he would better relations with the United States as the solution to several problems. But Ahmadinejad stood firm, insisting that only Iran could control the controversial fuel cycle.

"If they accept our legitimate right [to enrich], we will cooperate," he told supporters. "Otherwise, nothing will force the Iranians to comply with their demands. The world should know that it cannot contain this effort."

Ahmadinejad meant it. The week after his inauguration, Iran began enriching uranium again after a two-year suspension. Although the president is just one member of the Supreme National Security Council, the results of Iran's presidential election had altered the atmosphere. The hard-liners and ideologues dominated the internal debate. And they were far less willing to buckle to the West.

Tensions with the outside world quickly began building again.

In 2006, Europe and the United States crafted a carrot-and-stick compromise with broad incentives: Iran could keep its energy program, but Russia would control the uranium enrichment fuel cycle to ensure that the key process was not diverted for a weapon. The West would also throw in economic and diplomatic perks, including talks that would bring the United States and Iran to the negotiating table for the first time in decades. The alternative was the threat of increasingly punitive United Nations sanctions.

Tehran balked. It did not want to be dependent on the often hostile outside world.

Many Iranians, not just senior officials, feared the West would use access to the fuel to pressure Iran into future concessions. Many Western officials believed Iran's rejection of the offer only further confirmed Tehran's quest for a weapon.

Ahmadinejad actually had almost no decision-making control over Iran's nuclear program. Major security and foreign policy questions are decided by the supreme leader and the Supreme National Security Council. But the new president scored points, even among some who did not like or trust him, for standing up publicly against the world. He played to the strong Iranian yearning to restore the country's standing as a center of science, independent development, and learning; he capitalized on the Iranian belief that the West wanted to hold Iran back.

On his poorly translated English-language Web site, the president complained that he grew up at a time when the shah had "slavishly" tried to Westernize Iran, making it a "market for Western commercial goods, without any progress in the scientific field.... They decided to make this noble and tenacious culture weak, gradually, so that Iran be attached strongly to the West as far as its economy, politics and culture was concerned."[36]

Ahmadinejad dismissed the West's incentives package as "walnuts for gold." The threat of United Nations sanctions did not make Iran back down either.

In the heat of the showdown in September 2006, Ahmadinejad flew to New York to deliver a combative speech at the opening session of the United Nations General Assembly. He took on the outside world, particularly the United States, with a cocky certainty and an evangelical zeal.

"The Almighty," he said, standing at the green marble podium in the Security Council chamber,

> has not created human beings so that they could transgress against others and oppress them. . . . Some seek to rule the world relying on weapons and threats, while others live in perpetual insecurity and danger. Some occupy the homeland of others thousands of kilometers away from their borders, interfere in their affairs, and control their oil and other resources and strategic routes, while others are bombarded daily in their homes, their children murdered in the streets and alleys of their own country, and their homes reduced to rubble. Such behavior is not worthy of human beings, and runs counter to the truth, justice, and human dignity.

The defiant tone was a stark contrast to Khatami's appeal for dialogue among civilizations.

Ahmadinejad reflected the most reactionary element to emerge from three tumultuous decades of an Islamic republic. His rants were often far more inflammatory than militant clerics' rhetoric. In two particularly stunning pronouncements, he questioned whether the Holocaust really happened and then said Israel should be "wiped off" the map.

I met Ahmadinejad the evening after his UN speech at a small and controversial supper with the Council on Foreign Relations. He strode into the chandeliered ballroom of a New York hotel surrounded by aides and security, including his American Secret Service detail. He was the smallest among them, but he set the pace.

Over an open-necked shirt, he was wearing a drab suit coat that looked big on his small frame. The shah had relied heavily on an elite Westernized class called the *kravatis*—after cravat, meaning "tie-wearers"—who symbolized the modernization mandated by the Pahlavi dynasty. Ahmadinejad deliberately went tieless, keeping with revolutionary attire. During his campaign, he had insisted that his clothing be indistinguishable from a street sweeper's.[37] Tehran stores soon began carrying the "Ahmadinejad jacket."

The diminutive president waved briefly, sat down quickly, and was intent on business.

Islamists often preface remarks at public appearances with "In the name of God, the most merciful, the most compassionate." But as he did in his United Nations speech, Ahmadinejad added an additional line.

"O Mighty Lord," he intoned, "I pray to you to hasten the emergence of the Promised One, that perfect and pure human being, the one that will fill this world with peace and justice."

The Promised One is the missing Mahdi, the twelfth and last of the original Shiite imams descended from the Prophet Mohammed. He disappeared in the eighth century. Shiites pray for his return the same way that Jews await the Messiah and Christians await the Second Coming. Shiites believe the Mahdi is in a state of "occultation"—or hidden by God—and will return to cleanse a corrupt world on Judgment Day. After the revolution, the main Tehran boulevard that cuts across the entire capital was renamed Vali-e Asr, or "the expected one."

Ahmadinejad had a deep devotion to the Shiite messiah. "Our revolution's main mission is to pave the way for the reappearance of the twelfth imam, the Mahdi," he told a meeting of clerics four months after taking office.

"Today," he said, "we should define our economic, cultural, and political polices based on the policy of Imam Mahdi's return."[38]

Ahmadinejad's meeting with thirty members of the Council on Foreign Relations was supposed to be a civil and informal conversation. But it quickly became politely hostile. The disconnect was often scary.

Pressed on his comments denying the Holocaust, Ahmadinejad noted that a total of sixty million people had been killed during World War II. "Why was such prominence given to such a small portion?" he asked.

Maurice Greenberg, who headed the world's largest insurance and financial services corporation, told the Iranian president that he had seen Dachau concentration camp as Germany fell.

"How old are you?" Ahmadinejad asked.

"Eighty-one," Greenberg replied.

"You were there, and you survived. Congratulations," Ahmadinejad said coldly, and then smiled, as if that was enough proof to dispel the enormous body of evidence that six million Jews had been murdered during World War II.

More proof was still needed, he added, proposing that an "impartial" group investigate. Three months later, Ahmadinejad convened a conference in Tehran on the Holocaust. Among those who attended was David Duke, former Imperial Wizard of the Ku Klux Klan.

Ahmadinejad also rebuffed attempts to discuss conditions in his own country. Questioned on the regime's growing arrest of dissidents, newspaper closures, and clampdown on human rights groups, he launched a small tirade about the comparative freedoms in the United States and Iran.

"Please don't allow yourself to be involved in the domestic politics of other countries, or there is much more we can all say. If you think you can affect our people with your statements, you are wrong," he said sternly, scolding us to "correct our mentality" about Iran.

"We had free elections—I spoke with people, and they chose me. This is a unique, pure democracy, which is impossible in your country. Which country is freer and more democratic? I would like to ask you whether anyone outside the two ruling parties has reached the American presidency.... The whole U.S. administration is in the hands of two groups."

On the two issues that most divide Americans and Iranians, Ahmadinejad was chilling.

On Iraq, Ahmadinejad warned that the United States had lost its way, alienating the entire Muslim world in the process. "U.S. policy in the Middle East has brought only the rage, hatred, and hostility of over one billion people," he told the group.

And on Iran's nuclear program, Ahmadinejad was dismissive. "The age of the nuclear bomb has ended, and anyone investing in it has made a mistake," he said. "Today, nuclear weapons don't bring superiority."

As the discussion ended, the Iranian president reprimanded the council. "In the beginning of the session, you said you are an independent group, and I accepted that," he told us. "But everything you said seems to come from the government perspective."

He got up and walked as briskly out of the room as he had come in.

The ground rules for the session barred recording devices and cameras. After he arrived home, however, Ahmadinejad put an incomplete and poorly translated copy of the meeting up on his Web site. He held many events and interviews in New York, but the evening with the council was the only one he wrote about. He ended the entry with his own analysis, expressing disappointment in the session.

"It was again proven to me that the actual reason for the failure of U.S. policy in politics and foreign relations is their lack of information regarding the world's realities. Decision-makers are caught up in their own fabricated and false political propaganda." Many at the council meeting felt the same way about him.

In his rhetoric and actions, Ahmadinejad was increasingly a throwback to the angry militancy and misadventures of the revolution's early years. The Revolutionary Guards were increasingly the instrument of mischief—not only in securing the country's borders. They became a pivot around which central parts of the system turned.

Their rise mirrored Ahmadinejad's evolution into the presidency, as the young men who had fought in the Iran-Iraq war grew into middle age. Politically, Revolutionary Guards officers moved from the battlefield into mayoralties, governates, and management of ministries.[39] Economically, an old-boys' network of current and former commanders staked claims in the oil and gas sectors, won bids on major government construction contracts, and even gained lucrative franchises, such as Mercedes-Benz dealerships.

Within the military, the Revolutionary Guards also evolved from the days when they had served mainly as human minesweepers and cannon fodder in the war with Iraq. By 2007, they controlled Iran's deadliest arms, including missiles with ranges of up to 1,200 miles and programs for both chemical and biological weapons. They were also widely reported to be involved in attempts to acquire a nuclear weapons capability.[40]

The Revolutionary Guards became a critical arm of Iran's foreign policy, too. As tensions with the outside world increased, its elite and secretive wing, the Quds Force, became increasingly active in dozens of countries. Quds is Arabic for Jerusalem, a name symbolic of its mission.

The Quds Force was tasked with exporting the revolution. It had at least eight separate directorates, charged with activities from Afghanistan and the Arabian Peninsula to Iraq, from Lebanon and the Palestinian territories into North Africa, and including a unit for Europe and North America. It had operatives in most embassies abroad, and ran Iran's camps to train foreign militias in unconventional warfare.[41]

Little is reliably known about the force. Its roots lie in Iran's first campaign in Lebanon in the 1980s, when 2,000 Revolutionary Guards deployed after the 1982 Israeli invasion and spawned Hezbollah. It was reportedly called the Lebanon Corps at the time. Its most entrenched operation is still in Lebanon. It supplied Hezbollah with missiles and trained its militia before the 2006 Hezbollah war with Israel, the longest conflict the Arabs ever fought with Israel.

The largest Iran opposition movement claims the Revolutionary Guards' foreign operations were consolidated into the Quds Force in about 1990, when the military regrouped after the end of the Iran-Iraq war.[42] It was initially a comparatively small corps. In 2007, it reportedly tripled in size, from 5,000 to 15,000 troops and operatives.[43]

The special-forces unit reflected the greatest fears elsewhere in the Middle East about Iran. Although it worked with Sunni movements like Hamas and Palestinian Islamic Jihad, its most threatening operations were mainly in Shiite communities—penetrating west into Iraq, Syria, and Lebanon and south along the eastern Arabian Peninsula into Kuwait, Bahrain, and Saudi Arabia.

Jordan's King Abdullah, a Sunni, told me of his fears that the balance of power between Sunnis and Shiites dating back to the seventh century was on the verge of an upheaval. He was the first Arab leader to call the potential danger "the Shiite crescent." It was a fear shared among several Sunni regimes, even though the general Arab antipathy toward Persians, even among Shiites, was also a strong counterweight.

But the Quds Force did symbolize a kind of regional Cold War taking shape. It pitted the United States and its Middle East allies against Iran and its proxies. It played out in the 2006 war between Hezbollah and Israel. It was most intense, however, in Iraq.

The U.S. invasion of Iraq was a shocking jolt to Iran. As much as it loathed Saddam Hussein, the presence of up to 165,000 American troops along its western border alarmed the Tehran regime. With

American and NATO forces on its eastern border in Afghanistan since 2001, Iran was suddenly sandwiched between foreign armies. After the quick fall of both Kabul and Baghdad, Tehran initially feared it might be next.

The Quds Force was the unit deployed to challenge the United States presence. It operated throughout Iraq, arming, aiding, and abetting Shiite militias. The three largest Shiite movements in Iraq—the Supreme Council for Islamic Revolution in Iraq, Dawa, and the personal movement built around renegade cleric Moqtada Sadr—all had close ties to Iran, some dating back decades. During Saddam Hussein's quarter century in power, Iran was the only reliable ally for Shiite dissidents.

But the Quds Force also worked openly with the Kurds and even secretly armed some of the Sunni insurgents. Many of the roadside explosives that maimed or killed American troops as well as innocent Iraqis, the Pentagon charged, came from Iran.

In 2006, Iran-American tensions inside Iraq spawned a conflict within a conflict. It played out in unconventional ways. American troops countered with their own raids on Quds Force offices in Iraq, detaining its intelligence agents and seizing equipment and computers. During the first raid in December 2006, an American team in Baghdad nabbed two of the highest ranking Quds Force commanders; they were operating in the compound of Iraq's largest Shiite political party. Under Iraqi pressure, the two were released a week later.

But on January 11, 2007, helicopter-borne American troops swooped down on Iran's diplomatic liaison office in the northern Kurdish city of Irbil. The goal was to seize two of Iran's highest-ranking security officials—General Minojahar Frouzanda, chief of Revolutionary Guards intelligence, and Mohammed Jafari, the deputy of Iran's Supreme National Security Council. The two men's frequent visits to Iraq predated the U.S. invasion. They came to Iraq with the full knowledge of Iraqi officials. They had just met with the two Kurdish leaders, Masoud Barzani and Jalal Talabani. Talabani was also Iraq's president.

The two Iranians eluded capture. But U.S. troops netted five junior officers of the Quds Force. Iran clamored for their release, initially to no avail.

After ten weeks and intense pressure on allies in the Iraqi government, Iran announced that it expected the five to be freed for the Iranian New Year of *Nowruz,* a celebration on the spring equinox, March 21, dating back more than 3,000 years. It is the most important Iranian holiday of the year; Persian in its origins, it is shared by all faiths and ethnicities. It lasts two weeks and includes bonfires to celebrate the light winning over darkness, visits to neighbors, and feasts of special foods with friends.

But the Iranians—who became known as the Irbil Five—were not released on *Nowruz.*

Three days later, a British naval team conducted a routine inspection of a ship in the Persian Gulf to ensure it was not smuggling goods. The British were the closest American allies and the second-largest force in Iraq. They operated in Shiite strongholds in southern Iraq and the Persian Gulf. The navy team, fourteen men and one woman on two small motorboats, were headed back to the HMS *Cornwall* when they were overtaken by six vessels of the Revolutionary Guards. The fifteen British sailors were taken hostage.

Iran claimed the British sailors had crossed into its waters, which was not unprecedented. It had happened in 2004, when eight British sailors were held for three days. But Britain claimed global satellite tracking proved its patrol boats were almost two miles inside Iraqi waters.

The abduction was interesting in another respect. It came one day before the United Nations voted on a new resolution to impose sanctions on Tehran for failing to suspend uranium enrichment. The sanctions were narrow, targeting banks, institutions, and twenty-eight officials believed to be involved in Iran's suspected nuclear program. Among the individuals were the top seven Revolutionary Guard commanders of its ground forces, navy, air force, intelligence unit, and Quds Force.

Iran and Britain both insisted there were no connections between the seizure of the Irbil Five, the UN sanctions resolution and the capture of the fifteen Brits. But the common denominator was the Revolutionary Guards. Its Quds Force operatives were being held by the United States. Its top leaders had been sanctioned by the United Nations. And its naval unit had taken the British hostage.

Over the next two weeks, the hostage drama became an international incident. The United Nations Security Council issued a statement of concern. Pope Benedict wrote to appeal for the sailors' freedom. Leaders from Islamic countries urged Tehran to release them. Even Syria weighed in.

For all the attention generated outside Iran during the drama, the internal reaction was telling. Unlike the 444-day ordeal after the American embassy takeover in 1979, the regime could not generate public fervor about the capture of British soldiers in 2007.

A small rent-a-crowd of less than 200 showed up outside the British Embassy for a noisy but comparatively tepid demonstration. It was a one-day affair. This time, the Iranians were more interested in their holiday. Iranian television showed videos of the British in captivity, and radio covered the diplomacy—but often not as the top story or at great length. Many of the papers were not published during the two-week New Year break, but when they resumed, the editorials focused on other issues and offered no encouragement to prolong the standoff.

The buzz of Tehran was the lack of buzz.

Two weeks later, on April 4, Ahmadinejad held a press conference. With lavish praise, he pinned medals on the Revolutionary Guards naval commanders who had captured the Brits. The Iranian president then rambled on to reporters for thirty-five minutes. He railed at America's destruction of Iraq, the United Nations failure to protect the Palestinians, the world's failure to help the Lebanese during Hezbollah's war with Israel—and Iran's innocent intentions on its nuclear program.

Near the end, in what almost seemed an afterthought, he announced that the Brits would be freed—in celebration of the upcoming birthday of the Prophet Mohammed and Easter. "This pardon of the British soldiers," he pronounced, "is a gift."

The broader confrontation was not over, however. Iran had milked that crisis for all it could get; the costs of holding the British military personnel began to outweigh the benefits. So Tehran shifted its focus. One month later, in May 2007, Iran began imprisoning Americans.

Ali Shakeri, a California businessman who went to college in Texas, was the first one. He had returned to Iran to see his ailing mother before she died; he stayed long enough to bury her. He was detained at

Tehran's International Airport after he had already checked in his bags for the flight to Los Angeles, in the wee hours of May 8. He was taken to Tehran's notorious Evin Prison, a forbidding compound of buildings in the foothills of the Elburz Mountains. Hours later, Haleh Esfandiari, a diminutive grandmother who had been visiting her ninety-three-year-old mother, was ordered to report to the intelligence ministry. The director of Middle East programs at the Smithsonian's Woodrow Wilson Center in Washington, she too was jailed in Evin's Ward 209, the section where political detainees are held in solitary confinement. Three days later, New York social scientist Kian Tajbakhsh was imprisoned. Tajbakhsh, a consultant for George Soros's Open Society Institute, had actually been trying to help Iranian government ministries on HIV/AIDS prevention and other health projects. Parnaz Azima, another grandmother and a correspondent for United States-funded Radio Farda, was also visiting an ailing mother. She was not jailed, but was forced to put up the deed to her mother's home as bail to stay out of prison.

They were odd choices. All four were dual nationals who had lived for decades in the United States and taken American citizenship, but each had maintained extensive contacts in Iran and traveled back and forth frequently. Esfandiari and Tajbakhsh particularly had worked hard to bridge the gaps between the United States and Iran and to encourage dialogue at many levels.

Weeks passed before Tehran acknowledged that it had taken action against the four Americans—and why. Iran denied, however, any knowledge about Robert A. Levinson, a former FBI agent—more than a decade in retirement—who had flown in March to Iran's Kish Island. Kish was a free-trade zone and popular vacation area where Iranian visas are not required. Levinson was on a private business trip. Through diplomatic contacts, the State Department and Levinson's family repeatedly pressed for information on him—to no avail.

Tehran eventually charged the four dual American-Iranian nationals with unspecified "crimes against national security." Iranian intelligence and judiciary officials accused them of promoting the kind of "soft revolution" witnessed in Eastern Europe in the late 1980s and early 1990s. Iran was especially suspicious about a seventy-five-million-dollar program unveiled by the Bush administration in 2006 to promote democracy in Iran. The imprisoned Americans, however, had no connections to the funding. With sometimes uncanny similarities to tensions between Washington and Tehran after the 1979 revolution, the new "soft hostages" became pawns to bigger issues.

Throughout the Middle East, the United States and Iran were by 2007 effectively engaged in a new Cold War. It was a race for supremacy in ideology and influence. And it played out over the full array of issues.

For the United States, the biggest problems were Iran's alleged nuclear program, its arms and aid to extremist groups, its increasing role in Iraq, its rejection of the Middle East peace process, and its attempts to export a militant ideology. Washington's goal was to contain Iran, prevent it from developing a nuclear weapon, and changing the regime's behavior.

For Iran, the immediate issues were two U.S. invasions that positioned more than 150,000 American troops in neighboring Afghanistan and Iraq, a large U.S. naval force in the Persian Gulf, arms sales to the six Gulf sheikhdoms worth tens of billions of dollars, and attempts to influence several leaders in countries far from American shores. Iran's goal was to get U.S. troops to leave the region, ensure friendly governments rules in Iraq and Afghanistan, and contain American influence.

In key ways, the Middle East's strategic balance had begun to tilt in Tehran's favor for the first time. In the Palestinian territories, Iranian-backed Hamas won the most democratic election ever held in the Arab world, then militarily routed its secular, American-backed rivals in Fatah to seize control of the Gaza Strip. In Lebanon, Hezbollah used Iranian weaponry to fight Israel—and fought to a draw, despite Israel's vastly superior U.S. weaponry. In Syria, Iran's closest ally let foreign jihadists cross into neighboring Iraq, funnel Iranian arms to Hezbollah, and support radical Palestinian groups opposed to peace—undermining Washington's top strategic goals in the region. And in Iraq, Shiite militias armed and trained by Iran made Baghdad's streets and the fortified Green Zone unsafe, even for the U.S. military.

The United States, however, remained the world's most powerful country. When Tehran failed to suspend its uranium enrichment, Washington pushed for a series of UN resolutions that sanctioned top Iranian officials and institutions. It used its own economic clout to squeeze foreign banks and businesses to make a choice—business with the United States or Iran. More than forty major banks in Europe and Asia backed away from Iran. In a bold move to drive home its own determination, Washington even imposed its own sanctions on the Revolutionary Guards and the Quds Force.

In the run-up to President Ahmadinejad's trip to the United States to give another speech at the United Nations in September 2007, the four American Iranians were released, in phases, from prison or allowed to leave the country. Yet tensions between Iran and the United States only continued to deepen. Indeed, the Cold War increasingly looked like it could become a hot confrontation.

nine

MOROCCO

The Compromises

All governments—indeed, every human benefit and
enjoyment, every virtue and every prudent act—is
founded on compromise and barter.

—British philosopher Edmund Burke

You can only protect your liberties in this world
by protecting the other man's freedom.
You can only be free if I am free.

—American lawyer Clarence Darrow

The great debate in the Middle East is whether the region is really ready for democracy. It has become a chicken-and-egg argument.

Almost all leaders argue that conditions are not yet ripe for big change: Countries are either not stable enough for the initial shocks of democracy, or economies are not rich enough to meet expectations, or societies are not developed enough to wisely use democratic rights, or the region is simply too volatile to introduce a new political order.[1] They contend that voters will merely elect new tyrants or undemocratic populists—as Germany did in electing Adolf Hitler in 1933 or Venezuela did in voting for Hugo Chavez in 1998.[2]

Yet public-opinion polls, academic discourse, newspaper editorials, and overwhelming anecdotal evidence all indicate a yearning for real political change. Some call it reform. Others call it democracy. All agree it must be more than token or tepid steps. Their driving fear is what will happen down the road in the absence of change.

The debate is likely to rage for years to come.

Yet it is already clear that governments in the Middle East will have to cultivate compromise—now, or very soon—to survive in any form. Initiating action on three controversial issues—political prisoners, women's rights, and political Islam—can start the process. Cooperation will signal intent to change. It will require ceding some power. And it will redefine the social contract between ruler and ruled.

It will still mark only a beginning, however. Without serious follow-up on other fronts, governments will only be buying a bit more time.

Morocco is the only country that has attempted action on all three—although largely in reaction to imaginative local actors and strong outside pressure.

The first compromise is for regimes to account for the secrets and abuses of their past. Reforms for the future will not be enough. They must also come clean about decades of injustice to build credibility and establish trust. The old adage can be adapted: The truth will set societies free.

Morocco took the first step in 2004, when Driss Benzekri received a summons from King Mohammed VI. The dapper young monarch wanted to discuss human rights abuses in Morocco, particularly during the rule of his father and grandfather.

The invitation, Benzekri later told me, was the last thing he expected.

Born in 1950, Benzekri was one of Morocco's most noted political rebels. He was a wanted man by the time he turned twenty-five. Benzekri is a tall, trim man who wears rimless glasses and has a translucent white mustache. He has the long, lean face of many who live in the

Maghreb, the vast region of arid desert and spiny mountains stretching across North Africa from the Nile River to the Atlantic. He also
has the frail physique and hunched weariness of a survivor. His manner
is subdued; he responds to questions in a quiet voice and not at great
length. You have to keep asking to get him to tell a little bit more of his
story. He expresses himself best, he says, through poetry. He seems to
vent by chain smoking.

Benzekri grew up during what Moroccans call the Years of Lead, a
notorious era of rule by the gun, when King Hassan II dealt ruthlessly
with opposition by labor activists, leftists, tribal rebels, and his own
military. He imposed a state of emergency in the mid-1960s that lasted
five years. In the 1970s, the king survived two assassination attempts
and a failed coup by military officers that deepened repression by the
ruling clique in Morocco, which is known as the *makhzan,* Arabic for
"storehouse"—as in storehouse of power.

During the Years of Lead, the monarchy's secret police arrested,
abducted, or executed thousands who dared to criticize or challenge
the king. The plotters of the 1972 coup attempt were executed by firing squad, live on national television.

A linguistics student, Benzekri became a Marxist and youth activist
who organized protests against autocratic rule on campuses across the
country.

"I was the generation that came of age in the late 1960s and 1970s.
We were the first generation after the independence of Morocco, and
there was a need to do something," he told me. "We came to Marxism
through the literature of what was happening in France at the time and
in San Francisco during the war on Vietnam.

"So we decided," he said, drawing quietly on a cigarette, "that we
wanted to make a proletarian revolution."

In 1975, secret police went after Benzekri too. On a cold January
day, they tracked him down to a hideout in Casablanca.

Over the next eighteen months, he endured prolonged solitary confinement and frequent torture—beatings, electric shock on the geni-
tals, hanging for hours by rope, head immersed in buckets of chemicals
or dirty water, and the rest of the time living with his head hooded, his
hands tied tightly behind his back, his body left prone on the ground.

"There was a rhythm to it. The technique depended on the questions they asked and the answers they wanted," Benzekri recalled, without emotion. "Sometimes they wanted a confession or specific information. Other times they wanted to humiliate and break your will."

Benzekri was eventually tried for belonging to a subversive group and plotting against King Hassan II. He was sentenced to thirty years. He ended up at Kenitra Central, a prison notorious for its filthy conditions and ruthless guards. It was built for 5,000 but it held almost twice as many. Kenitra has often been called the Abu Ghraib of Morocco.[3]

"One day, they put us in a common room to shave our heads, and while I was waiting my turn I saw one of the guards beating a young boy brutally. I was really outraged, so I detached myself and pushed the guard away from the boy," Benzekri recounted three decades later.

"To punish me they tied me like a lamb, with four limbs together, and beat me until I was hemorrhaging. They tore the muscles in my leg. My feet were so swollen and bleeding I couldn't walk. I had to be hospitalized."

Benzekri languished in prison for the next eighteen years. He was released in a 1991 amnesty by King Hassan after pressure by international groups about Morocco's political prisoners. When he was freed, he established the Moroccan Organization for Human Rights and an association for former political prisoners.

Thirteen years later, in 2004, the palace called.

King Hassan, who took only tepid moves to improve human rights toward the end of his reign, had died in 1999. When Mohammed VI assumed the throne, he immediately pledged major reforms. In one of his boldest steps, the new king told Benzekri that he wanted to establish an Equity and Reconciliation Commission to investigate abuses by secret police, intelligence, and the military from 1956 until 1999. The four-decade period began with Morocco's independence from France. It covered both the five-year rule of his grandfather, Mohammed V, and the thirty-eight-year reign of his father, Hassan II.

The idea was unprecedented in the Middle East. It was modeled on similar panels in other countries coming out of repressive eras, most famously the South African Truth and Reconciliation Commission that addressed the atrocities and assassinations during the apartheid era.

Argentina and Chile conducted similar probes into torture and disappearances after their military dictatorships ended.

But no Arab government had ever confessed to widespread abuses, much less tried to investigate the past or reconcile with its victims.

The young king asked Benzekri to be president of Morocco's commission.

So in 2004, Benzekri went back to prison—in fact, every prison, detention center, and major jail in Morocco—this time to document the abductions, disappearances, torture, and executions of thousands of Moroccan political prisoners. He and sixteen other former political prisoners and human-rights activists on the new commission investigated more than 20,000 cases.

At times, it was a journey into his own past. With other former prisoners, Benzekri went to the detention center where he had first been tortured. Several of his friends broke down and wept. Benzekri did not.

"Now they are only walls," he told me several months after the visit.

"The jail is in a poor neighborhood in Casablanca. The area is very famous for its cultural richness. It gave birth," he added, with a rare grin, "to many bands that play music like Bob Dylan. So in collaboration with the police and the local people, we agreed to turn it over to be used as a community center."

Benzekri also met his torturers. He knew most of them only by their voices, since prisoners were usually blindfolded or hooded. Some of them apologized and said they were only executing orders.

I asked if he believed them.

"It has no importance for me any longer," Benzekri replied. "They had lost their humanity.

"The important thing is that there is no longer the same culture of impunity, no executive privilege for top officials—not even for the king. In the past, the king was sanctified. No longer."

"This is not the same Morocco that arrested, tortured, and oppressed me," he said.

The commission then heard testimony—some of it broadcast live on Moroccan television and radio—from victims who detailed torture, families who recounted deaths of loved ones in prison, and wives and children who appealed for help in tracking down loved ones who had simply disappeared one day.

The testimony that gripped Benzekri the most, he told me when we first met in 2006, was from a woman in her seventies who was still searching for her husband. He had disappeared in 1957. She recounted to the commission every detail, every appeal, every official she talked to for almost a half century to find her husband.

Through official documents, Benzekri discovered that the man had been abducted by Morocco's secret services and murdered. He made it a personal mission to find out where her husband had been secretly buried.

When we talked a second time several months later, Benzekri said the commission had recently located the concealed grave and matched the DNA.

In the end, the two-year probe concluded that the state had systematically used torture as part of deliberate political repression and "gross" violations of Moroccan law. Benzekri and his colleagues uncovered the fate of almost 800 political prisoners who died from torture, many after being abducted—the so-called "forced disappearances." Prisoners who died or were executed were usually buried at night, without notification to families of their deaths or burial places, the commission revealed. Many families had not even known that their relatives had been seized by security services.

The reconciliation commission, its final report concluded, "achieved a substantial leap forward in establishing the truth about many events in this period of time, as well as about violations which had remained until then marked by silence, taboo, or rumors."

To make amends, the commission proposed that the monarchy pay compensation to almost 10,000 victims or their beneficiaries.

Among the most poignant cases for compensation was Ahmed ben Saleek, whose father and grandfather both disappeared in the 1950s. Saleek went to search for them when he was thirteen, but he, too, ended up detained and tortured.[4] The two older men never returned home.

The commission called for many victims to be covered in a special health-care program because of their permanent injuries or disabilities. It also proposed a system of collective reparations—in the form of economic projects—to revive communities particularly affected by government abuses.

Finally, the commission recommended bold steps to ensure that the Years of Lead were truly over. It called for a legal ban on arbitrary detention, disappearances, torture, cruel and inhumane treatment of detainees, and all other crimes against humanity. It recommended that international human-rights law should have priority over Moroccan law. It demanded constitutional amendments to separate government powers, particularly to ensure an independent judiciary. It proposed massive revisions in the penal code, including the basic assumption of innocence until proven guilty. It called for an overhaul in the training and oversight of the nation's diverse security services.

And, to get the ball rolling, the commission created a new body to track the government's performance and monitor future abuses.

"To create a democratic society, people have to know the truth and their history. This is the only way to achieve a culture of transparency and the only way for people to know how to choose their future," Benzekri said. "The report marked a fundamental rupture with Morocco's past."

But that was also the commission's biggest limitation. Its mandate was restricted to the past—and just documenting it, not doing anything about it. Former political prisoners were not allowed to name specific guards, officials, or other individuals who engaged in abuse. Victims could detail the most gruesome torture. But they were barred from identifying or describing their jailers.

Benzekri also had no legal power to hold anyone to account once their abuses were revealed. The commission could not refer torturers for investigation, charges, or trial.

The commission also had no power to compel testimony from people in high places to answer questions. There was no penalty imposed on institutions or individuals who did not come forward with the truth. And there was also no incentive to cooperate, such as the amnesty granted by South Africa's Truth and Reconciliation Commission.

The final report in 2006 complained about inadequate cooperation, "deplorable" records, and the failure of key officials to come forward.

The government clearly had no interest in trying anyone for abuse or breaking the law, according to several former political prisoners I visited in Rabat, the Moroccan capital. As a result, many political prisoners opted to stay away.

Among them was Ahmed Marzouki, one of fifty-eight junior officers charged with a minor role in the 1972 coup plot. He was sentenced to five years, but King Hassan ignored the judgment. Marzouki ended up in prison for almost nineteen years, all in solitary confinement. The king had had a secret desert prison especially constructed in Tazmamart for the perpetrators of the coup. It became the toughest prison in Morocco.

In his book *Tazmamart, Cell 10,* Marzouki graphically describes the decay of unwashed bodies, the slide toward insanity, and the deterioration from untreated disease.

For almost two decades, King Hassan denied that the Tazmamart prison existed. Under pressure from international human-rights groups, the government finally acknowledged the secret facility. When the military officers were released, less than one half of the men emerged alive.

Marzouki opted not to testify on grounds that his account would have no impact.

In the end, the reconciliation commission found out only part of the truth about Morocco's past. No officials stepped forward to admit wrongdoing, name wrongdoers, or provide evidence of wrongdoing. The commission merely confirmed what most already knew: Morocco abused, horrifically. It was just no longer an official secret.

In 2006, in front of an audience of victims and families of the disappeared, King Mohammed VI accepted the report. Moroccans, he said, "must all of us draw the necessary lessons from it in a way that will shield our country from a repetition of what happened and make up for what was lost." He called for full implementation of the commission's recommendations.

But the king did not apologize. And many of Morocco's human-rights activists claimed the outcome fell far short of its promise.

In Rabat, a city of wide boulevards and whitewashed buildings, I called on Mohamed Sebbar, a short man with a bushy black mustache who chews gum with vigor to cut down on cigarettes. A lawyer, he heads the Forum for Justice and Truth, the group of former political prisoners founded by Benzekri before he left to head the reconciliation commission.

Sebbar believes the commission failed. "We had to bargain to get this much truth," he told me. "What we got is the truth decided and provided by the state.

"The process failed to create a new climate for the future," he said. "We wanted boundaries on the king's powers. But, instead, we are still living with the same regime and the same state that the commission was investigating. In other countries that went through this process, in South Africa and Latin America, they have a different kind of government. We don't."

"And," he sighed, "there are still many secrets out there."

I asked if he felt that he was still under scrutiny from the Mukhabarat, or secret police.

"Of course," he said, laughing at the question. "The Mukhabarat is still listening to my phone."

Since assuming the throne, King Mohammed has made more promises of change and introduced more reforms than any of his predecessors and most other leaders in the region. In a 2004 address marking his fifth anniversary on the throne, he used the word "democracy" eighteen times to describe his hopes for Morocco's future.[5]

But even under a younger and more open-minded king, Morocco remains an absolute monarchy run by the oldest dynasty in the Arab world. Monarchy dates back 1,200 years in Morocco. The current Alouite dynasty dates back to the seventeenth century. Morocco's king is arguably the most powerful Muslim leader in the Middle East because of his multiple sources of authority. He is head of state. He is commander-in-chief. He appoints the prime minister and his cabinet. Both foreign and domestic policy comes from the palace. Judges are appointed on the recommendation of the Supreme Council, which is presided over by the king. The rubber-stamp parliament debates, but it has little power and even less oversight of government performance. The king can legislate new laws without parliament. And he can dismiss it at will.[6] He still has the powers of a despot.

Morocco's monarch has another whole separate set of powers, however. The royal family descends from the Prophet Mohammed and has for centuries invoked its religious position. King Mohammed, who is widely referred to as "His Majest-ski" for his love of jet-skiing, carries the title of Commander of the Faithful. It is Morocco's top religious position, and he has supreme religious authority.

To prepare his son for a religious role, King Hassan enrolled him in Koranic school at the age of four in 1967. Mohammed's official biography says he memorized the entire Koran.

No other Middle East leader holds total powers of state and mosque, even in Saudi Arabia. Only Iran's supreme leader comes close. Iran popularly elects its president, however, and its parliament has oversight rights, which it has frequently used to reject cabinet appointments, question ministers in office, or dismiss them.

Masmuh is the Arabic world for "allowed" or "permissible." It reflects the central flaw in the commission—and Morocco's broader attempt to open up.[7] Change is only what is *masmuh,* or what the king permits.

The king has acknowledged that he does not intend a political overhaul.

"One should not think that a new generation will turn everything upside down or bring everything into question. Let us not forget that in our countries, tradition is very strong," he told *Time* in 2000, in a rare interview the year after he assumed power.[8]

"Trying to apply a Western democratic system to a country of the Maghreb, the Middle East or the Gulf would be a mistake. We are not Germany, Sweden or Spain. I have a lot of respect for countries where the practice of democracy is highly developed. I think, however, that each country has to have its own specific features of democracy. . . . There should be a Moroccan model specific to Morocco."

After the commission's report was released, the seventeenth king of the Alouite dynasty did nothing significant to share power. The traditional power brokers, including the king's court, the intelligence and security services, and an oligarch elite—continued to dominate Moroccan politics. The king did not significantly strengthen other branches of government, at least in ways that checked his own. And the electorate still had little leverage through independent institutions.

Even as the king invited Benzekri to probe the past, the Moroccan regime was again secretly engaged in many of the same human-rights abuses used during the Years of Lead—this time to face a new threat.

On May 16, 2003, twelve suicide bombers struck targets throughout Casablanca, Morocco's bustling commercial and industrial center. It was the largest terrorist attack in the country's history. Dozens were killed, more than 100 injured.

The single deadliest bombing was at a Spanish restaurant, but the Islamist extremists also hit a five-star hotel, a Jewish community center, and a Jewish-owned restaurant. Most of the targets had Western or Jewish ties. The bombers allegedly belonged to an offshoot of the Moroccan Islamic Combatant Group and had links to al Qaeda. The bombings followed a broadcast from Osama bin Laden in which he branded Morocco an "apostate nation." The bombers were all Moroccans, most in their early twenties, and all from a Casablanca shantytown.

In the biggest sweep since the Years of Lead, the government arrested up to 5,000 Moroccans. The government later confirmed that more than 2,000 people—including more than 400 who were already in detention centers on other charges when the bombs went off—were charged with trying to subvert the state. More than 900 were convicted. Seventeen were sentenced to death.[9]

Moroccans again whispered tales of torture and additional mysterious deaths.

"The May 16 bombings were the beginning of the period of regression on human rights," said Sebbar, the gum-chewing lawyer and human-rights activist. "The government again started illegal detentions and torture. Many were arrested simply because they had beards.

"We also had problems again with freedom of speech, as the government arrested journalists accused of giving false information on the events."

I later asked Benzekri about the criticism—and if he had any fears that he and the reconciliation commission had been used by the palace.

"I am not a marionette, a puppet," he replied, drawing on a cigarette. "The truth is that the violations committed while arresting the

Islamists were not systematic or deliberate repression, as they were in our day." He paused briefly, then added, "We are concerned about this issue, although we consider these two distinct eras.

"Look," he said, "what is passionate about our experience is that we have moved from a stage of nurturing ideals or dreaming about what it is to be a democratic state to a phase of concrete initiatives."

In a theme I heard on every stop, in every country, Benzekri anguished over how long change will take in the Middle East.

"There is a new dynamic within society, but it is limited in its advocacy power. It doesn't have a voice yet," he explained, "There is a decision in Morocco to go ahead with democratization and reform, including separation of powers, but we are still debating a time frame and how to go about it.

"Look at Spain," he said, referring to the democratic transition after the 1975 death of General Francisco Franco ended a long dictatorship. "It took a decade to become a sustainable democracy, as it separated powers and established checks and balances. It's the same with South Africa. It didn't happen suddenly in 1993 with the end of apartheid. It took the rest of the decade, and South Africa is still struggling."

Yet in Morocco, progress also does not seem inevitable: Under King Mohammed, local and international human-rights groups again began to document charges that the secret police were engaging in arrests without warrants, and abductions. Held incommunicado, many suspects were put on a fast track to conviction after torture forced false confessions, human-rights groups complained.

Morocco also reportedly collaborated with the Central Intelligence Agency in holding terrorist suspects that the United States had apprehended abroad. The monarchy allowed U.S. intelligence to use at least one Moroccan facility as part of a covert foreign prison system set up after the September 11, 2001, attacks.[10] As the reconciliation commission released its report, Morocco was secretly detaining not only its own citizens but also suspects from other countries.

"Morocco's campaign against suspected Islamist militants," Human Rights Watch concluded, "is undermining the significant human rights progress the country has made in recent years."[11]

The second compromise is removing restrictions on women. No government in the twenty-first century can claim legitimacy without giving its female population personal and political rights.

On their own steam, women are already an imaginative force for change in the Middle East. Some of the transitions are quite stunning.

Fatima Mernissi grew up in a harem.

"I was born in 1940 into a traditional house, a harem, which was a luxury of the bourgeoisie," she told me, when I visited her in Morocco. Mernissi talks and writes about her life with a storyteller's delight, re-creating the innocence of her childhood and another way of life practiced not so long ago. She grew up in Fez, a city founded in the ninth century that is still the cultural heart and center of Islamic orthodoxy in Morocco. Many doors and walls in Fez's fabled Old City are painted green, the color of Islam.

Hers was not the exotic imperial harem of bygone dynasties, with eunuchs, slaves, and concubines reclining on pillows. She was raised in the traditional harem of an extended family; it was a place of seclusion for a patriarch, his adult sons, and all their wives and children residing together. Harem life was contained behind the *hudud,* or sacred frontier, protected by high walls and strong iron gates. Ahmed, the door-keeper, was the enforcer. The layout reflected life's hierarchy: Formal events, dining, and the men's world played out in salons on the ground floor, around the courtyard with Arabesque pillars, tiled archways, and a fountain. The two sons' family quarters were on the second floor. Widows and divorced women lived on the third.

Mernissi's early life was confined to the women's quarters with her mother, aunts, cousins, and a grandmother who had been one of her grandfather's nine wives—some, but not all, at the same time. The females rarely went out, usually just for religious festivals, only with permission, and always veiled and escorted by a male family member. They otherwise kept busy with beauty rituals, sewing, and creating little plays of what they imagined the outside world to be. They performed for each other.

As a child, Mernissi was told by her father that the sexes, rightly, had been segregated by God. Harmony required that each gender respect the prescribed limits of the other. Trespassing, he warned her, would lead only to sorrow.

"We live in difficult times, the country is occupied by foreign armies, our culture is threatened," he told her, during the days Morocco was still ruled by France. "All we have left is these traditions."[12]

For the women, however, life's obsession was escape. "Ahhh," Mernissi recalled, "but we dreamed of trespass beyond the gates all the time."

In her memoir, *Dreams of Trespass: Tales of a Harem Girlhood,* Mernissi recounted her mother's yearning.

"I would wake up at dawn," mother would say now and then. "If I only could go for a walk in the early morning when the streets are deserted. The light must be blue then, or maybe pink, like at sunset. What is the color of the morning in the deserted, silent streets?" [13]

The women's view of the sky was confined to a patch visible by looking up from the courtyard. Most windows were shuttered or draped so the outside world could not peek inside.

Their one connection to the outside world was a large radio. It was supposed to be for the men's ears only; it was locked in a large cabinet when they were out. But the girls eventually found the key and, when the men were away, they turned it on—and danced to local music, sang along with a Lebanese chanteuse, or listened to the news on Radio Cairo.

"The news became very important to me," Mernissi recalled, as she sipped a cup of sweet mint tea. She still remembers hearing on the radio about World War II for the first time.

"They were killing each other on such a big scale! This is why we were scared of the Europeans," she told me.

Her father eventually found out about the females' secret pastime. He grumbled that they would next find a key to open the front gate.

That's exactly what Mernissi did—with her mother's help.

Mernissi's mother was illiterate, but she was an independent spirit. She rejected restrictions on her life as an absurdity, and male superiority as anti-Islamic.

"Allah made us all equal," she would say, with indignation.

"My mother didn't know the alphabet, but that didn't make her ignorant. She knew *A Thousand and One Nights* by heart," Mernissi told me. "She was *very* clever."

Her mother ensured that Mernissi, from the age of three, was enrolled in Koranic school. It was the only form of education for females at the time. The family was devout. She shared her first name, Fatima, with one of the Prophet Mohammed's daughters. Many revere Fatima as the greatest Muslim woman who ever lived.

"I memorized many parts of the Koran as a child," Mernissi told me. "I say to women to this day: Swallow history and use it. You have to *sing* the Koran. It gives you a good memory."

She rose off a little divan and, in full theatric voice, recited from the forty-first chapter, or sura, of the Koran. "Respond to aggression with softness," she said, "and you will see your worst enemy become your fervent partner."[14]

The key out of the front gate—and eventually the harem—was education. When the Moroccan government opened public education to girls in the 1950s, Mernissi's mother pleaded with her husband to let their only daughter attend the new school. That meant learning arithmetic and foreign languages and even playing sports in shorts, none of which was allowed in religious school.

It also meant crossing the *hudud,* the sacred frontier, after which there was no going back.

Mernissi's father called a family council of senior male members. Debate was heated, but the council eventually decreed that Mernissi—as well as her ten female cousins—could go to public school.

"If I had been born two years earlier," Mernissi told me, "I would not have obtained an education."

Modernization only went so far; tradition still restricted personal freedom. When the Mernissi women were allowed to attend their first movie, the men bought tickets for four rows, so all the seats both in front of and behind the females were empty. The women spent hours doing their makeup and hair for the outing—only to have to don veils, or *hejab,* to cover it all.

Her mother once tried to change their *hejab,* replacing the heavy white cotton that impeded breathing with a lighter, sheer black chiffon. But her father resisted, Mernissi wrote.

> *"It's so transparent! You might as well go unveiled. It is like the French women trading their skirts for men's pants. And if women dress like men, it is more than chaos, it is the end of the world."* [15]

Mernissi's mother was never able to break out of the harem prison. When she appealed for permission to attend literacy classes, the family council turned her down. So she turned around and advised her daughter to learn to "shout and protest" just as she had learned to walk and talk.

"She would turn to me and say, 'You are going to transform this world, aren't you? You are going to create a planet without walls and without frontiers, where the gatekeepers have off every day of the year,'" Mernissi recalled. [16]

At the time, the Middle East offered few feminist role models for its women. Indeed, the groundbreaker was arguably a man.

Qasim Amin was an Egyptian judge, cofounder of Cairo University, and an activist in Egypt's nationalist movement. He is also considered the father of Arab feminism. He wrote *The Liberation of Women* in 1899 to argue that the education and liberation of women were pivotal in ending British colonial rule. In *The New Woman,* published in 1900, he then boldly condemned Arab societies for their attitudes and treatment of females. The book resonates with a single word—slavery.

> *The woman who is forbidden to educate herself save in the duties of the servant or is limited in her educational pursuits is indeed a slave, because her natural instincts and God-given talents are subordinated. . . . The one who is completely veiled—arms, legs, body—so that she cannot walk, ride, breathe, see, or speak except with difficulty is to be reckoned a slave.* [17]

It was much harder for women to campaign for their rights. Among the early critics was Aisha Taymour, an Egyptian born in 1840 who was never able to leave the harem. She spent her life penning angry poems against the veil in Arabic, Persian, and Turkish—languages otherwise largely useless since she could not leave her confinement to speak them in public.

Zaynab Fawwaz grew up in a Lebanese village. Through self-instruction and the men she married, she eventually became a noted literary figure. In the 1890s, she wrote a 500-page volume of women's biographies entitled *Generalizations of Secluded Housewives.*

Hoda Shaarawi was married at thirteen and lived sequestered for years in an Egyptian harem, yet she dared to gradually challenge convention. She organized the first lectures for women, founded the Intellectual Association of Egyptian Women, led women's street protests against British occupation in 1919, campaigned successfully to have the age of marriage raised to sixteen, and, in 1923, dared to publicly remove her veil. Shortly before her death, in 1947, she founded the Arab Feminist Union.

In the 1950s, Mernissi's mother was dogged about her daughter's future. She prodded her husband to allow Mernissi to go on to high school, then college, and next to the Sorbonne in Paris for graduate work. Mernissi ended up working on a doctorate at Brandeis University, where she began to write about the Middle East's harem culture—and, more to the point, how to break out of it.

Along the way, Mernissi told me with a chuckle, she also got her own radio.

Mernissi was in the last generation born into the traditional Moroccan harem and the first to break out of it. She soon emerged as one of the most audacious feminists in the Arab world.

Mernissi has grown into a defiantly flamboyant woman. I first met her in the mid-1990s. She generates energy, speaks in long, rambling, stream-of-conscious sentences that cover many subjects in a single breath, and is usually an idea or two ahead of most people around her. She is as sure of herself as any woman I've ever met. She is larger-than-life physically, too. She has high cheekbones and a long leonine nose; her hair is a mass of frizzy curls, rinsed in warm, auburn henna. She dresses in the deep, bright colors of Morocco, rich dark red, burnt orange, or dark violet. She is usually adorned with big jewelry, long dangling earrings, a chunky Bedouin necklace, and large rings. She wears neither scarf nor veil.

Her modest apartment in Rabat is filled with Berber carpets and big pillows. But when I visited her in 2006, what struck me the most were the big windows.

"Yes," she laughed, "I paid a lot to have this view. I love to see the sky. I have to see it, especially the moon."

Liberated from harem traditions, Mernissi now has the certainty of a convert. She has poured her obsession into a torrent of books that are the essential feminist primers in the Middle East. *The Forgotten Queens of Islam* chronicles the lives of fifteen female rulers in the medieval Islamic world—from Asia to North Africa, from Queen Arwa of Yemen to the sultanas of India and Persia—to refute misogynist claims that it is un-Islamic for women to lead. *The Political Harem: The Prophet and the Women* tackles the taboo subject of human sexuality.

Her most ground-breaking works challenge traditional interpretations of women's rights. In *The Veil and the Male Elite,* Mernissi offers a feminist interpretation of Islam. Most Arab governments have banned it. In it, she argues that the Prophet Mohammed actually sought equality between the sexes and gave a place to women in public life for the first time. In the period before Islam—known as the Jahaliya, or period of ignorance—females were treated brutally. They could claim no rights. They could be sold, stolen, abandoned, or claimed as booty in warfare. Female infanticide was common; unwanted baby girls could be buried alive.[18]

Islam revolutionized the treatment of women with new laws. It gave females the right to inherit, divorce, own and operate businesses, have partial custody of children, and pray in mosques.

"You can't blame the repression of women on the Prophet," Mernissi told me. "By comparison, he liberated women!"

And just how were women of other faiths treated in the eighth century? she asked.

In *Women and Islam,* Mernissi applied the mores of the early Islamic era to the present—with a vastly different spin than the region's conservative sheikhs and imams.

*Women fled aristocratic tribal Mecca by the thousands to enter Medina,
the Prophet's city in the seventh century, because Islam promised equality and dignity for all, for men and women, masters and servants. Every
woman who came to Medina when the Prophet was the political leader of
the Muslims could gain access to full citizenship, the status of "sahabi,"
companion of the Prophet. Muslims can take pride that in their language
they have the feminine of that word, "sahabiyat," women who enjoyed
the right to enter into the councils of the Muslim umma [community], to
speak freely to its Prophet-leader, to dispute with men, to fight for their
happiness, and to be involved in the management of military and political
affairs. The evidence is there in the works of religious history, in the bio-
graphical details of sahabiyat by the thousands who built Muslim society
side by side with their male counterparts. . . .*

*We Muslim women can walk into the modern world with pride,
knowing that the quest for dignity, democracy, and human rights, for full
participation in the political and social affairs of our country, stems from
no imported Western values, but is a true part of Muslim tradition.*[19]

Practices discriminating against women, she told me with dismissive self-confidence, are misinterpretations of the Koran and Muslim
traditions added by despots, dynasties, sheikhs and sultans, fundamentalist preachers—and husbands—over the centuries.

"You find in the Koran hundreds of verses to support women's rights
in one way or another and only a few that do not. They have seized on
those few and ignored the rest," Mernissi said.

The first convert to Islam, she noted, was Khadija, a prominent
businesswoman who ran trade caravans across the Middle East. She
hired Mohammed, eventually proposed marriage to him, and after his
revelations became a Muslim. After his death, his third wife Aisha provided roughly one-quarter of the hadith, the traditions of the Prophet
that are still considered as authoritative as the Koran in guiding the
way a good Muslim should live. Aisha also raised an army, gave fiery
speeches, and even went to the battlefield in a litter behind a camel.

Islam's original egalitarian values, Mernissi insisted, are actually the
best vehicle for change in the Middle East.

"Equality isn't a foreign idea and doesn't need to be imported from other cultures. It is at the heart of Islam, too. Allah spoke of the two sexes in terms of total equality as believers," she said. Muslim politicians who scream that equality for women is alien to Muslim tradition, she added, are like those who protested a century ago that banning colonial slavery was anti-Islamic.

It does not bother her that many Muslim scholars, past and present, interpret Islamic history and the Koran differently than she does. "Men have no monopoly on knowing what is right."

The first United Nations report on the status of Arab women, published in 2006, called Mernissi's work "pioneering" and described her as a "luminary" in the Islamic world.[20] Yet the same report also revealed how far Arab women still have to go. More than five decades after Morocco's public schools were opened to girls, over sixty percent of its female population still could not read and write—even though public opinion overwhelmingly supported equal education.[21]

Morocco is not an exception. Across the region, almost one half of all Arab females, almost seventy million, were illiterate in 2006—even though females in the Middle East outperform their male counterparts when given the chance. "Arab girls are the better learners," the United Nations report concluded.

In her indomitable way, Mernissi told me that she believes women in the Middle East have at least turned a corner.

"It's very simple, really. I reduce everything to information," she said, tossing her hennaed head. "Historically, only the king and his advisers had information, and beyond that everything was rumor. But technology brought us access to information. In 1991, I got a satellite dish. It brought CNN, but it was also the year of the first Arab satellite stations, and suddenly all the boundaries between private and public, between palace and street, and all the other dichotomies vanished.

"In *A Thousand and One Nights,* Scheherazade told the stories at night, as the daytime was the period of men's power. Women had influence only in the night. Now, Scheherazade can speak at any time! There's no more separation of day and night. And the number of women on television—it's amazing," she continued.

"The change that took centuries in the West took only a decade in the Third World because of technological advances. And no one can stop it. When I brought a fax here from Paris, I put a scarf on the machine when the telephone guy came to put in a line. But six months later, the government couldn't ban the fax.

"You know," she mused, "I recently asked the young woman working for me what she likes to do as a pastime. She told me she listens to tapes to learn French. She was almost illiterate, but with technology she is becoming self-taught. She chats on the Internet.

"Women ten years younger than I am," Mernissi said, "are from another planet!"

Family harems may have largely disappeared, but the rules that spawned them have not. Most Middle East countries still have two sets of separate and often conflicting laws. One set governs society; the other dictates to women.

After it became independent in 1956, Morocco adopted many French laws inherited from colonial rule. Article Eight of its constitution, for example, stipulates that men and women "enjoy equal political rights." In 1957, King Mohammed V also unveiled his eldest daughter—though not his wife—in public to signal that the next generation of women need not be hidden away.

At the same time, however, the new government passed a separate set of laws to codify traditions that had governed private life for centuries. It was the king's compromise: He adopted certain civil and criminal laws to modernize. But under pressure from traditional clerics who wanted a complete restoration of Islamic law once the French left, the king also agreed to enshrine in the law Muslim cultural practices about personal life.

In Morocco, the second set of laws is called the Moudawana, or Code of Personal Status. It relegated females to haremlike status.

The two sets of laws meant that women could vote under the constitution, but remained lifelong minors under the Moudawana. Fathers, husbands, brothers, and even sons were their legal guardians. Females needed written permission to open a business, obtain a passport, or leave the country. A woman could be divorced at the whim of her husband, without a reason, by simple public repudiations without going to court—and even without her knowledge. An unmarried woman who gave birth was sentenced to six months in jail, and the baby was put in an orphanage.

Often referred to simply as "family law," the Moudawana has been the biggest legal impediment to empowering women.

In the 1980s, an iconoclastic Moroccan dissident named Latifa Jbabdi decided to take on the Moudawana. It became an epic battle. I first heard about Jbabdi in a footnote on page thirty-seven in Mernissi's memoir. I finally met her in 2006. She is a striking woman, tall and big-boned but largely unadorned. Her jaw is strong; her brown eyes are piercing. She dresses with handsome femininity. She was in a blue suit with soft pinstripes, and a silk blouse. She was wearing no makeup and no jewelry beyond small stud earrings, and her short, brown hair fell in a natural wave. She, too, lived in Rabat.

If Mernissi is phase one, then Jbabdi is phase two.

Jbabdi started out as a communist in the 1970s. As a teenager, she organized strikes by high school students and factory workers.

"We dreamed of revolution," she told me. "We wanted a rupture with the past. It was the seventies—the traumatic time after the 1967 Arab-Israeli War and during the Vietnam War and dissent worldwide.

"We even raised money for Angela Davis," she chuckled.

Jbabdi read Lenin and Sartre and, for a while, attended meetings of a secret communist cell. "I was looking for a magic formula to change the world. But this group of old men was too Soviet. When it rained in Moscow, they took out their umbrellas in Morocco," she said, laughing again. "They focused on the elites. It was not what I was looking for to help the working class." She soon dropped out and joined an emerging group of leftists.

Jbabdi spent more than a decade being tailed, harassed, or hunted by Morocco's security forces for her dissident activities and strike mobilizations. Once she hid in a Christian cemetery for twelve days, relying on a graveyard worker to bring her bread and tea. Another time she hid in the mountains.

"We lived like wild animals," she told me, matter-of-factly.

Eventually captured, she was in and out of prison from 1977 until the early 1980s. Occasionally, she was detained preemptively until a protest strike was over. Her worst stint was six months in Casablanca's notorious prison. Torture was routine; she was blindfolded the entire time.

"They erased completely your femininity. They gave each of us a man's name," she recalled. "I was called Saeed."

Jbabdi was released on medical grounds for heart trouble; she received a pacemaker while still in her twenties. She remained on parole until she was granted an amnesty in 1990.

As she continued to push for political change, however, Jbabdi again grew frustrated with her political allies.

"There was a generation of young women born on the eve of Morocco's independence or shortly afterwards. We really believed we were equal, but even progressive parties and unions weren't open to the issue of women's rights," she told me. "They all proved to be misogynist."

"That," she added, "is when we came up with our own initiative."

In 1987, Jbabdi founded the Union of Feminine Action to confront the taboo of family law.

"You can't have a constitution that says we can be elected to parliament and decide the direction of the country, but under the Moudawana we have to have a guardian and can't make basic decisions on the most intimate issues of our lives," she told me.

In the Middle East, where mosque and state are still deeply intertwined, the Moudawana is the essence of the conflict between modernity and tradition, secular and religious. Unlike civil or criminal law, family law is based on interpretations of the Koran, which is quite specific on subjects ranging from a woman's menstrual cycle to suckling a baby and the taboo of incest. Conservative clerics argue that, as sacred text, the *Moudawana* cannot be altered because it is the literal word of God.

The Moudawana's holy origin has made the status of women the most intractable issue of change in the Middle East.

Jbabdi had to start from scratch. The Union of Feminine Action launched a newsletter that evolved into a magazine. It lobbied lawmakers. It held workshops for women in cities, villages, and shantytowns across Morocco to explain that poverty, domestic abuse, illiteracy, and dependence on men for the most basic decisions were tied to the Moudawana.

"Illiterate women and mothers and housewives came to our meetings in the poorest homes of a shantytown, and when we explained how the Moudawana ruled their lives, a lot of them started knocking on doors too," Jbabdi told me. "Many became even more active than we were."

To prove growing support for their cause, the movement launched a petition to demand change. By 1990, it had accumulated one million signatures—forty percent of them from men.

But the petition also sparked the first serious backlash. Conservative clerics preached against the Union of Feminine Action in mosques, appealed to the prime minister to ban it and punish its members, called for police to block the women's activities—and even issued a fatwa condemning Jbabdi to death.

"We were getting death threats all the time," she said. "It's hard to make progress when you're worried about your life."

In 1992, King Hassan intervened. In a nationwide television broadcast, he acknowledged that women had legitimate complaints, agreed to meet with them, and pledged to amend the Moudawana.

He also admonished the clerics, "Do not mix religion and politics."

A year later—after consulting with an all-male panel of senior clerics—the king announced reforms. They were few and modest. Among them: Brides had to consent to marriage. Husbands needed a wife's permission to take other wives.

More important was the principle. "The Moudawana was no longer so sacred. It could be debated and changed, like any other law," Jbabdi explained. "We had opened the door."

Peaceful change rarely comes with a single act or decision, particularly in the Middle East and particularly on women's rights.

Jbabdi persevered, as did a burgeoning array of women's groups that had sprung up among the middle and lower classes. She also adapted her tactics. As a former communist, Jbabdi initially blended Marxist ideas, the tactics of Western feminists, and the principles of international laws, including the 1979 United Nations Convention on the Elimination of All Forms of Discrimination Against Women.

Then she added Islam.

"We realized the movement would not be successful if it was based on women's rights alone. We began to repossess our Islamic heritage and to read the Koranic texts again, this time from a feminist perspective," she told me. "We did this for more than two years, and we found many verses that emphasize equality."

Like other sacred texts, the Koran offers a variety of messages about everything from personal relations to peace. A lot depends on how it is read—or who reads it.

The fourth chapter of the Koran, for example, is entitled "Women." Verse thirty-four says that men are "maintainers of women." But verse thirty-two also decrees, "Men shall have the benefit of what they earn and women shall have the benefit of what they earn." And, although their shares are not equal, verse seven requires, "Men shall have a portion of what the parents and near relatives leave and women shall have a portion of what the parents and the near relatives leave, whether there is little or much of it."

On the sensitive subject of polygamy, for which Islam is most criticized by the outside world, Muslim feminists now interpret the Koran as preferring one wife—and more than that only in a certain context.

Verse three stipulates, "If you fear that you cannot act equitably towards orphans, then marry such women as seem good to you, two and three and four; but if you fear that you will not do justice, then marry only one or what your right hands possess; this is more proper, that you not deviate from the right course."

On divorce, longstanding custom allows a man to end his marriage by simple repudiation, repeating "I divorce thee" three times. But the Koran also says, "If you fear a breach between the two, then appoint a judge from his people and a judge from her people."

The new generation of feminists argues that the Koran may even be an ally.

"We discovered that Islamic law is really a set of guiding principles open to interpretation," Jbabdi told me. She is as slow and deliberate in her speech as Mernissi is fast and frenetic.

"After that," Jbabdi added, "we tried to build all our arguments around Islam and prove that all change was rooted in Islamic principles."

For another seven years, Morocco's feminists continued to mobilize other women, lobby publicly, and pressure the monarchy to act. Then in 1999, King Hassan died. In one of his first acts, Morocco's new young monarch promised changes for women, whose "interests are still denied." His prime minister soon introduced a 118-page plan to address illiteracy, poverty, political discrimination, and reproductive health problems among women.

The plan polarized Moroccans, however. Feminists and modernists were pitted against conservatives and fundamentalists—and their differences spilled over onto the streets.

On March 12, 2000, Morocco witnessed two of the biggest demonstrations in its history. In Rabat, sixty women's groups, unions, and human-rights organizations rallied more than 300,000 people to support the government plan. Jbabdi was the coordinator. Six government ministers participated.

"No to reactionaries. Yes to equality," they shouted, as they streamed down the capital's tree-lined boulevards.[22]

In Casablanca, conservative Islamist groups mobilized at least one million Moroccans to protest the plan. They marched down the streets of Morocco's commercial center in separate columns, men in one, women in *hejab* in the other.

"The feminists said it was all or nothing—and the fundamentalists said it was nothing," Jbabdi recalled. "This was our period of labor pains."

The plan was shelved. As a compromise, King Mohammed formed a royal commission to come up with its own reforms to the Moudawana. Jbabdi was one of three women—out of fifteen members, including theologians—appointed by the king.

"Three is nothing for Americans," she recalled. "But for us this was revolutionary because we were going to be changing what was accepted as Islamic law. This was almost inconceivable."

The commission labored two years and produced almost 100 proposals.

Jbabdi worked outside the commission too. To pressure male members, she orchestrated an intensive lobbying campaign by women's groups.

They tracked down abused women and conducted a statistical analysis of the violence—and sent copies of their findings to the commission members.

They identified more than 10,000 women whose court cases for domestic abuse, financial abandonment, homelessness, and other family problems had lingered for up to fifteen years—and then flooded commission members with thousands of postcards detailing each case and its court number.

They held and videotaped mock trials, showing the problems women face with real lawyers, juries, and judges, to illustrate the legal limbo for women—and sent the videos of the proceedings to commission members.

"We became quite creative as lobbyists," Jbabdi recalled. "It had an extraordinary impact."

In 2003, Morocco's feminists got an unexpected break from an unlikely source—al Qaeda. The Casablanca bombing, the deadliest terrorist attack in Moroccan history, put all Islamist groups on the defensive. It changed the political atmosphere completely. Women were among the first to take to the streets to protest against extremism. The government soon cracked down on extremists, introduced education reforms, and moved on the Moudawana.

Five months later, King Mohammed VI took the royal commission's recommendations and proposed far-reaching changes in family law.

"The proposed legislation is meant to reconcile lifting the iniquity imposed on women, protecting children's rights and safeguarding men's dignity," he said in a speech to the opening of parliament.

This time, there was little resistance. Parliament passed the law in 2004.

The new Moudawana raised the minimum age of marriage from fifteen to eighteen. Marriage became an act of free will, and women could wed without consent of a male family member. Men and women entered marriage with equal rights, and husbands and wives were equally responsible for their households and families. The language requiring a wife to obey her husband was abolished. Marriage was certified by a judge, not a religious clerk—as was divorce. Men could no longer simply abandon their wives.

After a twenty-year battle, Moroccan women became among the most legally protected females in the Middle East—at least in theory.

Jbabdi called the new Moudawana "the moment of enlightenment, the harvest, not just for women. It is the biggest democratic step forward for Morocco.

"The family space is the heart and anchor of society, the place where behaviors and values and societal norms are established, and now the Moudawana will educate future generations on equality. This is the seed for everything else in democracy."

In a touch of irony, the women's movement had taken a toll on Jbabdi's personal life. The mother of two teenage boys, she was going through her own divorce as the new laws passed.

The new Moudawana opened the way to other changes. In 2006, Morocco graduated its first class of fifty female Muslim preachers, or guides, to work among the poor, bring women into a sacrosanct profession, and help counter the drift toward Islamic extremism.[23]

In practice, however, most Moroccan women still faced serious disadvantages. Women still had unequal access and grounds to divorce. Polygamy was still legal, although it had to be authorized by a family judge. Sexual relations outside marriage still made women liable for up to a year in jail, and criminal prosecution of a pregnant unmarried mother was still on the books—while the father faced no penalty. Unequal inheritance traditions did not change. A divorced woman could still lose custody of her children over the age of seven if she remarried. And illegitimate children still had citizenship problems.[24]

The bigger problem was that women had little access to information about the new laws. With up to eighty percent of rural women illiterate, they could not even read them, much less take action. And the government did little to educate women about the changes. Several judges stuck to traditional ways. And many families adhered to the old rules, including virginity tests before marriage.

Millions of Moroccan women also remained trapped in poverty. In 2005, Human Rights Watch reported that some 600,000 female children, some as young as five years old, worked as domestic help. Morocco's labor code did not regulate domestic work, nor did inspectors enter private homes to check.[25] The idea of girls assuming control over their lives remained a far-fetched dream.

Morocco's new feminist movement and the Moudawana reforms it produced were a starting point, not an end.

The third great compromise is détente with Islamists willing to work within the system and with other parties. It is also a risky step—for both sides.

Political Islam, in its disparate forms, will be the most energetic idiom of opposition in the Middle East for at least the next generation. Governments will pay a growing price for ignoring, isolating, or persecuting nonviolent movements, which could end up making them even more popular. The Islamist trend will only evolve or burn out under two conditions: When parties willing to work within the system and with other parties are allowed to participate, and when the desperate problems that fuel political unrest are addressed.

More than thirty years after the rise of political Islam, a growing number of Islamic movements have begun searching for compromise with Middle East governments. They need to be given political space. Some may be, in the end, the most effective barrier against the Jihadi militants. Secular and liberal and pro-Western forces clearly have proven that they, together, cannot defeat bin Ladenism.

"Islamists on principle and on pragmatic grounds must be included in any democratic transformation of the region," Egyptian democratic activist Saad Eddin Ibrahim said at a 2005 briefing on Capitol Hill in Washington.

> *They are substantial. They are on the ground. They are disciplined. They are committed. And they have been performing very important social services for the poor, for the needy. And they have managed to project an image of a corruption-free political force in contrast to regimes that are plagued by corruption. . . . They are substantial constituencies and they have to be included in any scheme for political governance.*[26]

One of the most interesting experiments in compromise is the Party of Justice and Development in Morocco. It may offer a new model.

"We are a political party, *not* a religious party," Saadeddine Othmani, the party chairman, insisted with the same hand-waving insistence the first, second, and third time we talked. "We are the most moderate party in the Arab world with an Islamic reference," he said. "But we are *not* Islamist!" He makes the point repeatedly in speeches, interviews, and private discussions to counter stereotypes that any party with an Islamic base automatically has a religious agenda, is made up of fanatics, and is inherently undemocratic.

Othmani cofounded the party. Born in 1956, he is a thin man who moves and speaks with quick energy. His face is narrow; his dark hair is very, very short, as is his beard. He grins easily and often, revealing a row of pearly white teeth. He is a psychiatrist by training; he worked for many years in a government hospital.

The party's headquarters is in a converted home set behind a tawny-gold stucco fence on a tranquil, tree-lined street in Rabat. It has no security at the door, no bodyguards for officials, no searches, no metal scanners, no monitoring cameras. The understated office has no posters of religious sheikhs, no framed Koranic verses written on black velvet, no models of the Dome of the Rock in Jerusalem. The walls are decorated instead with large drawings of the party symbol—an old-fashioned kerosene lamp, a light burning in its belly. A floor-to-ceiling version dominates the conference room.

The only picture on any wall is of Morocco's king.

The Party of Justice and Development, popularly called the PJD, is trying to carve out a new political niche in the Middle East as a Muslim movement neither militant nor assertively Islamist. It is not trying to topple the monarchy. It acknowledges the king as Commander of the Faithful. It accepts his power to handpick the entire government. It does not seek to impose Islamic rule. Women members do not have to wear *hejab*. Members do not even have to be Muslim.

The Party of Justice and Development grew out of Islamist organizations formed in the 1970s, when Islam moved into the political arena regionwide. They metamorphosed in the 1980s and then merged into a conservative party with Islamic values in 1992.

"You could compare us with the Christian Democratic parties in Europe," Othmani explained, switching from Arabic to French. "They base their goals on principles in their faith, but their platforms center on civil, not religious, issues."

The party takes a similar approach to the contentious issue of imposing Islamic law. "Unfortunately, to many people, Sharia has come to mean only the penal code," Othmani explained. "We derive our principles—justice and dignity and human development—from the essence of Islamic law. But we've moved away from using it explicitly in the party charter."

The party has redefined Morocco's messy political landscape, which teems with more than two dozen political parties. Most are built around political cliques. The majority are socialist or liberal—and fairly unproductive. Many have been co-opted by the monarchy.

In its electoral debut in 1997, the party deliberately limited the number of races it contested to prevent a political panic. But it still shook up—and shocked—the system by winning fourteen seats in parliament.

At the next election in 2002, the party tripled its numbers. It came in third in a huge field, even though it ran in only sixty percent of electoral districts. When the top two winning parties joined a coalition government, the Party of Justice and Development became the official opposition—arguably the first serious opposition since Morocco gained independence.

Like most other Middle East countries, Morocco's political parties are all ultimately beholden to the same autocratic leader. Since independence, parliament has never dared to test either the monarchy or its own powers because the king has the right to dissolve the legislature at his discretion. Under King Hassan, every parliament in four decades was either suspended or indefinitely "extended" to defer an election.[27] The idea of having a genuinely diverse, independent, and outspoken parliament as a check and balance on the executive has been virtually alien.

But the PJD injected momentum and a new discipline into Moroccan politics. For one thing, its legislators actually showed up—in a body rife with absenteeism. Legally, legislators are supposed to provide written excuses for absence or be docked pay, but the rule had long been ignored.

"If we didn't attend sessions, nobody would be in parliament," Othmani said, with a chuckle.

Among its own members, each of the forty-two legislators is required to draft one question about government performance to be asked orally in parliament each week, to submit one written question monthly for a ministry to formally answer, and to propose one new bill each year. It also requires all its legislators to give twenty percent of their government paychecks back to the party—one half for local party work and one half for national activities.

"We are a poor party," Othmani said, with a shrug and another grin.

The party focused heavily on three issues central to real change in Morocco: dirt-poor poverty among more than ten million Moroccans, corruption endemic among the political elite, and constitutional reform to empower parliament as a separate body not controlled by the monarchy.

"We have no problem with the king, but we do need to have a balance between powers in the state," Aziz Rebbah explained the day I visited party headquarters. Rebbah is a Canadian-educated information technology engineer who heads the party's youth organization.

"That's why we're trying to start a national debate on constitutional reform," he said. "The objective is not to limit the power of the king, but to enhance the ability of the government and the prime minister to act."

Public-opinion polls regularly predict steady growth for the PJD—potentially even winning the largest vote in future elections. A 2006 poll by the International Republican Institute in Washington showed that up to forty-seven percent of Moroccan voters leaned toward the PJD—a huge number in a field of more than two dozen parties.[28] Getting even twenty percent could provide a decisive plurality.

The party has since scrambled to emphasize that a victory would not lead to an overhaul of Moroccan politics.

"Parties like ours have a duty to take part in political reform, but not to impose religious solutions," Othmani told me.

Elected to head the party in 2004, Othmani campaigned both at home and abroad to allay fears. He outlined the party's vision at a 2006 speech in Washington, D.C.

The state in Islam can by no means be described as a religious type.... In Islam, the ruler does not derive legitimacy from some supernatural force. Rather, the ruler is an average individual, who derives power from the nation that willingly selected him and to which he is responsible in this world. ...

Islam has no fixed form of governance or of citizen participation. Instead, this has been left for human creativity and to be decided by man's ever-changing circumstance.... The people's will is the decisive criterion.[29]

Among Middle East parties, the difference between fundamentalist, Islamist, and an "Islamic reference" can seem a semantic shill to skeptics. The differences often seem nuanced. Definitions also vary by party; context varies by country. But the distinction is the essence of an emerging political trend in the Middle East.

"If you compare us with the Muslim Brotherhood, there is a big difference. Oh, yes!" Othmani told me. "The leader of the Brotherhood has the job for life. In our party, I can serve *only* two terms."

"We're also democratic in the way we elect our officials and decide policy," he added. "Every official is selected from a local, regional, or national conference, not picked from the top." Othmani was elected in a three-way contest by 1,600 members of his party.

"All together, we vote on policy, too!" he said.

The search for compromise by Islamic parties began in the late 1990s. Among most, it is still at a tentative stage. Reasons for a shift range widely.

The first major factor is the reaction to past confrontations.

In Algeria, a civil war between Islamic extremists and the military government killed almost 200,000 people between 1992 and 2002—and solved little. The war erupted after the 1992 military coup aborted Algeria's democratic transition, just as a nonviolent Islamic party running in a field of fifty-four parties was about to sweep parliamentary elections. The popular Islamic Salvation Front was banned, and its leaders were detained. The Islamist trend then splintered, spawning extremists who fought the military, sabotaged its government, and terrorized the public. The violence was often bestial. No one was safe.

A stark message rippled through the region: Confrontation can be costly in human life and to the cause of change. When the war ended, an autocratic government was still in place. And the chronic problems of the poor were only worse.

Morocco, which shares a 1,000-mile border with Algeria, shivered as Algeria was badly shaken by turmoil and brutality.

"Our party is trying to do something good for the country. That's why you'll hear our members talk a lot about not wanting Morocco to repeat the Algerian experience," Abdelkader Amara, a young member of parliament and head of the party's political section, told me.

Other Islamist movements—Egypt's Center Party and Muslim Brotherhood, the Iraqi Islamic Party and Dawa, Jordan's Islamic Action Front and Center Party, Kuwait's Islamic Constitutional Movement, Turkey's Justice and Development Party, and Yemen's Reformist Union—have begun running for office and working within government institutions. Even groups with provocative names, such as the Supreme Council for the Islamic Revolution in Iraq, now participate in secular politics. Their transition is only beginning. But they have rejected violence and distanced themselves from extremists.

A second factor is the rise of reform movements.

The 1997 surprise victory of reformers in Iran, where the revolution had launched political Islam a generation earlier, gradually inspired rethinking regionwide. Even though reformers were ousted in 2005, the mere fact of diversity in Iranian politics demonstrated the possibility of options. Reform entered the Islamist lexicon.

Philosophically, Othmani identifies with Soroush, Iran's leading philosopher, but he goes one step further. "We want renewal, which goes beyond reformation," Othmani told me. "Reform means using what you have and making small new interpretations. Renewal means radical change, to produce whole new ideas, not just to fix the core."

He takes an especially bold stand on the relationship between mosque and state. Jihadists want to blend the two after ousting the autocrats. But Othmani argues that the Prophet Mohammed had separate roles as religious leader and political chief of the new community of Muslims. "When we distinguish between these two behaviors, it gives us the precedent to separate political and religious institutions," Othmani explained.

The third factor is the reaction to al Qaeda.

After September 11, 2001, the gap widened among Islamists. Activists were forced to take a definitive stand on terrorism. Public alienation also increased as extremism took a mounting toll on Muslims themselves. Between 2002 and 2005, public-opinion polls found opposition to violence against civilians in the name of Islam had soared. Disapproval grew in pivotal countries such as Morocco, Turkey, Pakistan, Indonesia, and Lebanon, according to the Pew Research Center.

Opposition was highest in Morocco, where it more than doubled— to almost eighty percent. The shift followed the 2003 Casablanca bombings by an al Qaeda ally. The survey also found support waning in most countries for Osama bin Laden.[30]

A fourth factor is the impact of the stunning Islamist upset in the Palestinian elections.

The Hamas victory in 2006 scared many Islamic groups. Its win only deepened Palestinian problems. The cutoff of international aid left seventy percent unemployed, sparked deadly new clashes with Israel, and ended up threatening the existence of the Palestinian Authority.

Hamas made a mistake, several officials in Morocco's Party of Justice and Development told me.

"It would have been much better for the Palestinians, and also for the situation in the Middle East, if they had come into government gradually," said Amara, the parliamentarian, who is also a veterinary specialist in the pathology of ornithological diseases, such as bird flu.

"I think they were taken to power by what we call The Wave. The same thing could happen in Morocco. It's the reason that we ran candidates in only sixty percent of the districts in 2002," Amara explained. "We did it deliberately to prevent being taken to power by The Wave."

Other factors foster political compromise: Geographic proximity to democratic governments, notably Mediterranean countries close to Europe; historic political experience and ties to the outside world, even through colonialism; cultural diversity that exposes communities to each other; and economic need.

Morocco reflects a special confluence of factors.

A country slightly larger than California with a 1,200-mile coast bordering both the Atlantic and the Mediterranean, Morocco straddles two worlds. It is both Arab and African. In the seventh century, the invading Arabs called it the Farthest Land of the Setting Sun.

To this day, Morocco remains the westernmost outpost for both Islam and the Arab world.

It is also the closest Arab gateway to Europe, just fourteen miles from the Strait of Gibraltar. Ties between Arab and Western cultures date back to the eighth century—via Morocco.

After sweeping across North Africa, the Arab army used Morocco as a base and Morocco's Berber tribes as recruits to move into Europe. The Arabs penetrated the Iberian Peninsula, then came within 200 miles of Paris. They controlled the region for the next 500 years. The rich Moorish culture that took root in Spain borrowed heavily from the Berbers as well as the Arabs. Andalusia eventually declared its independence from the Abbasid dynasty in Baghdad and established its own caliphate in Córdoba in the tenth century. It was the largest and the most culturally sophisticated polity in Europe at the time.

Morocco's proximity to Europe has had an enduring impact. Spain occupied northern Morocco in the nineteenth century. Morocco then became a French protectorate in 1912. Since independence in 1956, Morocco's troubled economy has been dependent on tourism by Europeans and Americans plus remittances from Moroccan workers in Europe.

The crosscurrents remain strong.

Morocco is also the least Arab country in the diverse Arab world. The vast majority of Morocco's thirty-three million people are also at least part Berber, a non-Arab ethnic group that can be traced to North Africa since Neolithic times. Up to one half are pure Berber, and Berber is still widely spoken. The king's mother was Berber. Othmani is Berber. Driss Benzekri is part Berber. The Berber roots reflect the country's African identity. Morocco is as much of a player in the African Union as it is in the Arab League.

Morocco is also far from the front lines of the Arab-Israeli conflict, the main reason that the monarchy has been willing to deal with Israel and mediate peace talks. King Hassan broke with the Arab world to host Israeli Prime Minister Shimon Peres in 1986. Israel opened a small diplomatic mission in Morocco in 1994. King Hassan also brokered talks between Israel and Yasser Arafat in 1995. And when the king died in 1999, Israeli Prime Minister Ehud Barak and Moroccan-born Foreign Minister David Levy attended the funeral.

Morocco is, in many ways, one the most obvious places for a compromise to flourish.

But compromises also come down to making choices—and to leadership.

Othmani was among Morocco's early Islamic activists. He came from a religious family. His father was a professor of Islamic law. As a student, Othmani was a leading figure in Islamic Youth, the first major Islamist movement in Morocco. Founded in 1972, its focus was Sunni students. Its agenda was antiregime. When the youth group spawned a militant wing in 1981, however, Othmani quit.

"It embraced violence and undemocratic activities," he told me, "so many of us split off and organized ourselves in the Islamic Association."

He paid a price for his activism. He was jailed for almost five months in 1981, while still in medical school. After he was released, he spent the next decade organizing Islamic activists in civil-society groups, running an Islamic magazine, and exploring ways to form a legal Islamic party.

"I never, *never* envisioned I'd be in parliament," he told me.

But in 1992, the groups he helped pull together took over a moribund party that still had legal status and turned it into Morocco's first Islamic political party. He was one of fourteen who won a seat in parliament in 1997.

Othmani has since been a consensus builder, crafting compromises on issues that make Islamic parties most controversial—and preventing the party from being outlawed.

Women's rights is one of the most contentious issues. The party helped to mobilize almost one million men and women to protest changes to the Moudawana in 2000. It labeled the initial draft "a bid to corrupt Moroccan families" that would foster a "culture of dissoluteness" by eliminating Islam-inspired provisions in Moroccan law.[31] But when the king made it part of his 2003 agenda, the party debated it—heatedly, Othmani conceded—and in the end supported the new Moudawana.

Ironically, the Party of Justice and Development is among the most inclusive to women. It has a fifteen-percent quota for women in all branches, the highest of any party. Among the forty-two party members who won seats in parliament in 2002, six were women, matched only by the Independence Party. And after the 2003 local elections, it had the highest number of women in local councils.

The most contentious foreign-policy issue for Islamic parties throughout the Middle East is Israel. In a 2006 speech in Washington, Othmani spoke at length about Islam's early relations with Jews. He cited the Medina Charter, often considered the first constitution in Islam. It was enacted by the Prophet Mohammed following his migration to Medina in 622. The Charter, Othmani noted, stipulates:

> *Any Jew who may follow us shall be supported and treated equally and fairly. . . . The Jews may pay as much as the Muslims shall pay at times of war. The Jews of Bani-Auf are a believing nation. The Jews have their own religion and the Muslims likewise. This goes for themselves, goes for their followers, save whoever may commit a crime.*[32]

Islam intends to insure, Othmani concluded, that "Every man has the right to believe in any religion and shall not be harassed."

I asked Othmani if his party was willing to accept Israel's right to exist—or even use the word Israel, which Islamist parties elsewhere refused to do.

"Yes, yes, we use the word Israel. Israel exists, of course," Othmani said. "What we need to find is a solution for both parties."

A two-state solution? I asked him.

"Why not?" he replied. "We need mutual recognition."

The party's biggest compromise is its go-slow policy. Under pressure from the government, it agreed to run candidates for only one quarter of city council seats in the 2003 local elections. Autocratic governments are often most wary of devolving power because Islamist groups build strong local bases; they often deliver more of what they promise in terms of local services and development.

When I visited party headquarters, the leadership was in the midst of a similar debate—over how many seats to contest in 2007 national elections for parliament. Othmani favored running a full slate. Aziz Rebbah, the Canadian-educated engineer, argued against it.

"The population's expectations from our party are bigger than our capacity," Rebbah told me. "We also need time to create trust between us and other actors in the country, like the business community.

"We should have at least five more years in government, to create more confidence at home and to convince American and French decision makers that we are not dangerous and can discuss mutual interests between us," he added. "So I think we need to be one of the main parties, but not the main party."

The party's compromises, however, have made it vulnerable to charges of being co-opted by the monarchy—and failure. It has not only stood by the king; several PJD officials work in government ministries.

"The monarchy has the support of the Moroccan public. We feel it doesn't contradict democracy," Othmani told me. "There are many monarchies in Western democracies."

The compromises, so far, have been largely one-sided. The monarchy has given the Party of Justice and Development a bit of public space but retained all power. Even if it won a parliamentary election, the PJD might not be able to either lead a government or pass legislation, since the king appoints the prime minister and can dissolve parliament at his whim.

The failure to share power or enact political reform puts the monarchy in a precarious position, for the Party of Justice and Development is neither the largest Islamic movement in Morocco nor the biggest threat to the royal palace.

Despite its traditionally moderate brand of Islam, Morocco has several other more hard-line movements. The most militant is the Moroccan Islamic Combatant Group, an ally of al Qaeda sired by Moroccan dissidents trained in Afghanistan. In the 1990s, many of its members returned home and cultivated new cells, particularly in the cinderblock slums of Casablanca that teem with more than 300,000 people.

The group also has cells in Europe. Besides the 2003 Casablanca attacks, the group's militants are linked to the 2004 bombings in Madrid, when ten bombs went off simultaneously on four commuter trains at rush hour. Almost 200 were killed, almost 2,000 injured. It was the worst terrorist attack in Spanish history.

The Moroccan militants want an Islamist regime to replace the monarchy. They also support al Qaeda's confrontation with the West.[33]

The largest and most popular Moroccan Islamist group is Justice and Charity. The movement is nonviolent but refuses to participate in politics.[34] It was founded by Sheikh Abdesalam Yassine, a charismatic cleric, who is widely compared to Iran's Ayatollah Khomeini. Both led campaigns against powerful monarchies in the 1960s and 1970s. Both called for a monarchy to be replaced by a republic. Both men also went to jail, fueling their popularity.

Yassine launched his party with a 120-page open letter to King Hassan in 1974. It accused the monarchy of tolerating corruption. It condemned the regime for allowing Western-style moral decay. And it warned that an Islamic deluge would sweep the monarchy from power.

For much of the next quarter century, Yassine was intermittently locked up in a state psychiatric hospital, imprisoned, or under house arrest. His message of good works for the poor nevertheless tapped into deep discontent among the poor and triggered a groundswell of support, as his daughter carried on the campaign in his absence.

In 2000, shortly after his father died, King Mohammed released Yassine and other political prisoners. But the sheikh did not repent. He penned another long open letter charging that the late king had looted billions from the national treasury and calling on the King Mohammed to save his father from eternal damnation by returning the people's "legitimate belongings" to alleviate Morocco's enormous poverty.[35]

Yassine's powerful challenge has given Justice and Charity credibility among Islamists—and posed the biggest challenge to both the monarchy and the PJD.

When he inherited power, King Mohammed VI pledged to become the "king of the poor." "We are firmly determined to lead our people to a democracy which involves all participants and incites everybody to take part in the economic and social Jihad," he told parliament in 2000.

But little changed. One third of Moroccans still live below the poverty line. One in five is still unemployed. Infant mortality rates are very high. And prospects for rapid improvement are limited, because roughly one half of Moroccans are still illiterate, putting significant progress a generation away, at least.

The young king also tightened the cordon around political Islam after the Casablanca bombings. In 2003, the government introduced an antiterrorism law that allows it to monitor mosques, religious leaders, and the religious content of textbooks. "Apologizing for terrorism," widely interpreted as explaining it in terms of local conditions, became a crime.[36]

In 2005, the regime proposed another law that barred all religious and ethnic references in party platforms. It effectively blocked any group more ambitious than Othmani's movement—and even put it on notice.

Othmani acknowledged the tensions—and the growing limitations. "As an opposition party, we have no ability to get our bills enacted," he told me. "Our approach is to have gradual progress and avoid haste and shortcuts, which is a major mistake committed by many leftists, nationalists, and Islamist movements over the decades."

"The strategy for us is to be patient," he said. "The question now is whether the population has enough patience to stick with us."

In Morocco's 2007 parliamentary elections, in a field of thirty-three parties, the PJD did not do as well as it had expected. Yet the Islamists won more votes than ever. And the PJD improved its position in parliament. It officially became Morocco's second most popular party.

TEN

IRAQ AND THE UNITED STATES

The Furies

Democracy cannot be brought on the back of a tank.

—Syrian dissident Riad al Turk[1]

A new Middle East? The way I'm looking at this new Middle East, I'm seeing what is happening in Gaza, I see what's happening in Lebanon, I'm seeing what's happening in Iraq. This is a new Middle East?[2]

—Jordan's King Abdullah

For the foreseeable future, the Middle East will be engulfed in a contest between the familiar and the feared, between the comfort of long-standing local traditions and the lure of global political trends. In a region where ways of life date back millennia, it will be a tug-of-war, bloody at times.

Along the way, change will often require sorting out the past or at least trying to move beyond it. Progress will otherwise be overpowered.

Iraq is the starkest case.

In November 2002, during the buildup to the Iraq war, I went to see Barham Salih, the prime minister of Kurdistan. The northern region of Iraq, about the size of Switzerland or twice the size of New Jersey, was then isolated from the outside world, so it took a while to get there. I flew first to Iran, spent several days in Tehran getting assorted permissions, then flew west to Iran's Kermanshah province, and finally took a three-hour cab ride to the border with Iraq. In a cold, drizzling rain, I checked in at a hut used mainly by truckers and smugglers who ferried goods into Iraq in defiance of United Nations sanctions. I was asked to sign my name in an old-fashioned ledger to note that I was leaving the country. Then I walked across a no-man's-land—illegally, since I did not have a visa—into Saddam Hussein's Iraq.

I was not the only American in Kurdistan. U.S. intelligence and Special Forces officers were already secretly in the northern Iraqi province, almost six months before the invasion and as diplomacy was only midstream at the United Nations. The Americans were conducting reconnaissance, negotiating access with Kurdish leaders, checking out four unused airfields, setting up listening posts, probing the strength of Kurdish troops, and becoming familiar with the starkly beautiful region of craggy mountains and tranquil lakes.

The American experiment in creating a democracy in the Middle East was already in the works.

I stopped first in Sulaimaniyah, a bustling city with tree-lined streets and its own Ferris wheel, about four hundred miles north of Baghdad. Sulaiman is the Islamic version of Solomon. The suffix -*iyah* citifies a name. Sulaimaniyah was named after an eighteenth-century Kurdish prince. It is one of two Kurdish capitals. Irbil is the other.

Born in 1960, Barham Salih is an erudite man with a smoothly bald pate; the sides and back of his hair are neatly barbered, as is his mustache. He speaks the Queen's English, is a dapper dresser, and has a penchant for fine red wines and cigars. Arrested twice by Saddam's regime, he graduated from the University of Cardiff in Wales and did graduate work at the University of Liverpool. He was a Kurdish representative in Washington before returning to join the government. I had known him for more than a decade, and we had been debating the future of Iraq through most of it.

Salih invited me to his family house in Sulaimaniyah so we could watch the American election results. He was closely monitoring the 2002 vote, in part to see if it would have any impact on U.S. plans in Iraq. He was both nervous and excited by the prospects of American intervention.

"We still have a precarious relationship with the West in this part of the world. Our admiration is shaded by suspicion from past experience," he told me. "But we're hoping the United States will be a partner in bringing about a better Iraq. And I'd be surprised if the United States allows this opportunity to go down the tubes."

I asked him if he had any reservations. He hesitated for a moment.

"Living in the West was a very useful opportunity for me to see debate in the British Parliament and America's Congress. It was wonderful!" he said, with a laugh. "But as I am reminded daily since I returned to Iraq, your Western societies took hundreds of years to get that far. Modernity is the rejection of so many traditions and sources of identity. We are not anywhere near this point.

"As prime minister," he added, as the U.S. election results on CNN streamed across the bottom of his television, "I spend a *lot* of time with traditional people who want to build a mosque when my instinct is to build a school. I fully believe that the Middle East can't continue in the way of the past. There's simply too much change taking place everywhere, and globalization makes us part of it, whether leaders like it or not. But there's no place the saying that 'old habits die hard' is truer than in the Middle East.

"My concern," he said, "is that removing a dictatorship does not mean democracy will work—right away or perhaps at all. I have been warning the Americans about this. But I don't know whether they understand."

Kurdistan was a model for both the potential and the dangers of change in Iraq.

The world's largest ethnic group without a state, the Kurds were particularly keen on ousting Saddam Hussein. They had never wanted to be part of Iraq in the first place.

An Indo-European people, the Kurds are closer ethnically to Persians than Arabs. Kurdish tribes have inhabited the inhospitable mountains for millennia. An early mention of the Kurds—people in "the land of Karda"—was found in cuneiform writings of the Sumerians some 3,000 years before Christ. Saladin, arguably the greatest warrior in Middle East history, was a Kurd. Born in the twelfth century, he came from Tikrit, which, ironically, was also Saddam Hussein's home town. Saladin went on to become the vizier of Egypt. He recaptured Jerusalem from the Crusaders. Ever since, leaders in the region have coveted the idea of being the next Saladin.

After the Ottoman empire's collapse, the 1920 Treaty of Sèvres promised the Kurds their own country. But the agreement fell apart. Today, the estimated thirty million Kurds—although estimates vary widely—are divided up among four countries: More than one half are in Turkey. Iraq and Iran each have about twenty percent. More than five percent are in Syria. Smaller numbers are in Azerbaijan and Armenia. The Kurdish diaspora includes significant numbers in Europe as well as Israel, Afghanistan, and Lebanon.[3]

For the Kurds, life in modern Iraq was never easy. They always felt like outsiders, as non-Arabs, and continuously agitated for real autonomy. Relations with Baghdad were often tense. But Saddam Hussein's rule was the most brutal.

In the 1980s, Saddam's army razed hundreds of Kurdish villages. More than 180,000 Kurds were detained. Thousands were executed, their bodies dumped in mass graves, their families never notified. In 1987 and 1988, the Iraqi military fired chemical weapons on two dozen Kurdish towns and villages.[4] The grisliest attack was in Halabja, where some 5,000 Kurds died from mustard gas and the nerve agents tabun and sarin. The bodies of mainly women, children, and the elderly littered the streets where they had dropped. Guy Dinmore of *The Financial Times* recorded the gruesome scene when he arrived shortly afterward.

It was life frozen. Life had stopped, like watching a film and suddenly it hangs on one frame. It was a new kind of death to me. You went into a room, a kitchen, and you saw the body of a woman holding a knife where she had been cutting a carrot.

The aftermath was worse. Victims were still being brought in. Some villagers came to our chopper. They had fifteen or sixteen beautiful children, begging us to take them to hospital. So all the press sat there and we were each handed a child to carry. As we took off, fluid came out of my little girl's mouth and she died in my arms.

Halabja ranked as the most devastating chemical weapons attack against a civilian population in modern times. The city was under Salih's jurisdiction, just down the road from Sulaimaniyah. It served as a constant reminder of the Kurds' vulnerability.

In 1991, the Kurds rose up one last time against Saddam in response to an appeal by President George H. W. Bush to topple the Iraqi leader after a U.S.-led campaign had forced him to retreat from Kuwait. But Baghdad quickly crushed the Kurdish revolt, again killing thousands and forcing one million to flee to the borders of Turkey and Iran. Baghdad then punished the five million Iraqi Kurds by cutting off funds, food, fuel, electrical power, and any human traffic in or out of their landlocked enclave. Saddam wanted the Kurds starved into submission.

The threat of military action hung over every action the Kurds took. "If the current government in Baghdad remains in power, the prospect of another genocide is very real," Salih told me. "Iraqi tanks are literally an hour or so away. Most Kurds have contingency plans for what they'll do if something should happen again."

The Kurds lived under double sanctions. As part of Iraq, they also came under the toughest punitive measures ever imposed by the United Nations.

The Kurds, as a famous proverb laments, had no friends left but the mountains.

Yet the rugged people of northern Kurdistan, some of whom still wear the baggy pants and colorful turbans of tribal tradition, are a scrappy lot. In the 1990s, they slowly began transforming the north, reconfiguring what they had and smuggling in the rest to survive.

Outside Sulaimaniyah, a little oil refinery assembled from the cannibalized parts of cement, sugar, and soft-drink factories noisily pumped out 3,000 barrels of oil a day. Its slogan: "Where there's a well, there's a way." Unable to get passports, Kurdish officials converted time abroad as students or workers into second nationalities. Salih had a British passport, his minister of education was a Swede, the ministers of reconstruction and of human rights were Germans. Other officials were Belgian, French, Italian, Spanish, Austrian, and Swiss.

"I don't think there are any Portuguese among us," reflected Defense Minister Sherdl Hawezey, seriously.

The Kurds also adapted their skills. Salih was a civil engineer and statistician. His intelligence chief, Khasro Mohammed, was a former veterinarian specializing in poultry diseases.

"Both jobs require research and investigation," Mohammed told me, somewhat bemused.

To compensate for having no postal system, dozens of Internet cafés had opened in the previous three years. The Internet elsewhere in Saddam Hussein's Iraq was heavily censored and required a police permit to get full access, but Kurds had cheap, unrestricted connections. Satellite dishes, perched atop mud-brick homes in the countryside and dangling with laundry off apartment balconies in the cities, brought in the outside world. As we watched the U.S. election results, Salih flicked between CNN, Fox, MSNBC, and the BBC with his remote. The Kurds had also launched their own television stations, some with satellite links on Kurdsat that beamed into the United States and Europe. One station aired an equivalent of *Saturday Night Live* with irreverent pokes at Kurdish politicians.

Kurdistan, which was divided into eastern and western regional governments, had the early trappings of democracy. One of the first signs was a decision by the two regional governments to form a united front and hold elections in 1992 for a single new Kurdish legislature. Although two parties dominated politics, others contributed to feisty public and parliamentary debates.

Freedoms of the press, speech, and assembly were also taking root. Several regional newspapers began questioning policies and politicians.

"Every week, someone comes through my office asking me to do something about the papers," Salih told me, with a sigh.

Hawlati, or The Citizen, was the particular bane of Kurdish politicians after its launch in 2000—on a 1967 printing press. It exposed a military commander's illegal kickbacks on government contracts. It published secret government communications. Its investigation of a Kurdish official led to his arrest for kidnapping and murder. And its editorials blasted government inefficiency, corruption, and heavy-handedness.

"Politicians understand that allowing criticism is more important than stopping criticism—no small thing in Iraq," *Hawlati's* editor Aso Hardi told me. Some papers were independent; others were tied to political parties. "But at least we have a lot of parties," Hardi said. The rest of Iraq was then ruled by the all-powerful Baath Party, which controlled every media outlet, print or broadcast.

Free enterprise had also produced a taste of globalization in Kurdistan. A new fast-food outlet, complete with golden arches, had introduced Big Macs and Happy Meals—but as MaDonal's.

"I have to wait until sanctions end to make it the real thing," explained owner Suleiman Kasab, a former hamburger flipper at a McDonald's in Austria.

Kurdistan was hardly self-sufficient. The Kurds relied heavily on the United Nations, which under the sanctions arrangement channeled thirteen percent of Iraq's oil revenues back into the north and provided a daily food ration for every Kurd (and every Iraqi). The income helped rebuild the villages that Saddam had destroyed. It paid for new schools, clinics, a justice ministry, and a Central Bank independent of Baghdad. It helped develop agriculture, pave roads, and plant three million trees.

The Kurds, however, did figure a way to generate revenue by turning the tables on Saddam, who also relied on illicit trade to circumvent international sanctions. The Kurds taxed smugglers bringing sanctions-busting goods across from Turkey and Iran, through Kurdistan, into the rest of Iraq—to the tune of one million dollars a day.

"Our dinar—the old one, without Saddam's picture on it—is now stronger than the currency in the rest of Iraq," Salih told me.

Kurdistan had evolved into a state within a state. It had done so well that many Kurds, who made up about twenty percent of Iraq's twenty-six million people, liked to boast that the north could be a prototype for the rest of Iraq.

"Kurdistan has traditionally been the least developed part of Iraq, economically, politically, and socially," Salih reflected. "If we could achieve this in Kurdistan, we could easily achieve it in the rest of Iraq."

Yet Kurdistan also reflected a core tension within Iraq and the wider Middle East. Two often-rival forces—traditional clans and modern parties—shaped local politics. They were not always a good fit. Despite their unity in opposition to Saddam Hussein, they divided Kurdistan into two halves for a reason.

Politics in the western sector—which bordered Turkey and had its capital in Irbil—was dominated by tribe and clan, specifically the Barzani clan.

Mustafa Barzani, a charismatic, dagger-wielding fighter, launched the Kurdish nationalist movement in Iraq. He founded the Kurdish Democratic Party in 1946. In 1961, he led an armed struggle against Baghdad to win autonomy from Arab-dominated Iraq. In the 1970s, the United States initially encouraged the uprising to pressure Baghdad, only to turn around and negotiate a deal between Iraq and Iran in 1975 that pulled the rug from under the Kurds. Baghdad crushed the rebellion. Barzani was forced into exile; he died four years later in Washington, D.C. His son Masoud, who still wore the traditional Kurdish baggy pants and turban, inherited power.

"Until 1975, the Kurds looked at the West as saviors," Salih told me. "But after the Kurdish rebellion collapsed, the United States became synonymous with the notion of betrayal." Henry Kissinger, who crafted both sides of the policy flip-flop, was still a dirty word in northern Iraq almost three decades later.

"We're afraid the United States will get involved, make promises, and then betray us again," Salih said.

Politics in the eastern sector—which bordered Iran and had its capital in Sulaimaniyah—was defined by Kurdish intellectuals who broke away from the Barzanis after the 1975 Kurdish rebellion was quashed.

They formed the Patriotic Union of Kurdistan, a modern, leftist, and less clan-based party. It was led by Jalal Talabani, a portly and congenial lawyer with wavy hair who preferred Western suits.

The two sectors collaborated when Saddam cut off north Kurdistan in 1991. Yet they remained serious political and economic rivals. Both also had their own branches of the Peshmerga, a Kurdish militia whose name means "those who face death." In 1995, tensions erupted into open clashes between the two parties over disputes about land and revenue sharing from their taxes on smuggling. Fighting continued sporadically for two years. Barzani finally turned to Baghdad. Although Iraqi troops had earlier killed three of his brothers, twenty-nine family members, and some 8,000 Barzani clansmen, he invited Saddam's forces into the north in 1996 to regain territory lost to Talabani's militia.[5] Talabani damned Barzani as a traitor to the Kurdish cause.

It took years to really patch things up. The month before my visit, the Kurdish legislature had held its first meeting in six years. The driver who took me from Sulaimaniyah through the stark, brown mountains to Irbil had never been to the western sector. For him, it was like going to a foreign capital. He was quite nervous.

I called on Barzani at his scenic mountaintop villa overlooking Irbil. I asked him if fighting among the Kurds was really over.

"Yes, it was an unfortunate thing to happen," he told me. Born in 1946, Barzani is short and still rather cherubic looking, although he is widely reputed to be stubborn and tough. He also prefers to speak in Kurdish and rarely leaves Kurdistan.

"Because of confidence-building measures," he said, "trust has come back to people. The rank and file of the Kurdish parties have been convinced that war leads to the destruction of their people."

With peace among the Kurds and U.S. intervention looming, the bigger question had become whether the Kurds wanted out of Iraq altogether.

On the eve of a war likely to determine Iraq's fate for years to come, one way or the other, I asked Barzani if Kurdish leaders were willing to give up his own father's dream of an independent Kurdistan and remain in a new Iraq. The answer could also determine the future of Iraq.

"We do want self-determination," he replied, sitting back against a brocade settee in an ornate reception hall. The Kurds wanted a "voluntary union" in a federal framework. "There is a desire and will to preserve the unity and territorial integrity of this country within the state of Iraq. We never asked for an independent Kurdish state," he added. "These are only accusations of neighbors."

Separately, when we had crossed paths in Tehran, I had also asked Talabani if the Kurds felt they would be better off on their own.

"No," Talabani told me. "That's very shortsighted. What we have is not stable or permanent. We need to...reunite with Iraq for a permanent democratic life."

Landlocked, economically stranded, and politically hostage to the demands, quirks, and preferences of neighboring countries, the Kurds had learned the exorbitant costs of going it alone during a dozen years of isolation, he said. The Kurds needed the clout and seaports of Iraq. They also needed a share of Iraq's resources.

The leaders, however, seemed to reflect a minority view.

Everywhere I traveled in northern Iraq, the overwhelming majority of students, shop owners, government employees, Peshmerga fighters, and people on the streets expressed a preference, even a yearning, to live in their own Kurdish nation. Many acted as if they already had one. With sixty-five percent of the Kurds under twenty-five, many had no memory of the days under Baghdad's control. For them, Saddam had ruled far away and long ago—even though he was still in power.

"I only know about him from stories my father tells," Sawsan Ali, a University of Irbil freshman, told me, virtually dismissing one of the region's most powerful dictators. "We were just children when he ruled here."

After Saddam cut off the Kurds in 1991, the Kurdish language made a full comeback in government, schools, and workplaces. The Kurds flew their own flag, a red, green, and white tricolor with a big yellow sun in the middle. School curriculum was "Kurdicized."

What the Kurds do will determine whether Iraq can move beyond the primordial instincts that have defined the Middle East for millennia and ultimately hold together as a country. Iraq's fate may ultimately be decided in Kirkuk. A multiethnic city of almost one million people,

Kirkuk is claimed with equal vehemence by the Kurds, the Arabs, and minority Turkomans backed by Turkey.

Kirkuk is the Jersualem of Iraq.

The city's importance was hinted at in the Old Testament. King Nebuchadnezzar cast the Jews of Babylon into a "burning fiery furnace," a site some Middle East scholars believe was the endless flame from Kirkuk's natural gas, a clue to oil deposits discovered twenty-five hundred years later that gave modern Iraq its economic and strategic importance.

Kirkuk holds the second largest oil fields in Iraq. The area has produced up to one million barrels a day; it has another ten billion barrels of proven reserves. Oil analysts believe other rich fields have yet to be discovered nearby.

Saddam Hussein went to imaginatively ruthless extremes to secure Kirkuk for the Arabs. His Arabization campaign—many Kurds called it ethnic cleansing—began with mass Kurdish deportation from the city. After the outside world protested, the regime used more subtle tactics: Employers were coerced into firing Kurdish staff. Landlords were squeezed into turning out Kurdish tenants. Kurdish children were detained until parents agreed to leave the city. Kurdish food-ration cards were confiscated to cut off access to UN aid. As Kurds fled, their homes and jobs were filled with Arabs brought up from the south. In a "nationality correction" scheme in the late 1990s, the Baghdad government also forced minorities applying for anything from school enrollment to marriage licenses and car registrations to sign a form changing their national identity to Arab. Newborns were not allowed to be registered with non-Arab names.[6]

The regime then adopted bizarre tactics to erase the Kurdish presence. To provide a false sense of how long Arabs had been there, tombstones with non-Arab names were rubbed out and Arab names engraved in their place. In 2002, local relief groups told me, the government offered Arab families an extra incentive, including land, if they would dig up the remains of ancestors and rebury them in a Kirkuk graveyard.

More than 120,000 Kurds had been expelled since 1991, UN officials and human rights groups told me. I drove to checkpoints in both the eastern and western Kurdish sectors and saw more families walking across. Many had been dumped at the frontier, with virtually no possessions, clothing, or furniture. The United Nations had set up tent camps with communal water and toilets, but waiting lists were long. Thousands of evicted Kurds ended up homeless. I saw one newly arrived family with six small children scouring the ground for rocks to build a hovel in a mountain clearing where other families were living under roofs of cardboard and plastic sheeting. In Kurdistan, the brutal winters can sink to twenty degrees below zero.

The Kurds were intent on getting Kirkuk back. The process of Arabization, Barzani made a point of telling me, would have to be reversed.

"It doesn't mean that apart from the Kurds there should be nobody else in Kirkuk. It's an Iraqi city like Baghdad or Basra. There could be Arabs, Turkomans, and Shiites living there," Barzani said. "But what we are not ready to compromise on is the city's identity. Kirkuk is part of Kurdistan.

"For others, Kirkuk's importance is that it lies on a sea of oil," Barzani added. "For us, Kirkuk is important because it lies on a sea of our blood."

Change in today's Middle East is likely to succeed only when all major players—not just the majority—believe they have a stake in the new order. Rival identities will otherwise derail it. The sense of common nationhood is still too fragile. Suspicions run too deep.

Iraq is a telling, and tragic, precedent.

In September 2003, five months after the fall of Baghdad, I flew back to Iraq with Secretary of State Colin Powell. It was the first visit by an American secretary of state in a half century. There was still freedom of movement in Baghdad back then. *The New York Times* correspondent and I walked out of the Green Zone, met *The Washington Post* Baghdad bureau chief, and wandered around the sprawling capital. Powell, too, left the Green Zone for a meeting with Iraqi leaders. We stayed for a couple of nights in the legendary al Rashid Hotel. I visited Iraqis and former exiles who had moved back to the capital. I meandered around the Green Zone oasis of palm-fringed streets and villas. And I stopped by Vendors' Alley, where dozens of Iraqis flogged memorabilia from Saddam Hussein's rule. A military medal, hung from grosgrain ribbon in the red, white, and black colors of Iraq's flag, went for ten bucks.

For the Bush administration, from a great distance, Iraq had seemed a logical candidate for change. Neoconservative theorists called it "Iraqi exceptionalism."[7] Saddam Hussein had been so ruthless at home, they argued, that "liberation" would be welcomed. The Iraqi leader was also vulnerable because he was in violation of more than a dozen United Nations resolutions spanning a dozen years. So, they concluded, Iraq would be an exception to all the dangers of a foreign army overthrowing a Middle East government.

Iraq generally also seemed to have appealing requisites for change.

It had the allure of past greatness. A cradle of early civilization, advanced cultures flourished in ancient Mesopotamia long before the empires of Egypt, Greece, or Rome. They invented writing. They figured out how to tell time. They founded modern mathematics. They were the first people to build cities. For centuries, they wrote some of the greatest poetry, history, and literature in the world.

Abraham, the father of the three great monotheistic religions, came from the Mesopotamian city of Ur. Some four thousand years ago, the Code of Hammurabi introduced the world's first codified laws. It included trials and witnesses and judges accountable for their decisions; protection for the weak, widows, and orphans; an eye-for-an-eye punishment; and contracts, deeds, and receipts for ownership.

Iraq also had a comparatively literate society. The area along the Euphrates and Tigris rivers had long been a center of education. For more than a millennium, Baghdad was considered one of the world's most civilized cities. It had the first school for astronomers. In the ninth century, its universities imported teachers from throughout the civilized world to teach medicine, mathematics, philosophy, theology, literature, and poetry. Until Saddam drained the country's coffers, Iraqis had the largest percentage of well-educated people in the Arab world.

Slightly larger than California, modern Iraq also had economic riches. It had the third largest proven oil reserves in the world. It had rich agriculture. And as home to the two holiest sites in Shiite Islam, it also had tourism. Hundreds of thousands of religious tourists poured into Iraq even in the worst of times. Najaf was the burial site of Ali, the first Shiite imam, after whom the sect is named; Karbala was where his son Hussein lost his battle against the Omayyad dynasty. Iraq was flush with wealth when Saddam Hussein seized the presidency in 1979. By Middle East standards, it had well-equipped hospitals and new industries. New apartment blocks and housing complexes offered modern standards of living. The arts, heavily subsidized with petrodollars, were thriving. The middle class was robust and rapidly growing. Iraq was flooded with luxury goods, from Mercedes-Benz cars to imported Camembert cheese and the latest technology.

"Iraq has the elements of either an amazing success or an outstanding disaster," Barham Salih told me just weeks before the American invasion. "That's the irony of Iraq."

To the outside world, many Iraqis also appeared ready for change.

During his quarter-century rule, Saddam Hussein made more mistakes—at home and in the region—than any other Middle East leader. In 1980, he invaded Iran, a country four times the size of Iraq with almost three times the population. Baghdad boasted that the conflict would be over in weeks because Iran's revolutionary regime was still fragile and fractured. The war instead dragged on, exhausting Iraq's wealth and weaponry. Baghdad had to borrow heavily from Saudi Arabia and Kuwait, and take loans from Moscow to buy Russian arms.

In the mid-1980s, I covered Saddam's campaign to get Iraqi women to donate their jewelry to pay for the war. Nightly television programs showed women turning in family heirlooms, gold bracelets bestowed at the birth of a child, and even their bridal dowry jewelry.

The war carried political costs too, as Saddam cracked down brutally to keep Kurds in the northern mountains and Shiites in the southern marshes along the Iranian border in check. Opposition outside the country—western-educated exiles in Europe, clerics and refugees in Iran, and Baathist rivals in Syria—gained new momentum.

In 1986, it began to look as if Baghdad could even lose the war as Iranian troops gained ground inside Iraq for the first time. It took Iraq two years—and massive amounts of mustard gas and poisonous nerve agents—to repel them. In a decisive 1988 Iraqi offensive to recapture the strategic Fao Peninsula, thousands of Iranian Revolutionary Guards were killed by chemical weapons, in part because gas masks did not fit snugly enough over their beards. During the two-year interval, Iraq had received an unusual combination of Arab, Soviet, European, and American assistance—funds, arms, training, and intelligence—motivated largely by shared fear of an Iranian victory. Tehran reluctantly agreed to a UN-brokered cease-fire four months after the battle at Fao Peninsula.

After eight years of the bloodiest modern Middle East war, however, neither side gained a square inch of territory—at the cost of more than one million casualties. The war had been for naught.

Owing billions, Saddam demanded that Saudi Arabia and Kuwait forgive his debts. He played to historic rivalries, claiming to have fought the Shiite Persian revolutionaries on behalf of all Sunni Arabs. When his neighbors balked, the Iraqi leader first accused Kuwait of stealing oil from wells along their common border. He then revived a long-standing claim to Kuwait as Iraq's nineteenth province. And finally, in 1990, he invaded the little city-state.

Operation Desert Storm, led by the United States and including troops from three dozen countries, liberated Kuwait in 1991. Afterward, Washington tried to exploit the Iraqi leader's vulnerability by calling on Shiites and Kurds to rebel against him. They did. But the United States had not required the grounding of Iraq's air force in the cease-fire. So Saddam dispatched his helicopter gunships to put down the uprisings, bloodily. Thousands died. Hatred deepened.

After two wars, Iraqis and their treasury were spent—only to then face the toughest international economic embargo ever imposed, when Saddam Hussein refused to allow UN inspectors to track down his deadliest weapons programs. Over the next dozen years, Iraqis paid the price as daily life began to break down. By 2002, more than one quarter of the population struggled with poverty or need; per-capita income was estimated at less than one quarter of what it had been in 1980.[8] Malnutrition was rampant. Child mortality soared.

In 2002, Saddam Hussein was given one more chance by the United Nations to cooperate. Again, he invoked the rights of sovereignty rather than allow UN inspectors to freely search his realm—even though by then he no longer had active chemical, biological, or nuclear programs. It was an extraordinarily arrogant bluff.

So by 2003, the American advocates of war argued, a confluence of factors made Iraq ripe for new direction. Ousting the regime in Baghdad would also be a catalyst for wider change throughout the Middle East. Paul Wolfowitz, then deputy defense secretary, told *The New York Times:*

> *I don't think it's unreasonable to think that Iraq, properly managed...
> really could turn out to be, I hesitate to say it, the first Arab democracy... I
> think the more we are committed to influencing the outcome, the more
> chance there could be that it would be something quite significant for Iraq.
> And I think if it's significant for Iraq, it's going to cast a very large
> shadow, starting with Syria and Iran, but across the whole Arab world.[9]*

Operation Iraqi Freedom, launched on March 20, 2003, was initially easier than anticipated. The Iraqi military used no chemical or biological weapons, as had been widely feared. Resistance from Iraqi troops was limited. Many either disappeared or failed to put up much of a fight.

The U.S. blitz to Baghdad took only three weeks.

On April 9, as U.S. troops poured into the Iraqi capital, Iraqi weight-lifting champion Kadhim al Jubouri rallied his neighbors to go to Firdous Square to bring down the statue of Saddam Hussein, a twenty-foot bronze of the Iraqi leader with his arm raised above the city he ruled. Jubouri, who had spent nine years in Saddam's jails, reflected the initial relief of many Iraqis.

"There were lots of people from my tribe who were also put in prison or hanged," he told reporters. "It became my dream ever since I saw them building that statue to one day topple it."[10]

Over and over and over again, Jubouri slammed a sledgehammer into the massive concrete plinth beneath the statue until his hands bled. An American tank eventually rumbled in to help bring it down. Although Saddam managed to escape Baghdad, the toppling of the huge statue symbolized the end of his rule.

Yet by the time Powell arrived in Baghdad, six months after Saddam's ouster, Iraq was rapidly unraveling.

Ali Allawi understood why. He saw it happening from the inside.

Allawi was just the kind of Iraqi the United States wanted to lead the new Iraq. He bridged the two worlds. A tall, trim man with salt-and-pepper eyebrows, Allawi is usually attired in well-made suits and looks the businessman he is. Born in Baghdad in 1947 to a wealthy Shiite family, he spent large chunks of time in the West after the monarchy was toppled in 1958. He attended the Massachusetts Institute of Technology, the London School of Economics, and Harvard Business School. He worked at the World Bank, then in finance in London and Kuwait. But he was also a practicing Shiite. His wife Munya wore a head scarf and modest Islamic dress even when she visited the West.

Allawi went back to Baghdad three days before Powell's visit to take part in rebuilding Iraq. He initially believed in the dream.

"I returned on September 11, 2003. It was the culmination of something I had been working toward for years," Allawi later recalled, almost wistfully. He agreed to serve under the U.S. occupation government, the Coalition Provisional Authority. He became the first minister of trade.

"My expectation was that we'd help in stabilizing the country short-term. We'd build a foundation for post-Saddam Iraq, realizing there were shortcomings in the Iraqi state, not just the dictatorship. This would be the first step," he told me.

Allawi kept a diary of his impressions and Iraq's prospects. He very soon began chronicling the political shadows accumulating over Iraq.

"Within a month, I was dissuaded, as I saw the incoherence of the American project. By October, the whole thing seemed to be spinning out of control," he recounted, with polite anger. "I became very dispirited."

Like many Iraqis, Allawi concluded that the United States made two basic mistakes that doomed any early success—and possibly the long-term mission. The first was miscalculating the dynamics within Iraqi society.

"The United States embarked on its invasion with very little understanding of the country," Allawi told me. "The Americans didn't even grasp that Iraq had been through this before."

Iraq is a microcosm of many Middle East countries. It was artificially created in 1920 with the decline of the Ottoman empire. Britain won the mandate for Iraq, which was formed by the merger of three Ottoman regions—with disparate populations—centered in Mosul, Baghdad, and Basra.

Iraq challenged foreign rule from its earliest days. Both Sunnis and Shiites rebelled against the British in waves of attacks. Iraqi militias, clerics, and politicians all had a piece of the action. In an eerie foreshadowing of the American experience, *The London Times* editorialized in 1920, "How much longer are valuable lives to be sacrificed in the vain endeavor to impose upon the Arab population an elaborate and expensive administration which they never asked for and do not want?"

The 1920 revolt took four months to put down. By the time it ended, some 6,000 Iraqis and 500 British troops were dead.[11]

In 1921, the British installed King Faisal I to govern Iraq. The choice riled Iraqis for many reasons, foremost because Faisal was not Iraqi. Born in what is today western Saudi Arabia, he had been a representative for Jeddah in the Ottoman parliament. During World War I, he worked with the allies—in a role later made famous in the epic film *Lawrence of Arabia,* in which he was played by Alec Guinness. For a few months in 1920, Faisal was made king of Greater Syria, until France won the mandate for Syria and expelled him. Britain then put Faisal on the throne in Baghdad.

Iraq was still a predominantly tribal society. Tribal sheikhs were unfamiliar with the concept of modern statehood, uncomfortable with recognizing a higher authority, and unwilling to cede control, resources, or revenues with uncertain return—especially to a foreign king. Winning their fealty proved difficult.

In the young state, Islam was the most common denominator, although it too often divided rather than unified. Faisal and his British-backed entourage were largely Sunni, but the majority of the population was Shiite.

"In 1920, the Shiites rose against the British, but found themselves on the losing side of the power equation. They were disempowered for the next eighty years," Allawi told me. "That history has haunted Shiites ever since."

Identity became a constant in Iraqi politics, with the Kurds believ-
ing they had been cheated of their own state and a host of other minorities wanting a secure stake in the new system too.[12] In 1932, the year of
Iraq's independence from Britain, King Faisal I lamented:

> *With my heart filled with sadness, I have to say that it is my belief that
> there is no Iraqi people inside Iraq. There are only diverse groups with no
> national sentiments. They are filled with superstitious and false religious
> traditions with no common grounds between them. They easily accept
> rumors and are prone to chaos, prepared always to revolt against any
> government. It is our responsibility to form out of this mass one people
> that we would then guide, train and educate. Any person who is aware of
> the difficult circumstances of this country would appreciate the efforts that
> have to be exerted to achieve these objectives.[13]*

Faisal died a year later. The monarchy went through two more
kings but continued to struggle with resentment against it and deep
rifts within Iraqi society. In 1958, the monarchy was overthrown.

Thirty years later, a Library of Congress report in Washington
assessed the long-term damage.

> *Ultimately, the British-created monarchy suffered from a chronic legiti-
> macy crisis: the concept of monarchy was alien to Iraq. Despite his Islamic
> and pan-Arab credentials, Faisal was not an Iraqi, and, no matter how
> effectively he ruled, Iraqis saw the monarchy as a British creation. The
> continuing inability of the government to gain the confidence of the people
> fueled political instability well into the 1970s.[14]*

The Baath Party also failed to coalesce Iraqi society. Baath is Arabic for "renaissance." Founded in 1951 as an underground offshoot of
Syria's Baath Party, the socialist movement sought to modernize Arab
societies and eventually unite them in a regional political collective.
After a false start in 1963, Iraq's Baathists came to power in a 1968
coup. Some Shiites signed up, but the Baath Party over the next thirty-
five years was really about entrenching Sunni domination.

So by 2003, eighty years after the state's creation, Iraq's national identity was still precarious. "It's hard to have a strong national state," Allawi told me, "when large numbers feel alienated from government."

The second mistake, which played off the first, was plotting Iraq's future.

"There was only cursory prewar planning. Iraqis were unrealistically expected to adapt quickly to the premises of Western democracy," Allawi later reflected in his own book. "A massive opportunity was lost."[15]

The United States initially counted on tapping into a functioning state, including government ministries, a police force, and public services—just without Saddam and his inner circle. The political strategy became known as "plug and play." The plan for Iraq's military forces was to get rid of Saddam's henchmen, downsize the armed forces, and use thousands of troops for reconstruction.[16] The strategy was nicknamed "purge and protect." The military would be the primary tool of nation rebuilding.[17]

"We'd continue to pay them to do things like engineering, road construction, work on bridges, remove rubble, demining, pick up unexploded ordnance, construction work," explained retired Lieutenant General Jay Garner, a mild-mannered Vietnam veteran who had earlier worked in Kurdistan and was originally dispatched to administer postwar Iraq. "The regular army has the skill sets to match the work that needs to be done."

At a press conference before leaving Washington, Garner said he did not want to immediately demobilize the military and "put a lot of unemployed people on the street."

Little about Iraq went as planned, however.

Two decades of wars and economic sanctions left the Iraqi state chronically corroded. After Saddam fled, the capital crumbled into chaos and wild looting. By the time American administrators arrived in Baghdad, little of government was left to plug into. Seventeen of twenty-one Iraqi ministries had basically evaporated in the postwar anarchy. Files, documents, and records disappeared. Government buildings in the Arab world's second largest city were looted down to bathroom fixtures, utility wires, and light bulbs. There wasn't a single chair to sit on.

Iraq literally means "well-rooted" country. Like many modern Middle East states, Iraq was rooted around two institutions—the ruling party and security forces. For thirty-five years, almost half of Iraq's life as a modern country, the two institutions had employed the largest number of people, many of the best educated personnel, and a huge chunk of the middle class.

The Baath Party penetrated politics, the economy, the professions, the tribes, and both big cities and remote villages. Membership had been the best way—and sometimes the only way—to get a decent education, find a job or win a promotion, and prevent harassment by security services. Membership estimates ranged as high as two million.

Yet two months after the fall of Baghdad, Washington dispatched a new governor whose first acts pulled up Iraq's remaining roots.

In May 2003, only four days after his arrival, American governor L. Paul Bremer III issued Order No. 1. It disbanded the Baath Party. It also fired senior and midranking members from any job receiving a government paycheck and banned them from ever being employed in the public sector again—in a socialist state. Overnight, civil servants, judges and hospital administrators, principals and university deans, provincial governors and city managers, and heads of state industries and banks were out of jobs—with no one ready to step in and no private sector to provide alternative employment. The decree then stipulated that Baathists were subject to criminal investigation.[18]

Sunnis cried foul. Most estimates put the true believers in the party at less than ten percent of its membership. As a result, many Sunnis believed the sweeping decree against all Baathists targeted them, vindictively, as a sect.

"In the early months, when I thought that I should participate in a new political order, one of the central features was to dismantle the Baathist state," Allawi later told the Council on Foreign Relations. "I was a firm believer—and still am—in the depravity of the Baath Party and its mismanagement. It was a prop for authoritarian rule. But de-Baathification became equated with de-Sunnification."[19]

The process was selectively applied and manipulated. Rather than help define a just new political order, de-Baathification became the instrument of new injustice.

"It was a blunderbuss approach. It went over the top," Allawi added. "All kinds of people were thrown out, many unjustly. Sweeping de-Baathification led to a group of angry people. The way the party was dismantled has come back to us—with a vengeance.

"By the end of 2003, Sunni opinion basically rejected the authority created after the invasion and occupation," he reflected. "The insurgency was rooted in the community's sense of disempowerment."

During his second week in power, Bremer issued Order No. 2. It dissolved the entire Iraqi military.

Iraq's land, air, and naval forces were was almost as important as the party. The military not only secured the state. It was also the single largest employer in Iraq, with more than 400,000 troops—and at least two million more family members dependent on that income. They instantly lost both pay and pensions, again in an economy with no private sector to absorb them.

Bremer argued that the Iraqi army had basically already disbanded. "By the time the conflict was over, that army, so-called, didn't exist anymore," he told me.

The second decree stunned Iraq's military. Many Iraqi officers had been telling anyone who would listen—foreign journalists, U.S. diplomats, and American military officials—that they were simply waiting to be ordered back to their barracks.[20] Many felt they had actually contributed to the American blitz through Iraq. Thousands of soldiers had gone home after the United States air-dropped millions of leaflets urging them not to fight.

Once again, Sunnis felt specifically targeted. The reaction was swift and angry. Tens of thousands of former troops took to the streets of Baghdad almost before the ink was dry on the decree.

DISSOLVING THE IRAQI ARMY IS A HUMILIATION TO THE DIGNITY OF THE NATION, cried one of the banners borne by former soldiers who gathered almost daily outside the Green Zone.

"Instead of us using these personnel against terrorism, terrorists are using them against us," lamented former Iraqi Special Forces Major Mohammed Faour, an exile who advised the United States. "You can't put half a million people with families and weapons and a monthly salary on the dole. You can't do this in any country. They'll turn against you."[21]

The two decrees backfired, undermining any prospect of winning support from Iraq's major players. The unfinished war in Iraq soon got much messier. For the United States, enemies proliferated: An insurgency was led by loyalists to Saddam Hussein and fueled by Sunni disaffection. Foreign fighters throughout the region—from as far away as Morocco and Algeria in North Africa, and as close as neighboring Saudi Arabia and Syria—crossed the border to aid Arab brethren against a foreign army widely seen as occupying Iraq. And al Qaeda set up a new extremist network in Iraq.

The common denominator was that they were all Sunni.

The tactics of war also grew nastier. Suicide bombs and roadside explosives—never before problems in Iraq—became regular features. Unlike the U.S. invasion, there were no neat front lines. Every site was a target. And no one, Iraqi or foreigner, was safe.

On a sweltering summer day a month before Powell's visit, a cement truck had approached United Nations headquarters in Baghdad. It was a clever choice; a cement truck was welcome anywhere because it signaled reconstruction. Only this one carried a massive bomb. Two of my friends were inside the building. Ghassan Salameh, the chief UN adviser on Iraq, had just returned to his office when the explosives went off. He scrambled through the thick smoke and flying brown debris to search for Sergio Vieira de Mello, the charismatic Brazilian diplomat who headed the UN mission, and who many thought could one day become Secretary-General. He found de Mello, who was crushed from the waist down between slabs of collapsed concrete but still had the presence of mind to use his cell phone to call for help. Rescuers could not extract him in time; he died three hours later. Almost two dozen were killed in the attack.

The UN bombing was an early turning point. Unable to protect its people, the United Nations evacuated staff. Aid groups became reticent about setting up big operations in Baghdad. Other countries were reluctant about opening embassies.

The two decrees also created a triple long-term challenge.

First, they created a vacuum in personnel.

The United States scrambled to find new and untested management to rebuild every arm of government, occasionally from scratch. American advisers, many of whom did not speak Arabic and had never been to Iraq before, were tasked to get ministries up and running again—often with Iraqis who had never worked in the ministries either. Several were exiles, including Allawi, who had not even been in Iraq for years.

Second, the two decrees left a vacuum on security at one of the most vulnerable moments in Iraq's history. The early looting gave way to rampant criminality—theft, kidnappings, rape, and murder.

"Imagine waking up and finding that your leaders have dismantled all police and military. As a result, there is not one police or law-enforcement agent or guard or army to protect you," Iraqi Vice President Tariq al Hashemi, the highest-ranking Sunni in government, told me. "That's what has happened in Iraq."

The United States did not have sufficient troops to restore order and patrol the streets of a country with twenty-seven million people, much less end an escalating war. American soldiers initially had orders *not* to police Baghdad. The absence of an established army and police paved the way for illegal militias—all with sectarian loyalties—to step in and take over neighborhoods and carry out their vendettas. And once they exerted control, it proved very difficult to fully dislodge them.

Finally, the biggest challenge was the new political disorder.

The two decrees were designed to prevent the old regime's return and to create political space for others to emerge. But abruptly dismantling the Sunni-dominated party and military—without new cross-confessional and multiethnic institutions ready to begin taking their place—just as abruptly shifted the balance of power. Virtually overnight, control swung from minority Sunni to majority Shiites, and from secular to religious parties.

The Baath Party and the military had been the two most secular institutions in Iraq. In their place, the largest new political forces were all Shiite, Islamist, and aligned with Iran—the opposite of what the United States originally intended. In the new Iraq, Sunni and Shiite were split in ways unprecedented since the country was created in 1920.

Many of Allawi's early allies were Shiite brethren in Islamist parties. Yet he noted the dangers of their one-sided dominance in his diary. "Once it was clear that the Shiites were going to follow a sectarian agenda, the violent response was inevitable," he later explained. "I have a diary entry in 2003 when I say to myself that...we are heading toward a far clearer definition of sectarian community identity."[22]

The war steadily escalated throughout 2003 and 2004, even after the United States pulled out its governor and handed over control to a U.S.-appointed Iraqi council. The first prime minister was Allawi's cousin, Ayad Allawi, a secular Shiite and a bear of a man who had worked closely with the Central Intelligence Agency during his years in exile. Ali Allawi became defense minister.

The first real hope was offered in 2005. It was the year of elections to put in place a permanent government.

Iraqis took fairly well to democracy as voters went to the polls three times: In January 2005, they elected an interim parliament. It was the first multiparty elections in fifty years. Despite escalating violence, fifty-eight percent of Iraqis voted. The enthusiasm was inspiring.

"I would have crawled here if I had to. I don't want terrorists to kill other Iraqis like they tried to kill me," said Samir Hassan, a young man who had lost a leg in a car bomb attack. "Today I am voting for peace."[23]

The downside was the clear pattern of voting—or not—by cultural identity. Shiites and Kurds turned out in throngs to vote for candidates from their own communities. Groups of Kurdish men danced outside polling stations as they waited to cast ballots. Smiling Shiite women proudly held up purple ink-stained fingers to be filmed or photographed. But the majority of Sunnis boycotted the election.

Allawi, one of the winners, became minister of trade. He had run in an alliance with Shiite Islamist parties. The outcome, he noted, was not what the United States had anticipated.

"One of the principal myths that underlay justification for the invasion and occupation of Iraq lay in ruins. When given the choice, the Shia did not vote for the secular, liberal or pro-western parties," Allawi later noted in his own account. "Instead, they voted in ways diametrically opposed to the original hypothesis of the war's ideological promoters."[24]

The short-lived government's main job was to craft a new constitution. It was pulled together in three months. Debate was intense. In the end, many contentious issues—including how much power to grant the Shiite, Sunni, and Kurdish regions—had to be postponed until later.

In October 2005, Iraqis went to the polls a second time to vote on the document. Sixty-three percent turned out at the referendum. This time Sunni Arabs went to the polls, although mainly to vote against the constitution. It squeaked through.

The final vote was held in December 2005 for a permanent government. This time, nearly eighty percent of Iraqis turned out, the highest tally so far. In a stark contrast from Saddam Hussein's one-party rule, 228 parties and nineteen coalitions competed for the 275-seat parliament. The downside was that Iraq's divisions were deeper than ever—sometimes within a sect as well as between them. Religious parties fared better than secular groups.

The largest Shiite and Sunni winners were Islamist parties. Ali Allawi, who left the Shiite alliance, lost his seat.

The hope spawned by the three elections in 2005 faded early in 2006. Iraq steadily unraveled.

History may well judge that the tipping point for the U.S. intervention in Iraq was on February 22. It happened at the Shrine of the Two Imams in Samarra, a city along the Tigris River some sixty miles north of Baghdad. The shrine, famed for its bulbous gold dome and pastel blue tiles, was the burial site in the ninth century for the tenth and eleventh Shiite imams, both direct descendants of the Prophet Mohammed.[25] A million Shiites annually made pilgrimages to the Samarra's golden-domed shrine.

During the night of February 22, a handful of men dressed in military uniforms sneaked into the mosque, tied up the caretaker in a side room, and carefully planted explosives to have maximum impact on the golden dome. Then they fled. At 6:55 A.M., the bombs went off. The dome collapsed; the shrine was destroyed.

"For Iraqis, it was like 9/11 was for the United States," Adel Abdul Mahdi, one of Iraq's two vice presidents, later told me.

Even the White House recognized the potential impact. "Violence will only contribute to what the terrorists sought to achieve by this act," President Bush said in a written statement. "I ask all Iraqis to exercise restraint in the wake of this tragedy."

Ironically, no one died in the attack, which was tied to al Qaeda. But it provoked a massive slaughter, as Shiite men poured onto the streets to seek vengeance. More than twenty Sunni mosques were attacked across Iraq. Several Sunni clerics were dragged onto streets and beaten or murdered. More than 1,000 Iraqis—about one third the number who died on 9/11—died in retribution killings.

After Samarra, sectarian passions accounted for the bulk of killings. Many died after grotesque torture, body parts mauled, axed, or power-drilled. On any given day, dozens of bodies were found dumped on roadsides or in remote fields. A man traumatized by the sight of hundreds of gruesome bodies in the hunt for his missing uncle decided to have his name, address, and telephone number tattooed on his thigh, the one place still likely to be distinguishable after torture.[26] It started a widespread trend.

By the end of 2006, more than two dozen militias ruled the streets, intimidated society, dictated to businesses, and defied the government.

The new constitution did not prohibit alcohol or impose Islamic dress. But even in cosmopolitan Baghdad, shops selling alcohol were bombed or attacked. Music shops received warnings from gunmen; many closed down. Leaflets threatened women who did not wear *hejab,* while barbers were murdered for shaving men. The constitution stipulated freedom of speech and the press. But dozens of Iraqi reporters, photographers, and cameramen were killed. Many journalists became afraid of telling the truth; fear led to self-censorship.

In politics, sect became a more important criterion for filling a job than training or experience. Shiite parties purged Sunnis in government ministries under their control and fired Sunni generals in the army. Sunnis were denied treatment at hospitals. As the war entered its fifth year, the Organization for the Care of the Displaced estimated more than 40,000 Sunni families had fled Baghdad to other parts of the country.[27] Many Sunnis who stayed sought false papers, expunging telltale Sunni names, such as Omar.

The tensions and dangers alienated even some Shiites. In June 2006, Allawi once again left Iraq.

"When I left, I knew a new chapter was beginning in Iraqi politics. At that point I didn't want to belong," he told me. "It was clear that Iraq was moving into an era where the Shiite dominance of the state was being cemented through the help of the United States. It was good in some ways in reversing discrimination, but not good for crafting a common identity for Iraq."

In 2007, the Bush administration deployed 28,000 additional troops in Iraq to try to restore order to Baghdad and quell the sectarian strife. The reinforcements were still arriving as the Iraq war entered its fifth year, surpassing America's engagement in World War II.

For Allawi, however, the dream had already died. Drawing on his diaries of the transition in Iraq, he marked the anniversary by publishing his own assessment.

"America's 'civilizing' mission in Iraq stumbled, and then quickly vanished, leaving a trail of slogans and an incomplete reconstruction plan," he wrote in *The Occupation of Iraq: Winning the War, Losing the Peace* in 2007.[28]

The billions that American had spent went unrecognized, and therefore not appreciated. Iraqis heard about the billions, like some memorable banquet to which only a few are invited. But what they experienced was the daily chaos, confusion, shortages and the stark terrors of life. Death squads now compounded vicious attacks by terrorists. Opinions and divisions were hardening. No-go areas, ethnic cleansing, emigration, internal displacements were now happening under the watch of 150,000 MNF troops.[29]

Allawi was just as critical of his own people.

The new Iraqi political establishment was notably silent about how to extricate the country from its current predicament. . . . The Iraqi political class that inherited the mantle of the state from the Baathist regime was manifestly culpable in presiding over the deterioration of the conditions of the country. . . . There was no national vision for anything, just a series of deals to push forward a political process, the end state of which was indeterminate. There was no governing plan. The corroded and corrupt state of Saddam was replaced by the corroded, inefficient, incompetent and cor-rupt state of the new order.[30]

As he toured the United States to promote his book, I asked Allawi to look down the road to what Iraq might look like in a decade.

The best-case scenario, he said, would be an electoral democracy dominated by Shiite Islamist parties, with an angry but accepting Sunni minority that worked along with government even as it tried to under-mine it, and Kurds on their merry way but not as an independent state.

But the bottom line, he said, was that "Iraq cannot, by any stretch of the imagination, be seen as a model for anything worth emulating."

Allawi's bleak assessment was not unusual. As the war entered its fifth year, the national weightlifting champion who had wept with joy as he brought down Saddam Hussein's statue angrily told reporters that the U.S. invasion had all been a horrible mistake.

"I really regret bringing down the statue. The Americans are worse than the dictatorship," Kadhim al Jubouri reflected. "Every day is worse than the previous day."[31]

Change is always better homegrown. Whatever its shortcomings, it is more legitimate, more familiar, more adaptable, and more accountable. It will also be far less suspect.

The American experiment in Iraq was the ultimate proof.

In October 2006, I made my fourth postwar trip to Iraq with Sec-retary of State Condoleezza Rice. The visit was so secret that the dozen journalists accompanying her had only a few hours notice; we weren't allowed to tell anyone, including editors and family. We flew first to a military base in western Turkey and switched to a lumbering mili-tary cargo plane equipped with antimissile technology for the ninety-minute flight to Iraq. Over Baghdad, we circled for almost an hour because mortars had struck near the airport. When we finally landed, we donned heavy flak jackets and helmets for the short hop to the Green Zone in Black Hawk helicopter gunships armed with three machine-guns poking out of windows. The road was too unsafe to drive.

With each trip, dangers increased, freedoms shrank. This time, I couldn't wander *inside* the fortified Green Zone, much less outside it. A trip beyond the blast-proof concrete walls and razor-wire perimeter, even if for only a few hours, cost 25,000 dollars a day for security, an American official told me. The Green Zone was no longer safe either; rocket and mortar attacks were increasing. The al Rashid Hotel had been hit during the visit of Deputy Defense Secretary Paul Wolfowitz; we stayed instead in trailers on the palace grounds. The alley bazaar had closed, the victim of one of two almost simultaneous suicide bombings inside the Green Zone that killed ten, including four Americans. New armed checkpoints had been set up every few yards throughout the Green Zone.

A "Welcome to Iraq!" packet included instructions to "seek cover in the nearest bunker or hardened shelter" or hide "under a desk or bed, away from any window" to avoid being hit during an attack inside the Green Zone. The threat, the handout warned, "is very real and ever present."

Saddam Hussein's sprawling Republican Palace compound, which was the temporary United States Embassy, had been thoroughly militarized. Staff took weapons or security guards everywhere. Saddam's old pool, where American staff occasionally went to work out or relax, boasted a large and somewhat bizarre sign advising, NO DRINKING WHILE ARMED. I was assigned an escort, who was armed, to walk across the hall from the palace media center to the ladies' bathroom.

"Enjoy your stay in Iraq!" the welcome packet added, noting that the palace dining facility now carried Baskin-Robbins ice cream.

By 2006, the catastrophic turning point, the United States was spending roughly one hundred billion dollars a year—almost two billion dollars a week—on Iraq. But the war only escalated. The kind of grisly terrorism spectaculars that first shook Beirut twenty years earlier—three over an eighteen-month period—had become everyday events in Baghdad. Rice's entourage was even more barricaded inside the Republican Palace than Saddam Hussein had been in his last days before his ouster.

The most ambitious and costly U.S. foreign intervention since the end of World War II felt like it was in free fall.

The Iraqi press openly mocked the American vision. A Baghdad newspaper ran an editorial cartoon of a mother with a baby, symbolizing democracy, in a doctor's office. "Doctor, it is three years old," the mother complains, "but it's not growing. It's getting smaller. Is there a cure?"[32]

Iraq's democratically elected government was deeply flawed. The 2007 State Department Human Rights Report conceded that its allies in Baghdad were guilty of some of the same "serious" human-rights violations committed by Saddam Hussein's regime, including torture, electrocution, and sexual assault of detainees. Corruption was also rampant. Billions of dollars had simply gone missing. Among those indicted was an early defense minister. In 2006, Transparency International's Corruption Perceptions Index put Iraq at the very bottom of 163 countries. On a ten-point scale, it rated 1.9. Only Haiti and Myanmar ranked lower.

Rather than create a new democracy and a strategic partner in the Middle East, the American intervention ignited a deep fury in Iraq. As the war entered its fifth year, more than eighty percent of Iraqis polled said they had little or no confidence that the United States or its troops could fix their country. More than half of those surveyed in a nationwide poll in 2007 said it was "acceptable" to attack American troops, triple the number in 2004.[33]

The vital tools to build a democratic future were caught in the crossfire of political tensions and horrific violence. American plans to build a civil society struggled to get off the ground because Iraqis were too scared to leave their homes, meet in public places that might be targeted by suicide bombers, or be associated with Americans.

The United States spent 100 million dollars to rehabilitate 3,000 schools and educate a new democratic generation. But education was disrupted by fighting on or near school grounds, student abductions, and murders of staff. In one gruesome episode, five Baghdad schoolteachers were executed in 2005 by gunmen dressed as police officers who burst into their school and shot them in an empty classroom. By the war's fourth anniversary in 2007, almost 200 university professors had been murdered in sectarian warfare, suicide bombings, or assassinations. Hundreds of schools either opted or were forced to close down for weeks at a time; thousands of families began keeping children at home.[34]

The middle class—an essential component in a healthy democracy— was fleeing. Iraq's chaos produced more refugees than were unleashed in 1948 when Palestinians fled the new state of Israel during the region's first modern war. By 2007, almost four million people—out of twenty-six million—had either fled Iraq or fled their homes to other parts of the country, according to the United Nations. Up to 50,000 were fleeing each month. Syria had taken in one million Iraqis, adding five percent to its population. Jordan took some 700,000, swelling its population by twelve percent. The United States had taken in less than 500 Iraqis.[35]

The danger was not only the numbers. Most were the best educated, the most skilled, and the people most needed to convert Iraq from dictatorship to democracy. One third of the country's 40,000 doctors had fled by 2007. The hemorrhaging was so serious that the government stopped issuing graduation certificates to new doctors to prevent them from leaving the country—a tactic used during Saddam Hussein's rule.[36]

Their main freedom, Iraqis complained, was the freedom to suffer. Daily life was an increasing struggle.

The early U.S. decision to abruptly dismantle Iraq's state-run enterprises and open up the marketplace had backfired. Violence discouraged investment by either Iraqis or foreign corporations—leaving no alternative when state industries were shut down. The economic miscalculation contributed significantly to thirty-percent unemployment in safe areas, up to sixty percent in danger zones.[37] Oil could not compensate. Production was falling short by one million barrels per day.[38] And by the war's fourth anniversary, up to thirty percent of it was being smuggled either out of the country or into Iraq's own black market.[39]

One third of Iraqis lived in poverty by 2007. The average Iraqi fared significantly worse than the day Saddam Hussein left power. In a nationwide poll, more than six out of ten said their lives were going badly—double the figure just a year earlier.[40]

By 2007, electricity barely met half the demand. Before the war, in 2003, Baghdad had electricity for at least sixteen hours and up to twenty-four hours a day. In 2007, the capital had power for about five hours a day.[41] Nationwide, eighty-five percent of Iraqis lacked a stable source of electricity, the United Nations reported. To cook, Iraqis were returning to the use of *tanoors,* the traditional mud ovens heated by glowing wood coals, because supplies of both electricity and propane fuel were unreliable.[42]

Meanwhile, Iraq's various insurgents had become self-sufficient. Through criminal activity, kidnapping for ransom, counterfeiting, and oil smuggling, they made up to 200 million dollars a year, *The New York Times* reported.[43]

The military scorecard of tactical successes and failures aside, Iraq was a crumbling state. And Iraq was becoming America's greatest foreign policy failure—ever.

But the toll was not limited to Iraq. Its disintegration affected the entire Middle East.

The United States had originally calculated that ousting the Middle East's most notorious dictator would shake arrogant regimes and passive populations out of their political lethargy. The new momentum, according to Washington's advocates of war, would in turn help "drain the swamp" of both old autocrats and new Islamic radicals. After Saddam's demise, they argued, reformers in neighboring Iran were more likely to rally against the theocrats. Emboldened democratic activists would be encouraged to demand truly free and fair elections in Egypt. Syria's regime would be squeezed into easing its oppressive rule. Even the conservative sheikhdoms would have to recognize the trend.

The new forces unleashed would in turn counter the wave of militant Islam. Both religious fanatics and autocratic hard-liners would be so weakened, the argument went, that a regionwide peace could finally be negotiated with Israel.

It was instead quite the opposite. Everywhere I went, I heard a similar refrain from people of all political parties and religious affiliations: In Iraq, the world's mightiest democracy had undermined—even sabotaged—prospects for political change.

In Morocco, the Equity and Reconciliation Commission chief, Driss Benzekri warned that democracy was being discredited. "When the principles of democracy are memorialized with the images of war, people become disillusioned," the former political prisoner told me. "They leave a distorted image of democracy."

Saadeddine Othmani, the Islamist head of Morocco's Justice and Development Party, fretted that militants would gain ground. "The United States has chosen an approach," he said, "that will crush moderate Muslims and produce only extremism."

In Lebanon, Harvard-educated political analyst Paul Salem worried that the Iraq experiment could even undo progress made in the past. "Any real election in the Middle East today is likely to produce an anti-American government. That's just the mood now," he said. "If you pushed the Egyptians to have a fair election, you'd probably find the new government abrogating the peace treaty with Israel, and then we'd all be back in a different universe."

Kefaya, the best known Egyptian democracy movement, launched a campaign in 2006 to amass one million signatures on a petition demanding that Egypt annul its peace treaty with Israel.[44] *Al-Masri al-Youm,* Egypt's most independent newspaper, ran an opinion piece declaring, "America, we hate you."

"Iraq will not be an easy thing for the Middle East to survive," Salem added. "And the United States is stuck in the Middle East it created."

Iraq's overall impact was to taint the United States even more than the region's odious autocrats. "However opposed Syrians are to our own regime," warned Syrian dissident Yassin Haj Saleh, "they now distrust the Americans more."

In six countries with solid American ties—Egypt, Jordan, Lebanon, Morocco, Saudi Arabia, and the United Arab Emirates—only twelve percent of the people surveyed had a favorable opinion of the United States.

"The vast majority of people in every country believe the Middle East has become less democratic than it was before the Iraq war," said Shibley Telhami, who conducted the survey with Zogby International.[45]

In an extraordinary twist, Arab anger was greater at American leadership than at Israel. When asked what foreign leader they disapproved of most, President Bush scored the highest—more than three times higher than then Israeli Prime Minister Ariel Sharon.[46]

There was little gratitude for the past. In Kuwait, which had been liberated under American leadership in 1991, protesters burned the American flag in front of the United States Embassy during Hezbollah's war with Israel in 2006. Several thousand protesters carrying Hezbollah flags and posters of Nasrallah gathered outside parliament and chanted anti-American slogans. They were joined by several members of parliament.[47]

Throughout the region, the Iraq experiment also strengthened, even emboldened, the antidemocratic forces the United States had intended to contain or defeat.

President Bush cited the "war on terrorism" as a justification for the Iraq war, but al Qaeda and Iran actually benefited. Iraq became al Qaeda's most active base of operations. Challenging the United States became a cause capable of luring thousands of new recruits and deepening Islamic militancy regionwide.

"The United States was not too long ago seen by Muslims as a partner and as a model of democracy, even when it was criticized," said Aziz Rebbah, head of the youth wing of Morocco's moderate Party for Justice and Development.

"Today, if we had no borders in the Arab world, thousands of people would be willing to go to Iraq. Nobody thinks you really want democracy in Iraq."

In the biggest irony, Iran's theocrats reaped the most out of Operation Iraqi Freedom. The United States had hoped to put in place a secular, multiconfessional, pro-Western democracy; Iraq ended up with an elected government led by Shiite Islamists, including many who had lived in exile for years in Tehran. The militias trained and armed by Iran ruled many streets. Iranian-trained clerics were powerful players.

The United States was increasingly caught up in damage control—not only in the Middle East. No foreign-policy initiative had been more disastrous to core American values, interests, goals, and status around the world.

On the eve of President Bush's 2007 State of the Union speech, global opinion of the United States had plummeted. Almost three quarters of those polled in a survey of twenty-five countries on six continents disapproved of American intervention in Iraq.[48] More than two-thirds said the Iraq war had done more harm than good.

In Britain, America's closest ally, more than eighty percent opposed the U.S. intervention. Almost three out of every four Britons said America's presence in the Middle East provoked more conflict than it prevented. And almost sixty percent said the United States played a mainly negative role in the world.

"It's been a horrible slide," Doug Miller, president of international GlobeScan polling company, told *The Washington Post*.[49]

By 2007, virtually every goal set by the United States for its intervention in Iraq was more illusive than on the eve of war in 2003. Terrorism was a far greater threat. Proliferation of weapons of mass destruction was a graver danger. Iraq was more unstable, with the war itself looking increasingly unwinnable. The sectarian divide across the Middle East was threatening to redraw the Middle East map.

"We are at a potentially historic moment when the modern Arab state order that was created by the Europeans in 1920 has started to fray at its edges and its core, perhaps in what we might call the Great Arab Unraveling," opined Rami Khouri, the Lebanese political columnist who dotes on American sports. "Shattered Iraq is the immediate driver of this possible dissolution and reconfiguration of Arab states that had held together rather well for nearly four generations."[50]

Strategically, the United States was also more vulnerable, as it held less credibility and influence in the Middle East than at any time since its oil needs and alliance with Israel took it deep into the region after World War II.

If the 1956 Suez Canal crisis marked the demise of Europe's influence in the Middle East, the Iraq War could well mark the demise of American influence. The United States may still be the major player, but mainly by default and largely on paper. Washington will be unable to threaten the use of sustained force or confrontation again anytime soon for fear of even greater backlash.

The U.S. experiment with force to create democracy also took a heavy toll on the agents of change. It stranded new activists and movements regionwide. As Iraq disintegrated, the region's autocracies acted as if they had carte blanche to do as they pleased. Several of the dissidents I interviewed for this book, particularly in Egypt and Syria, were subsequently detained for their activities. Most were still held as this book went to press, some for more than a year. Anwar al Bunni, the Syrian human-rights lawyer, was sentenced to five years.

"The complete failure in Iraq," said Syrian political analyst Sami Moubeyed, "will only keep other regimes in power longer."

Some of the new democrats felt American aid or support was downright dangerous. In 2005, during Iranian writer Akbar Ganji's long hunger strike, President Bush issued a statement expressing concern about his deteriorating health in prison and demanding his unconditional release for medical treatment. The White House appealed to human-rights activists around the world to rally to the Iranian writer's cause.

"His valiant efforts should not go in vain," the statement said. "Mr. Ganji, please know that as you stand for your own liberty, America stands with you."

But in 2006, during Ganji's first trip to Washington to pick up a freedom-of-speech award, he stayed as far away from the White House as he could.

"You people have great accomplishments," the diminutive Iranian dissident told me. "But no one trusts the American government now. Many people wanted to set up meetings while I was here. All the dissidents in Iran asked me not to."

Iranian activists felt betrayed by America's tactics, he said, especially compared with their own peaceful efforts. "Violence and force," Ganji said, "can never by themselves create genuine beliefs."

Yet Ganji was not giving up his campaign for democratic change. Nor were others.

Ghada Shahbender, the Egyptian mother who formed a group to monitor presidential and parliamentary elections, came to Washington in 2007. Despite growing obstacles in Cairo, she had persevered—and was making something of a name for herself in the region. When Yemen held elections in 2006, she was invited to help monitor its polls.

She was also planning long-term. "Democracy is not about one-time elections," she told me as we had dinner overlooking the Potomac.

Shayfeencom (We're Watching You) had recently launched a campaign against Egypt's endemic corruption. The government countered with a warning not to cross into politics. But then her group, Shahbender told me with a chuckle, discovered a simple discrepancy. The

UN Convention Against Corruption, which Egypt formally ratified in 2005, stipulated that it had to be published by every signatory to inform its citizens of their rights in fighting corruption—which Egypt had not properly done. So We're Watching You turned around and took the government to court.

"Even if we don't win, we've made a point," Shahbender said. "It's a step."

Shahbender had brought sixteen teenagers with her to Washington. They were part of her latest venture—Kid-mocracy 2007. It was a trial program that she and a few friends pulled together in less than three months to expose young Egyptians to democratic practices.

"Students in Egypt don't know what a constitution is. They simply aren't required to learn about it," she told me. "I didn't even read the whole thing until we organized this program. So what we need is basic civic education."

Shahbender's group launched a competition for students aged thirteen and fourteen. Kids studied democracies around the world and then wrote an essay evaluating four countries, based on United Nations criteria. Two of them had to be Egypt and the United States. The sixteen winners won a two-week trip to the United States—one week at a Massachusetts school to do a joint human-rights project with their American counterparts, the other week touring Washington, New York, Boston, and Philadelphia. The students saw both Republicans and Democrats on Capitol Hill. They experienced local government at the Boston State House. They saw the Liberty Bell and Independence Hall in Philadelphia. And they watched international diplomacy at the United Nations.

"Our resources are flimsy, so we have become professional beggars among our friends," Shahbender said. "My god, can't you just imagine what the 500 billion dollars the Americans have spent in Iraq would do if it had been used for real promotion of democracy!"

I asked Shahbender what impact the Iraq experiment with democracy had on her efforts.

"In Iraq, Bush set back democracy and freedom in the region more than any other American president," she told me. "Most Egyptians now raise their eyebrows and speak quite sarcastically about American democracy."

If change eventually took root in the region, she added, it would be despite what the United States did in Iraq, not because of it.

So what, I asked, would she do next?

"Keep trying," she replied.

ACKNOWLEDGMENTS

This book is the result of more than three decades of living and traveling throughout the Middle East. I am grateful to the thousands of people in two dozen countries who have shared their stories and offered their insights. I owe the most to the subjects of this book who met with me, sometimes at great personal risk.

My editors at *The Washington Post*—Leonard Downie, Liz Spayd, Susan Glasser, and Scott Vance—supported my project and graciously gave me the time to work on this book. My colleagues Thomas Ricks and Dana Priest offered thoughtful advice, and Glenn Kessler often had to do the work of two people so that I could take time off.

I am particularly grateful to the Brookings Institution's Saban Center for Middle East Policy, which provided a peaceful refuge to think and write as well as the research staff to help. I am enormously indebted to Strobe Talbott, Martin Indyk, and Kenneth Pollack for their thoughtful support and interest. At Brookings, Bilal Saab was a doting, determined, and thorough researcher who poured himself into this project. Christopher DeVito and Shai Gruber were diligent and imaginative assistants. All three worked long hours to come up with both historic and current material to supplement my field research and reporting.

During a pivotal year of travels through the region, I was fortunate to work with an array of talented people in each country. I also benefited from the personal perspective of many Middle East experts. It would take a whole chapter to name them all.

For the historic Palestinian election, Waleed Agel put aside his jazz and his studies long enough to guide me around the territories and through the local political networks. We had a great adventure. Nathan Brown of the Carnegie Endowment for International Peace and Robert Malley of the International Crisis Group, who were both international election monitors, generously shared their insights. Palestinian legislator Ziad Abu Amr, with whom I've had a running discussion about political Islam for two decades, was immensely helpful.

In Egypt, good-natured Nagwa Hassan spent long hours ensuring I saw everyone and went everywhere I needed for the book. We accumulated some wonderfully poignant stories. Amr Hamzawy at the Carnegie Endowment for International Peace shared his great expertise on his homeland and on political trends throughout the region.

In Lebanon, Nayla Khoury had the ability to navigate Beirut's crazed traffic—moving a stick shift with one hand that also held a pen to jot down names, directions, or phone numbers on a notebook balanced on her lap, while getting information in any of three languages on a cell phone in the other hand, leaving her knees to steer the car. She redefined multitasking. Augustus Richard Norton, noted author of his own books on Hezbollah, read through the Lebanon material and made many helpful suggestions. Julia Choucair at the Carnegie Endowment for International Peace and Emile el Hokayem of the Henry L. Stimson Center offered extensive advice. Nicholas Noe, Hezbollah expert and editor in chief of Mideastwire.com in Lebanon, helped track Hezbollah documents.

In Syria, sweet Dalia Haidar often had wise thoughts after tough interviews. I admire her determination and courage. Joshua Landis generously opened up his Rolodex so that I had a full range of contacts on all sides of the debate in Damascus.

My wonderful friends Shaul Bakhash and Haleh Esfandiari have guided me for almost twenty years on the subject of Iran. The intrepid Lily Sadeghi has been my right hand on many trips there. I learned much from the Hadi Semati, who is the joyful Shirazi spirit personified, and Najmeh Bozorgmehr, a colleague at the Brookings Institution.

Karim Sadjadpour of the International Crisis Group always provided sage counsel.

In Morocco, Driss Aissaoui was a helpful assistant in Rabat. Stephanie Willman Bordat, who has done groundbreaking work, steered me through the minefield of women's rights. Dalia Mogahed of the Gallup polling organization also helped me understand the broader attitudes on women's issues throughout the Middle East. I'm particularly sorry that the noble human-rights activist Driss Benzekri passed away shortly before this book was published; he was such an inspiration.

On Iraq, Ellen Laipson, Henri Barkey, Robin Raphel, and I have spent years debating Iraq and U.S. policy; they always enriched my knowledge and stimulated my thinking. In Baghdad, Barham Salih was pivotal in helping me delve deeper into Iraq, as was Adel Abdul Mahdi. Charles Duelfer also shared his expansive firsthand knowledge after a decade in Iraq, both during and after the rule of Saddam Hussein. Anthony Cordesman is unparalleled in the output of thoughtful data and analysis and always generous with his time.

On the many sides of change in the Middle East, I'm especially grateful to the democracy project at the Carnegie Endowment for International Peace, particularly Marina Ottaway and Paul Salem. Their work on democracy is the most comprehensive undertaken by any U.S. institution. At Brookings, Shibley Telhami is an encyclopedia of vital polling data tracking public opinion throughout the Middle East. Peter Singer was helpful on the precarious state of relations between the United States and the Islamic world.

At Penguin Press, Scott Moyers was a patient and nurturing editor. His advice and ideas made this a much richer book. I feel especially privileged to have worked with him before he left the field of editing. Esther Newberg, my agent, is always a wonderful shoulder; over the years, in other ways, she's also taught me a great deal about the joys of charity.

No one has done more to inspire me than my mother, who encouraged her children from an early age to taste the world and understand all its people. She never hesitated to visit me in many of the war zones I lived in. And she is always my first—and best—manuscript reader. She would have been much better at what I do if she'd had the same opportunities. I can never thank her enough.

NOTES

PROLOGUE: THE MIDDLE EAST: THE PROSPECTS

1. Akbar, Ganji The Middle East: "Money Can't Buy Us Democracy," *The New York Times,* Aug. 1, 2006.
2. "Bloggers May Be the Real Opposition," *The Economist,* Apr. 12, 2007.
3. Final statement of a conference, Arab Reform Issues: Vision and Implementation, held March 12–14, 2004 at the Bibliotheca Alexandrina in Egypt. Participating organizations included: the Arab Academy for Science and Technology, the Arab Business Council, the Arab Women's Organization, the Economic Research Forum, and the Arab Organization for Human Rights. This text is available at arabreformforum.com in Arabic and English.
4. "Stop Terror Sheikhs, Muslim Academics Demand," *Arab News,* Oct. 30, 2004.
5. Brian Murphy, "Moderate Muslims Using Quran to Wage 'Counter-jihad' against Radicals' Interpretation of Islam," Associated Press. Mar. 28, 2006.
6. Rami Khouri, "A Sensible Path to Arab Modernity," distributed by Agence Global, Aug. 21, 2005.
7. *Arab Human Development Report 2004: Towards Freedom in the Arab World* (New York: United Nations, 2005).
8. Samir Kassir, *"Being Arab"* (New York: Verso. 2006), p. 28.
9. Jim Krane, "Voters in United Arab Emirates Set to Vote in Historic Elections Saturday," Associated Press, Dec. 15, 2006.
10. Marina Ottaway, "Tyranny's Full Tank," *The New York Times,* Mar. 31, 2005.
11. Rami Khouri, "From Paris to Sydney, Baywatch to Bombers," column distributed by Agence Global, Nov. 2005.
12. Ibid.
13. "How to Beat the Terrorists: Lessons from a Journey Across the Arab World," Rami Khouri, column distributed by Agence Global, July 20, 2005.
14. Interview with pollster Nader Said of Birzeit University in Ramallah, Jan. 23, 2006.
15. *Arab Media: Tools of the Governments, Tools for the People?* United States Institute of Peace, Virtual Diplomacy Series, No. 18, Apr 12, 2005.
16. Robin Wright and Peter Baker, "Iraq, Jordan See Threat to Election from Iran; Leaders Warn Against Forming Religious State," *The Washington Post,* Dec. 8, 2004.
17. Hugh Poulton, *Top Hat, Grey Wolf and Crescent: Turkish Nationalism and the Turkish Republic* (New York: New York University Press, 1997), p. 93.

CHAPTER ONE: THE PALESTINIANS: THE CONUNDRUM

1. Two of the eight factions in the Palestine Liberation Organization were founded and led by Christians. The Popular Front for the Liberation of Palestine was founded by George Habash, and the Democratic Front for the Liberation of Palestine was founded by Nayif Hawatmeh.

2. Janet Wallach and John Wallach, *Arafat: In the Eyes of the Beholder,* (New York: Carol Publishing Group, 1990), p. 108.

3. Robin Wright, "Jeans and Dolls Put PLO into the Big Money," *The Sunday Times* (London), Oct. 4, 1981.

4. Nathan J. Brown, *Requiem for Palestinian Reform: Clear Lessons from a Troubled Record,* Carnegie Papers Middle East Series, No. 81, Democracy and Rule of Law Program, Carnegie Endowment for International Peace, Feb. 2007.

5. Khalil Shikaki, "The Future of Palestine," *Foreign Affairs,* vol. 83, no. 6, Nov.–Dec. 2004.

6. "Palestinian Corruption," *Middle East Reporter,* Feb. 6, 2006.

7. Shikaki's work has been groundbreaking in identifying trends and surveying public opinion among Palestinians. The United States Institute of Peace, the congressionally created and funded think tank in Washington, D.C., has supported his research and hosted his speeches in Washington. It described him as "one of the foremost authorities on Palestinian national politics." The Ford Foundation is among several American and European funders of his projects. He has been a fellow at the Brookings Institution's Saban Center for Middle East Studies and was the first appointment by Brandeis University's new Crown Center for Middle East Studies in 2005. He has conducted joint projects with Hebrew University and worked with other Israeli academics.

   Khalil Shikaki would not discuss his estranged brother more than a decade after his death. His brother's extremism has haunted his own career. In the early 1990s, before returning to the West Bank, Shikaki taught at Columbia, the University of Wisconsin, Milwaukee, and the World and Islam Studies Enterprise, a University of South Florida think tank. But Campus Watch, a group that monitors courses, faculty, and writings about the Middle East on American campuses, published allegations in 2006 that the younger Shikaki in the early 1990s also had connections to Islamic Jihad, had maintained covert contact with his brother, and had contributed funds that ended up with the extremist group. Khalil Shikaki, the report charged, was "a key intermediary in the organization of the American arm of the Palestine Islamic Jihad."

   Brandeis University immediately issued a strong denial. Khalil Shikaki, it said, is "among the most serious, responsible, credible, committed and courageous observers of Middle East politics. For more than a decade and a half, he has been at the forefront of numerous attempts to help reach a peaceful resolution of the Palestinian-Israeli dispute." He had often briefed American officials and had specifically reached out to Israeli and Jewish groups in the United States, it noted, including the Anti-Defamation League and the America-Israel Public Affairs Committee (AIPAC). The allegations, the university countered, were based entirely on "unsubstantiated claims, mischaracterizations, innuendos, and guilt by association."

8. Palestinians charged the crash was deliberate; the accident followed the stabbing of an Israeli shopping in Gaza a few days earlier.

9. The interview was posted on the Internet several years later: http://www.palestineremembered.com/al-ramla/zarnuqa/story455.html.

10. The turning point was a controversial visit by Ariel Sharon to the Temple Mount, the site of the Dome of the Rock and the al Aqsa mosque. Al Aqsa is the third holiest site in Islam. Muslims believe the prophet Mohammed ascended into heaven from a rock at the mosque to hear the word of God. The Dome of the Rock—a spectacular gold-domed structure built around the rock and decorated with azure blue and teal green tiles—is the dominant landmark on Jerusalem's skyline. But both structures are also built on a plateau above the Jews' First and Second Temples, the holiest site in Judaism. Competing claims to the thirty-five-acre plateau make it the most contested religious site in the world.

    Sharon, the rotund former general who then led the Israeli opposition, reportedly had Palestinian approval for the visit but had been warned that the Palestinians could not provide protection. So Sharon was accompanied by hundreds of well-armed Israeli police. Soon after his half-hour visit, clashes broke out on the Temple Mount between rock-throwing Palestinians and Israeli troops responding with tear gas and rubber bullets.

Many Palestinians thought Sharon's visit was political, since he was under assault from right-wing rivals in the Likud Party and was likely to face a national election soon. Five months later, in fact, he won a landslide victory and became Israel's prime minister—in part because of insecurity sparked by the new intifada. Many Israelis, in turn, charged that the Palestinian Authority encouraged confrontation to deflect attention from Arafat's failure to make peace. The official media called on Palestinians to support their brothers who had taken a stand at the Temple Mount.

11. Daniel Williams, "The Second Uprising," *The Washington Post,* Jan. 21, 2001.
12. According to statistics from the Israeli Foreign Ministry and Human Rights Watch, some 120 Israelis were killed in attacks between 1994 and the outbreak of the uprising in September 2000. Between 2000 and 2005, hundreds of Israelis were killed in dozens of attacks each year. In the spring of 2005, the main Palestinian militant factions declared an unofficial cease-fire or *hudna.*
13. The al Qassam Brigade was named after Izz al-Din al-Qassam, a Syrian-born cleric who had led attacks against British colonial officials and Jewish targets in the 1920s and 1930s. He was killed by British forces after he murdered a Jewish policeman.
14. International Crisis Group, *Enter Hamas: The Challenges of Political Integration,* Middle East Report No. 49, Jan. 18, 2006; and *Hamas,* Council on Foreign Relations, June 8, 2007, http://www.cfr.org/publication/8968.
15. Khalil Shikaki, "The Future of Palestine," *Foreign Affairs,* vol. 83, no. 6, Nov.–Dec. 2004.
16. Jim Hoagland, "Friends of the CIA," *The Washington Post,* Apr. 7, 2002.
17. United Nations Information System on the Question of Palestine, "Chronological Review of Events Relating to the Question of Palestine: Monthly Media Monitoring Review," July 2001.
18. Hanna Rosin, "Schools' Links to Hamas Give Arafat Dilemma," *The Washington Post,* Jan. 2, 2002.
19. Greg Myre, "Political Sibling Rivalry: Hebron Parliamentary Race Pits Brother Against Brother," *The New York Times,* Jan. 24, 2006.
20. International Crisis Group, *Enter Hamas: The Challenges of Political Integration,* Middle East Report No. 49, Jan. 18. 2006.
21. The full text of the March 19, 2005 Cairo Declaration:

(1) Those gathered confirmed their adherence to Palestinian principles, without any neglect, and the right of the Palestinian people to resistance in order to end the occupation, establish a Palestinian state with full sovereignty with Jerusalem as its capital, and the guaranteeing of the right of return of refugees to their homes and property.

(2) Those gathered agreed on a program for the year 2005, centered on the continuation of the atmosphere of calm in return for Israel's adherence to stopping all forms of aggression against our land and our Palestinian people, no matter where they are, as well as the release of all prisoners and detainees.

(3) Those gathered confirmed that the continuation of settlement and the construction of the wall and the Judaization of Jerusalem are explosive issues.

(4) Those gathered explored the internal Palestinian situation and agreed on the necessity of completing total reform in all areas, of supporting the democratic process in its various aspects and of holding local and legislative elections at their determined time according to an election law to be agreed upon. The conference recommends to the Legislative Council that it take steps to amend the legislative elections law, relying on an equal division (of seats) in a mixed system, and it recommends that the law for elections of local councils be amended on the basis of proportional representation.

(5) Those gathered agreed to develop the Palestine Liberation Organization on bases that will be settled upon in order to include all the Palestinian powers and factions, as the organization is

the sole legitimate representative of the Palestinian people. To do this, it has been agreed upon to form a committee to define these bases, and the committee will be made up of the president of the National Council, the members of the PLO's Executive Committee, the secretaries general of all Palestinian factions and independent national personalities. The president of the executive committee will convene this committee.

(6) Those gathered felt unanimously that dialogue is the sole means of interaction among all the factions, as a support to national unity and the unity of the Palestinian ranks. They were unanimous in forbidding the use of weapons in internal disputes, respecting the rights of the Palestinian citizen and refraining from violating them, and that continuing dialogue through the coming period is a basic necessity toward unifying our speech and preserving Palestinian rights.

22. International Crisis Group, *Enter Hamas: The Challenges of Political Integration,* Middle East Report No. 49, Jan. 18. 2006.
23. *Hamas,* Council on Foreign Relations, June 8, 2007, http://www.cfr.org/publication/8968; and "Hamas Terrorist Attacks," Israeli Ministry of Foreign Affairs, Mar. 22, 2004, www .mfa.gov.il/mfa/terrorism.
24. Secretary of State Condoleezza Rice, press briefing en route to London, Jan. 29. 2006.
25. "Hamas: Palestinians Suffering Moral Crisis," interview with Sheikh Nayef Rajoub, aljazeera.net, Jan. 17, 2006.
26. International Crisis Group, *Enter Hamas: The Challenges of Political Integration,* Middle East Report No. 49, Jan. 18. 2006.
27. Interview with Italy's *La Repubblica* cited by Samia Nakhoul, "Arabs Face Stark Choice: Reform or Ruin," Reuters, Mar. 25, 2004.
28. Mohammed Yaghi, "The Growing Anarchy in the Palestinian Territories," Washington Institute for Near East Policy, May 16, 2006.
29. Mathew Levitt, "Hamas's Hidden Economy," *Los Angeles Times,* July 3, 2007.
30. Khaled Mashaal, "We Will Not Sell Our People or Principles for Foreign Aid," *The Guardian,* Jan. 31, 2006.
31. Dion Nissenbaum, "Islamic Fundamentalist Group Suspected of Killing Prostitutes," McClatchy Newspapers, Mar. 1, 2007.
32. Jake Lipton, "The War of Words Between Hamas and al Qaeda," The Washington Institute for Near East Policy, June 28, 2007.
33. Nathan J. Brown, "The Peace Process Has No Clothes: The Decay of the Palestinian Authority and the International Response," Carnegie Endowment for International Peace, June 14, 2007.
34. Jake Lipton, "The War of Words Between Hamas and al Qaeda," The Washington Institute for Near East Policy, June 28, 2007.
35. "Israel-Palestinians Q & A," The Associated Press, June 13, 2007.
36. Nidal al-Mughrabi, "Bloody Day in Gaza Raises Civil War Fears," Reuters, June 12, 2007.
37. Nidal al-Mughrabi, "Hamas Gunmen Hunt Down Fatah Rivals in Gaza Strip," Reuters, June 14, 2007.
38. Dion Nissenbaum, "Hamas Fighters Tighten Hold on Gaza," McClatchy Newspapers, June 13, 2007.
39. Nidal al-Mughrabi, "Hamas Defeat Fatah in Gaza, Abbas Declares Emergency," Reuters, June 14, 2007.
40. Dion Nissenbaum, "Hamas' Rule over Gaza Begins with Promises, Pillaging," McClatchy Newspapers, June 15, 2007.
41. Scott Wilson, "Fatah Gunmen Assert Authority in West Bank," *The Washington Post,* July 8, 2007.
42. Dion Nissenbaum, "Hamas Fighters Tighten Hold on Gaza," McClatchy Newspapers, June 13, 2007.
43. "Mashaal: Hamas to Work with Fatah," *Alalam News,* June 15, 2007.
44. Craig S. Smith and Greg Myre, "Hamas May Find It Needs Its Enemy," *The New York Times,* June 17, 2007.

CHAPTER TWO: EGYPT: THE TURNING POINTS

1. "Shayfeen.com Report on Egypt's First Presidential Campaign" (English), Sept. 7, 2005.

2. "Shayfeen.com Report on Egypt's First Presidential Campaign" (English), Sept. 7, 2005, and "Shayfeen.com Special Report" (Arabic), Sept. 8, 2005.

3. Reem Nafie, "Illiteracy Revisited: A Major New Project Aiming to Significantly Reduce Illiteracy Has Just Been Launched," *Al-Ahram Weekly,* Sept. 4–10, 2003.

4. "2005 Human Rights Report: Egypt," U.S. Department of State, Mar. 8, 2006.

5. Interviews with United States officials in Cairo, Feb.–Mar. 2006.

6. "Egypt: Flawed Election But...," *Democracy Digest,* vol. 2, no. 9, Sept. 13, 2005.

7. "2005 Human Rights Report: Egypt," U.S. Department of State, Mar. 8, 2006.

8. Telephone interview with a senior Western diplomat in Cairo who stipulated that I could use the information only if I protected his name and nationality, Mar. 2, 2006.

9. "Multiple Violations in the Third Round and the Responsibility of the Security Services," Shayfeen.com, Dec. 3, 2006.

10. "The Last Days of the Elections Are the Worst," Shayfeencom, Dec. 8, 2005.

11. "Egypt: Fear of Torture or Ill-Treatment/Incommunicado Detention," Amnesty International, Apr. 16, 2003.

12. Megan K. Stack, "Pain of Political Change," *Los Angeles Times,* Dec. 7, 2005.

13. "Egypt: Human Rights Developments," Human Rights Watch, World Report 2001.

14. Charles Levinson, "Brotherhood Blues," *Cairo Times,* vol. 7, no. 28, Sept. 18–24, 2003.

15. Samia Mehrez, "Take Them Out of the Ball Game: Egypt's Cultural Players in Crisis," Middle East Report No. 219, Middle East Research and Information Project (MERIP), vol. 31, no. 2, Summer 2001.

16. Mohamed Sid-Ahmed, "The Intelligentsia and Politics," *Al-Ahram Weekly,* no. 517, Jan. 18–24, 2001.

17. Gamal Essam el-Din, "Brotherhood in the Crossfire," *Al-Ahram Weekly,* no. 620, Jan. 9–15, 2003.

18. "Egypt: Country Reports on Human Rights Practices 2004," Human Rights Report, U.S. Department of State, Feb. 28, 2005.

19. Stack, "Pain of Political Change."

20. Ibid.

21. Nathan J. Brown and Hesham Nasr, "Egypt's Judges Step Forward," Carnegie Endowment for International Peace, Policy Outlook, Democracy and Rule of Law Project, May 2005.

22. Dina Shehata, "Egyptian Judges Test the Government's Commitment to Democratic Reform," Al-Ahram Center for Political and Strategic Studies, no. 36, June 28, 2005. http//www.ahram.org./eg/acpss/Eng/ahram/2004/7/5/ESYP43/htm.

23. Brown and Nasr, "Egypt's Judges Step Forward"; and Shehata, "Egyptian Judges Test the Government's Commitment to Democratic Reform."

24. Telephone interviews with the two lawyers in the case, Yosry el Sawy, Mar. 16, 2006, and Ayman el Foly, Mar. 14, 2006.

25. Megan K. Stack, "Some Judges in Egypt Lend Voice to Chorus for Reform, *The Los Angeles Times,* May 2, 2005; and Mona El-Nahhas, "Judges of Character," *Al-Ahram Weekly,* Dec. 29, 2005–Jan. 4, 2006.

26. Mona el-Nahhas, "Judges of Character."

27. Mona el-Nahhas, "Judicial Stand-off," *Al-Ahram Weekly,* no. 783, Feb. 23–Mar. 1, 2006.

28. Nadia Abou el-Magd, "Egyptian Judges Protest Lack of Freedom," Associated Press, Mar. 17, 2006.

29. "Egypt Judges Take Protest to the Streets," aljazeera.net, Mar. 17, 2006.

30. Nadia Abou el-Magd, "Egyptian Judges Protest Lack of Freedom."

31. "Mandate," Baheyya: Egypt Analysis and Whimsy: Commentary on Egyptian Politics and Culture by an Egyptian Citizen with a Room of Her Own, Baheyya.blogspot.com, Dec. 20, 2005.

32. "Egypt Threatens Journalists over Referendum Violence Complaints," Agence France Presse,

June 14, 2005; and Amira Howeidy, "Zero Tolerance for Torture," *Al-Ahram Weekly,* no. 749, June 30–July 6, 2005.

33. Amira Howeidy, "Zero Tolerance for Torture."

34. *Amnesty International Report 1989* (London: Amnesty International Publications, 1989), p. 253.

35. Ibid.

36. Glenn E. Perry, "Challenging Islamic Fundamentalism: The Writings of Muhammad Said al-Ashmawy," Ethnic NewsWatch, *Digest of Middle East Studies* (*DOMES*), July 31, 1999; and Rose Ismail, "Political Islam a Deviation?" *The New Straits Times* (Malaysia), Apr. 21, 2000.

37. Pamela Nice, "Finding the Right Language: A Conversation with Syrian Filmmaker Usama Muhammad," *Al Jadid,* vol. 6, no. 31, Spring 2000.

38. Alan Sipress, "Creativity Under Siege in Egypt," *The Philadelphia Inquirer,* Feb. 28, 1994.

CHAPTER THREE: EGYPT: THE PLAYERS

1. Ziad Munson, "Islamic Mobilization: Social Movement Theory and the Egyptian Muslim Brotherhood," *The Sociological Quarterly,* vol. 42, no. 4, Fall 2001, pp. 487–510.

2. Interview with Assistant Foreign Minister Sallama Shaker, Feb. 21, 2006.

3. Amira Howeidy, "Politics in God's Name," *Al Ahram Weekly,* no. 247, Nov. 16–22, 1995.

4. Daniel Williams, "Egypt's Muslim Brotherhood May Be Model for Islam's Political Adaptation," *The Washington Post,* Feb. 3, 2006.

5. Ibid.

6. Sarah Gauch, "Egypt's Opposition Targets Reforms," *The Christian Science Monitor,* Mar. 23, 2006.

7. Amira Howeidy, "Muslim Brotherhood Flexes Muscles," *aljazeera.net,* Dec. 5, 2005.

8. http://www.ummah.net/ikhwan.

9. Robin Wright, *Sacred Rage: The Wrath of Militant Islam* (New York: Simon & Schuster, 2001), p. 178.

10. Amira Howeidy, "Politics in God's Name," *Al-Ahram Weekly,* no. 247, Nov. 16–22, 1995.

11. http://www.u-s-history.com/pages/h2177.html

12. Sayyid Qutb, *Milestones* (Indianapolis: American Trust Publications, 1990).

13. Ibid.

14. Steve Coll, "Letter from Jedda. Young Osama: How He Learned Radicalism, and May Have Seen America," *The New Yorker,* Dec. 12, 2005.

15. Robin Wright, "Quiet Revolution: Islamic Movement's New Phase," third of a five-part series, "Politics in the Name of God," *The Christian Science Monitor,* Nov. 6, 1987.

16. John Walsh, "Egypt's Muslim Brotherhood: Understanding Centrist Islam," *Perspectives on the United States: A Splintered Mirror, Harvard International Review,* vol. 24, Winter 2003.

17. Robin Wright, *Sacred Rage: The Wrath of Militant Islam* (New York: Simon & Schuster, 2001), pp. 175–178.

18. Ibid.

19. Ibid.

20. Omar Sinan, "Al Qaeda Touts U.S. Troop Cuts in Iraq in a New Zawahiri Tape," Associated Press, Jan. 6, 2006.

21. Steven Stalinsky, "Egyptian Support for Killing American Soldiers in Iraq," Middle East Media Research Institute, Dec. 2, 2004.

22. www.harakamasria.org, www.harakamasria.net. and www.harakamasria.com.

23. Shaden Shehab, "Gomaa's Last Stand," *Al-Ahram Weekly,* Apr. 6–12, 2006; and Miret el-Nagger, "Standoff Deals Blow to Secular Parties in Egypt," Knight Ridder, Apr. 7, 2006.

24. Ron Nordland, "The Pharaoh and the Rebel," *Newsweek,* Dec. 30, 2005.

25. Ayman Nour, "Letter from Prison: Did I Take Democracy Too Seriously?" *Newsweek,* Mar. 14, 2005.

26. "Egypt: Focus on Second Week of Campaigning," IRINnews.org, United Nations Office for the Coordination of Humanitarian Affairs, Aug. 25, 2005.

27. Daniel Williams, "Mubarak's 2005 Election Rival Sits in Jail as Movement Withers," Bloomberg News, Mar. 6, 2007.

28. Gamal Essam el-Din, "Re-introducing Gamal Mubarak," *Al-Ahram Weekly,* Mar. 30–Apr. 5, 2006.
29. The reign of Ramses II was the longest, at more than sixty years in the thirteenth century B.C. That of Mohammed Ali was the second longest, at forty years in the nineteenth century. From Saad Eddin Ibrahim at the Capitol Hill Conference Series on U.S. Middle East Policy, Hart Senate Office Buildling, Apr. 22, 2005.
30. Gamal Essam el-Din, "It Won't Happen Here," *Al-Ahram Weekly,* no. 672, Jan. 8–14, 2004.
31. Gamal Essam el-Din, "Re-introducing Gamal Mubarak."
32. Gamal Essam el-Din, "It Won't Happen Here," *Al-Ahram Weekly,* no. 672, Jan. 8–14, 2004.
33. Nevine Khalil, "Young Minds, Open Debate," *Al-Ahram Weekly,* no. 637, May 8–14, 2003.
34. Daniel Williams, "Egyptians Wonder If Dynasty Is Near; Mubarak's Son Gaining Prominence," *The Washington Post,* Sept. 24, 2004.
35. "Book Eulogises Mubarak's Son," Agence France Presse, Mar. 9, 2004.
36. Tom Perry, "Egypt Islamist Sees Mubarak's Son Seeking Presidency," Reuters, Feb. 27, 2006.
37. Rod Nordland, "The Pharaoh and the Rebel," *Newsweek,* Dec. 30, 2005.
38. Interview with Mohammed el-Sayed Said, deputy director of the Al-Ahram Center for Political and Strategic Studies.
39. "Egypt Detaining More People, Rights Council Says," Reuters, Apr. 5, 2006.
40. Hannah Allam, "Egyptian Reformer's Experience a Cautionary Tale, Knight Ridder Newspapers, Mar. 30, 2006.
41. Amira Howeidy, "I Fear For Egypt," *Al-Ahram Weekly,* no. 786, Mar. 16–22, 2006.
42. Hannah Allam, "Egyptian Reformer's Experience a Cautionary Tale."
43. Abigail Hauslohner, "Egypt Monitoring Group Reports Vote Fraud." *Reuters,* June 13, 2007.
44. Paul Schemm, "Egyptian-American Academic Fears Arrest if He Returns Home from U.S." Associated Press, Aug. 26, 2007.
45. Saad Eddin Ibrahim, "Egypt's Unchecked Repression." *The Washington Post,* Aug. 21, 2007.

CHAPTER FOUR: LEBANON: THE DREAMERS

1. "Index Ranks Middle East Freedom," BBC News, Nov. 18, 2005. *The Economist* Intelligence Unit ranked twenty countries based on fifteen indicators of political and civil liberty. The ratings were:

     Israel 8.20
     Lebanon 6.55
     Morocco 5.20
     Iraq 5.05
     Palestine 5.05
     Kuwait 4.90
     Tunisia 4.60
     Jordan 4.45
     Qatar 4.45
     Egypt 4.30
     Sudan 4.30
     Yemen 4.30
     Algeria 4.15
     Oman 4.00
     Bahrain 3.85
     Iran 3.85
     United Arab Emirates 3.70
     Saudi Arabia 2.80
     Syria 2.80
     Libya 2.05

2. Ramsay Short, *A Hedonist's Guide to Beirut* (London: Filmer, 2005), p. 134.

3. "Censors Raid Beirut's Virgin Megastore," BBC News, Jan. 7, 2002.

4. *Background Notes: Lebanon,* U.S. Department of State, Aug. 2005, p. 2. The United States reports that as many as seven percent of Lebanon's population was killed during the war, which is higher than most estimates. The generally accepted figures range from 100,000 to 150,000 killed, with some 100,000 injured or handicapped, and up to 17,000 missing.

5. Susan Sachs, "Rafiq Hariri Is Dead at 60; Ex-premier of Lebanon," *The New York Times,* Feb. 15, 2005.

6. Ghassan Charbel "The Long Interview: Rafiq al Hariri," *Al Hayat,* reprinted in English in *The Journal of Turkish Weekly,* Feb. 17, 2005.

7. Gary C. Gambill, and Ziad K. Abdelnour, "Dossier: Rafiq Hariri," *Middle East Intelligence Bulletin,* vol. 3, no. 7, July 2001.

8. Ghassan Charbel, "The Long Interview: Rafiq al Hariri." Hariri told *Al Hayat* that his personal contribution to reconstruction of Beirut's war-ravaged commercial district downtown was $125 million, or about seven percent of the total.

9. Ethan Bronner, "A Builder in Lebanon; New Prime Minister Wealthy, Fiercely Dedicated," *The Boston Globe,* Mar. 22, 1993.

10. Oussama Safa, "Lebanon Springs Forward," *Journal of Democracy,* vol. 17, no. 1, Jan. 2006, pp. 28–34.

11. Nora Boustany, "Lebanon's Sorrow: Hariri's Murderers Were Targeting Democracy," *The Washington Post,* Feb. 20, 2005.

12. Oussama Safa, "Lebanon Springs Forward."

13. Gary C. Gambill and Ziad K. Abdelnour, "Dossier: Rafiq Hariri."

14. Ethan Bronner, "A Builder in Lebanon."

15. Oussama Safa, "Lebanon Springs Forward."

16. Robin Wright and Colum Lynch, "Syria Blamed in Death of Hariri; U.N. Also Faults Lebanese Officials," *The Washington Post,* Oct. 21, 2005.

17. United Nations Security Council report by investigator Detlev Mehlis, circulated Oct. 20, 2005.

18. Hassan M. Fattah, "Wails at Loss of Lebanese Leader, Cries for His Vision," *The New York Times,* Feb. 17, 2005.

19. Megan K. Stack, "Mourners in Lebanon Say Syria Must Go," *Los Angeles Times,* Feb. 17, 2005.

20. Megan K. Stack, "Son of Slain Former Leader Triumphs in Beirut Vote," *Los Angeles Times,* May 30, 2005.

21. Lally Weymouth, "The Next Prime Minister?" *The Washington Post,* May 29, 2005.

22. Scott MacLeod, "Days of Cedar," *Time Europe,* vol. 166, no. 15, Oct. 10, 2005.

CHAPTER FIVE: LEBANON: THE SHADOWS

1. David Ignatius, "An Interview with Sayyed Hasan Nasrallah," *The Washington Post,* Feb. 3, 2006.

2. Of the fourteen, four are independents who are aligned with Hezbollah and vote with the party. Two are Sunni and one is Maronite.

3. Hassan Nasrallah, speech addressing the nation on the publication of cartoons about the Prophet Mohammed, Al Arabiya television, Feb. 9, 2006.

4. Richard Armitage, "America and the World Since 9/11," luncheon speech at the United States Institute of Peace, Sept. 12, 2002. In reply to a question, Armitage, the Bush Administration's first deputy secretary of state, said, "Hezbollah may be the A-Team of terrorists, and maybe al Qaeda is actually the B-Team. They're on the list, and their time will come. There is no question about it. They have a blood debt to us...and we're not going to forget it, and it's all in good time. We're going to go after these problems just like a high-school wrestler goes after a match: We're going to take them down one at a time."

5. Sami Moubayed, "Nasrallah and the Three Lebanons," *Asia Times,* Aug. 3, 2006.

6. Julie Goodman, "Cleric's Disappearance Sensitive Issue for Shiites," International Reporting Project, Johns Hopkins University School of Advanced International Studies, Fall 2004.

7. Augustus Richard Norton, "Hizballah: From Radicalism to Pragmatism?" *Middle East Policy Council Journal,* vol. 5, no. 4, Jan. 1998.

8. The spark for Israel's invasion, somewhat ironically, was an assassination attempt on its ambassador to Britain by a Palestinian renegade group led by Abu Nidal. His group had split from the Palestine Liberation Organization and later tried to kill Yasser Arafat, too. But the attack on Israel's ambassador provided the pretext to deal with the long-standing problem of the PLO in neighboring Lebanon.

9. Al Manar television, Mar. 20, 2002, on www.islamicdigest.net.

10. Robin Wright, *Sacred Rage: The Wrath of Militant Islam* (New York: Simon & Schuster, 2001), pp. 69–110.

11. Robin Wright, *Sacred Rage,* p. 73.

12. "An Interview with Yitzhak Rabin: They Want Lebanon, Let Them Enjoy It," *Time,* Feb. 11, 1985, p. 44; and Robin Wright, *Sacred Rage,* p. 233.

13. Enno Franzius, *History of the Order of the Assassins* (New York: Funk & Wagnalls, 1969) and Bernard Lewis, *The Assassins: A Radical Sect in Islam* (New York: Basic Books, 1968, 2002; London: Al Saqi Books, 1985).

14. Bernard Lewis, *The Assassins.*

15. Robert Fisk, "Dialogue Is No Longer Enough; Muslims in the Arab World Are Despairing of the West's Attitude to Them," *The Independent,* Dec. 7, 1993.

16. The first American taken hostage in Lebanon—and the only one taken to Iran—was David Dodge, the president of American University of Beirut. He was kidnapped when four Iranian diplomats went missing in Lebanon days after Israel's 1982 invasion. Tehran demanded pressure by the international community to free them; when nothing happened, Dodge went missing. He was held for 366 days. Syria mediated his release. The four Iranians, whose vehicle with diplomatic plates had been stopped at a checkpoint run by a right-wing Christian militia, were never heard from again. In the search for information to win the release of American hostages, U.S. diplomats were told that the four had been murdered.

17. "An Open Letter: The Hezbollah Program," *As Safir,* Feb. 16, 1985; and Augustus Richard Norton, *Amal and the Shi'a: Struggle for the Soul of Lebanon* (Austin, TX: University of Texas Press, 1987).

18. "An Open Letter: The Hezbollah Program"; and Augustus Richard Norton, *Amal and the Shi'a.*

19. "Return to the Lion's Den," CNN On-Air, Dec. 1, 1996.

20. "Patterns of Global Terrorism 2001," *Background Information on Designated Foreign Terrorist Organizations,* Appendix B, U.S. Department of State.

21. Augustus Richard Norton, "Hizballah: From Radicalism to Pragmatism?" *Middle East Policy Council Journal,* vol. 5, no. 4, Jan. 1998.

22. "Hezbollah Leader Addresses Election Rally in Beirut's Southern Suburb," excerpt from report by Hezbollah Radio, *BBC Summary of World Broadcasts,* Aug. 26, 1992.

23. The quotation is actually by Heraclitus, fragment 41 from *On the Universe*: "You could not step twice into the same river..."

24. Gary C. Gambill and Ziad K. Abdelnour, "Hezbollah: Between Tehran and Damascus," *Middle East Intelligence Bulletin,* vol. 4, no. 2, Feb. 2002.

25. Sami Moubayed, "Who Is Hasan Nasrallah?" *World Politics Watch,* July 17, 2006.

26. "Treasury Designation Targets Hizballah's Bank," U.S. Treasury Department, Sept. 7, 2006.

27. Jeffrey Goldberg, "In the Party of God: Hezbollah Sets Up Operations in South America and the United States," *The New Yorker,* Oct. 28, 2002; "Hezbollah and the West African Diamond Trade," *Middle East Intelligence Bulletin,* vol. 6, no. 6–7, June–July 2004; and Douglas Farah, "Hezbollah's External Support Network in West Africa and Latin America," International Assessment and Strategy Center, Aug. 4, 2006.

28. "Hezbollah Leader Says Lebanon at a 'Dangerous Stage,'" excerpts from a report in *As Safir, BBC Summary of World Broadcasts,* Dec. 29, 1997.

29. "Hezbollah Leader Addresses Beirut Rally, Sees End of Israeli 'Dream,'" al Manar television Web site in Arabic, May 7, 1998.
30. Avi Jorisch, "Al-Manar: Hizbullah TV 24/7," *Middle East Quarterly,* vol. 11, no. 1, Winter 2004; and Avi Jorisch, "Terrorist Television," *National Review,* Dec. 22, 2004.
31. Robin Wright, "Iran Shipping Arms to Hezbollah," *Los Angeles Times,* Apr. 18, 1996; and Robin Wright, "Iran Boosts Arms Supplies to Hezbollah," *Los Angeles Times,* Dec. 13, 1996.
32. In 1993, via Syria, the United States brokered an unwritten deal: Israel ended attacks on Lebanese civilians, while Hezbollah limited operations to Israelis in Lebanon. It broke down in 1996 in a brutal sixteen-day onslaught by both sides. The United States renegotiated the same deal, this time in writing.
33. Oscar Serrat, "Argentine Prosecutors Seek Arrest of Former Iranian President in Jewish Center Bombing," Associated Press, Oct. 25, 2006.
34. Richard Engle, "Hezbollah Guerrillas Taunt Israeli Soldiers, Loot Abandoned Border Posts," Agence France Presse, May 24, 2000.
35. Deborah Sontag, "Retreat from Lebanon: The Triumphal Procession, Israel out of Lebanon after 22 Years," *The New York Times,* May 24, 2000.
36. "Hezbollah Leader Calls for Muslim-Christian Coexistence," Lebanese Broadcasting Corp., broadcast aired May 26, 2000, and published by *BBC Summary of World Broadcasts* May 27, 2000.
37. Daniel Sobelman, "Hezbollah Two Years After the Withdrawal—A Compromise Between Ideology, Interests, and Exigencies," *Strategic Assessment,* Jaffee Center for Strategic Studies, Tel Aviv University, vol. 5, no. 2, Aug. 2002.
38. Daniel Sobelman, "Four Years After the Withdrawal from Lebanon: Refining the Rules of the Game," *Strategic Assessment,* Jaffee Center for Strategic Studies, Tel Aviv University, vol. 7, no. 2, Aug. 2004.
39. Robin Wright, "Most of Iran's Troops in Lebanon Are Out, Western Officials Say," *The Washington Post.* Apr. 13, 2005.
40. Daniel Sobelman, "Hezbollah After the Syrian Withdrawal," *Strategic Assessment,* Jaffee Center for Strategic Studies, Tel Aviv University, vol. 8, no. 1, Aug. 2005.
41. "The Electoral Program of Hezbollah 1996," Distributed by al Manar television, online at http://almashriq.hiof.no/lebanon/300/320/324/324.2/hizballah/hizballah-platform .html.
42. Hassan Nasrallah, speech addressing the nation on the publication of cartoons about the Prophet Mohammed, al Arabiya television, Feb. 9, 2006.
43. Will Rasmussen, "Hezbollah Hasn't Moderated, but It Has Been Humbled," *The New Republic Online,* Jan. 4, 2006.
44. "Hizbullah Risks Becoming Part of 'Business as Usual' in Beirut," *The Daily Star* editorial, July 8, 2006.
45. Interview with Egyptian television, June 2, 2000.
46. Daniel Sobelman, "Hezbollah Two Years After the Withdrawal": Daniel Sobelman, "Four Years After the Withdrawal from Lebanon"; and Reuven Pedatzur, "Plays by the Rules," *Haaretz,* Aug. 16, 2004.
47. Daniel Sobelman, "Hezbollah Two Years After the Withdrawal."
48. *Nightline,* ABC News, Oct. 19, 2000.
49. "Lebanese Hezbollah Leader Views Capability of New Drone to Bomb Israel," al Manar Television, Nov. 12, 2004, published by *BBC Worldwide Monitoring,* Nov. 13, 2004.
50. Daniel Sobelman, "Four Years After the Withdrawal from Lebanon."
51. "Factbox: How Hizbollah Captured Israeli Soldiers," Reuters, July 13, 2006.
52. "Nasrallah: We Are Working on Making This Year the Year to Free Our Brothers in Israeli Detention," *The Daily Star,* Feb. 10, 2006.
53. Greg Myre and Steven Erlanger, "Israelis Enter Lebanon After Attacks," *The New York Times,* July 13, 2006.
54. Amir Oren, "The Longest Month," *Haaretz,* Aug. 18, 2006.
55. Jon Finer, "Israeli Soldiers Find a Tenacious Foe in Hezbollah," *The Washington Post,* Aug. 8,

2006; and Lin Noueihed, "Israel Faces Invisible Enemy in Southern Lebanon," Reuters, Aug. 2, 2006.

56. "Nasrallah: No Second Round," *As Safir,* Aug. 28, 2006, translation of interview on New TV by Miriam al Bassam.

57. Adam Entous, "More Than 60 pct of Israelis Want Olmert to Quit—Poll," *Reuters,* Aug. 25, 2006.

58. "Poll Finds Support for Hizbullah's Retaliation: Opinions Diverge on Sectarian Lines—But Not Completely," Beirut Center for Research & Information, July 29, 2006.

59. Edward Cody, "Staying Power Adds to Hezbollah's Appeal," *The Washington Post,* Aug. 2, 2006.

60. Steven Erlanger, "Israeli Officer Says Army Aims to Kill Nasrallah," *The New York Times,* Aug. 20, 2006.

61. Zeina Karam, "Hezbollah Leader Says He Wouldn't Have Ordered the Capture of Two Israeli Soldiers Knowing It Would Lead to Such a War," *Associated Press,* Aug. 27, 2006; and "Nasrallah Regrets War in Hindsight," *The Daily Star,* Aug. 27, 2006.

62. "Hizbullah Shuts Down Posts Near Shabaa Farms, Moves Out Weapons," Agence France Presse, quoted by *Naharnet,* Aug. 28, 2006.

63. Nadia Abou El-Magd, "For Majority of Arabs, Hezbollah Won, Israel Army No Longer Unbeatable," *Associated Press,* Aug. 17, 2006.

64. Ibid.

65. David Rising, "Hezbollah's Fierce Resistance Giving Rise to Increased Arab Support," Associated Press, July 30, 2006.

66. Nadia Abou El-Magd, "Nearly a Month Into Lebanon Fighting, Arab Anger at Their Governments Grows," Associated Press, Aug. 7, 2006.

67. Mohammed Bazzi, "Some Fear a Thousand New Bin Ladens," *Newsday,* Aug. 1, 2006.

68. Interview with Hassan Nasrallah, al Jazeera, Sept. 12, 2006.

69. Robin Wright and Peter Baker, "Iraq, Jordan See Threat to Election from Iran: Leaders Warn Against Forming Religious State," *The Washington Post,* Dec. 8, 2004.

70. Hassan Hassan and Abdullah Taa'i, "Hizbullah in the Eyes of Syrians During the War," written for SyriaComment.com, Sept. 6, 2006.

CHAPTER SIX: SYRIA: THE OUTLAWS

1. Patrick Seale, *Asad: The Struggle for the Middle East* (Berkeley: University of California Press, 1988), p. 153.

2. Patrick Seale, *Asad,* pp. 3–8.

3. Gary C. Gambill, "Riyad al-Turk: Secretary-General of the Syrian Community Party Political Bureau," *Middle East Intelligence Bulletin,* vol. 3, no. 9, Sept. 2001; and Ranwa Yehia, "The Shackles of Leadership," *Al-Ahram Weekly,* no. 563, Dec. 6–12, 2001.

4. Patrick Seale, *Asad,* pp. 441–460.

5. Michael Jansen, "Spring Time in Syria," *Al-Ahram Weekly,* no. 526, March 22–28, 2001.

6. Inaugural Address, Syrian Arab News Agency, July 17, 2000.

7. "Statement by 99 Syrian Intellectuals," *Al Hayat,* Sept. 27, 2000.

8. Eli Karmelli, and Yotam Feldner, "The Battle for Reforms and Civil Society in Syria—Part I," Middle East Media Research Institute, no. 47, Feb. 9, 2001.

9. Flynt Leverett, *Inheriting Syria: Bashar's Trial by Fire* (Washington D.C.: Brookings Institution Press, 2005).

10. Deborah Amos, "Syria's Efforts to Reform Its Economy," *All Things Considered,* National Public Radio, Aug. 2, 2005.

11. Sami Moubayed, "Dateline Damascus: Threatened by Its Neighbors, Damascus Clamps Down on 'Opinion of the Other,'" *Washington Report on Middle East Affairs,* Dec. 2001.

12. Rhonda Roumani, "Syria Frees Five Political Activists," *The Washington Post,* Jan. 19, 2006.

13. Patrick Seale, *Asad,* pp. 3–8.

14. Yassin Haj Saleh, "Don't Rush the Revolution," *The New York Times,* June 4, 2005.

15. Howard Schneider, "For First Time, a Pope Sets Foot in a Mosque," *The Washington Post,* May 7, 2001.

16. Zeina Karam, "Planner of Assault on Munich Olympics Has No Regrets," Associated Press. Feb. 23, 2006.

17. Gary C. Gambill, "The Syrian Muslim Brotherhood, *Mideast Mirror,* vol. 1, no. 2, Apr.–May 2006.

18. The Muslim Brotherhood was also banned during Syria's union with Egypt between 1958 and 1961, but allowed to run after the United Arab Republic crumbled.

19. Patrick Seale, *Asad,* pp. 316–338.

20. Ibid.

21. *The Massacres of Hama: Law Enforcement Requires Accountability,* Syrian Human Rights Committee, Feb. 1, 2005.

22. Thomas L. Friedman, *From Beirut to Jerusalem* (New York: Farrar, Straus & Giroux, 1989), p. 80.

23. *The Massacres of Hama;* and interviews with human rights groups in Damascus, Apr. 2006.

24. "Mid-Range Wars and Atrocities of the Twentieth Century," http://users.erols.com/mwhite28/warstat4.htm.

25. Ibrahim Hamidi, "Islamist Streams on the March in Syria," *Al Hayat,* Jan. 4, 2006.

26. Anthony Shadid, "Inside and Outside Syria, a Debate to Decide the Future," *The Washington Post,* Nov. 9, 2005.

27. Deborah Amos, "Exiled Opposition Leader for Democracy in Syria," National Public Radio, Dec. 1, 2005.

28. Ibrahim Hamidi, "Islamist Streams on the March in Syria."

29. Charles Glass, "Is Syria Next?" *London Review of Books,* vol. 25, no. 14, July 24, 2003.

30. Flynt Leverett, "Syria's Wobbly Godfather Jr.: Will the Hariri Affair Be a Turning Point in the Assad Family Saga? *The Washington Post,* Oct. 30, 2005.

31. Bouthaina Shaaban, "Outside View: Who Killed Hariri?" *United Press International,* Feb. 19, 2005, and www.bouthainashaaban.com, Feb. 22, 2005.

32. Gary C. Gambill, "The Kurdish Reawakening in Syria," *Middle East Intelligence Bulletin,* vol. 6, no. 4, April 2004.

33. Christine Spolar, "Fearful Iraqis Seek Haven in Syria," *The Chicago Tribune,* May 22, 2006.

34. Dr. Nimrod Raphaeli, "The Syrian Economy under Bashar al Assad," Middle East Media Research Institute, no. 259, Jan. 13, 2006.

35. Matthew Levitt, "Syria and the War on Terrorism: Challenges for U.S. Policy (Part II)," PolicyWatch No. 596, The Washington Institute for Near East Policy, Jan. 24, 2002.

36. Thomas L. Friedman, *From Beirut to Jerusalem,* p. 80.

37. Albert Aji, "Prominent Syrian Human Rights Lawyer Among 6 Detained in Large Roundup," Associated Press, May 17, 2006; and Mohammed Bazzi, "Syria Cracks Down on Dissidents," *Newsday,* May 19, 2006.

CHAPTER SEVEN: IRAN: THE REVOLUTIONARIES

1. Hamid Algar, *Islam and Revolution: Writings and Declarations of Imam Khomeini* (Berkeley, CA: Mizan Press, 1981), pp. 169–173.

2. Ironically, the loan was largely to buy American arms.

3. Hamid Algar, *Islam and Revolution,* pp. 181–88.

4. Muqtedar Khan, "Two Theories of Ijtihad," Common Ground News Service, Mar. 22, 2006.

5. Other faiths are deliberately excluded, notably the Baha'i, and often persecuted. The Baha'i are particularly viewed as heretics. They are also resented politically, as many were close to or worked for the monarchy.

6. The Soviet Union and Britain invaded Iran in 1941 and forced Reza Shah to abdicate in favor of his twenty-two-year-old son. Reza Shah Pahlavi fled to South Africa, where he died three years later.

7. Akbar Ganji, *Republican Manifesto,* Sept. 2, 2002.

8. Akbar Ganji, *Republican Manifesto II,* May 30, 2005.

9. Akbar Ganji, "Second Letter to the Free people of the World," July 10, 2005.

10. Akbar Ganji, "Letter to America," *The Washington Post,* Sept. 21, 2006.

CHAPTER EIGHT: IRAN: THE REACTIONARIES

1. Robin Wright, *In the Name of God: The Khomeini Decade* (New York: Simon & Schuster, 1989), p. 227.

2. "Abolishing the Ruling Islamic Party: Why and for Whose Sake? *The Middle East Reporter,* July 11, 1987, pp 13–15.

3. Cheryl Benard and Zalmay Khalilzad, *The Government of God: Iran's Islamic Republic* (New York: Columbia University Press, 1984), p. 110.

4. Shaul Bakhash, *The Reign of the Ayatollahs: Iran and the Islamic Revolution* (New York: Basic Books 1989), p. 75.

5. "Chronology," *Middle East Journal,* vol. 36, no. 1, Winter 1982, p. 75.

6. Among the Web sites collecting these are http://www.khamenei.de and http://www.khamenei.ir.

7. Youssef M. Ibrahim, "Montazeri's Evolution: An Heir Is Gone," *The New York Times,* Apr. 2, 1989.

8. Patrick E. Tyler, "Ten Days of Dawn, Ten Years of Struggle," *The Washington Post,* Feb. 2, 1989.

9. "Ayatollah Khomeini's Criticism of the Government," *The Echo of Iran,* Oct. 18, 1988, p. 9.

10. The fatwa, read on Tehran Radio afternoon news, also called for the death of all those involved in the book's publication. "I call on zealous Muslims to promptly execute them on the spot they find them, so that no one else will dare to blaspheme Muslim sanctities," his fatwa declared.

11. Elaine Sciolino, "Montazeri, Khomeini's Designated Successor in Iran, Quits Under Pressure," *The New York Times,* Mar. 29, 1989.

12. Nazenin Ansari, "An Ayatollah Under Siege in Tehran," *Open Democracy,* Oct. 4, 2006; and Nazila Fathi, "Iran Arrests Outspoken Cleric Who Opposes Religious Rule," *The New York Times,* Oct. 9, 2006.

13. Nazila Fathi, "Qum Journal: Where the Austerity of Islam Yields to a Yen for Chic," *The New York Times,* June 7, 2005.

14. Shaul Bakhash, "Iran's Unlikely President," *The New York Review of Books,* vol. 45, no. 17, Nov. 5, 1998.

15. Neil MacFarquhar, "Iran Leader Vows to Enact Reforms in His Second Term," *The New York Times,* Aug. 9, 2001.

16. "Khatami Threatens Resignation over Power Struggle with Hard-Liners: Move Comes in Response to Widespread Dissatisfaction," *The Daily Star,* July 14, 2003.

17. Joe Klein, "Who Is Winning the Fight for Iran's Future?" *The New Yorker,* Feb. 18–25, 2002.

18. Karl Vick, "Iranian Elections Marked by Secular Messages, Apathy," *The Washington Post,* June 15, 2005.

19. Naysan Rafati, "Iran's President Election: The Candidates Speak," The Washington Institute for Near East Policy, June 23, 2005.

20. Shaul Bakhash, "Reading Jefferson in Tehran," *The Washington Post,* Aug. 13, 2006.

21. "Iran's Revolutionary Manager: Ahmadinejad in His Own Words," Agence France Presse, June 25, 2005.

22. Michael Slackman, "Winner in Iran Calls for Unity; Reformists Reel," *The New York Times,* June 26, 2005.

23. Shaul Bakhash, "Iran's Unlikely President," *The New York Review of Books,* vol. 45, no. 17, Nov. 5, 1998.

24. Nasser Karimi, "Iran's President Bans Western Music on Radio and Television," Associated Press, Dec. 19, 2005.

25. "Iran's Revolutionary Manager: Ahmadinejad in his own words," Agence France Presse, June 25, 2005.

26. Karl Vick, "A Man of the People's Needs and Wants; Ahmadinejad Praised in Iran as Caring Leader," *The Washington Post*, June 3, 2006.

27. Neil MacFarquar, "Iran's New Ideal: Small Families," *International Herald Tribune*, Sept. 9, 2006.

28. Anthony Shadid, "Iran's Population Program Cited as a Model," *Associated Press*, Feb. 6, 1995.

29. Robert Tait, "Ahmadinejad Urges Iranian Baby Boom to Challenge West," *The Guardian*, Oct. 23, 2006.

30. Ibid.

31. www.ahmadinejad.ir/en/autobiography.

32. Robin Wright, "Chemical Arms' Effects Linger Long After War," *Los Angeles Times*, Nov. 19, 2002.

33. Robin Wright, "Years After Exposure, Germ Warfare Victims Deteriorate," *Los Angeles Times*, Nov. 27, 2002. In a declassified report, the CIA estimated in 1991 that Iran suffered more than 50,000 casualties, including untold thousands of deaths, from Iraq's use of several chemical weapons. But Iran claims the tally has since soared as both troops and civilians have developed the telltale symptoms up to fifteen years later because low-dose exposure deferred physical deterioration or collapse.

34. Brenda Shaffer, "Iran at the Nuclear Threshold," *Arms Control Today*, November 2003; and interview with Robert Einhorn, former State Department Assistant Secretary for Nonproliferation, Apr. 9, 2007.

35. Ali Akbar Dareini, "Iran Issues New Bank Note with Nuclear Symbol, Amid Standoff with the West," Associated Press, Mar. 12, 2007.

36. http://www.ahmadinejad.ir

37. John Daniszewski, "Iran's Runner-Up Puts Fundamentalists in the Race," *Los Angeles Times*, June 21, 2005.

38. Paul Hughes, "Iran President Paves the Way for Arabs' Imam Return," *Reuters*, Nov. 17, 2005.

39. Interview with Kenneth Katzman, March 2007; and Kenneth Katzman, *The Warriors of Islam: Iran's Revolutionary Guards* (Boulder, Colo.: Westview Press, 1993).

40. Anthony Cordesman and Martin Kleiber, *Iran's Assymetric Warfighting Capabilities* (Washington, D.C.: Center for Strategic and International Affairs, 2007).

41. Ibid.

42. "Quds Force: Iranian Regime's Instrument for Extraterritorial Terror Activities," National Council of Resistance of Iran, Dec. 26, 2006, http://www.ncr-iran.org/content/view/2686/69.

43. Anthony Cordesman and Martin Kleiber, *Iran's Assymetric Warfighting Capabilities*. Washington, D.C.: Center for Strategic and International Affairs. 2007.

CHAPTER NINE: MOROCCO: THE COMPROMISES

1. Thomas Carothers, "The 'Sequencing' Fallacy: How Democracies Emerge," *Journal of Democracy*, vol. 18, no. 1, Jan. 2007.

2. Hitler actually never won more than forty-four percent in popular elections. He came to power through coalitions.

3. "Human Rights in Morocco," press conference of Driss Benzekri, National Press Club, Washington D.C., Jan. 19, 2006.

4. Geoff Pingree and Lisa Abend, "Morocco Moves Gradually to Address Past Repression," *The Christian Science Monitor*, Sept. 23, 2005.

5. "Gradual Reform in Morocco," *The Economist*, Aug. 7, 2004.

6. Marina Ottaway, "Morocco: From Top-down Reform to Democratic Transition?" Carnegie Paper Middle East Series No. 71, Carnegie Endowment for International Peace, Oct. 2006.

7. Charles Levinson, "Letter from Rabat," MEIonline.com, Sept. 15, 2005.

8. Scott MacLeod, "Whatever I Do, It Will Never Be Good Enough," *Time Europe*, vol. 155, no. 15, June 26, 2000.

9. "Human Rights after the Casablanca Bombings," Human Rights Watch, Oct. 2004.

10. Dana Priest, "CIA Holds Terror Suspects in Secret Prisons: Debate Is Growing Within Agency About Legality and Morality of Overseas System Set Up After 9/11," *The Washington Post,* Nov. 2, 2005.

11. "Morocco: Counter-terror Crackdown Sets Back Rights Progress," Human Rights Watch, Oct. 21, 2004.

12. Fatima Mernissi, *Dreams of Trespass: Tales of a Harem Girlhood* (New York: Basic Books, 1994), p. 78.

13. Ibid., p. 22.

14. Translations of the Koran vary (as do translations of the Bible). The authorized English translation of Sura (or chapter) 41, verse 34 reads: "Not equal is the good response and the bad response. You shall resort to the nicest possible response. Thus, the one who used to be your enemy may become your best friend."

15. Fatima Mernissi, *Dreams of Trespass* pp. 118–19.

16. Ibid., pp. 200–1.

17. Ted Thornton, "Qasim Amin," *History of the Middle East Database,* Aug. 7, 2006; and Susan Muaddi Darraj, "Understanding the Other Sister: The Case of Arab Feminism," *Monthly Review,* vol. 53, no. 10, Mar. 2002.

18. Fatima Mernissi, *The Veil and the Male Elite: A Feminist's Interpretation of Women's Rights in Islam* (Cambridge, Mass.: Perseus Books, 1987), p. 102.

19. Fatima Mernissi, *Women and Islam: An Historical and Theological Enquiry* (Malden, Mass.: Blackwell, 1991).

20. *The Arab Human Development Report 2005* (New York: The United Nations, Dec. 2006), pp. 9, 106–7.

21. Ibid., pp. 7–8, 72–83, 305–7. In contrast, only thirty-eight percent of Moroccan men are illiterate.

22. Iman Ghazalla, *Sculpting the Rock of Women's Rights: The Role of Women's Organizations in Promoting the National Plan of Action To Integrate Women in Development in Morocco* (Minneapolis: University of Minnesota Hubert H. Humphrey Institute of Public Affairs, 2001).

23. "Morocco Gets First Women Preachers," Agence France Press, Apr. 28, 2006.

24. Rabea Naciri, "Morocco," in *Women's Rights in the Middle East and North Africa: Citizenship and Justice,* Sameena Nazir and Leigh Tomppert, eds. (New York: Freedom House, 2005).

25. "Morocco: Hidden Child Workers Face Abuse: Girls Working as Domestics Denied Basic Rights." Human Rights Watch, Dec. 20. 2005.

26. Middle East Policy Council, Capitol Hill Conference Series on U.S. Middle East Policy, Hart Senate Office Building, Apr. 22, 2005.

27. Rachid Idrissi Kaitouni, "The Moroccan Parliamentary System," 107th Interparliamentary Conference, Marrakech, Mar. 17–23, 2002.

28. Roula Khalaf, "Morocco Sees the Rise of 'Acceptable' Islamist Party, *The Financial Times,* May 23, 2006.

29. Saadeddine Othmani, "Islamist Political Parties and Winning the Challenge of Democratic Reform," Paper delivered at the 2006 annual conference of the Center for the Study of Islam and Democracy, Washington, D.C., May 5, 2006.

30. "Islamic Extremism: Common Concern for Muslim and Western Publics: Support for Terror Wanes Among Muslim Publics," Pew Research Center Global Survey, July 14, 2005.

31. "Landmarks in the Party's History," on the Justice and Development Party Web site, http://www.pjd.ma.

32. Saadeddine Othmani, "Islamist Political Parties."

33. "In the Spotlight: Moroccan Combatant Group," Center for Defense Information, May 21, 2004; "Fighting Back: The Hunt for Terrorists in Spain and France," *The Economist,* Apr. 7, 2004; and Peter Finn and Keith B. Richburg, "Madrid Probe Turns to Islamic Cell in Morocco," *The Washington Post,* Mar. 20, 2004.

34. Marina Ottaway, "Morocco: From Top-down Reform to Democratic Transition?" Carnegie Paper, Middle East Series, no. 71, Carnegie Endowment for International Peace, Oct. 2006.

35. Bruce Maddy-Weitzman, "Islamism, Moroccan Style: The Ideas of Sheikh Yassine," *Middle East Quarterly,* vol. 10, no. 1, Winter 2003.

36. Geoff Pingree and Lisa Abend, "Morocco's Rising Islamist Challenge," *The Christian Science Monitor,* Nov. 23, 2005.

CHAPTER TEN: IRAQ AND THE UNITED STATES: THE FURIES

1. Joshua Landis, "Riad al Turk Interview: 11 March 2005," www.syriacomment.com, Mar. 19, 2005.

2. BBC interview by Lise Doucet, Aug. 8, 2006.

3. Country studies, *CIA Factbook.*

4. "Whatever Happened to the Iraqi Kurds?" Human Rights Watch, Mar. 11, 1991.

5. Saddam's intervention also forced the United States to abandon a large CIA covert operation supporting an opposition coalition based in Kurdistan.

6. Robin Wright, "Families Are Harassed or Starved Out: A Decree Allows Minorities to Change Their Ethnicity," *Los Angeles Times,* Dec. 3, 2002.

7. Isam al Khafaji, "The Myth of Iraqi Exceptionalism," *Middle East Policy,* vol. 7, no. 4, October 2000; Phoebe Marr, "Comment on Isam al-Khafaji's 'The Myth of Iraqi Exceptionalism,' *Middle East Policy,* vol. 7, no. 4, October 2000; and George Packer, "Dreaming of Democracy," *The New York Times Magazine,* Mar. 2, 2003.

8. Ellen Laipson, "Assessing the Long-Term Challenges," The Stimson Center, www.stimson.org, Sept. 2002.

9. Bill Keller, "The Sunshine Warrior," *The New York Times Magazine,* Sept. 22, 2002.

10. Audrey Gillan, "The Regrets of the Man Who Brought Down Saddam," *The Guardian,* Mar. 19, 2007.

11. Helen Chapin Metz, ed., *A Country Study: Iraq,* Library of Congress, Nov. 8, 2005.

12. Islam was not the only religion in the new Iraq. When the country was carved out of the Ottoman empire, one third of Baghdad was Jewish. Modern Iraq's first finance minister was Jewish, as was much of the symphony orchestra and chamber of commerce. Christian denominations included Assyrians, Chaldeans, and Catholics.

13. Abd el Karim al Uzri, "The Problem of Governance in Iraq," self-published, London, 1991, pp. 2–9; and Ali Allawi, *The Occupation of Iraq: Winning the War, Losing the Peace* (New Haven Conn.: Yale University Press, 2007), p. 17.

14. Ronald L. Kuipers, "Entrance to the Ruins of Babylon," in *A Country Study: Iraq,* Helen Chapin Metz, ed. Library of Congress, May 1988.

15. Ali Allawi, *The Occupation of Iraq,* p. 162.

16. In the most extensive advance planning, a panel of Iraqis organized by the State Department in the Future of Iraq Project recommended that 100,000 soldiers should form the nucleus of a new defensive military force. Special Forces should be adapted for work in counterterrorism, antinarcotics, and peacekeeping. Intelligence units could work with American forces in cleaning up any postwar security problems. Military police could focus on internal vulnerabilities, such as pipeline security. Conscripts could be used for agricultural development, postwar reconstruction, and the serious environmental damage that was part of Saddam's legacy.

17. Mark Fineman, Warren Vieth, and Robin Wright, "Dissolving Iraqi Army Seen by Many as a Costly Move," *Los Angeles Times,* Aug. 24, 2003.

18. Mark Fineman, Robin Wright, and Doyle McManus, "Washington's Battle Plan: Preparing for War, Stumbling to Peace, *Los Angeles Times,* July 18, 2003.

19. Council on Foreign Relations, Washington, D.C., Apr. 10, 2007.

20. Mark Fineman, Warren Vieth, and Robin Wright, "Dissolving Iraqi Army Seen by Many as a Costly Move."

21. Ibid.

22. Council on Foreign Relations.

23. "Iraq War, the Notable Quotes, Reuters, Mar. 8, 2007.

24. Ali Allawi, *The Occupation of Iraq,* p. 393.

25. The shrine was also one of the places where Shiites believe the twelfth and final imam, the Mahdi, went into occultation, or hiding, to return before the Day of Judgment to deliver perfect justice.

26. Nancy A. Youssef, "These Tatoos Aren't Artful—They Help Identify Iraq's Dead," McClatchy Newspapers, Nov. 1, 2006.

27. Leila Fadel and Mohammed al Dulaimy, "Violence, Fear Pervade Once-Vibrant Baghdad," McClatchy Newspapers, Mar. 18, 2007.

28. Ali Allawi, *The Occupation of Iraq,* p. 457.

29. Ibid., pp. 459–60.

30. Ibid.

31. Audrey Gillan, "The Regrets of the Man Who Brought Down Saddam," *The Guardian,* Mar. 19, 2007.

32. Vanessa Arrington, "Iraqi Political Cartoonists, Free from Fear of Saddam, Now Face Death Threats from Extremists," Associated Press, May 13, 2006.

33. Cameron W. Barr, and Jon Cohen, "Poll Shows Iraqis Feel Quality of Life Has Plunged," *The Washington Post,* Mar. 19, 2007.

34. Solomon Moore, "A Battlefield Called School: Iraq Violence Threatens Teachers and Students: Campuses are Closing," *Los Angeles Times,* Dec. 16, 2006.

35. "A Look at the Iraqi Refugee Situation," Associated Press, Feb. 12, 2007; and Hamza Hendawi, "Iraq War Spawns a Growing Refugee Problem for Its Neighbors," Associated Press, Feb. 4, 2007.

36. Karin Brulliard, "Iraq Reimposes Freeze on Medical Diplomas in Bid to Keep Doctors," *The Washington Post,* May 5, 2007.

37. Christian Berthesen, "Study: One-third of Iraqis Live in Poverty," *Los Angeles Times,* Feb. 19, 2007; and "Iraq: Unemployment and Violence Increase Poverty," UN Office for the Coordination of Humanitarian Affairs, Oct. 17, 2006.

38. At its peak in the 1970s, the country with the world's third-largest oil reserves produced 3.7 million barrels per day. Production varied, but on the war's fourth anniversary, it produced just over half that—about 2.1 million barrels per day.

39. Charles J. Hanley, "Bush Plan's $1 Billion in Aid Would Make Small Dent in Iraq's Needs," Associated Press, Jan. 14, 2007.

40. Cameron W. Barr, and Jon Cohen, "Poll Shows Iraqis Feel Quality of Life Has Plunged," *The Washington Post,* Mar. 19, 2007.

41. "Key Figures About Iraq Since the War Began in March 2003," Associated Press, Mar. 1, 2007.

42. Laith Hammoudi, "Traditional Mud Oven Makes a Comeback in Iraq," McClatchy Newspapers, Mar. 8, 2007.

43. John F. Burns, "U.S. Finds Insurgency Has Funds to Sustain Itself," *The New York Times,* Nov. 26, 2006.

44. Hamza Hendawi, "Egyptian Activists Turn from Democracy Campaign to Bitterness at Israel and the U.S.," Associated Press, Sept. 14, 2006.

45. Capitol Hill Conference Series on U.S. Middle East Policy, Hart Senate Office Buildling, Apr. 22, 2005. The poll was conducted by Zogby International and Shibley Telhami, who holds the Anwar Sadat Chair of Peace and Development at the University of Maryland and is a fellow at the Brookings Institution's Saban Center for Middle East Policy.

46. Carol Giacomo, "Polls Show Arabs Dislike Bush, See U.S. as a Threat," Reuters, Feb. 8, 2007.

47. "Kuwait Marchers Slam Lebanon War, Back Hezbollah," Reuters, Aug. 7, 2006.

48. The twenty-five countries were Argentina, Australia, Brazil, Chile, China, Egypt, France, Germany, Great Britain, Hungary, India, Indonesia, Italy, Kenya, Lebanon, Mexico, Nigeria, the Philippines, Poland, Portugal, Russia, South Korea, Turkey, the United Arab Emirates, and the United States.

49. Keith Sullivan, "Worldwide Poll Shows Most Dislike U.S. Policy," *The Washington Post,* Jan. 22, 2007.

50. Rami Khouri, "The Great Arab Unraveling," *The Jordan Times,* Mar. 2, 2007.

BIBLIOGRAPHY

ARTICLES AND REPORTS

Abaza, Khairi. "Presidential Elections in Egypt: The Day After." Washington Institute of Near East Policy, Sept. 8, 2005.

———. "Reform Prospects During Mubarak's Fifth Term." Washington Institute of Near East Policy, Sept. 26, 2005.

Adams, Gordon. "Prime Numbers: Iraq's Sticker Shock." *Foreign Policy,* no. 159, Mar.–Apr. 2007.

Aita, Samir. "Syria: What Reforms While a Storm is Building." Arab Reform Initiative Brief, no. 6, Apr. 2006.

Aly, Abdel Monem Said. "Prelude to Change: Egyptian Democratization, 2005." Brandeis University Crown Center for Middle East Studies, Middle East Brief, no. 2, Jan. 2006.

Anderson, Jon Lee. "Letter from Beirut: The Battle for Lebanon." *The New Yorker,* Aug. 7 and 14, 2006.

———. "Letter from Iraq: Out on the Street." *The New Yorker,* Nov. 15, 2004.

Altman, Israel Elad. "Democracy, Elections and the Muslim Brotherhood," in *Current Trends in Islamist Ideology,* vol. 3. Hudson Institute, Feb. 16, 2006.

Amuzegar, Jahangir. "Khatami: A Folk Hero in Search of Relevance." Middle East Policy, vol. 11, no. 2, June 22, 2004.

"A Discussion with Yasser Arafat," *Journal of Palestine Studies,* vol. 11, no. 2, Winter 1982, pp. 3–15.

Bakhash, Shaul. "Letter from Evin Prison." *The New York Review of Books,* Sept. 22, 2005.

Baram, Amatzia. "Who Wins in Iraq: Israel." *Foreign Policy,* no. 159, Mar.–Apr. 2007.

Barsalou, Judy. "Islamists at the Ballot Box: Findings from Egypt, Jordan, Kuwait, and Turkey." United States Institute of Peace, Special Report No. 144, July 2005.

Bennet, James. "The Enigma of Damascus." *The New York Times Magazine,* July 10, 2005.

Bronner, Ethan. "Living with the Palestinian Catastrophe." *The New York Times,* Apr. 23, 1998.

Brown, Nathan J. "Requiem for Palestinian Reform: Clear Lessons from a Troubled Record." Carnegie Papers Middle East Series No. 81, Democracy and Rule of Law Project, Carnegie Endowment for International Peace, Feb. 2007.

———. "Aftermath of the Hamas Tsunami." Carnegie Endowment for International Peace, Policy Outlook, Feb. 2006.

————. "Evaluating Palestinian Reform." Carnegie Papers Middle East Series No. 59, Democracy and Rule of Law Program, Carnegie Endowment for International Peace, June 2005.

Brown, Nathan J., and Hesham Nasr. "Egypt's Judges Step Forward." Carnegie Endowment for International Peace Policy Outlook, Democracy and Rule of Law Project, May 2005.

Brown, Nathan J., Amr Hamzawy, and Marina Ottaway. "Islamist Movements and the Democratic Process in the Arab World: Exploring the Gray Zones." Carnegie Papers Middle East Series No. 67, joint publication of the Carnegie Endowment for International Peace and the Herbert Quandt Stiftung, Mar. 2006.

Brown, Nathan J., and Hesham Nasr. "Egypt's Judges Step Forward." Carnegie Endowment for International Peace Policy Outlook, Democracy and Rule of Law Program, May 2005.

Butko, Thomas. "Unity Through Opposition: Islam as an Instrument of Radical Political Change." *Middle East Review of International Affairs,* vol. 8, no. 4, Dec. 2004.

Byman, Daniel. "Should Hezbollah Be Next?" *Foreign Affairs,* vol. 82, no. 6, Nov.–Dec. 2003.

————. "Who Wins in Iraq: Al Qaeda." *Foreign Policy,* no. 159, Mar.–Apr. 2007.

Carothers, Thomas. "The 'Sequencing' Fallacy: How Democracies Emerge." *Journal of Democracy,* vol. 18, no. 1, Jan. 2007.

Choucair, Julia. "Lebanon: Finding a Path from Deadlock to Democracy." Carnegie Papers Middle East Series No. 64, Carnegie Endowment for International Peace, Jan. 2006.

Ciezadlo, Annia. "Beirut Dispatch: Sheik Up." *The New Republic,* Aug. 7, 2006.

Cobban, Helena. "Hizbullah's New Face: In Search of a Muslim Democracy." *Boston Review,* Apr.–May 2005.

Cole, Juan. "A Shiite Crescent? The Regional Impact of the Iraq War." *Current History,* Jan. 2006.

Coleman, Isobel. "The Pay-off from Women's Rights." *Foreign Affairs,* vol. 83, no. 3, May–June 2004.

————. "Women, Islam and the New Iraq." *Foreign Affairs,* vol. 85, no. 1, Jan.–Feb. 2006.

Cordesman, Anthony H. "Lebanese Security and the Hezbollah." Center for Strategic and International Studies, July 15, 2006.

————. "Preliminary Lessons of the Israeli-Hezbollah War." Center for Strategic and International Studies, Aug. 16, 2006.

————. "A Visit to the Israeli-Lebanese Front: Lessons of the War and Prospects for Peace and Future Fighting." Center for Strategic and International Studies, Aug. 17, 2006.

————. "Reconstruction in Iraq: The Uncertain Way Ahead." Center for Strategic and International Studies, Feb. 7, 2007.

————. "Contrasting the New NIE on Iraq with the Assumptions in the New Bush Strategy." Center for Strategic and International Studies, Feb. 2, 2007.

————. "The Impact of the Iraqi Election." Center for Strategic and International Studies, Dec. 31, 2005.

————. "US Strategy in Iraq: 'Losing' While 'Winning'?" Center for Strategic and International Studies, Feb. 1, 2007.

————. "The New Bush Strategy in Iraq: The Details and the Risks." Center for Strategic and International Studies, Jan. 12, 2007.

Danner, Mark. "Iraq: The War of Imagination." *The New York Review of Books,* vol. 53, no. 20, Dec. 21, 2006.

Darraj, Susan Muaddi. "Understanding the Other Sister: The Case of Arab Feminism." *Monthly Review,* vol. 53, no. 10, Mar. 2002.

de Bellaigue, Christopher. "Defiant Iran." *The New York Review of Books,* vol. 53, no. 17, Nov. 2, 2006.

Eisenstadt, Michael, and Jeffrey White. "Assessing Iraq's Sunni Arab Insurgency." Washington Institute for Near East Policy, Policy Focus No. 50, Dec. 2005.

El-Hokayem, Emile. "Hizbollah and Syria: Outgrowing the Proxy Relationship." Center for Strategic and International Affairs, *The Washington Quarterly,* vol. 30, no. 2, Spring 2007.

Emmott, Bill. "Who Wins in Iraq: The Price of Oil." *Foreign Policy,* no. 159, Mar.–Apr. 2007.

Fearon, James D. "Iraq's Civil War." *Foreign Affairs,* vol. 86, no. 2, Mar.–Apr. 2007.

Frum, David. "Who Wins in Iraq: Samuel Huntington." *Foreign Policy,* no. 159, Mar.–Apr. 2007.

Gambill, Gary C., and Ziad K. Abdelnour. "Hezbollah: Between Tehran and Damascus." *Middle East Intelligence Bulletin,* vol. 4, no. 2, Feb. 2002.

———. "The Counter-revolution of the Cedars." *Mideast Monitor,* vol. 1, no. 2, Apr.–May 2006.

Ganji, Akbar. "Republican Manifesto: A Model for a Way Out of a Political Dead End." *Nimruz* and http://freeganji.blogspot, Sept. 9, 2002.

———. "Republican Manifesto II." http://freeganji.blogspot, May 30, 2005.

Gause, Gregory F., III. "Can Democracy Stop Terrorism?" *Foreign Affairs,* vol. 84, no. 5, Sept.–Oct. 2005.

Gavrilis, George. "The Forgotten West Bank." *Foreign Affairs,* vol. 85, no. 1, Jan.–Feb. 2006, pp. 66–76.

Ghazalla, Iman. "Sculpting the Rock of Women's Rights: The Role of Women's Organizations in Promoting the National Plan of Action to Integrate Women in Development in Morocco." University of Minnesota, Hubert H. Humphrey Institute of Public Affairs, 2001.

Glass, Charles. "Is Syria Next?" *London Review of Books,* vol. 25, no. 14, July 24, 2003.

Goldberg, Jeffrey. "In the Party of God, Part One: Are Terrorists in Lebanon Preparing for a Larger War?" *The New Yorker,* Oct. 14, 2002.

———. "In the Party of God, Part Two: Hezbollah Sets Up Operations in South America and the United States." *The New Yorker,* Oct. 21, 2002.

———. "From Peace Process To Police Process." *The New York Times Magazine,* Sept. 14, 1997.

Haass, Richard. "The New Middle East." *Foreign Affairs,* vol. 85, no. 6, Nov.–Dec. 2006.

Hamzawy, Amr. "The Key to Arab Reform: Moderate Islamists." Carnegie Endowment for International Peace, Policy Brief No. 40, August 2005.

———. "Opposition in Egypt." Carnegie Endowment for International Peace, Democracy and Rule of Law Project, Policy Outlook, Oct. 2005.

Hamzawy, Amr, and Nathan J. Brown. "Can Egypt's Troubled Elections Produce a More Democratic Future?" Carnegie Endowment for International Peace, Democracy and Rule of Law Project, Policy Outlook, December 2005.

Hamzawy, Amr, Marina Ottaway, and Nathan J. Brown. "What Islamists Need to Be Clear About: The Case of the Egyptian Muslim Brotherhood." Carnegie Endowment for International Peace, Democracy and Rule of Law Program, Policy Outlook, Feb. 2007.

Henderson, Simion. "Women in Gulf Politics: A Progress Report." Washington Institute for Near East Policy, June 28, 2005.

Hersh, Seymour M. "Annals of National Security: The Redirection." *The New Yorker,* Mar. 5, 2007.

Howeidy, Amira. "Politics in God's Name. *Al-Ahram Weekly,* no. 247, Nov. 16–22, 1995.

Human Rights Watch. "Egypt: Election Offers Public Debate, Not Free Choice." Sept. 2, 2005.

———. "Morocco: After Truth Commission, End Impunity." Nov. 28, 2005.

———. "Morocco: Convictions Show Limits on Press Freedom." May 9, 2006.

———. "Morocco: Hidden Child Workers Face Abuse: Girls Working as Domestics Denied Basic Rights." Dec. 20, 2005.

———. "Morocco: Counter-Terror Crackdown Sets Back Rights Progress." Oct. 21, 2004.

———. "Morocco: Human Rights after the Casablanca Bombings." Vol. 16, no. 6(E), October 2004.

———. "Morocco: Human Rights at a Crossroads." Oct. 21, 2004.

Ibrahim, Anwar. "Universal Democracy and MuslimValues." *Journal of Democracy,* vol. 17, no. 3, July 2006.

Ibrahim, Saad Eddin. "An Islamic Alternative in Egypt: The Muslim Brotherhood and Sadat." *Arab Studies Quarterly,* no. 4, 1982, pp. 75–93.

International Crisis Group. "After Mecca: Engaging Hamas." Middle East Report No. 62, Feb. 28, 2007.

———. "Enter Hamas: The Challenges of Political Integration." Middle East Report No. 49, Jan. 18, 2006.

———. "Lebanon: Managing the Gathering Storm," Report No. 48. Released in Amman and Brussels, Dec. 5, 2005.

———. "Palestinian Refugees and the Politics of Peacemaking." Middle East Report No. 22, released in Amman and Brussels, Feb. 5, 2004

———. "Reforming Egypt: In Search of a Strategy," Report No. 46. Released in Brussels and Cairo, Oct. 4, 2005.

———. "Understanding Islamism." Middle East/North Africa Report No. 37, Mar. 2, 2005.

Jorisch, Avi. "Al-Manar: Hizbullah TV 24/7." *Middle East Quarterly,* vol. 11, no. 1, Winter 2004.

Karmon, Ely. "Fight on All Fronts: Hizballah, the War on Terror, and the War in Iraq." Washington D.C.: Washington Institute for Near East Policy, 2003.

———. "The U.S. Indictment of Palestinian Islamic Jihad Militants: The Iranian Connection." Washington D.C.: Washington Institute for Near East Policy, Policy Watch No. 718, March 3, 2003.

Khouri, Rami G. "Islamist Democrats." Agence Global, Dec. 10, 2005.

Kitfield, James. "The Decline Begins." *The National Journal,* May 18, 2007.

Kodmani, Bassma. "The Dangers of Political Exclusion: Egypt's Islamist Problem." Carnegie Paper Middle East Series No. 63, Democracy and Rule of Law Project, Carnegie Endowment for International Peace, October 2005.

Kramer, Jane. "Letter from Morocco: The Crusader." *The New Yorker,* Oct. 16, 2006.

Maddy-Weitzman, Bruce. "Islamism, Moroccan Style: The Ideas of Sheikh Yassine." *Middle East Quarterly,* vol. 10, no. 1, Winter 2003.

Makiya, Kanan. "Iraq's Democratic Prospects." Foreign Policy Research Institute, June 7, 2006.

Malka, Haim. "Forcing Choices: Testing the Transformation of Hamas." *Washington Quarterly,* Autumn 2005, pp. 37–54.

Marr, Phebe. "Democracy in the Rough." *Current History,* Jan. 2006.

Malley, Robert. "A New Middle East." *The New York Review of Books,* Sept. 21, 2006.

Moroccan Equity and Reconciliation Commission. "Summary of the Findings of the Final Report," Kingdom of Morocco, Dec. 2005.

Munson, Ziad. "Islamic Mobilization: Social Movement Theory and the Egyptian Muslim Brotherhood." *The Sociological Quarterly,* vol. 42, no. 4, Fall 2001, pp. 487–510.

Muravchik, Joshua. "And the Walls Came Tumbling Down." *The American Enterprise,* vol. 16, no. 3, Apr.–May 2005.

Murphy, Brian. "Hamas' Participation in Palestinian Elections Challenges Militants to Be Democrats." Associated Press, Oct. 9, 2005.

Nasr, Vali. "When the Shiites Rise." *Foreign Affairs,* vol. 85, no. 4, July–Aug. 2006.

———. "Who Wins in Iraq: Iran." *Foreign Policy,* no. 159, Mar.–Apr. 2007.

Noe, Nicholas. "The Relationship between Hizbullah & the United States in Light of the Current Situation in the Middle East." Master of Philosophy Thesis, Cambridge University Centre for International Studies, July 2006.

Norton, Augustus Richard. "Hizballah and the Israeli Withdrawal from Southern Lebanon." *Journal of Palestine Studies,* vol. 30, no. 1, Autumn 2000, pp. 22–35.

———. "Hizballah: From Radicalism to Pragmatism?" *Middle East Policy Council Journal,* vol. 5, no. 4, Jan. 1998.

———. "Hizballah of Lebanon: Extremist Ideals vs. Mundane Politics." New York: Council on Foreign Relations, Muslim Politics Project, 1999.

———. "Walking Between Raindrops: Hizballah in Lebanon," *Mediterranean Politics,* vol. 3, no. 1, pp. 81–102.

Othmani, Saadeddine. "Islamist Political Parties and Winning the Challenge of Democratic Reform." Paper delivered at the 2006 annual conference of Center for the Study of Islam and Democracy, Washington, D.C., May 5, 2006.

Ottaway, Marina. "Evaluating Middle East Reform: How Do We Know When It Is Significant?" Carnegie Papers Middle East Series No. 56, Carnegie Endowment for International Peace, Feb. 2005.

———. "Morocco: From Top-down Reform to Democratic Transition?" Carnegie Papers Middle East Series No. 71, Carnegie Endowment for International Peace, Oct. 2006.

———. "Who Wins in Iraq: Arab Dictators." *Foreign Policy,* no. 159, Mar.–Apr. 2007.

Pargeter, Alison. "The Islamist Movement in Morocco." *Terrorism Monitor,* vol. 3, no. 10, May 19, 2005.

Remnick, David. "Letter from the West Bank: The Democracy Game." *The New Yorker,* Feb. 27, 2006.

Saad-Ghorayeb, Amal. "Hizbollah's Outlook in the Current Conflict, Part One: Motives, Strategy, Objectives." Carnegie Endowment for International Peace Middle East Program, Policy Outlook, Aug. 2006.

———. "Hizbollah's Outlook in the Current Conflict, Part Two: Accommodating Diplomacy and Preparing for the Postwar Context." Carnegie Endowment for International Peace Middle East Program, Policy Outlook, Aug. 2006.

Safa, Oussama, "Getting to Arab Democracy: Lebanon Springs Forward." *Journal of Democracy,* vol. 17, no. 1, Jan. 2006, pp. 22–37.

Salem, Paul. "The Future of Lebanon." *Foreign Affairs,* Nov.–Dec. 2006.

Samii, Abbas William. "Shiites in Lebanon: The Key to Democracy." *Middle East Policy,* vol. 13, no. 2, Summer 2006, pp. 30–37.

Samuels, David. "In a Ruined Counry: How Yasir Arafat Destroyed Palestine." *The Atlantic Monthly,* Sept. 2005.

Schenker, David, ed. "Countering Islamists at the Ballot Box." Washington Institute for Near East Policy, Policy Focus No. 61, Nov. 2006.

Shanahan, Rodger. "Hizballah Rising: The Political Battle for the Loyalty of the Shi'a of Lebanon." *Middle East Review of International Affairs,* vol. 9, no. 1, Mar. 2005.

Shikaki, Khalil. "The Future of Palestine." *Foreign Affairs,* vol. 83, no. 6, Nov.–Dec. 2004.

———. "Palestinians Divided." *Foreign Affairs,* vol. 81, no. 1, Jan.–Feb. 2002.

———. "The Palestinian Electorate: Islamists Are More Capable of Leading the Reform and State Building Process." Arab Reform Initiative Brief, Mar. 12, 2006.

———. "The Politics of Paralysis II: Peace Now or Hamas Later." *Foreign Affairs,* vol. 77, no. 4, July–Aug. 1998.

———. "Willing to Compromise: Palestinian Public Opinion and the Peace Process." United States Institute of Peace Special Report 158, Jan. 2006.

Sobelman, Daniel. "Four Years After the Withdrawal from Lebanon: Refining the Rules of the Game." Jaffee Center for Strategic Studies Strategic Assessment, vol. 7, no. 2, Aug. 2004.

———. "Hizbollah After the Syrian Withdrawal." Jaffee Center for Stratgic Studies Strategic Assessment, vol. 8, no. 1, Aug. 2005.

———. "Two Years After the Withdrawal—A Compromise, Interests, and Exigencies." Jaffee Center for Strategic Studies Strategic Assessment, vol. 5, no. 2, Aug. 2002.

Takeyh, Ray. "Time for Détente with Iran." *Foreign Affairs,* vol. 86, no. 2, Mar.–Apr. 2007.

United States Institute of Peace. "Arab Media: Tools of the Governments? Tools for the People?" Virtual Diplomacy Series No. 18, Apr. 12, 2005.

Walsh, John. "Egypt's Muslim Brotherhood: Understanding Centrist Islam," in Perspectives on the United States: A Splintered Mirror. Harvard International Review, vol. 24, Winter 2003.

Wegner, Eva. "Morocco: PJD Works at Being New and Different." Carnegie Endowment for International Peace, *Arab Reform Bulletin,* vol. 4, no. 3, Apr. 2006.

Wittes, Tamara Cofman. "The Promise of Arab Liberalism." *Policy Review,* July 2004.

Wright, Robin. "Iran's Greatest Political Challenge: Abdol Karim Soroush." *World Policy Journal,* Summer 1997.

———. "Iran's New Revolution." *Foreign Affairs,* vol. 78, no. 1, Jan.–Feb. 2000.

———. "Islam and Liberal Democracy: Two Visions of Reformation." *Journal of Democracy,* April 1996, pp. *64–75*

———. "Letter from Teheran: We Invite the Hostages to Return." *The New Yorker,* Nov. 8, 1999.

Yaghi, Mohammad, and Ben Fishman. "The Consequences of Fatah's Chaotic Primaries." The Washington Institute for Near East Policy, Special Report on the Arab-Israeli Peace Process, Dec. 6, 2005.

————. "Fatah's Primary Results: Lessons from the First Round." The Washington Institute for Near East Policy, Special Report on the Arab-Israeli Peace Process, Nov. 29, 2005.

Zakheim, Dov. S. "Blending Democracy: The Generational Project in the Middle East." *The National Interest,* Fall 2005.

Zelikow, Philip. "Saudi Arabia, the United States and Political Reform in the Arab World." Keynote address, Center for Strategic and International Studies, Washington, D.C., May 24, 2005.

BOOKS

Abdo, Geneive. *No God But God: Egypt and the Triumph of Islam.* New York: Oxford University Press, 2000.

Abouzeid, Leila. *Return to Childhood: The Memoir of a Modern Moroccan Woman,* trans. by author with Heather Logan Taylor. Austin: University of Texas Press, 1998.

Abu Amr, Ziad. *Islamic Fundamentalism in the West Bank and Gaza: The Muslim Brotherhood and Islamic Jihad.* Bloomington, Ind.: Indiana University Press, 1994.

Abu Sharif, Bassam, and Uzi Mahnaimi. *Bests of Enemies: The Memoirs of Bassam Abu* Sharif and Uzi Mahnaimi. New York: Little, Brown, 1995.

Ahmed, Leila. *Women and Gender in Islam: Historical Roots of a Modern Debate.* New Haven, Conn.: Yale University Press, 1993.

Ahmed, Rifaat Sayyed. *Rebel from the South: Hassan Nasrallah.* Damascus and Cairo: House of the Arab Book, 2006 [in Arabic].

Ajami, Fouad. *The Foreigner's Gift: The Americans, the Arabs and the Iraqis in Iraq.* New York: Free Press, 2006.

Algar, Hamid. *Islam and Revolution: Writings and Declarations of Imam Khomeini.* Berkeley, Cal.: Mizen Press, 1981.

Allawi, Ali A. *The Occupation of Iraq: Winning the War, Losing the Peace.* New Haven, Conn.: Yale University Press, 2007.

Alterman, Jon, and Haim Malka. *Arab Reform and Foreign Aid: Lessons from Morocco.* Washington, D.C.: Center for Strategic and International Studies, 2006.

Amin, Nasser. *Egypt's Court System: A Study of Court Divisions and Training of Judges.* Cairo: Amin Law Firm, 2004.

Baker, James A., III, and Lee H. Hamilton. *The Iraq Study Group Report.* New York: Vintage Books, 2006.

Benard, Cheryl, and Zalmay Khalilzad. *The Government of God: Iran's Islamic Republic.* New York: Columbia University Press, 1984.

Blanford, Nicholas. *Killing Mr. Lebanon: The Assassination of Rafiq Hariri and Its Impact on the Middle East.* London: I. B. Tauris, 2006.

Byman, Daniel L, and Kenneth M. Pollack. *Things Fall Apart: What Do We Do If Iraq Implodes?* Washington D.C.: Brookings Institution Saban Center, 2006.

Carothers, Thomas. *Critical Mission: Essays on Democracy Promotion.* Washington, D.C.: Carnegie Endowment for International Peace, 2004.

Chandrasekaran, Rajiv. *Imperial Life in the Emerald City: Life in the Green Zone.* New York: Knopf, 2006.

Clawson, Patrick, and Michael Rubin. *Eternal Iran: Continuity and Chaos.* New York: Palgrave Macmillan, 2005.

Cordesman, Anthony, and Martin Kleiber. *Iran's Assymetric Warfighting Capabilities.* Washington, D.C.: Center for Strategic and International Affairs, 2007.

Diamond, Larry. *Squandered Victory: The American Occupation and the Bungled Effort to Bring Democracy to Iraq.* New York: Times Books/Holt, 2005.

Diamond, Larry, Marc F. Plattner, and Daniel Brumberg. *Islam and Democracy in the Middle East.* Baltimore and London: Johns Hopkins University Press, 2003.

Ebadi, Shirin. *Iran Awakening: A Memoir of Revolution and Hope.* New York: Random House, 2006.

Fisk, Robert. *Pity the Nation: The Abduction of Lebanon*. New York: Nation Books, 2002.

Friedman, Thomas L. *From Beirut to Jerusalem*. New York: Farrar, Straus and Giroux, 1989.

Fukuyama, Francis. *America at the Crossroads: Democracy, Power and the Neo-Conservative Legacy*. New Haven, Conn.: Yale University Press, 2006.

Gerecht, Reuel Marc. *The Islamic Paradox: Shiite Clerics, Sunni Fundamentalists and the Coming of Arab Democracy*. Washington, D.C.: American Enterprise Institute Press, 2004.

Gheissari, Ali, and Vali Nasr. *Democracy in Iran: History and the Quest for Liberty*. New York: Oxford University Press, 2006.

Hamzeh, Nizar. *In the Path of Hizbullah*. Syracuse, N.Y.: Syracuse University Press, 2004.

Harik, Judith Palmer. *Hezbollah: The Changing Face of Terrorism*. London: I. B. Tauris, 2005.

Hourani, Albert. *A History of the Arab Peoples*. Cambridge, Mass.: Harvard University Press, 1991.

Howe, Marvine. *Morocco: The Islamist Awakening and Other Challenges*. New York: Oxford University Press, 2005.

Huntington, Samuel. *The Clash of Civilizations and the Remaking of World Order*. New York: Simon & Schuster, 1996.

Jaber, Hala. *Hezbollah, Born with a Vengeance*. New York: Columbia University Press, 1997.

Kaplan, Robert D. *The Coming Anarchy: Shattering the Dreams of the Post Cold War*. New York: Vintage, 2001.

———. *The Ends of the Earth: A Journey at the Dawn of the Twenty-first Century*. New York: Random House, 1997.

Kassir, Samir. *Being Arab*. New York: Verso, 2006.

Katzman, Kenneth. *The Warriors of Islam: Iran's Revolutionary Guards*. Boulder, Colo.: Westview Press, 1993.

Keddie, Nikki. *Women in the Middle East: Past and Present*. Princeton, N.J.: Princeton University Press, 2006.

Kepel, Gilles. *Jihad: The Trail of Political Islam*. Cambridge, Mass.: Harvard University Press, 2002.

———. *Muslim Extremism in Egypt: The Prophet and Pharaoh*. Berkeley, Cal.: University of California Press, 1993.

Kepel, Gilles. *The War for Muslim Minds: Islam and the West*. Cambridge, Mass.: Harvard University Press, 2004.

Laipson, Ellen, and Maureen S. Steinbruner, eds. *Iraq and America: Choices and Consequences*. Washington, D.C.: Henry L. Stimson Center, 2006.

Leverett, Flynt. *Inheriting Syria: Bashar's Trial by Fire*. Washington, D.C.: Brookings Institution Press, 2005.

Levitt, Matthew. *Hamas: Politics, Charity, and Terrorism in the Service of Jihad*. New Haven, Conn.: Yale University Press, 2006.

Lewis, Bernard. *The Crisis of Islam: Holy War and Unholy Terror*. New York: Random House, 2004.

———. *Islam and the West*. New York: Oxford University Press, 1994.

———. *What Went Wrong? The Clash Between Islam and Modernity in the Middle East*. New York: Harper Perennial, 2003.

Mernissi, Fatima. *Beyond the Veil: Male-Female Dynamics in Modern Muslim Society*. Cambridge, Mass.: Schenkman, 1975.

———. *Dreams of Trespass: Tales of a Harem Girlhood*. Reading, Mass.: Addison-Wesley, 1994.

———. *The Veil and the Male Elite: A Feminist Interpretation of Women's Rights in Islam*. Cambridge, Mass.: Perseus Books, 1991.

Munson, Henry. *Religion and Power in Morocco*. New Haven, Conn.: Yale University Press, 1993.

Nazir, Sameena, and Leigh Tomppert, eds. *Women's Rights in the Middle East and North Africa: Citizenship and Justice*. New York: Freedom House, 2005.

Norton, Augustus Richard. *Hezbollah*. Princeton, N.J.: Princeton University Press, 2007.

Pipes, Daniel. *Greater Syria: The History of an Ambition*. New York: Oxford University Press, 1990.

———. *In the Path of God: Islam and Political Power*. New York: Basic Books, 1983.

Pollack, Kenneth M. *The Persian Puzzle: The Conflict between America and Iran.* New York: Random House, 2004.

Rabil, Robert G. *Syria, the United States and the War on Terror in the Middle East.* Westport, Conn.: Praeger Security International, 2006.

Ricks, Thomas E. *Fiasco: The American Military Adventure in Iraq.* New York: Penguin Press, 2006.

Rubin, Barry M. *The Long War for Freedom: The Arab Struggle for Democracy in the Middle East.* Hoboken, N.J.: Wiley, 2006.

Rubin, Michael. *Into the Shadows: Radical Vigilantes in Khatami's Iran.* Washington, D.C.: Washington Institute for Near East Policy, 2001.

Ruthven, Malise. *Fundamentalism: The Search for Meaning.* New York: Oxford University Press, 2004.

Saad-Ghorayeb, Amal. *Hizbullah: Politics and Religion.* London: Pluto Press, 2002.

Salibi, Kamal. *A House of Many Mansions: The History of Lebanon Reconsidered.* Berkeley, Cal.: University of California Press, 1990.

Schmierer, Peter J. *Iraq: Policy and Perceptions.* Washington, D.C.: Georgetown University Institute for the Study of Diplomacy, 2007.

Seale, Patrick. *Asad: The Struggle for the Middle East.* Berkeley, Cal.: University of California Press, 1988.

Servold, Gary M. "The Muslim Brotherhood and Islamic Radicalism," in *Know Thy Enemy: Profiles of Adversary Leaders and Their Strategic Cultures,* Barry R. Schneider and Jerrold M. Post, eds. Montgomery, Ala.: Maxwell Air Force Base Counterproliferation Center, 2003.

Shadid, Anthony. *Legacy of the Prophet: Despots, Democrats and the New Politics of Islam.* Boulder, Colo.: Westview Press, 2002.

Soroush, Abdolkarim. *Reason, Freedom and Democracy in Iran: Essential Writing of Abdolkarim Soroush,* Mahmoud Sadri and Ahmad Sadri, eds. and trans. Oxford: Oxford University Press, 2000.

Takeyh, Ray. *Hidden Iran: Paradox and Power in the Islamic Republic.* New York: Times Books, 2006.

United Nations. *Arab Human Development Report 2004: Towards Freedom in the Arab World.* New York: United Nations, 2005.

United Nations. *The Arab Human Development Report 2005: Toward the Rise of Women in the Arab World.* New York: United Nations, Dec. 2006.

Wadud, Amina. *Qur'an and Woman: Rereading the Sacred Text from a Woman's Perspective.* London: Oxford University Press, 1999.

Wallach, Janet, and John Wallach. *Arafat: In the Eyes of the Beholder.* New York: Carol Publishing Group, 1990.

Wieland, Carsten. *Syria—Ballots or Bullets? Democracy, Islamism and Secularism in the Levant.* Seattle: Cune Press, 2006.

Wright, Robin. *In the Name of God: The Khomeini Decade.* New York: Simon & Schuster, 1989.

———. *The Last Great Revolution: Turmoil and Transformation in Iran.* New York: Knopf, 2000.

———. *Sacred Rage: The Wrath of Militant Islam.* New York: Simon & Schuster, 2001.

INDEX